FEMINISM AND AFFECT
AT THE SCENE OF ARGUMENT

FEMINISM AND AFFECT
AT THE SCENE OF ARGUMENT

*Beyond the Trope
of the Angry Feminist*

Barbara Tomlinson

TEMPLE UNIVERSITY PRESS
PHILADELPHIA

Temple University Press
1601 North Broad Street
Philadelphia, Pennsylvania 19122
www.temple.edu/tempress

COVER ART: "Enchanted Rider." Artist: Bob Thompson. Smithsonian American Art Museum Accession Number: 1975.21. Gift of Mr. and Mrs. David K. Anderson. Martha Jackson Memorial Collection. Used with the kind permission of the Smithsonian American Art Museum.

Library of Congress Cataloging-in-Publication Data

Tomlinson, Barbara, 1941–
    Feminism and affect at the scene of argument : beyond the trope of the angry feminist / Barbara Tomlinson.
        p. cm.
    Includes bibliographical references and index.
    ISBN 978-1-4399-0246-2 (cloth : alk. paper) — ISBN 978-1-4399-0247-9 (pbk. : alk. paper)   1. Feminism.   2. Women—Psychology.   3. Sex role. I. Title.
    HQ1155.T66 2010
    305.42—dc22

                                                                2009048504

Printed in the United States of America

2 4 6 8 9 7 5 3 1

Contents

Acknowledgments

Thanks to my wonderful colleagues and students in the Department of Feminist Studies at the University of California, Santa Barbara. It has been exhilarating to be part of the critical project that we are creating together. I am especially appreciative of all the work that department chairs Leila Rupp and Eileen Boris have done to welcome me into the department and to build a program of which we can all be proud. My research, writing, and teaching have all been enhanced by working with Laury Oaks, Barbara Herr Harthorn, Jacqueline Bobo, Grace Chang, Ellie Hernandez, Mireille Miller-Young, Christina Toy, and Lou Anne Lockwood. Claudine Michel, Maria Herrera-Sobek and William Warner made me feel especially welcome went I first arrived on campus, and sharing ideas with them as well as with Felice Blake, Paula Ioanide, Heidi Hoechst, Gaye Johnson, and Esther Lezra has been a wonderful experience. Thanks as well to Dean Melvin Oliver whose unique blend of research distinction, professional leadership, and personal integrity sets a high standard for the rest of us to emulate. It has also been wonderful to learn with—and from—a new generation of scholars, especially Denise Gill, Katrina Kimport, Joan Budesa, Jason Pfeifle, Angela Baez, and Darlene Craviotto.

Scholars across the disciplines have been generous with comments, criticisms, and questions that have helped me hone and refine my ideas. Among them are Nancy Armstrong, Rise Axelrod, Steven Axelrod, Susan Castillo, Kimberle Crenshaw, Angela Davis, Susan Gilman, Wlad Godzich, Luke Harris, Bruno Latour, Elizabeth Long, Steven Mailloux, Emily Martin, Elaine

May, Susan McClary, Helene Moglen, Tricia Rose, Dick Terdiman, and Sharon Traweek. I appreciate the comments from audiences at the British Association for Cultural Studies in Nottingham, UK; the Institute for Cultural Research at Lancaster University, UK; Brazilian National Seminary of Univ. Professor. of English Language & Literature at Atibaia, Brazil; Second Fulbright American Studies Conference, University of Waikato, Hamilton, NZ; New Zealand-U.S. Educational Foundation Lectures at University of Victoria, Massey University, and the University of Aukland, NZ; Pacific Coast Ancient and Modern Language Association, Conference on College Composition and Communication, the University of Illinois, and UC Santa Cruz.

Thanks for sharing years of feminism and affect to George Lipsitz, Kerry Tomlinson, Matthew Tomlinson, Lisa Choy Tomlinson, Rebecca Leigh Tomlinson, Emily Rae Tomlinson, and Kevin James Tomlinson.

Janet Francendese has been an ideal editor. I am deeply grateful to her for her faith in this book, for her wonderful work in support of it, and for the professionalism and wisdom that she has displayed in every single one of our interactions. An especially helpful reader's report from an anonymous reviewer has strengthened this book tremendously and I very much appreciate the time and care that this reviewer devoted to my work.

Some of the material that follows has been taken from previous versions and revised. Due to the sometimes lengthy process of journal publication, earlier versions may not yet be published.

"Intensification and the Discourse of Decline: A Rhetoric of Medical Anthropology." *Medical Anthropology Quarterly* 13.1 (March 1999): 1–25. Thanks to the American Anthropological Association.

"Phallic Fables and Spermatic Romance: Disciplinary Crossing and Textual Ridicule." *Configurations: A Journal of Literature, Science, and Technology* 3.2 (May 1995): 105–134. Thanks to Johns Hopkins University Press.

"The Politics of Textual Vehemence, or: Go to Your Room Until You Learn How to Act." *Signs: A Journal of Women in Culture and Society* 22.1 (Autumn 1996): 86–114. © 1996 The University of Chicago.

Review of Lisa Jean Moore, *Sperm Counts: Overcome by Man's Most Precious Fluid.* (New York: New York University Press, 2007). *Cultural Sociology* 3.1 (March 2009): 198–200. © 2009 SAGE Publications Ltd. All rights reserved.

"Tough Babies or Anger in the Superior Position." *Cultural Critique* 39 (Spring 1998): 151–188. © 1998 Oxford University Press.

"Transforming the Terms of Reading: Ideologies of Argument and the Trope of the Angry Feminist in Contemporary U.S. Political and Academic Discourse." *Journal of American Studies.* Thanks to Cambridge University Press.

CHAPTER ONE

Transforming the Terms of Reading

Ideologies of Argument and the
Trope of the Angry Feminist

ontemporary U.S. political and academic discourse abounds with a recurring set of formulaic claims that feminist scholars (and feminists in general) are angry, unreasoning, shrill, humorless, ugly, man-hating, perverse, and peculiar. This "trope of the angry feminist" is designed to delegitimize feminist argument even before the argument begins, to undermine feminist politics by making its costs personal, and to foreclose feminist futures by making feminism seem repulsive to young women.[1] The trope is a convention, a plot trick, a setup, a narrative structure, a character type.[2] Its incessant repetition constitutes part of a *cultural training program* that makes antifeminism and misogyny a routine element in everyday speech and written argument. Instigated by expressly *political* opposition to feminism, deploying affectively charged strategies that float free of evidence, clichés like the angry feminist put animosity—not argument—at the center of political discussions, interpellating readers as *always already antifeminist*. The repetition and circulation of such tropes produces a cumulative overdetermined quality that makes them seem already true before the moment of argument. One never encounters the feminist's argument for the first time because it comes already discredited. Because the trope of the angry feminist encourages unacknowledged ways of interpreting feminist affect, its inveterate irruption is consequential in journalism, entertainment, political, and quasi-intellectual arenas, as I describe in this introductory chapter. It is perhaps even more consequential in its influence on academic discourses, the subject of the remainder of the book: affect in academic discourses on social justice is often policed through "ideologies of style" that purport to be neutral but operate to entrench current conditions of power.

In this book I argue that we have failed to theorize adequately the role of such pervasive affective and ideologically encapsulated arguments in academic and political discourses. In consequence, we do not recognize that our conventional reading practices mislead us about ways to comprehend and counter them. I argue that *transforming the terms of reading* can reframe the problem, and propose for that purpose a critical toolkit that I call "feminist socioforensic discursive analysis."

My argument here constitutes a provocation to transform the terms of reading, to reframe interpretation of affect in both feminist and antifeminist writing. The trope of the angry feminist is a familiar conceit, like many similar phrases deployed to delegitimize social criticism, one that draws on a deep well of related clichés, affective rhetorical strategies, and familiar tropes. These discursive moves circulate as instantiations of power. The trope of the angry feminist presents itself as fresh each time it is uttered, its repetitious banality framed as mere reflection of the repetitious banality of the feminist's argument. This leads to the absurd but politically efficacious situation where readers are weary of arguments they have never heard. These argumentative tactics often succeed in part because our normal reading and writing practices lead us to object or counterargue in ways that fail to come to grips with the specific nature of the rhetorical situation that the tropes instantiate. Our conventional reading practices reinscribe ways of thinking that seem "logical" or "fair" because they are so familiar; they lead us to treat the tropes as surface features of discourse that serve to "skew" debate from its direct and proper form. These conventional practices, permeated by unacknowledged power relations, encourage us to respond to the tropes "normatively," with reproaches about textual etiquette, textual responsibility, or textual appropriateness, to complain about inadequate evidence, to provide counterexamples, or to condemn the person proffering the trope, as though its use violates an agreement about the proper nature of civic discussion, and as if there is a mechanism of accountability. None of this is the case. Responses that might chastise, correct, or even complain about the trope of the angry feminist are inadequate in part because they rest, ultimately, on an imaginary ideal: a discursive arena regulated by impartial principles in which utterances are adjudicated by unbiased observers.

Framing political and even academic discussion in this commonsense way treats rhetoric as a neutral technology to be deployed or evaluated in isolation from its conditions of production, the situations of speakers, or the general societal power relations that give utterances friendly to prevailing power relations an overdetermined "reasonableness" while rendering most oppositional arguments automatically suspect. Our reading practices *already* rest on uninterrogated and deeply gendered and racialized models of textuality, argument, authorship, politeness, and emotion. Under such conditions, affect is a potent tool of dominance, infusing the reading situation to teach us what power is, who has it, how to get it, how to be rewarded, and how to avoid the punishments power can deliver. Louis Althusser (1971) argues that concrete individuals become constituted as "subjects" through ideology, but the most powerful ideological influences do not come to us in the form of ideological pronouncements. That would make them visible, controversial, and refutable. Instead, he argues, the most powerful ideologies exist in "apparatuses," in practices, and these practices are always material. Reading, writing, and argument are social practices sedimented with ideologies of legitimacy, propriety and fairness so powerful and pervasive that we presuppose their value rather than examining their effects.

I have proposed a way of reading—feminist socioforensic discursive analysis–to reshape how we construe, critique, and transcend the always already gendered nature of public and scholarly texts, to call into question their interpretation, their disaggregation, and the consequences of their framing texts as "objective" or "subjective," as "scientific" or "political." As Karen Newman argues, ". . . it is not a question of seeing the woman, of putting 'woman' into discursive circulation, but of transforming the terms of reading by mobilizing a variety of texts and stories . . . We need a different kind of textual intercourse, a promiscuous conversation of many texts . . ." (1991, 146). Examining "a promiscuous conversation of many texts" with an eye toward the operations of affect and power allows us to talk about discursive patterns, about systemic ways of shaping arguments, about discursive technologies of power. It allows us to see how particular rhetorical strategies and discursive contexts are used and reused to create hierarchy and reestablish racialized and gendered authority. It helps us distinguish between the power of particular individuals and groups and the power of larger discursive arenas. Transforming the terms of reading focuses our attention on how the terms of the larger discursive arena can disable us, but also on how we can develop countermoves to negotiate these effects. It requires acknowledging that our arguments are always situated within fields of power.[3]

Feminist socioforensic discursive analysis provides a critique of the ideologies of argument that permeate both academic and political argumentation about issues of social justice. It is a form of descriptive theory that examines the contours of feminist and antifeminist controversies, treating them symptomatically and diagnostically to reveal how everyday and scholarly deployments of affect function as technologies of power.[4] It connects discursive arenas generally disaggregated by the disciplines to demonstrate the significant costs of our boundary practices: the promiscuous conversation of texts in social life compels any one utterance to function as a node in a broader discursive network. Feminist socioforensic discursive analysis seeks to enhance the work of the disciplines by challenging unacknowledged racialized and gendered ideologies of argument that frame and exclude certain kinds of claims and evidence in specific disciplines. The more fervently conventional practices shut down debate by defending themselves as neutral, the more their political nature is revealed.

The trope of the angry feminist draws from a deep well of related clichés, affective rhetorical strategies, and familiar tropes that are deployed routinely in our society to denigrate a broad range of political claims by people of color, antiracists, lesbians and gays, liberals, and even Democrats. In fact, conflating the claims of such disparate groups of social critics, as such tropes do, renders diverse political actors as united, multitudinous and powerful in a starkly Manichean worldview of good and bad people. The countless irruptions of the trope of the angry feminist and its equivalents do not simply emerge spontaneously from a simmering core of misogyny and racism. They are deployed deliberately as part of a set of productive tools carefully calculated for use on behalf of conservative social movements that have devoted enormous resources to reinforcing their own interests and to suppressing social movements that do not align with them.[5] To mask their defense of sedimented privileges, these discourses prime publics to see difference through a lens of antipathy. As a result, feminists and other social critics must make arguments about power and social inequities in a political arena animated by animus.

As a frankly "political" tool—a tool to shape social relationships involving authority and power—the trope is ready for deployment on any occasion when the term *feminist* is used, whether there is "provocation" or not. For example, in late September 2008, the University of California announced it had approved a graduate program at UC Santa Barbara that would offer master's and doctoral degrees in Feminist Studies.[6] The brief announcement soon came to the attention of talk radio host and syndicated columnist "Dr. Laura" Schlessinger. In a series of comments on her blog and in the *Santa Barbara News-Press*, Schlessinger presents herself as disheartened by the new program because it would be "sending graduates off into their lives as angry, bitter, paranoid harridans who cannot imagine being in any way dependent on or respectful of men and masculinity" ("Save Us from Feminist Studies," October 9, 2008).[7] Returning to this point on October 12, Schlessinger claims that a feminist studies degree only promotes "teaching more women to be angry and cynical" ("More on Feminist Studies," October 12, 2008).[8] Dr. Laura's use of the trope asserts that feminists are just angry, unhappy people who keep bringing up things like "oppression."[9] She directs feminists to what Schlessinger deems more appropriate targets for their anger: in this case, the Taliban; she would like us "locked and loaded" in Afghanistan allegedly to protect Afghan women from Afghan men.[10] Schlessinger does not disapprove of "anger" expressed *at* feminists, nor does she disapprove of feminist "anger"—or even killing—as long as it would be congruent with the aims of U.S. foreign policy. Affect is central to her means of persuasion: she uses "angry" rhetoric herself; she encourages readers' "anger" at feminist ideas and also at young women who do not adopt the most traditional of gender roles.[11] She does so to pinpoint which kinds of people are suitable for censure and which claims can be dismissed out of hand.

Schlessinger claims that feminist professors make their students "harridans"—women who are constantly finding fault, scolding, even vicious—while *enacting* such a role herself. The public shaming of women as harridans, shrews, and scolds has a long and dishonorable history. Karen Newman's research traces the practice to early modern England, where it served to warn women against acting freely or asserting their own ideas instead of knuckling under to the whims of their husbands. Identifying women as harridans and shrews went hand in hand with deeply misogynist fears about women's bodies. Newman notes that public rituals punished harridans similarly to adulteresses: "an open mouth and immodest speech are tantamount to open genitals and immodest acts" (Newman 1991, 11). The Dr. Lauras of the early modern era prescribed chastity, obedience, and silence as the traits appropriate for women, even advising those already silenced to repress facial expressions or gestures that might signal opposition to their spouses (Newman 1991, 9). Without reference to this exact history, our Dr. Laura knows enough to parrot its major premises, to warn women against behavior that might not please men. She contributes to a climate where young men are authorized to berate young women who assert themselves as feminists: "Oh, do you hate men? Do you shave your legs? Are you a lesbian?"

Schlessinger's adoption of the moniker "Dr. Laura" for her professional work as a talk-show host and commentator flags the distinction between a person, "Laura Schlessinger," and a public persona, "Dr. Laura." Distinguishing the two entities allows us to make more precise and productive claims about the kinds of evidence we have access to in examining a text. Schlessinger's writings provide considerable evidence to substantiate claims about

"Dr. Laura" the persona, but almost none to substantiate claims about Schlessinger the person. "Dr. Laura" is a *package* of rhetorical devices and arguments set in certain kinds of texts presented in certain kinds of venues within a larger cultural set of discourses. "Dr. Laura" stands for the production or enactment of a specific authorial position. Since I argue that *all* authors are enactments of rhetorical packages, emphasizing this distinction does not disparage either "Dr. Laura" or Schlessinger. What it does is redirect our analytic attention to the *nature of the package* itself instead of using that package as transparent evidence about a person. I use the term *persona* (from referring to a stylized mask worn by an actor), to describe the impression of the author that we infer from a textual package. The term *persona,* however, does not solve the problem I am addressing here, because it continues to imply that the purpose of our reading is to infer truths about an individual: the "real" person behind the mask. Our inordinate attention to inferring truths about the person leads us to pass too quickly over the argument itself, the claims that should be supported by reasons or evidence. We tend to treat the inferred merit of the person as if it can stand in for the merit of the argument. But it cannot.

Distinguishing between a person Schlessinger and the textual package of "Dr. Laura" is a useful move in analysis. First, it eliminates the notion that the qualities of an individual can stand in for the qualities of an argument. This is not to say that claims about the individual are not interesting (yes, Dr. Laura may have had something of a sordid past, a divorce, racy photos, etc.), but if we discard their arguments whenever individuals evince failings, we can go nowhere. In any case, valorizing or dismissing individuals does not solve social problems. It is not productive argument. Second, the distinction positions us to eschew claims about what the persona "cannot conceive," "fails to understand," "believes." Such claims cripple argument analysis because they make undue inferences about the thinking person who wrote the text. Argument is a social tool for thinking precisely because it articulates claims that may be clearer and less contradictory than could be said of what people "believe." Arguments are articulated at a specific point in time (although subject to revision). The "beliefs" of the person who wrote the text may be subsequently swayed by counterargument and evidence. Therefore claims about what someone "believes" are far less useful than claims about the characteristics and consequences of the argument being made. Finally, bracketing the truths of Schlessinger the person allows us to examine more carefully the strategies and arguments of the package presented as "Dr. Laura" to determine exactly how it projects the *impression* of a certain kind of person.[12]

Rather than dismissing a source such as "Dr. Laura" as nonserious discourse, we need to acknowledge newspapers, talk radio, and popular books as important points of circulation for antifeminist tropes.[13] These sites have all been infused with the discourse of contempt about academic feminism as part of a broader political and public relations campaign designed to counter the rise of antiracist and antisexist egalitarian social change in the second half of the twentieth century and the beginning of the twenty-first. There is no primary point of origin for the trope of the angry feminist. It migrates back and forth across various social domains, acquiring its aura of truth because it is immediately recognizable as something we have heard before. The shared features of the trope instantiate and demonstrate its truthfulness. It is a layered claim that references previous claims in order to intimidate. It is not substantiated by its connection to evidence but through its echo of previous claims. It is not an argument but merely a "citation," a "repetition," a discursive circulation of power based on previous uses of the trope (consider Butler 1990, 1997 *Excitable* and Derrida 1991). That is the nature of a trope as a "common or overused theme or device." Dr. Laura's column does not need actual evidence about feminist studies graduate programs, because the anger and unreasonableness of feminists have already been stipulated for her readers in innumerable nightclub acts, television shows, and talk radio programs. Schlessinger's deployment of the trope of the angry feminist illustrates a number of the trope's main features. Its purposes are openly political; it is available for immediate use; it is timeless and contextless; it requires no research; it is unfettered from evidence; it ignores inconsistency or contradiction; it makes no attempt to be "fair"; it is impossible to refute; it allows no mechanism for rebuttal. Part of the power of the trope is exactly that it is insulated from what we might think of as correction and counterargument. It "thumbs its nose" at such attempts and uses them to reemphasize the original claims of the trope. None of this undermines the impact of the trope of the angry feminist, because its purpose is repetition. The discourse of feminism and the counterdiscourse of Dr. Laura are closely linked; the latter is designed to hide the former. Schlessinger's use of the trope of the angry feminist is part of a political and economic apparatus designed to train everyday publics to distrust feminists, to position feminists as inappropriate citizens, "outside the economy of reason."

Using the trope as Schlessinger does functions as part of the cumulative political work of "pounding the base," solidifying group identity, and passing on conservative and antifeminist attitudes across generations.[14] It reinforces prejudices, using contempt and exasperation to affirm already-known "truths," taunting current feminists and threatening potential ones. It "poisons the well" for argumentative exchange about social justice. The issue is not whether the Angry Troper or the base it pounds "believes" such claims; rather, the claims themselves (whether made by men or women) *perform, enact,* and *instantiate* gendered power.

The trope of the angry feminist functions forcefully to constrain and even foreclose discussions of feminist arguments in both everyday and academic arenas. As with many successful methods of misdirection, we cannot reply to it without framing our claims according to the logic of the original trope. If a question is illegitimate, all answers are going to be shaped and shaded by its illegitimacy. Whether we claim that feminists are not angry or are legitimately angry, or that some feminists have a right be angry (though, perhaps, not all), *we are responding to the logic of the trope rather than challenging it.* Whether we claim that the Angry Troper does not have evidence, or that he does not have the right evidence, or that our evidence counters his, *we are treating his claim as worthy of consideration.* We are agreeing to consider whether the value of feminism can be linked to the proper behavior and rhetoric of feminists. We are agreeing that feminists must argue their relation to reason and emotion *before* they can be conceded the right to exist and have a political stake in their society. We are treating the commonplace product of a discourse saturated with power as though it were equivalent to a thoughtful academic argument, rather than a patently illegitimate claim functioning in a discourse that asserts rather than demonstrates truth or responsibility. We are allowing antifeminists to set the terms of feminist discussion, to substitute their claims for ours, to shape the economy of our attention, to play on our emotions, to steal our intellectual efforts. In Wahneema Lubiano's terms, we've been "mugged by a metaphor" (1996).

Popular discourse, the site of Dr. Laura's arguments, is a node in a network of communications that are structured in dominance. The trope of the angry feminist may appear convincing in journalism because it is echoed constantly in advertising, entertainment, public relations, political discourse, and scholarship. Whether we notice them or not, whether we accept them or not, these displays of dominant power are meant for all of us. They "hail" us as if we are certain kinds of people—or at least ought to be. They encourage us to find certain kinds of positions "coherent" and recognize their dominance.[15] While readers may adopt or resist the text's interpellation, they nonetheless "overhear" its argument and are affected by it.

This introductory chapter examines the migrations of the trope of the angry feminist from popular to quasi-intellectual discourses, but this book primarily focuses on its relevance for interpreting feminists' original discovery scholarship. I provide analytical tools to understand and counter the trope, but, more importantly, to reframe interpretation of both antifeminist and feminist textual affect. Feminist scholars and other women are constantly asked to defend our right to exist, our reasonableness, our emotional makeup. Accepting our assigned roles in these debates diverts scholars from more important tasks: from exploring how gender functions as a social force, revealing the mechanisms of denial and disavowal that protect unequal power, and producing ways of knowing and ways of being capable of moving us all to more just, decent, and honorable lives.

Antifeminist Affect and the Discourse of Dominance

Claims about untoward feminist emotion and irrationality are a nexus and a knot where various lines of argument are tied together. They form one of the most repeated elements inside contemporary antifeminist discourse. The trope of the angry feminist is not so much a "turn" in the use of words as a way to "turn" the argument: claims for social justice are "turned into" proof of bad character. The trope is always open to modification. Indeed, any unpleasant emotion can fit the slot of "angry," *since it is the* turn *that is important, not the charge itself.* The trope of the narcissistic feminist, for example, works to condemn contemporary feminists for their narcissism in comparison to the virtues of past feminists; yet those past feminists, in their own time, were argued to be narcissists in comparison to the selfless women of previous times (Tyler 2005).[16] Claims about "ideology"—a system of thought—serve an important function in such arguments.[17] They hold that if a feminist has an "ideology," she cannot think "for herself." She simply believes whatever feminist authorities say, their "dogma."[18] If feminist "ideology" is unhappy/pathological/resentful/hate-filled, then the feminist does not control her own thinking; her ideology controls her (the way unruly emotions do).

Consider, for example, Jeffrey Hart's review in *The New Criterion* (2002) of Carolyn Heilbrun's book of memoirs (2002). In her book, Heilbrun criticizes what she argues was the sexism that she experienced when she was a graduate student and then professor in Columbia University's English Department. Proclaiming that *he* was wholly satisfied with *his own experiences* at Columbia, Hart does not attempt to determine how things might have been different for a woman in academia at that time. Instead, he asserts that Heilbrun and other feminists are simply unreasoning, angry, humorless, man-hating, and whiny: they are virtually unhinged because their ideology has made them so. According to Hart,

> If the emotions and ideas that inform it [Heilbrun's book] came to prevail generally, *life would not be worth living.* . . . Her emotions have been *so wrenched out of shape by feminist dogma* that she cannot present to the readers of her books *a recognizable shared world.* . . . The sentences I have just quoted *drip with resentment and venom.* . . . Hers is a mind *losing active cerebral cells.* . . . In this book we witness the melancholy sight of *a mind in ideologically induced disintegration. Her mental lens is befogged.* She has *lost the ability to see the object itself as it actually is,* certainly the *preliminary to reasonable discourse.* She is a tragedy that has happened, unless, in a tough-minded way, you may regard her as a comedy without laughter. She is *besotted with feminism.* (2002, emphasis added)

Because Hart apparently cannot see himself (and his own privileges) in Heilbrun's account, he concludes that she is befogged and besotted. Like Dr. Laura, he presents the idea of feminism as already so intolerable that he need not acknowledge any actual feminist ideas; he presents them in caricature with a confidence that characterizes use of the trope.

Deploying what Albert Memmi calls "the mark of the plural" (1965, 81), these tropes of emotion "turn" *one* feminist into *all* feminists: she is depersonalized and made "collective"; anything said by one person deemed "feminist" can be attributed to anyone else deemed feminist. The "mark of the plural" authorizes the extension of a claim based on one feminist to condemn a mass of unknown women. For example, in her book, Heilbrun indicates that she was denied the chance to teach in Columbia's acclaimed honors course because she was a woman, although she longed to teach it. She notes that she was amused to find that women graduate students later assigned to teach it "hated almost every minute of it" (2002, 23). She provides no other information about these students. Hart, who as a graduate student taught the course, positions anyone who did not like to teach it as—literally—insane:

> Who were these "young women"? Clearly they were unsuited to be professors of literature, since they "hated" teaching some of the best things ever written. They surely *belonged in the Department of Abnormal Psychology,* not as teachers, to be sure, but *as objects for scientific study.* What *pathology blinded them* to the best that has been thought

and said. . . . Pretty clearly, they were *radical feminists* who were bored by great literature, "hated" it even, and instead *wanted to teach their gripes*. Harold Bloom has called this faction the *"party of resentment."* To permit one of these *vipers* into an academic department of literature was an act of tragic folly. (2002, emphasis added)

The confidence inherent to the persona of the Angry Troper gives the Troper license to attribute pathological emotions—insanity, self-absorption, resentment, and evil—to people the Troper has never encountered. Nonetheless, the Troper argues that their manifest irrationality reinforces the importance of walling feminists off from the "economy of reason."[19] Hart argues, in essence, that their inherent bad character and irrationality make it *impossible* for the angry feminists to be "reasonable," to join the body politic in applying logic, evidence, and shared value judgments to reach decisions. Feminists cannot even begin to reason, since they cannot apprehend the "object itself as it actually is." They cannot present "a recognizable shared world." If their world *were* shared, life would not be worth living.

Hart's argument constitutes the trope of the angry feminist as a constant play on binaries. On the first side is a life worth living, a recognizable shared world, participating in the best that has been thought and said. On the other side is pathological abnormality, irrationality, resentment, venom. On the first side is the human life of clear thinking and seeing. On the other side is a life of ideologically caused unreason: obscured mental acuity, blindness, mental disintegration, brain decay. On the one side is normality and humanity; on the other side, abnormality and Otherness or nonhumanity (a viper). Binaries have long been recognized as a central and damaging way of structuring Western thought, so feminists and other thinkers have provided us with tools for reconsidering them. Helene Cixous (1980), for example, argues that binaries such as male/female or sun/moon rest on hierarchical oppositions: the first term dominates the second. This is certainly evident in Hart's binaries. But Jacques Derrida (1978) makes a point that further clarifies how Hart's binaries create countersubversive force. Derrida argues that the second, unprivileged term of a binary is, in fact, *indispensible* in defining the privileged term. The first term cannot be defined, or exist, or function *without* the secondary term. In this argument, rationality or clear seeing, however "self-evidently" dominant, cannot exist without irrationality, abnormality, resentment. Hart's countersubversive discourse depends on the privileged first term to create the sense of an "ideal": the unitary, centered, significant way of living that must be saved. But that ideal depends also on the second term to reaffirm what it is *not*: the irrational other. Without his irrational feminist, Hart's rationality becomes unintelligible. Without her blindness, can he prove that what he sees is "the object as it really is"? Without her "venom," Hart's rhetoric might look like—venom. The logic of the binary depends on presenting as uniquely valuable and unitary its first, privileged term, dissolving the diversity of others into the disfavored secondary term. It is not surprising that examining the complexities suppressed in the second term has been a productive site for gender and racial politics that recognize and theorize difference.[20]

It would be hard to deny that Hart uses a misogynous representation of his angry feminist. But whether or not Hart is a misogynist is beside the point. If we bracket claims about the truths of Hart-the-person, we can see some interesting complications in the nature of his emotional appeals to his audience. His appeals to fear and aversion do not center on typical misogynist targets such as female bodies. What is it that Hart presents as horrifying? The feminists' mind as *collective*. Hart's argument about the angry feminist appeals to his audience's fear of "fungibility." For the work of the trope of the angry feminist is to establish the feminists as identical to one another, interchangeable, or "fungible." That is the point of Memmi's "mark of the plural." One feminist stands for all; any can be substituted for another. Like Memmi's colonial subjects, none of the feminists constituted by the trope can be an individual *subject*. In the terms of Hart's discourse, *that* is horrifying: the loss of individual subjectivity. There are multiple sources for the cultural influences that make plausible Hart's positioning of this loss as fundamentally intolerable. I use here Nancy Armstrong's argument about the role of the British novel in creating modern subjectivity. In *How Novels Think*, Armstrong argues that the history of the modern novel and the modern subject are virtually the same, as the novel developing in the eighteenth and nineteenth centuries created a kind of subject—"the individual"—by both appealing to and using that kind of subject:

> Simply put, this class- and culture-specific subject is what we mean by "the individual." . . . *To produce an individual, it was also necessary to invalidate competing notions of the subject—often proposed by other novels—as idiosyncratic, less than fully human, fantastic, or dangerous."* (2005, 3, emphasis added)

Hart and other Angry Tropers invalidate the feminist by defining her as less than an individual (she thinks with an "ideology," obeys a "dogma"). Her connection to others that has enabled her to effect social change positions her as a grotesque example, an individual folded into a group. Hart and the Angry Tropers employ what they present as the distorted subjectivity of the feminist as an admonishment. It serves the purpose that Armstrong notes of the popular romance that it "renders all alternatives to such [an individual] . . . as a monstrous life form capable of transforming the individual from a self-governing citizen into an instrument of group desire" (2005, 25). This is the hinge that connects the various "categories" of social critics—feminists, gays and lesbians, people of color—that the Troper and other "conservative" discourses conflate. By assuming their connection to a larger social aggregate, feminists and other social critics threaten this notion of the individual who is sovereign and self-governing. Armstrong argues that the novel served to limit our vision of other kinds of subjects. She argues that the novel's

> phobic representations of the human aggregate made it difficult for future novelists, their critics, and readers to imagine a society in which individuals can freely pursue their desires without encroaching on the rights of others. . . . [Now] at a time when individualism has clearly achieved hegemony . . . that model of individualism went on the defensive, as if to say that the modern individual could only define him- or herself as such in opposition to an engulfing otherness, or mass, that obliterated individuality. (2005, 25)

Fear of feminism's challenge to the idealized subject of the "individual" is part of the emotion that animates Hart's rhetorical appeals.

The stakes of redeploying affect in the cultural training program that depends on the trope of the angry feminist come into clear relief in cultural commentator Joseph Epstein's ridicule of feminists in the academy. Epstein, who has been lauded by William F. Buckley, Jr., as the wittiest writer alive, celebrated by the *Wall Street Journal* as America's leading essayist, and praised in the *Atlantic Monthly* as a "brilliant polemicist" (Gioia 1991), was awarded the National Humanities Medal in 2003 by President George W. Bush.[21] In an essay in the *Hudson Review* in 1991, Epstein presents a series of his famously "witty" remarks in an all too familiar form, "tweaking" members of the academy to emphasize what he presents as the debilitating left-wing culture of the university. Epstein claims that their emotions lead feminist academics to be irrationally out-of-control, so that "a reasonable feminist" is an oxymoron (13). Feminist academics are silly, oversensitive, and imagine themselves as victims, while actually being enormously powerful.[22]

Central to Epstein's effect is drawing on old sexist jokes to speak disparagingly of academic feminists as "angry":

> The feminists roll on, perpetually angry, making perfectly comprehensible the joke about the couple in their West Side Manhattan apartment who, having been robbed twice, determine to protect themselves, he wanting to get a revolver, she a pit bull, and so they agree to compromise and instead get a feminist. (28)

Feminists and other women are constantly faced with claims that they must forgive and overlook such "humorous" sexist commentary ("It's just a joke!"). The little girl who is teased should forgive the naughty boy who teases. Women who object to a joke need to "lighten up." Feminists "do not have a sense of humor." This chicanery rides on gendered notions about who should keep forgiving. It functions to misdirect attention from the grounds of the joke. It positions the jokester as always innocent, the joke itself as always funny, and the consequences of the joke as always harmless. Any objection by a feminist or other woman is eagerly taken up to "turn" the debate from whether the joke is puerile and insulting to why it is funny, why that makes it unimpeachable, and what is wrong with her if she does not think so. This sleight-of-hand hinges on mobile deployment of the notion that we all have agreed to hold "humor" as the highest value. It presupposes that we have agreed that a world of "humor" is not a political world. But it is.

Antifeminist jokes such as Epstein's function to recruit readers into discursive regimes of pleasure focused on hostility toward feminists, a kind of indirect discourse that assumes rather than argues. Thomas L. Dumm discusses Freud's theory of the joke in a way that may help us understand the economy of pleasure that Epstein offers. Freud places the third person, the audience of the joke, in a significant position. In the case of the obscene joke, the third person who laughs is "laughing as though he were a spectator of an act of sexual aggression" (Freud 1963, 97, quoted in Dumm 1994, 56). Epstein's joke encourages readers to laugh as witness to his aggression, to align themselves with his hostility. "Since we have been obliged to renounce the expression of hostility by deeds—held back by the passionless third person, in whose interest it is that personal security be preserved—we have, just as in the case of sexual aggressiveness, developed a new technique of invective, which aims at enlisting this third person against our enemy" (Freud 1963, 103, quoted in Dumm 1994, 56–57). The joke actually has two kinds of third-party onlookers. One is other men and sometimes women being recruited to join this aggressive dominant in order to enjoy the joke against the woman/feminist. But there is also the implicit onlooker of the woman/ feminist—the despised other—forced to watch and be unable to object. The feminist is always there, whether she reads the passage or not. The trope of the angry feminist always includes the puppet feminist as audience, using her invisible spectatorship to magnify the pleasure of the dominant display.

The appeal to the audience of the "third person" structured into Epstein's joke is central to its work as part of the coordinated public relations campaign funded and disseminated by conservative institutions. Masquerading as knowledgeable about scholarly debate, these commentaries are aimed primarily at readers who are not in the academy and do not read scholarly work. Derogating contemporary scholars (often in the name of traditional scholarly values or "common sense"), these commentaries work to marginalize the humanities and social sciences in social and political debate. They are particularly efficient for discrediting feminist, queer, and antiracist arguments for social justice, because they can be deployed opportunistically for dominance; they can rely on prevailing ideologies that appear "self-evident."

The contradictory claims and affects of those who use the trope of the angry feminist do not usefully serve as evidence that the Troper is "hypocritical." Rather they reveal themselves as acts of deliberate misdirection, not related to the aims and intentions of actual research but rather a form of discursive politics aimed at discrediting ideas and arguments that do not conform to the conservative and corporate agenda. Scholars who may feel their own intellectual positions are not highly regarded in the academy use contempt deliberately to appeal to more general publics, enlisting them as myrmidons in personal and political scholarly battles. Dennis Dutton, editor of the journal *Philosophy and Literature*, makes an appeal to the popular media through his "Bad Writing" contest, where selected sentences of politically deplored scholars become the scene of widespread ridicule and contempt. Mark Bauerlein reflected on the successful outcome of the 1999 contest, which promoted derisive commentary about Judith Butler's prose in the *Wall Street Journal*, the *New York Times*, the *Weekly Standard*, the *New Republic*, *Lingua Franca*, and *Salon*. According to Bauerlein, "Beyond the campus walls the 1999 Bad Writing Contest *did its job, solidifying the image of theorists* as an aimless coterie of pseudo-radicals playing to one another and inflicting shopworn countercultural messages on their captive students" (2004, 181, emphasis added). Here Bauerlein makes explicit the role of the Bad Writing Contest. It is one of the tools used by conservatives in a continuing campaign against their political opponents in U.S. higher education.[23] Conservatives use it to discredit the arguments of scholars whose political and intellectual positions they oppose, attempting to dislodge them from a place in the university that allows them to develop theoretical and intellectual alternatives to conventional arguments reflecting conservative discourses. This work attempts to make the academic life of the university operate by the sensibilities of an everyday public arena.

The trope of the angry feminist is not an argument about unseemly emotions; it is a tool of discursive politics designed to enact and reinforce patterns of social dominance. If it were actually an argument about unseemly emotions, the Troper would behave as if its own emotions were also to be evaluated. Yet in a contradiction also central to the trope, Tropers immerse themselves in emotionalism, irrationality, and self-righteousness in dismissing feminists as prisoners of emotion, irrationality, and self-righteousness. The internal contradictions of such a position do not undermine its discursive authority with its intended audiences, however, for the trope is not intended to persuade by mobilizing evidence into logical arguments. Instead, it is used for expressly political performance: displays of anger, contempt, and ridicule designed to warn potential malefactors about thinking in non-normative ways.

The trope of the angry feminist establishes itself as countersubversion. Like other tropes in the conservative "echo chamber" (see Jamieson and Cappella, 2008), it pops up persistently in punditry, political appeals, and popular journalism. It frames and polices the terms of public debate by focusing attention on claims about the unsatisfactory character of feminists rather than on unjust policies and practices. It protects power by ridiculing its critics, pandering to the anti-intellectualism of business leaders, journalists, and politicians to legitimate neoliberal schemes to privatize and corporatize the university, to replace the life of the mind with vocational training that subsidizes businesses by training and socializing a docile and uncritical labor force. Caricaturing the arguments and ideas of feminists and other social critics plays a central role in this work, not as actual argument about ideas but as a preemptive strike against potential opposition, confirming Lubiano's claim that we've been mugged by a metaphor. As she explains, "domination is so successful precisely because it sets the terrain upon which struggle occurs at the same time that it preempts opposition not only by already inhabiting the vectors where we would resist (i.e., by being powerfully in place and ready to appropriate oppositional gestures), but also by having already written the script we have to argue with and against" (1996, 66). Under these circumstances, we feminists frequently find ourselves tripped up by tropes and mugged by thugs.

Mugging requires *mugs*, a word with multiple meanings. A mug is not only a person who assaults and robs; the word also refers to someone who makes exaggerated faces in performing, as in a person "mugging" for the camera. When we encounter the trope of the angry feminist over and over again, it is important to bear in mind both senses of the word *mug*. When those who use the trope craft affective and emotional appeals riddled with contempt and hatred to describe feminists as "angry," they often produce in their own work the exaggerated intense affect that they purport to find so offensive in arguments by others. This use of affect can redirect the sense of nostalgia, loss, victimization, and failure that infuses so much conservative discourse. Disenchanted by the inevitable disappointments of the world that exists, one focuses contempt on subordinated targets, arguing that it is their presence, their agency, and their subjectivity that have spoiled the world one imagines could exist without them. One might even mug others because one fears one is being made a mug.

Because our roles are already structured according to the conventions of travesty, feminist responses to such sneers are also preframed as entertaining; women are free to debate our *own* right to be humans and citizens according to the illegitimate logic of the trope. Such antifeminist insults are not aimed at persuading feminists so much as performing a public shaming. They exhibit uncontrollable women for the amusement and reassurance of other men. By extension they exhibit a range of "political others" as worthy of shaming for "conservative" enjoyment, thus efficiently marking as unworthy an entire range of social arguments. The role of feminist academics is not incidental here. Encouraging readers of the general public to feel superior to academics is a practice to reinforce the challenges to and defunding of the university that has been accomplished also by other means. It positions its audience as *pleasured, participatory,* and *politically productive* in the *mere act of reading* that one's political opponents are simply silly, stupid scoundrels. In other words, it is not merely an argument provided *through* discourse; it is also a way of framing the act of reading itself—the act of responding affectively to derisive claims—to feel like it *counts* as "politics." These readers have been trained to mug. Trained to enjoy a discourse of animus in substitute for political argumentation, it turns out they have also been trained to *be* mugs.

Feminist Socioforensic Analysis of Discursive Authority

I have argued that a set of critical tools that I call *feminist socioforensic discursive analysis* is indispensible to understand and ultimately to counter the working of tropes like that of the angry feminist. Such a critical tool kit is necessary to reveal the ways that power infuses and limits the notion of reading, of writing, of critical thinking. If rhetoric is not a neutral technology, if ideas are sedimented in social life rather than packages available to deliver, if the ways we frame textuality, argument, authorship, politeness, and emotion emerge from and participate in gendered and racialized hierarchies, then we see that tools we have regarded as adequate and even robust must themselves come under examination.

Feminist socioforensic discursive analysis seeks to reshape how we construe, critique, and transcend the always already gendered nature of public and scholarly texts, their interpretation, their disaggregation, and the consequences of their framing as "objective" or "subjective," "scientific" or political." To reiterate: it argues for transforming the terms of reading by examining those terms more precisely. It examines what Newman characterizes as the "promiscuous conversation of many texts."

Transforming the terms of reading concentrates our analysis: we investigate how power infuses the scene of argument.[24] Socioforensic analysis requires us to ask questions about why the text exists, what it does, and what it *does not* do. This chapter has focused on how the antifeminist uses the trope of the angry feminist to define a field of interest, to establish what counts as a legitimate perspective, and to exclude as illegitimate other ways of thinking about the feminist. So I discuss questions useful for approaching these antifeminist discourses. Gunther Kress suggests starting with a series of productive questions: Why is the topic being written about? How is it being written about? What *other* ways of writing about the topic are there? (1985, 7, emphasis added). These questions focus the analyst's attention to identify important elements of the scene of argument: What strategy is involved in generating a particular discourse? What rhetoric does it use? *What alternatives are suppressed by this discourse?* (Cranny-Francis et al., 2003, 95, emphasis added). My added italics serve to emphasize that part of the analytic task that examines the "invisible": what *is not* in the discourse, what is framed, in fact, as *unnecessary* to it. Such sites are often particularly productive for revealing the effects of power. Discourses mobilize power relations to specific ends; they channel power relations to produce certain effects; the imbrication of power and effects often goes unacknowledged and unexamined. Under such circumstances, socioforensic discursive analysis makes discursive power available for critique. As Anne Cranny-Francis et al. note, "Being able to deconstruct discourse—to determine what knowledge is propagated by a particular discourse, what values are embedded in it, the rhetoric it uses—is simultaneously a way of analysing the operations of power in society" (2003, 94). So a feminist discourse can profit from bringing to light the ways that antifeminist discourses attempt to set the terms of debate. But the same questions and ways of approaching the scene of argument are productive for investigating feminist discourses too. Feminist discourses also draw on and deploy discursive power. In the core chapters of this book, I demonstrate how the tools of knowledge production in the disciplines are inflected by feminists to make compelling claims at the scene of academic argument.

Powerful interests do not acknowledge or give up their advantages willingly. They presume that their sedimented privileges have been earned—that if inequalities exist, these are natural, necessary, and inevitable. They position as irrational anyone who suggests otherwise. Dominant discourses recruit publics by encouraging them to read arguments as transparently personal and divorced from social power. They deny the ways that antifeminist arguments are enabled by and reinforce positions of domination. They deploy contempt routinely to *turn* all attempts at social and political critique *back on the arguer*, to suppress any claim that might be made on the reader. And why would they not? Why would a regime that seeks to naturalize power on the basis of gender, or race, or sexuality welcome challenge? As Cedric Robinson argues, regimes of power are "unrelentingly hostile to their exhibition" (2007, xii).[25] Their hostility is often displayed in discourses that encourage affiliation with dominant narratives through complex means of identification and repudiation.[26] Like other aggrieved and oppositional groups, feminists challenge power by attempting to work their way out of negative ascription and oppression, constructing long chains of signs and symbols that undo the damage done by dominant discourses.[27] The hostile terrain constrains us, but it need not define us.[28] Feminists turn hegemony on its head by turning the arguments designed to silence them into arenas where gendered power is exposed, critiqued, and countered. One of the places where this process takes place is at the scene of argument in academic and civic life.

This book identifies feminist and antifeminist textual affect as a rich site for considering how argumentative rhetorics create authority. It uses a tool kit of feminist socioforensic discursive analysis to challenge the limitations of normal reading practices, to encourage more precise definitions of textual affect, to examine the textual features that trigger attributions of "emotion" to particular texts, and to demand that we analyze textual "emotion" in the light of larger discourses about social power. This introductory chapter focuses on the trope of the angry feminist in a wide range of discourses in order to begin developing a kit of critical analytic tools to be used productively to transform the terms of reading affective argument. In subsequent chapters I consider the consequences of the trope of the angry feminist and other widespread antifeminist criticisms framing affective exchanges in the academic disciplines. Because academic arguments are not sealed off from the everyday world, the trope of the angry feminist also saturates the culture within which feminist *academic* argument takes place and occurs there also. Deployed against feminist scholars in *both* everyday and academic contexts, the trope demonstrates the interdependence in actual social life of discourses we are encouraged to disaggregate. The feminist scholar who argues about Beethoven, women's biology, or the Black family faces spite and contempt in everyday discourse along with other women and feminists. When a similar malicious discourse is deployed against her in the scholarly area, she may find that her colleagues overlook it, trivialize it, or treat it as idiosyncratic bad manners. Further, her own use of any rhetorical strategy that could be interpreted as "emotional" is overinterpreted and puts her at dramatic risk of dismissal, quite unlike the treatment of such rhetoric from those who have not been characterized as emotional. In the six chapters that form the core of this book, I use feminist socioforensic discursive analysis to reveal how the terms of debate set by the trope of the angry feminist shape the scene of argument in sociolegal studies, musicology, and science studies. I demonstrate how critics use strategies authorized by their unacknowledged gendered and racialized status to delegimate arguments about structures of dominance, attempting to shut down feminist inquiry through the very strategies of textual vehemence that they purport to condemn when used by feminists. Accompanying this analysis, I demonstrate how feminist scholars use affect in constructing alternative rhetorics of authority. Because the disciplinary and interdisciplinary settings of these arguments influence how we regard their use of affective rhetoric, I conclude with an argument about the nature of feminist interdisciplinarity.

Looking specifically at rhetoric that critics might flag for dismissal as "emotional" or "angry" when used in arguments for social equity, I argue for a more precise consideration of the nature of textual affect. Because we have become accustomed to framing textual affect as a means of revealing truths about the person who wrote the text, our analysis is truncated. We treat the task of reading as complete at the point when we make inferences about the authorial bundle, the person whose name the text carries. We also misconstrue what the text is doing because we have modeled it as the "expression" or "emotional style" of the individual whose name the text carries. This derails the analysis of particular social arguments by ignoring their participation in a discursive ocean of social arguments. So what happens when we bracket claims about the truths of the inferred writer, when we transform the terms of reading? We find that we have been treating as transparent (looking *through* instead of looking *at*) important questions with deeply political consequences: How are affect and argument constructed in the text? What is happening in the text that leads us to think of it as displaying "emotion"? What counts as proof that the text implies a particular kind of affect? What is a legitimate inference about the significance of textual affect? How do we situate the text in a larger set of disciplinary or interdisciplinary academic discourses? How does the role of the argument in larger public discourses influence our claims about affect? How do we account for our own positions? Our ability to answer these questions is politically significant exactly because the answers have been taken for granted or deemed unnecessary in a climate of contempt, where no provocation at all is necessary to set in motion the recirculation of claims: if one is a feminist, then one is angry about inappropriate things; to be angry about inappropriate things is to exhibit bad character; people with bad character are unworthy; we do not have to listen to unworthy people; therefore we can dismiss the arguments of the feminist as inappropriate. Because feminists are unworthy, it turns out, social inequities are to be vindicated and even celebrated.

Socioforensic discursive analysis takes a different tack.[29] It maintains that precise and productive claims about textual evidence require situating texts in larger social and discursive arenas and recognizing how their claims are authorized and deauthorized by various forms of social power. *Rhetoric* here refers to the use of speech or writing to persuade.[30] All the texts that I consider in this book are indeed trying to "persuade." They use arguments to encourage their audiences to embrace points of view or undertake courses of action. But in order to understand how affect functions in these arguments, we must transform the terms of reading. Conventional reading practices often leave us without the tools to ascertain exactly *what* kind of persuasion is going on and toward what goals. They encourage us to assume that we are in a position to *know whether* and *how* we are being persuaded. Yet too often we focus on the most obvious arguments without reflecting on what the entire text and its discursive setting are teaching us about what kind of persons we are and should be, about what kinds of arguments are "fair" (and how to ascertain that and treat unfair arguments), about which people and arguments are legitimate and which can be dismissed without being listened to.

Conventional practices for evaluating argument are especially impoverished.[31] They structure the goals of reading around reaching decisions framed as binary. For example, they encourage us to see our roles as "evaluators" in the sense of judging an argument as good or bad. This role usually positions "criticism" or "critical thinking" as "finding fault with someone's thinking" rather than being careful and exact in one's judgment.[32] But choosing either side, whether positive or negative, truncates analysis by allowing one to accept or refute an argument without any precise articulation of its claims. Our normal reading practices also implicitly frame the purpose of reading arguments as the adoption of a *position* (pro or con), rather than developing an understanding of what is at stake in a position or an argument, what kinds of evidence are made available, what arguments have been obscured by the way the debate is framed. The consumer role that permeates our broader cultural life influences these reading practices by leading us to read many arguments about cultural life as a consumer focused on liking and disliking. The task of reading is positioned as a consumer act focused on whether reading the argument is pleasurable for the specific reader: Did we find it interesting? Did we like or dislike it? Why? The readers' *reaction* to the text becomes the topic of interest, rather than the argument. These ways of approaching texts *mimic* analysis, but actually supplant it.

Feminist socioforensic discursive analysis brackets and blocks these taken-for-granted reading practices in order to develop an analytic stance toward argument. The analyst is concerned with different goals than the consumer: with how the argument is *constructed*, what evidence is used and how, what authorities are cited and why, what rhetorical devices are used to achieve particular effects, what the arguments open, what they occlude, where one could go with the argument. The analyst thus reads symptomatically, diagnostically. Transforming the terms of reading prepares us for analysis: it brackets consideration of the moral worth and psychology of the person who is presented as the writer, disallows the practice of centering our reaction to the text, denies the route of consumer evaluation, and demands that claims about affect be substantiated by reference to textual features and, therefore, be open to debate. Our analysis focuses, then, on the various "modulations" of textual resources: the constructed rhetorical package of the "author," the nature of argumentative claims, the sentence structures, the specific words used, and the like. "Modulation" involves the ways in which texts adapt or adjust or vary their pitch, intensity, tone, or volume. It emphasizes that the force with which a sound is made is *relative*, signaling that the same tone seems louder in a quiet room than in a noisy one. I frequently use the term *textual vehemence* to represent the kinds of textual "tempering" that create rhetorical affect in this context. While our interpretation of textual vehemence includes inferences about the impression created as an authorial package, or the "persona," it is the *text* that is marked, not a person. We have no evidence about an "angry" person here: not the feminist or the Troper. All authors are using affective textual features to make arguments. All write their texts over periods of time, with revisions, receive advice from colleagues and editors, and do all the things that create texts that cannot be reduced to their authors or the authors' emotions. This book argues that for both the feminist and the antifeminist, the various rhetorics of "textual vehemence"—moments of textual ridicule, irony, indignation, or intensification—work to create claims about the proper nature of our social life. It also argues that feminist claims are undervalued by conventional methods of reading. The feminist scholars whose work I discuss in this book carry out the important work of mobilizing multiple texts and stories to reveal how hegemonic power actually works and what we need to do to combat it: they have indeed moved far *beyond* "the trope of the angry feminist."

Discursive Authority and the Labor of Argument

Feminist socioforensic discursive analysis encourages us to think carefully and productively about the discourses we consume, confront, and contest. Public exchanges, academic debates, and interpersonal arguments and negotiations are sites where the social meanings of gendered identities and feminist identifications get produced. Specialized or expert knowledges such as academic discourses demarcate or "colonize" fields and establish how they can be discussed, including whose voices must be heard and whose can be ignored. Michel Foucault argues that specialized discourses do not produce "more truthful" knowledge, but rather different *kinds* of knowledge. Seeing discourse as connecting knowledge to power, he argues that "truth" "is to be understood as a system of ordered procedures for the production, regulation, distribution, circulation and operation of statements" (1980, "Truth," 133). Thus, for Foucault, "truth" "is linked in a circular relation with systems of power that produce and sustain it, and to effects of power which it induces and which extend it" (133). An academic "regime of truth" authorizes professors to speak about their topics; it does not authorize those studied to speak or to be heard other than as objects for study. This understanding of the frames of "regimes of truth" provides further insight if we revisit Hart's claim that his bad feminists "belonged in the Department of Abnormal Psychology . . . as objects for scientific study." Hart is explicitly *not* arguing that the bad feminists be silenced; rather, they should be required to submit to a regime of truth that defines anything they say as meaningless clamor, heard only as further evidence of their abnormality.

If the terms of inclusion in academic debate require the subordination of women, then feminists must be insubordinate. But that is not all they are. Modern feminism emerged out of a dialogue between institutionalized academic knowledge and what Foucault has aptly named "the insurrection of knowledges" (2003, 9). Foucault describes this insurrection as a rebellion against the power effects that come from the institutionalization of specialized knowledge. Foucault finds important situated knowledges among people who retain allegiances and draw insight from what he calls "subjugated knowledges," knowledges that have been disqualified, ridiculed, and dismissed. Foucault's interest was in the subjugated knowledge that prisoners have about incarceration or that psychiatric patients have about medicine, but scholars of gender and race find insight in the knowledges of other subordinated populations. Foucault cautions readers not to misunderstand his term. He insists that the insurrection of knowledges does not proclaim "the lyrical right to be ignorant," nor does it elevate immediate experience over evidence, ideas, and reflection. Instead, it emphasizes the importance of learning from discounted knowledges, knowledges that are local, regional, and otherwise particular and differential, knowledges that resist unanimity. The point here is not to seize power, but to interrupt, resist, and deconstruct it, to disturb the certainties of power with the contingencies of social experience (2003, 7).

Feminism is, at least in part, a product of the insurrection of knowledges and of insurrections by actual people against the injustices of gendered power. But it is also a form of scholarly interrogation and critique. It requires drawing on the history and techniques of disciplines while crossing boundaries to solve problems that are not limited to a particular disciplinary arena. Academic argument takes place in specific places in specific institutions at specific historical times through the concrete deployment of particular phrases, sentences, and ideas. This scene of argument is what Antonio Gramsci described as a site of "formation, of irradiation, of dissemination, and persuasion," a place where practical labor needs to be performed (1971, 192). The practical labor of feminist scholars includes overcoming discursive conventions designed to exclude them. But it also includes negotiating the residue of the trope of the angry feminist and other instances of the "prose of counterinsurgency" designed to position feminists outside the economy of reason, to invalidate their experiences, to suppress their subjectivities and subject positions. The *prose of counterinsurgency* is a term used by subaltern studies theorist and historian Ranajit Guha to explain how and why official government and academic discourse erases the subjectivity, interests, and actions of South Asian peasants from the historical record (1988). Guha argues that the conventions of dominant discourses deny any possibility of the legitimacy of the peasants' grievances or the worthiness of their actions.[33] Guha advises us that the erasures of the peasants' arguments cannot be understood unless one examines the discourse itself, to have "a close look at its constituting elements and examine those cuts, seams and stitches—those cobbling marks—which tell us about the material it is made of and the manner of its absorption into the fabric of writing" (1988, 47). In my book *Authors on Writing: Metaphors and Intellectual Labor*, I argued that metaphors like these about "cuts, seams and stitches" can tell us a great deal about the challenges we face as readers and writers (2005). They help us see the many minor and arduous tasks that exposition and argument require. In this book, it is my contention that the price of entry into academic debates by feminists from the 1990s to the present requires them to explore those "cuts, seams and stitches," to deploy the right tools for the particular jobs they have to do within a dialogue that began long before they entered it. They have to invite themselves to the party and then rearrange everything in the room once they have arrived. They must confront, contest, invert, and subvert the language of their enemies at the scene of argument.

Transforming the terms of reading necessarily requires transforming the terms of writing. In academic life, the scene of argument for feminists almost always entails dealing with the written word. Writing plays a central role in the work that scholars do, but we often take for granted the many different decisions that writers have to make. We focus on *what* authors create rather than on *how* they create it. Claims, arguments, and conclusions are indeed important, but they become legible to us in scholarship as a result of discursive practices, strategies, and performances. In *Authors on Writing*, I argued that writing needs to be seen as labor, as a concrete praxis performed to achieve discrete and finite ends. Writing may seem private and personal, but it is always a shared social practice, an activity with both critical and creative dimensions. Writers identify problems, pose solutions, inhabit subject positions, promote new subjectivities, appeal to potential allies and attempt to disarm potential enemies. They must appeal to publics new and old. But these publics are not simply already existing discrete social entities; rather, they are conceptual parts of a social imaginary produced through the actual work of writing, reading, and arguing (Michael Warner 2002).[34] Such publics are saturated with power—creating and created by institutions of circulation, ideologies of reading, textual genres, and the rhetoric of texts. Writing is a way of learning, a way of looking for allies who are looking for us, a way of winning recognition and resources vital to changing minds and changing social relations.

In the central chapters of this book I use the tool kit of feminist socioforensic discursive analysis to examine the rhetoric of particular disciplinary or cross-disciplinary arguments. Some of the cases I examine were published since 2000; others were published in the early 1990s, when feminists faced a pernicious and perilous history in the making. Lisa Duggan has identified the important larger societal goals of antifeminism linked with neoliberalism (2003). Duggan argues that the idealized glorification of an imaginary properly gendered, properly sexed, prosperous nuclear family serves as the New Right defense against government actions against sexism, racism, exploitation, and inequality. Within this ideology, bad social conditions are blamed on bad families, while good families are presumed to manage their problems privately without calling for any redistribution of power or wealth. Of course, this ideal private sphere does not actually exist, but is instead evoked through a countersubversive discourse and then promoted through tax and marriage laws that support and subsidize already-privileged groups. The neoliberalism of that time undergirded the much more widespread neoliberalism of the present, just as the discursive debates of the time are echoed in contemporary discourse and power relations (W. Brown, 2005).

Academic feminists in the 1990s tried to do their work as scholars in the face of this antifeminist mobilization. Their initial aims were more to change their disciplines than to change society, to do better scholarship by recognizing the importance of gender as an analytic category and structuring social force. Yet when attempting to address intersections of gendered, racialized, or class injustice, endeavoring to expose the sexist assumptions in the law that excused violence against women, to bring to light musicology's evasion of the centrality of gendered metaphors in musical compositions, or to explain how uncritical acceptance of gendered metaphors in scientific education and practice actually produced bad science, they encountered discursive and professional practices and politics that dismissed them without consideration. How scholars negotiated the rhetorical complications of these arguments forms an important part of the content of this book.

The book focuses on three specific academic scenes of argument: sociolegal studies, musicology, and science studies. All three have public concerns and constituencies that go beyond the academic. All three demonstrate differing notions of argument and evidence. All three demonstrate interplay among academic disciplines, critical social commentary, and more "general" newspaper or television discourses. The nature of these arguments—their general stance and their specialized knowledge—also demonstrate that feminist argument plays out differently in different settings according to this complex field of argument. It demonstrates the impossibility to defining what a "proper" feminist argument might be: To whom? In what setting? For what purpose?

The chapters that follow in this book occur in three sets of two. Each set focuses on a particular discursive politics that ultimately connects academic arguments with other "publics." Each set examines vehement rhetorics and methods of discursive policing at the interface of feminist and antifeminist arguments.

The first set, Chapters 2 and 3, concerns sociolegal studies and arguments about gender, race, consumerism, motherhood, and sexual violence. These are all arguments fraught with social and emotional complexity. Looking at their discourses and rhetorics socioforensically encourages us to see not isolated texts, but texts emerging from particular textual conditions, argumentative genealogies, and political and social conditions. Feminist sociolegal studies may emerge from academic and legal contexts, but it also speaks to wider "publics." Reception of these arguments therefore takes place at multiple discursive sites. Socially shared ideologies of reading often authorize negative commentary on the various arguments, rhetorics, and authors. I look in these two chapters at different structures of discursive policing and of rhetorical decision-making.

"Ideologies of Style: Discursive Policing and Feminist Intersectional Argument" (Chapter 2) argues that "ideologies of style" control how feminism at the scene of argument may be written and read. I examine how discursive policing is employed in three cases of intersectional feminist argument. When Patricia Williams describes how she was refused admittance to the store Benetton on the basis of her race, the editors of a law review and subsequent audiences attempt to control her argument and reduce its emotional resonance. When Dorothy E. Roberts claims that racism and sexism influence the removal of children from Black homes and inflict group harm, Lawrence M. Mead argues that such claims are uncivil, tantamount to libel. I demonstrate how intersectionality and affect influence the deployment of these ideologies of style at the scene of argument.

"Anger: Grammars of Affect and Authority" (Chapter 3) probes the notion of a unified vehemence of "anger" by contrasting the purposes and strategies of two scholars writing about sexual violence: Cynthia K. Gillespie, an attorney discussing the punishments meted out to women who have killed partners who battered them, and Julia Penelope, a linguist who argues that habits of grammar disguise and perpetuate sexual violence in society. I argue that the different effects of their rhetorics stem partly from their greatly differing purposes. Gillespie seeks to show how the language of the law silences women victimized by domestic violence and systematically nullifies women's judgments about the potential seriousness and threatening nature of male violence. Penelope contends that seemingly harmless grammatical constructions hide the agency of male perpetrators of child sex abuse and sexual violence, making it more difficult to hold them accountable and responsible for these acts. Their different rhetorical choices create different responses and demands on readers.

The next two chapters look at a specific moment in musicology in the early 1990s, when feminist research entered the scene of interdisciplinary argument and faced a dramatic response. Thinking of this argumentative moment socioforensically allows us to see how feminist arguments work in uneven terrain. Disciplinary histories can create climates that position as outrageous feminist arguments that have already been found productive in other disciplines. In effect, different disciplines have different "structures of feeling" that influence their reception of feminist arguments. "Structures of feeling," according to Raymond Williams, are composed of "affective elements of consciousness and relationships: not feeling against thought, but thought as felt and feeling as thought" (1977, 132). The structure of feeling that infuses a discipline may make it difficult even to argue for making room to include previously neglected women; it can create further barriers to arguments that using gender as an analytic category may also require interrogating and altering research paradigms. Disciplinary structures of feeling can infuse scenes of argument, as I demonstrate in Chapters 4 and 5.

"Tough Babies, or Anger in the Superior Position" (Chapter 4) explores the trope of the angry feminist as it has been deployed to discipline feminist musicologists, delivered through a persona I call the "Tough Baby" which engages in quite astounding vehemence of its own. The Tough Baby diverts attention away from feminist arguments, ideas, and evidence by substituting punditry for scholarly analysis. The Tough Baby evokes nostalgia for the old days when women allegedly knew their place, and proffers proclamations, recommendations, and condemnations designed to save conventional gender roles from scholarly critique. I delineate the characteristics of the Tough Baby as it is revealed in texts of Robert Craft, Eric Gans, and Pieter van den Toorn.

"Faux Feminism and the Rhetoric of Betrayal" (Chapter 5) examines how Leo Treitler and Paula Higgins use vehement rhetoric in an attempt to curb the challenges of feminist musicologist Susan McClary, whose work examines sexual codes in Beethoven, among other controversial subjects. Treitler and Higgins attempt to "quarantine" McClary and her work through discourses of betrayal and transgression—to recuperate a pure ideal of feminist musicology within the economy of reason in order to expel the "angry feminist" from this domain.

The next two chapters look at arguments about science and reproduction. Science studies—such as sociological studies of science and medical anthropology—represents a particularly complex discursive situation, an intersection of publics that maintain partial and to some degree contradictory perspectives on the relation of scientific, textbook, and popular discourses. Feminist arguments can, therefore, be policed from a variety of perspectives, perhaps most dramatically by exclusion: by claims that scientific arenas are sealed off from the social. According to this line of argument, because science represents "reality," it cannot be subject to gendered critique. In the face of claims of epistemological "purity," feminist critics have developed rhetorics designed specifically to "crack open" the claim that scientific narratives are divorced from gendered social attitudes.

"Intensification and the Discourse of Decline" (Chapter 6) scrutinizes the rhetoric used by medical anthropologist Emily Martin to counter deleterious visions of women still found in contemporary textbooks used in medical school and college physiology courses. Martin uses a complex of strategies that I call "intensification" to probe and distill this entrenched language in such a way that it can no longer be defended by scientists.

"Ridicule: Phallic Fables and Spermatic Romance" (Chapter 7) compares strategies used elsewhere by Emily Martin and by a group of scholars and students called the Biology and Gender Study Group with those deployed by a 1940s satirist, Ruth Herschberger. These three use intersecting strategies to ridicule "phallic fables" and the "spermatic romance," which describe the meeting of the sperm and the egg in the terms of a quest or romance. These critiques do not dispute the "facts" of scientific research, but instead show how the narratives that textbooks use to communicate research findings rely on highly gendered cultural stories that serve patriarchy and misrepresent science. They undermine simplistic stories about science in order to argue for more adequate and more accurate stories. I use these textured textual studies to emphasize that rhetoric is not a neutral tool that can be wielded effectively by anyone in any context, but rather that rhetoric is an effect of power and that it needs to be judged in relation to the interests that it seeks to advance, oppose, or displace.

The concluding chapter argues that feminist socioforensic discursive analysis provides an optic on the significantly different use of textual vehemence to create discursive authority in antifeminist and feminist academic argument.

Feminists cannot escape the gendered history of discourse, but we can destabilize it, explore its contradictions, and work through it to open up new possibilities. As Foucault argues, "We must make allowance for the complex and unstable process whereby discourse can be both an instrument and an effect of power, but also a stumbling block, a point of resistance and a starting point for an opposing strategy" (1980, *History,* 101).[35] The crux of Foucault's claim is that discursive effects cannot be known in advance or assumed to reflect the intentions of those who argue, that we cannot know fully the consequences of our own roles in the circulation of discourses. Yet these discourses are what we have—the sites, the circumstances, and the means—to understand ourselves and change our conditions. In *Bodies That Matter: On the Discursive Limits of "Sex,"* Judith Butler asks, "[H]ow is it that the abjected come to make their claim through and against the discourses that have sought their repudiation?" (1993, 224). We can contribute to an answer to Butler's question as it applies to this arena by looking closely at the scene of argument with the tools of feminist socioforensic discursive analysis. Transforming the terms of reading, sharpening our understanding of textual affect, acknowledging the role of labor in academic writing—these tools enable us to reposition ourselves within the agonistic structures of contemporary debate.

CHAPTER TWO

Ideologies of Style

*Discursive Policing and Feminist
Intersectional Argument*

The cultural training program exemplified in part by the trope of the angry feminist is a discursive technology of power that accounts for, swallows up, deflects, deflates, and redirects social criticism. Discursive technologies of power encourage affiliation with dominant discourses through complex means of identification and repudiation. They deploy affect as an important tool in that effort. Identifying this widely circulated discursive pattern is not to imply that dominant discourses speak in *one* voice, or from *one* position, or on behalf of *one* kind of social formation. It is not evidence of a monolithic alliance of antifeminists. I argue, in fact, the contrary. The trope is a tool that can also be used opportunistically as a means to further goals that are only peripherally related to antifeminism. In scholarship, tropes that carry the echoes of everyday punditry are deployed for a variety of political ends, including framing certain kinds of research claims as illegitimate or dramatically reining in calls for reframing the disciplines.

Judgments about which people or which claims can be labeled "emotional," which rhetorical strategies can count as vehement, and what textual affect is thought to accomplish are always deeply *political* and *rhetorical*. What subjects are open to discussion, who has the right to make certain kinds of claims, what counts as proper evidence are both scholarly and political questions.[1] Since debates take place in particular discursive arenas—say, within a particular discipline or connected set of disciplines—there are discursive norms that can appear to be violated by textual features and even by kinds of claims and evidence. Social relations of power are always at play in *readers'* decisions about affect. The trope of the angry feminist is one of many cultural resources that misdirect our attention to the emotions of the author rather than thinking about the emotions of the audience. One difficulty in understanding and countering the trope of the angry feminist is that conventional practices of reading unwittingly support the trope, rather than deconstruct it. I offer in this chapter some ways that our interpretive frames lead us into this situation. I therefore argue—perhaps counterintuitively—that the trope of the angry feminist is ultimately not about an opposition between emotion and reason, but rather about the relationships that link rhetoric to politics and power.

Shifting the terms of reading to think about politics and power rather than identifying and evaluating specific markers of textual affect offers a different set of interpretive possibilities. I develop in this chapter critical tools to help us recognize how *claims* about authorial "anger" and inappropriate affect have a *strategic rhetorical role* in the production and reception of arguments. In other words, claiming that one is "angry" or is expressing affect is a rhetorical device that deserves attention for its argumentative purposes. Claiming that one's agonist has inappropriate affect can be used for a variety of purposes, including "toning down" affect; it can also serve to dramatically evade a substantive argument by shifting to discussions of the author's integrity. Commonplace forms of discursive policing function to suppress challenges to unequal gender, racial, and class power at the scene of argument. Such policing is particularly prominent in issues central to women's traditional roles: bodies, consumption, motherhood, and what Tricia Rose calls "intimate justice" (2003).

I examine here two different cases where Black women scholars make claims about racialized and gendered injustice. In *The Alchemy of Race and Rights: Diary of a Law Professor* (1991), law professor Patricia J. Williams[2] describes an incident in which her embodied presence as a Black woman was used to deny her the opportunity to behave as a normative middle-class consumer: to shop for a sweater at Benetton. She writes that it made her angry. The issue for us is not whether Williams was "really" angry. Instead, what she tells us about her anger, her prose, her editing, and her audiences illustrates the connection of affect and social justice that Angry Tropers are trying to hide.

In the second case, I examine law professor Dorothy E. Roberts's[3] argument that those enacting child welfare policies use a racialized lens that leads to disproportionate destruction of Black families (2003). Roberts indicates that she sees the conditions she is addressing as damaging and wants policies to address them. Roberts does not say or write that she is "angry" or "emotional"; her text is congruent with disciplinary "norms" and shows no markers of vehemence. But the counterargument of responder Lawrence M. Mead III,[4] professor of political science, makes a dramatically vehement claim. He contends that an argument of the type Roberts has framed—questioning the role of racialized and gendered decision-making in welfare policies— should be barred from scholarly and public discussion. To the question of his title, "Is Complaint a Moral Argument?" (2003), Mead replies with a resounding "No!" The issue for us is not whether Mead is "really" angry or if he "believes" his claim; rather, his rhetoric productively instantiates my claim that arguments about inappropriate affect are discursive technologies of power deployed strategically to suppress claims for social justice.

Civil Society, Hegemony, and Dominant Discourses

Before turning to a closer examination of how affect works in the case of Williams and her experience at Benetton, as well as Mead's vehement condemnation of Roberts, we need more tools to apprehend the larger structures of power that set the stage for considering feminism and affect at the scene of argument. Concepts of civil society, hegemony, and dominant discourses are useful here. I am drawing on them to situate discursive authority as always fragmentary, flexible, and contested.

Claiming that power is in play in a field of discourse often evokes a vision of government or other monoliths using coercion and manipulation on subordinates. The power used by both feminists and antifeminists, however, is better understood as taking place in a field where social, political, and economic dominance is complex and contested. It is where we are persuaded to be certain kinds of citizens, to have certain visions of the good. It takes place in the discursive arena often called "civil society" or "civic culture," a contested and idealized site of debate. It is a sphere that is seen as neither family nor quite the government. It includes economic, religious, and intellectual institutions, the media, and so forth. Civil society includes all the scenes of argument that we consider here: journalism, punditry, advertising, entertainment, public relations, quasi-intellectual magazines, political discourse. It also includes the discourse of academic scholarship. It is important to recognize that scholarly debate is not hermetically sealed off from other discussions in civil society. Part of disciplinary debate is shaped by specialized tools for knowledge production, but part draws on norms common in civil society. Civil society is full of contestation and debate about what kinds of people we should be, what attitudes we should have, and what we should be doing. While academic debates necessarily draw on the norms of civil society, disciplinary specialists may undermine their ability to develop new paradigms of specialized knowledge if they do not interrogate their reliance on rhetorics permeated by sedimented histories of class, gender, race, and sexuality inequalities.

For a feminist socioforensic discursive analysis, it is particularly productive to think of the relations of power at play in civil society in terms of Antonio Gramsci's concept of "hegemony." Gramsci puts persuasion at the center of the process of creating conditions of social dominance. According to S. Kim,

> By "hegemony," Gramsci (1971) intended to conceptualize the pivotal role of cultural persuasion in acquiring, exercising, maintaining, or challenging power without resorting to physical coercion. . . . The essence of the concept of hegemony lies in the idea of subordinates' consent. According to Gramsci, the consent of subordinates is constructed when a dominant group's particular world view is accepted by the subordinate groups as their world view, and thus the dominant group's interests appear to be the interests of the society at large. As a result, the dominant group is seen as entitled to its ethical and intellectual leadership and arises as a hegemonic group in a particular historical period. (2001, 6645)

In Gramsci's view, argument is central to hegemony because it recruits subordinate groups into their own subordination. But the labor of argument is also central because it offers *other ways* of framing how things might be. Contestation and debate work on many fronts. Cultural categories, fantasies, and identities become part of the production of politics: places for persuasion, for constituting new ways of seeing, for establishing new joint interests, for creating new strategic alliances. Stuart Hall argues that by proliferating sites of power, modern capitalism creates more fields of social antagonism (1987, 20), opening new sites for argument. Hall argues that for Gramsci, politics "is where forces and relations, in the economy, in society, in culture, have to be actively *worked* on to produce particular forms of power, forms of domination" (1987, 20). The work of argument then is not merely to persuade others to one's point of view, but to build points of view conjointly with others. This is a view of politics centered on the *labor of argument*.

Given this arena of contest and debate, discursive technologies of power cannot be seen as monolithic, in automatic service to identified interests, or incontestable.[5] Dominant discourses are themselves fractured, changing, and in struggle.[6] Richard Terdiman contends that dominant discourses appear *transparent* (1985, 57):

The inherent tendency of a dominant discourse is to "go without say-ing." The dominant is the discourse whose presence is defined by the *social impossibility of its absence*. Because of that implicit potential toward automatism, the dominant is the discourse which, being every-where, comes from nowhere: to it is granted the structural privilege of appearing to be unaware of the very question of its own legitimacy. Bourdieu calls this self-assured divorce from consciousness of its contingency "genesis amnesia." (1985, 61, citing Bourdieu 1977, 79)

Part of my task in this book is to draw our attention to the way that dominant discourses provide us with conventional writing and reading prac-tices that "go without saying," that position specific and contingent ways of thinking about texts as universally applicable and reliable. Deploying uninter-rogated procedures of reading attenuates our ability to analyze power at the scene of argument. I have provided tools to counter some of these practices in Chapter 1 and will continue to do so as I turn to considering the cases of Williams as well as Roberts and Mead.

An Ideology of Style Rooted in a Social Text of Neutrality

In *The Alchemy of Race and Rights*, law professor Patricia J. Williams de-scribes her angry reactions when a teen-aged white sales clerk, seeing she was Black, refused to "buzz her in" to shop at the specialty store Benetton:

> It was two Sundays before Christmas, at one o'clock in the after-noon. There were several white people in the store who appeared to be shopping for things for *their* mothers. I was enraged. At that moment I literally wanted to break all of the windows in the store and *take* lots of sweaters for my mother. (1991, 45)

Williams explains how this insult registered itself in affective terms:

> I am still struck by the structure of power that drove me into such a blizzard of rage. There was almost nothing I could do, short of physi-cally intruding upon him, that would humiliate [that saleschild] the way he had humiliated me. No words, no gestures, no prejudices of my own would make a bit of difference to him. . . . He had no com-passion, no remorse, no reference to me; and no desire to acknowledge me even at the estranged level of arm's-length transactor. (1991, 45)

Williams's argument is explicitly about the production of affect—anger and humiliation—in the face of a *routine* and *unemotional* deployment of structural power. She describes herself as "enraged," using a term that implies very intense anger, and even presents a fantasy of violent window-breaking and theft. That claim is the basis of my argument in this chapter. For thinking about the "angry feminist," however, it is important to note what she does *not* say: she does not claim that she was "angry" when she wrote *about* the incident, or when she revised what she wrote, that she is in general an "angry person," or that she is "angry" today. While those things may or may not be true, there is no evidence for them in the text.

When Williams related her Benetton experience for a law review symposium on "Excluded Voices," her account did not fare well when subjected to the standards of rule-triggered strictures of style and argument. The editors of the law review deployed academic rules of textual propriety to curb her vehemence, to literally "rewrite" her vigorous and compelling arguments. First they muted the vehemence of the prose, adjusting the rhetorical strategies to suppress the "emotional content" of the experience. As she reports,

> From the first page to the last, my fury had been carefully cut out. My rushing, run-on-rage had been reduced to simple declarative sentences. The active personal had been inverted in favor of the passive impersonal. My words were different; they spoke to me upside-down. . . . [M]eanings rose up at me oddly, stolen and strange. (1991, 47)

The problem here is not the process of editing. Editing and comments about revision on texts in progress are a commonplace part of academic writing. Colleagues, friends, reviewers, editors—all suggest and even require revision. The law review's editing did not prevent Williams from "expressing her true self," because she was constructing a textual argument, not "expressing" herself. Her deployment of textual vehemence does *not* somehow "testify to its own authenticity," or frame her argument as unimpeachable. My claim is more precise: in rendering her textually vehement argument emotionally "neutral," the editors of the law review significantly changed the argument, most centrally what Williams presents as "rage" at being excluded on the basis of her race. Interpreting accurately what such exclusion means—and how that exclusion relates to Williams's social critique—requires one to grapple with her argument about anger and the experiences that it represents. In the light of her larger argument, when the editors of the law review use "neutral" rules about style to smooth over Williams's distress, to mute her vehemence, they engage (perhaps inadvertently) in political action of their own. Academic conventions applied like this—overlooking and obscuring political and ethical issues as matters of "style"—become deeply conservative.

At the next editing stage, "official" standards of evidence and fears of legal reprisal were mustered to suppress the events entirely:

> All reference to Benetton's had been deleted because, according to the editors and the faculty adviser, it was defamatory; they feared harassment and liability; they said printing it would be irresponsible. I called them and offered to supply a footnote attesting to this as my personal experience at one particular location and of a buzzer system not limited to Benetton's; the editors told me that they were not in the habit of publishing things that were unverifiable. (47)

Decisions to include or eliminate parts of arguments—in this case vivid moments that capture and crystallize central points—may make reference to academic "rules," but rules *always* require interpretation. When employed to delete evocative events from the protests of aggrieved parties, the suppression, again, becomes a political act. The editorial practices of any publication always represent a constellation of decisions that often appear invisible to outsiders but have developed from specific interactions and practices. Megan Knize, editor in chief of the *UC Davis Law Review* 2007–2008, argues that law review cultures work according to a "gladiator" ethos, "emphasizing competition over collaboration, prioritizing rules over relationships, and encouraging particularly 'masculine' leadership characteristics" (2008, 1). She indicates that participation in student-run law reviews is a prestigious way to advance one's career; historically, law review staffs have included a smaller proportion of women and students of color than in the school as a whole. It is thus misleading to envision Williams's editing as simply a conflict between an "emotional" author and an "emotionless" bureaucracy.

At the page proof stage, the editors used even more fine stylistic decisions to eliminate Williams's references to her own race, on the grounds that "editorial policy" did not permit "descriptions of physiognomy." An ostensibly "neutral" stricture about descriptions of physiognomy cuts deep into the reasons for Williams's argument, to the degree that, one would suspect, it could become not only less powerful but unintelligible. When Williams telephoned to protest the elimination of the information that she was Black, on the grounds that it was deeply significant to her argument, she was told by an editor:

"It's nice and poetic," but it does not "advance the discussion of any principle. . . . This is a law review, after all." Frustrated, I accused him of censorship; calmly he assured me it was not. "This is just a matter of style," he said with firmness and finality. (P. Williams 1991, 48)

While this decision was eventually reversed, its proffering as an academically and socially neutral policy goes far to illustrate the discursive policing enacted by what Williams calls "an ideology of style rooted in a social text of neutrality" (48). Claiming the decision is *just* a matter of style, he presents the formation of that style as apolitical, its origins obscured, its existence inevitable, its "objectivity" unchallengeable. But none of this is the case. The employment of academic styles to limit argument is a discursive technology of power that works to keep stable existing relations of power. Claims of "neutrality" paper over present inequalities and present the discursive situation as a "level playing field," where participants play games according to the same rules. But *readers* are not neutral. They are prepared to hear different arguments in different ways. Some arguments they are not prepared to hear at all. While ostensibly neutral, these prohibitions against textual vehemence in academic writing control what arguments can be acknowledged. They serve a socially conservative function. They hide the unequal access to power that makes people angry in the first place, isolate the forms of academic argument from their social causes and consequences, and deprive aggrieved groups and oppositional voices of the forceful, confrontational, affective language often required to displace entrenched ideas and interests.

The editing of Williams's Benetton report and her response to it expressly foreground the ways in which social relations of race, gender, and class can become occluded by academic writing conventions. Williams uses diverse rhetorical strategies to deploy anger, annoyance, and frustration *as rhetorical tropes* to inject race, gender, and class issues into discourses that systematically exclude them. Racial humiliation is at the center of the event. Clearly her race and probably its link to her gender prevented her from being buzzed in, not anything about her individual qualities, characteristics, or behavior. But in addition to their "neutrality" about descriptions of physiognomy, the editors of the law review, like many academic editors, sought "emotional neutrality," obliterating Williams's argument about the effects of being excluded.

Williams's reporting of the Benetton incident and its reception demonstrate how an ideology of argument can work in tandem with an ideology of style to define as "invisible" and "socially neutral" subject positions that are marked and constructed by gender, class, and race. The cognitive consequences of Williams's anger may *be exactly what academic conventions are designed to mute.* Williams's vehement narrative of her rejection at Benetton demands that readers confront their own positioning, that they recognize the degree to which they are implicated in the "sign" of race used as a criterion by the Benetton clerk. Her argument demands that readers see *themselves* as people whose routine privileges may be premised on the pain and humiliation of others. Williams's chapter revolves around the difficulty of registering the reverberations of this everyday insult, her rage, its implications, its consequences. For the discursive situation that Williams recounts is one that disables any argument she might make *prior to* its utterance: no matter how strong her argument, it is subject to prior veto by a teenaged worker authorized to decide whether a Black woman counts as a desirable shopper. Revealing the specificity of her marked identity and its humiliating consequences is the purpose of Williams's vehemence. She cannot speak neutrally, from "nowhere" (Haraway 1988), because the nature of the injury she wishes to expose can be seen only from a socially specific and situated standpoint.

Williams's *rhetorical strategies* are autobiographical, personal, evocative, "emotional." But her *arguments* are not. Providing remarkably little information about herself, she uses these rhetorical strategies to make arguments explicitly focused on long-standing racialized and gendered inequities. Much of the power and penetration of Williams's impassioned narratives rely on her vehement marshaling of her intersectional identities as a Black woman in public and private in order to expose ugly cracks in our civic life. Her rhetoric *enacts* as well as *makes* its arguments. Barbara Johnson, commenting on the very passages of Williams's *Alchemy of Race and Rights* that concern me here, argues, "It is not that Patricia Williams's style can be identified as black or female, but that her writing possesses a logic that makes perceptible the realities of difference subordinated behind the rhetoric of neutrality and impersonality. . . . In other words, the style of Patricia Williams is not the sign of her identity but the enactment of her critique" (1994, 262). Williams's strategies expressly violate claims that good academic prose can be "objective" because it can come from nowhere. In emphasizing her own position in inequitable social structures, she seeks to require the same of her readers, to make it clear that her readers too have a partisan position.

Citizens as Intersectional

Williams's critique confronts exclusion, but not, at its heart, her exclusion from Benetton. Benetton's exclusion is instead symptomatic, emblematic of her exclusion from inhabiting the liberal citizen-subject position of civil society.

While ideals of citizenship change, come under criticism, are debated, many citizens and scholars simply continue to proffer these ideals as if they are unchallenged, as if they always represent successful ways for people properly to participate in liberal democracy.[7] The apparent failure of the ideal, as in Benetton's policy, can be handled by argumentative strategies that save the ideal of citizen at the expense of the individual, for example, by branding the interests of the citizen that the ideal fails as being "partial," and therefore not of general concern.[8] The consequence of fashioning citizen-subjects in this way is to forestall challenges to the ideal that seek to make it account for actual treatment of citizens.

The site of exclusion denies Williams the opportunity to be a consumer. Rather than being peripheral to one's subjectivity as a citizen, consumption in our society is central to social membership. According to Toby Miller,

> The citizen and the consumer have shadowed each other as the *national* subject versus the *rational* subject—with politics rendered artificial and consumption natural, a means of legitimating social relationships (Marx 1994, 140). Adopting the tenets of the consumer, the citizen becomes a desirous, self-actualizing subject who still conforms to general patterns of *controlled* behavior. Adopting the tenets of the citizen, the consumer becomes a self-limiting, self-controlling subject who still conforms to general patterns of *purchasing* behavior. (2006, 30)

The consumer is positioned as flexible, mobile, free. Miller argues critically that this ideal positions the consumer as if he or she could be "the classless, raceless, sexless, ageless, unprincipled, magic agent of social value in a multitude of discourses and institutions, animated by the drive to realize individual desires" (2006, 31).[9] The liberal citizen-subject is also a market subject.

Shopping is a public sphere that is often presented as central to women's lives. The ideal of the liberal citizen-subject rests on the premise that part of what makes one "equal" is having consumer dollars to spend freely. In a capitalist society, we are told, the only color that should matter is the color of money. But Williams discovers otherwise. The injury is not that Benetton's corporate policy is "impolite." Rather, the injury is Benetton's demonstration that embodied identity trumps everything, that Williams's status as a law professor, her income, her demeanor, the cost of her clothing—all of which would qualify her as an ideal shopper—become invisible because the clerk sees only her race and gender. For Black women, so often subject to gendered racial profiling and defamed historically as nonnormative, unclean, untrustworthy, and immoral, the open humiliation of exclusion from the public sphere of shopping contains a special sting. Black women's long struggle for respect and respectability has often required them to "perform normativity" for their oppressors, to speak, dress, appear, and act "worthy," as if the roots of racism lay in their own deficiencies rather than in the pathological imaginations and actions central to white supremacy (Gaines 1996, Griffin 2001, Mitchell 2004). These performances of normativity often prove futile, as they did when Williams was refused access to Benetton.

Williams contests the prevailing model of the liberal citizen-subject as implicitly white and male; like other feminists, she argues that such a model works individually and atomistically to seal off the citizen-subject from responsibility for broader social injustice.[10] Like many critics, Williams presents a feminism and antiracism that do not merely argue that women and people of color can be liberal subjects, but interrogate how liberal citizenship masks group oppression and group injuries. In many of her writings, Williams exposes the inability of the model of the liberal citizen-subject to account for the contradictions in social relations that she experiences in everyday life.

As Williams's experience shows, the social constructions of gender and of race are both key building blocks in inequality and injustice, but neither works in isolation. In feminist intersectional analysis—like Kimberlé Crenshaw's insightful and uniquely generative concept of intersectionality (1989)—neither gender nor race appears alone.[11] At different times, different parts of our identities might matter more or less, yet identities are nonetheless tremendously important ways of positioning ourselves in relation to how power works. In these analyses, feminist arguments and responses to them are important not to advance the interests of all women as if women were a unified category, not to demonstrate that differences in biology produce differences in rhetoric, but to reveal what women know and experience about social and discursive relations. These relations are composite, uneven, and intersectional.

Intersectional analysis, central to women of color feminism, provides an *optic on power* that comes from experience and embodied identities but is not reducible to them. This optic does not explore who is the most oppressed or who has access to "truth," but seeks a maximally epistemologically sensitive position on how power works. Teresa de Lauretis makes a related argument in "Eccentric Subjects: Feminist Theory and Historical Consciousness" (1990), when she argues that lesbians notice the power of heterosexism in a way that heterosexuals do not; therefore, their situated knowledge provides everyone with a perceptive optic on its power. Similarly, arguments by women of color feminists and responses to them provide valuable ways of showing how we are actually governed, how raced and gendered power is exercised, and how more just and egalitarian social relations might be created. But part of the intersectional optic on power is an understanding of *readers' affects at the scene of argument*: their complacency about the capaciousness of the notion of the liberal citizen-subject, their desire to defend it at the expense of the individual who exposes its inadequacy. The rhetorical problem that authors face, then, is how to puncture readers' satisfaction with a concept that has served many of them well at the expense of others.

Williams's feminist intersectional analysis is uniquely suited to expose and contest discursive technologies of power—widespread conventions about argument etiquettes and civility that present as "ethical" and "neutral" an ideology of style requiring silence about social injustice. Rules of a "neutral" style serve as "hegemonic policing," suppressing social critique; framing this neutrality as "ethical"—which some do—masks its use to intimidate and silence voices from aggrieved groups.

Gender, Race, and Conventional Models of Emotion and Reason

In Chapter 1, I argued that feminist socioforensic discursive analysis provides tools to counter conventional reading practices that rest on uninterrogated and deeply gendered and racialized models of textuality, argument, authorship, politeness, and emotion. Our taken-for-granted deployment of these models signals their grounding in dominant discourses. Recall that Terdiman argues that the dominant discourse is "granted the structural privilege of appearing to be unaware of the very question of its own legitimacy" (1985, 61). The dominant discourses, "being everywhere, come from nowhere" (61). Denying their own contingency, these conventional tools of assessment present themselves as ready-made and always legitimate ways of evaluating arguments. Many of these tools offer themselves in the form of binaries: rational/irrational, objective/biased, sensible/emotional. The two terms are in a hierarchy, one depends on the other, and neither is adequately defined. Their purpose is clear, however, in terms of *what they do for the reader*. They are deployed to authorize *discarding* arguments. While such conventional tools are always available, they are not used uniformly. They are specifically brought into play to eject specific authors from the "economy of reason" in order to insulate readers from the challenges of social criticism. So one of the difficulties in clarifying textual vehemence as a rhetorical strategy is that readers tend to deploy complex, culturally based categories of evaluation as if they were self-evident and inflexible. Yet both "reason" and "emotion" are culturally and historically contingent. In the kinds of arguments under consideration in this book, they are always tools for *interpretation*, not *evaluation*.

Contemporary cultural models of reason are gendered and racialized, but not quite in the way that conventional reading practices imply. "Reason" is culturally positioned as an attribute of males, so women often must prove their "rationality." Cultural models also position "reason" as a set of self-evident rules. Foucault's discussion of "truth" turns our attention to specific features of reasoning: "a system of ordered procedures for the production, regulation, distribution, circulation and operation of statements" (1980, "Truth," 133). His formulation allows us to consider the different features that construct the procedures of thinking we call "reason," rather than simply use its name as a tool to dispatch an argument. Historical studies of scientific reasoning demonstrate that it changes over time.[12] Academic disciplines work according to different models of reasoning, with different kinds of claims and evidence and conclusions. They often criticize one another's methods. Genevieve Lloyd notes that the "connotations of 'rationality' are of objectivity, abstraction, detachment. Yet the term itself evokes strong emotions" (2000, 165). Feminists have called into the question claims that reason is unified, neutral, and universal by arguing that it rests on gendered norms. Lloyd argues,

> The most important upshot of the feminist critique of rationality has perhaps not been the emergence of—or even the aspiration to—a thought-style that is distinctively "female." Perhaps it has been rather a sharper articulation of the different strands—intellectual, imaginative, and affective—involved in human ways of thinking; a resistance to their polarization; and a greater appreciation of the strength and limitations of different ways of bringing them together. Different kinds of unity between intellect, imagination and emotion are appropriate or inappropriate in different contexts. (2000, 172)

Lloyd describes a kind of reasoning that is flexible enough to use for analysis of the kinds of arguments I examine here.

Contemporary cultural models of emotion are also gendered and racialized; they fail to account for historical changes in emotional styles and social conventions.[13] The cultural models suggest that emotion and reason operate separately, and that emotion *interferes* with reason, or that appeals to emotions are *other than* appeals to reason, rather than—as some would argue—*kinds of* appeals to reason.[14] Those not in dominant positions are particularly suspect under such cultural models: for example, such models tend to suggest that women are expected to demonstrate all emotions *but* anger, and men are expected to demonstrate few or no emotions *but* anger.[15] Children become aware of this stereotypical deployment and its implications even before kindergarten.[16] As a result of these models, the "emotional" utterances of women are treated differently than those of men:[17] both men and women tend to recode dominant and male emotion as "rational," or "justified," at the same time recoding virtually identical expression by women and aggrieved groups as "emotional," or "angry."[18] To achieve this recoding, people ignore evidence of men's cheering and prancing around with footballs, or their experiencing warmth, solidarity, bonding through drinking Bud and wearing Levi's Cotton Dockers—or, for that matter, the not-always-"irrational"-but-nonetheless-"unjustified" emotional reactions that may lead men to rape, assault, and kill.

The supposed gulf between emotion and reason is one warrant for disregarding the arguments of someone who appears to be angry or indignant. To discount or bracket research and arguments because the authors appear "angry" assumes that they *only* make these arguments *because* they are angry, and when reason takes hold again, they will come to see otherwise. But other ways of thinking about the roles of emotions in moral and conceptual thinking prove much more productive to the analysis of academic argument: the "cognitivist" point of view[19] holds that cognitive states—judgments or beliefs—are constituent of emotions. In such a case, being "angry" does not *preclude* reasoning, *interfere* with reasoning, or *substitute* for reasoning: it is a *motivation for*, an *element of*, and a *result of* reasoning.[20] Under such circumstances, emotions and reason together serve to establish social responsibility, not reflect social irresponsibility.

Considered this way, vehement emotions and their textual analogues may be valuable in clarifying the connection between specific arguments and the values upon which all arguments rest. Philosopher Elizabeth V. Spelman distinguishes between *rage* and *anger* (1989). She argues that the terms are used to condemn the emotions of subordinated groups and praise the emotions of those deemed worthy.[21] Spelman argues that

> analysis of the emotions, and of anger in particular, can be regarded as revelatory of important parts of our lives as moral agents in our social and political relationships with others. . . . [I]nsofar as dominant groups wish to place limits on the kinds of emotional responses appropriate to those subordinate to them, they are attempting to exclude

those subordinate to them from the category of moral agents. Hence there is a politics of emotion: the systematic denial of anger can be seen as a mechanism of subordination, and the existence and expression of anger as an act of insubordination. (1989, 270)

When the imbrications of emotion and ethical concerns are brought to the fore, it becomes evident that reasoning about one's own or another's situation may just as easily result in people *becoming* angry (Scheman 1980; Spelman 1989). Research or reasoning does not always lead one to consider the current state of affairs as justified; one can come to see it as unjustified, and therefore blameworthy.

Despite the existence of the cognitivist model and of other ways of seeing the links between ethical evaluation and "emotion," the salience of the dominant model is such that readers frequently assume that a textually vehement author is unable to "reason," even when there is considerable evidence to the contrary in the text: careful and logical progression of the argument, clear marshaling of evidence, and so forth. Readers' interpretive practices do not always allow them to recognize the value of vehemence to the argument, or to bracket the issue of an emotional argument and judge the argument apart from the vehemence of its presentation, or to check whether the impression of—or classification of—the "textual emotion" stands up under analysis. Yet to be vivid, to be emphatic, to be outraged, even to be wrong—none of these are "unreasonable."[22] In fact, I would argue that in some ways what is unfortunate (even "unreasonable") is for readers to shift attention *away from* the content of arguments to unconventionalities of rhetorical form or to the purported character failings of agonists. Such interpretive practices allow readers to direct their own and others' attention away from what I would contend is the significant ethical question: *Do the agonists have something to be angry about?*

Cultural ways of responding to gender that portray women as emotional and concerned with the personal sphere promote interpretations of feminist academic discourse that use the personalized cultural model rather than a rhetorical model. Since all discourse, including academic discourse, takes place in a social arena, readers cannot "bracket" their gender biases when they read formal and academic texts. The tendency to react to such arguments according to gender biases is a significant problem for academic argumentation as well as other types of public dispute. Literary critic Brenda Silver is only one of many who have noted that the definition of terms used to evaluate academic work varies according to gender: "One has the distinct feeling that men write cultural criticism but that women who criticize their culture only 'complain'" (1991, 356). Silver is drawing attention to the ways that social attitudes about gender are implicated in interpretation of academic texts. According to her study,

> [T]he perception and reception of a particular illocutionary act (or discursive document) must be seen as a matter of social and cultural contexts, among them the social relation of the speaker and the addressee and the interests at stake. Hence, whether a speaker is perceived as performing a legitimate cultural critique when she or he "complains" or merely as whining, will depend on "the intentions, attitudes, and expectations of the participants, the relationships existing between participants," including relationships of authority, "and, generally, the unspoken rules and conventions that are understood to be in play when an utterance is made and received." (1991, 360; Silver quotes from Pratt 1977, 86)

If readers classify textual vehemence as "expressive" rather than "rational," "outburst" rather than "argument," as many readers do, the consequences go beyond their reception of a specific line of argument. Such classification devalues the authors' political stances and turns their political arguments into personal "psychological" problems. The decision to do this serves political ends: if readers interpret these markers as revealing "anger," a personal, psychological trait of the author, they are conflating "emphatic," "disagreeable," or "demanding" with "unreasonable." They are, in effect, "depoliticizing" political speech (see Lyman 2004, 1981). This dynamic reinterprets political statements to demonstrate personal and psychological problems, to be solved at the level of the individual, not the social. It makes authors responsible for the "disturbance" caused by the affect in their arguments, rather than turning attention to the "disturbance" of the social injustices they protest. Authors who deploy affect as a vehicle of their prose style—such as Williams, with her claims of emotion, personal narrative, intersectional arguments about race and gender—appear to some to have "brought it on themselves," or "put themselves in the line of fire," because of their deployment of affect.

Those who argue about social injustice tend to be "marked" by their gender and race, and therefore considered open to discursive policing. I am building here on the insight of Carol Brooks Gardiner (cited in Feagin and Sikes 1994, 60) that women and Blacks are "open persons" in public, whose embodied identities place them under specific forms of surveillance. Intersectionality suggests that to be a woman *and* a Black makes one open to *additional* surveillance: as the intersectional category of "Black woman."

Their status as "open persons" allows readers and audiences to further chastise and instruct the author. Williams's argument about the Benetton incident and the law review's editing offers these opportunities. For when Williams objects to the insults that accompany her marked identity, her audiences often respond by reinforcing that open identity. Williams has spoken about this incident and its repercussions in public talks; she relates how her audiences present a panoply of strategies for deflecting her argument. Many members of her audiences appear perfectly willing to back up the clerk although what the clerk did is illegal—a clear violation of the public accommodations sections of the 1964 Civil Rights Act. Like antitrust violations and hate crimes, denying service to people because of their race or gender is considered a crime not just against the excluded individual but against the entire community as well because it inhibits the free movement, interaction, and commerce upon which the entire society depends. I believe that most people would be deeply offended if this policy were applied to them. Yet some audience members urge Williams to see that, from the store's own point of view, the policy is merely "prudent," "reasonable," and therefore excusable. Some endorse the abstract precaution of barring Blacks from these stores, while denying (of course) that they approve of *Williams* being barred. Others encourage Blacks such as Williams to imagine themselves in the *storeowners'* place—if *they* were the storeowners, they would *surely* believe it reasonable to exclude *themselves*. Some relentlessly reposition Williams's angry response as idiosyncratic, personal, "unverifiable," and "unfair." All these listeners are drawing on what might appear to be "neutral" tools of argument analysis to defend the status quo vigorously from the onslaught of Williams's critique—and, simultaneously, to avoid grappling with Williams's argument.

Williams's status as an "open person" authorizes not just the law review editors, not just some members of her audiences, but even casual acquaintances to feel free to comment on her private conduct. In one essay, Williams narrates her experiences at a dinner party hosted by a conservative couple, where the man invited as her dinner partner criticized all her beliefs and values, including her role as a mother. She says, "When he learned that I had adopted my son as a single parent, he opined that women who raised children without a husband were engaged in child abuse" (2004, 5). Under these circumstances, Williams has to defend her right to exist, to make decisions about her own life as a citizen-subject. Her dinner partner's posturing reveals dramatically that the liberal citizen-subject—white, male, and wealthy—feels authorized to treat all other intersectional identities as subject to his policing.

Tropes of Civility and Contempt

This line of argument suggests that those positioned as "open persons" must allow audiences to demand civility from them, while the audiences excuse incivility in themselves and others. Tropes of civility and contempt are used to reinforce exhausted binaries, to obscure the links between public and private, political and personal, individual and group that are core principles of women of color feminism. The tendency to frame "open persons" as responsible for the "disturbance" caused by their arguments justifies shifting the terms of debate: the question of the social injustices they scrutinize is preempted by interrogations of their integrity, their eligibility to ask such questions, and, ultimately, whether such questions should be permitted at all. To reiterate: *discursive technologies of power deploy tropes of civility and contempt to turn all attempts at social and political critique back on the arguer, to suppress any claim that might be made on the reader.*

A particularly pertinent example of this "turn" is provided by Lawrence M. Mead (2003) in a response to an article by Dorothy E. Roberts (2003). Roberts is a Black law professor whose work examines the racial harm caused by current raced and gendered structures of power deployed in child welfare policies. Roberts contends that a disproportionate number of Black children are removed from their homes and assigned to the child welfare system through an interplay of racialized and historically sedimented structures: conditions of poverty, legacies of discrimination, cultural misconceptions on the part of social workers and judges, and policies that focus on parental flaws rather than the economic, political, and social constraints on families. Significant factors are stereotypes about Black families and Black women in particular. These policies, according to Roberts, inflict on Blacks a *group* harm that is political; destruction of Black families eliminates an important site of oppositional solidarity and reduces Blacks' ability to mount collective responses to institutional discrimination. Roberts's argument is an intersectional one. She is arguing not about gender in general, nor about race in general, but about their intersection: Black women are disproportionately affected by the decisions of the child welfare system.

In his response to Roberts's argument, professor of politics Mead demonstrates how discursive technologies of power use tropes of civility and contempt to control and restrict public discussion of arguments for social justice. Mead's textual vehemence may not be designed actually to convince anyone as much as it is meant specifically to *discipline*: to have a chilling effect on the ability and willingness of scholars to seek more just social relations. Mead attempts to turn Roberts's argument for social justice back on her.

Deploying the dominant model of responsibility as "liability," Mead presents Roberts as civilly and perhaps criminally liable for her claims.

Mead signals (and therefore argues) his presupposition that Roberts's grievances are inappropriate by his title: "Is Complaint a Moral Argument?" (2003). Because he is unwilling to consider even the possibility of racialized policies or racialized consequences of policies, Mead claims that arguments like Roberts's—charging that racial attitudes influence decisions in contemporary society—cannot be defined as scholarly, political, *or* moral. In an interestingly authoritarian (though unwarranted) set of moves, Mead implies that arguments should be proscribed if they do not fall into those three categories, claiming that arguments such as those of Roberts should be eliminated from scholarly and public discussion, relegated to the courts and legislative committees. In effect, Mead argues that Roberts's claims should not be heard in public except under the liability model of responsibility. He implies that a political model of responsibility can never be appropriate for such an argument.

Mead ignores intersectionality to address Roberts only as a Black and not as a woman—and certainly not as a Black woman with specific knowledge and a unique set of grievances. Her argument, like that of Williams, demonstrates the failure of the concept of the liberal citizen-subject because of its inability to account for gender and race. Her prose style does not appeal to emotion or the personal through word choice and sentence structure, as Williams does. However, like many arguments about social justice, the argument that current social policies create significant ongoing group harms for Blacks on the basis of their race is affectively charged.

By ignoring intersectionality, Mead sets up impossible standards of proof: to make her claims, according to Mead, Roberts has to prove that there is some unique and conscious racial decision made on race alone, divorced from class and gender. According to this standard, Blacks cannot argue for racial harm unless they meet a standard of maximal injury in which the entire group has to suffer inequity equally, universally, and in every realm of society. Without this proof, their arguments for redress should be "dismissed out of hand" (144). But it is impossible to meet this standard of proof, Mead claims, and *only* if Roberts has met it should she be allowed to "complain."

Under the heading "Incivility," Mead argues that claims such as that of Roberts are "uncivil" because they pinpoint the specifically *racial* dimensions of social harms. Such claims—whatever their textual vehemence or nuance—are *always* tantamount to charges of racism from his perspective. He asserts,

I think this sort of argument ought to be excluded from moral and political discourse, whatever view one takes of the merits. The reason is that dispute over the facts defeats all dialogue. Arguments like Roberts's may or may not be true, but they are certainly abusive. They are contestable at such a level that they become uncivil. A civil argument is one in which one's hearers have a chance to respond. To claim racism is a trump card to which a civil reply is impossible. It creates an intellectual fait accompli that forecloses challenge. (139–140)

Mead invokes a double standard in which he can claim injury to himself and society, can claim that reproaching Blacks is *not* uncivil (because they may well deserve it), while reproaching whites *is* uncivil (because they cannot possibly deserve it). In fact, he argues, we cannot have a dialogue about something when the facts are in dispute. This is a rule that would eliminate most arguments, including Mead's own, since he presents as if they were facts what are actually his own highly questionable judgments about the complete success of the civil rights movement—judgments that most scholars would reject.

Mead argues that the existence of civil rights laws proves that society has rejected racism. He is so committed to a model of responsibility as individual "liability," so committed to the unchallengeable position that contemporary society is innocent of racial harm, that he finds any claim about racially disparate policies and behaviors to be indistinguishable from "libel." Therefore, he claims,

Roberts' complaint is already suit-like in character. She has not made a moral judgment against the society. Rather, she has libeled it. She alleges that it violates norms of fairness that it has already accepted. (145)

Mead's assumption that society is *innocent* translates into the consequent assumption that the *guilty* agent is Roberts, who will, in his vision, appeal to the courts for redress only to find herself condemned for "libel." For Mead, *charges* of racism are more abusive than *practices* of racism.

With this claim that Roberts has "libeled" "society," Mead reveals that he can see some kinds of intersectionality. His argument denying that there can be a particular Black woman's claim rests at the same time on the assumption that there can be an injury done to society in general and to white men specifically. When Black women argue for social justice, there can be no intersectionality; when white men want to suppress such claims, intersectionality and collectivity can be marshaled.

There is much at stake in what Mead is trying to suppress—both for him and for us. The argument for conservatives is that the properly ordered private life should not be interfered with by the state—it is what promotes social order. Roberts shows that this state of affairs is *already* raced, that it exists mainly for whites, and that the subordination of Black women's labor is, in fact, what makes the white family possible. Roberts reveals that the state punishes Black motherhood while elaborately subsidizing white motherhood. The state blames the effects of racism and classism on the Black community, on the putatively inadequate mothering of Black women. The state thus uses sexism and racism to make the white family normative and subsidized. All of this is what Roberts is revealing and what Mead wants to hide.

Mead does not want to hear "complaints" about how motherhood might be differentiated by race. For women, motherhood is what is supposed to be their identity. So there is a particularly raced, gendered, classed injury here when Mead tries to silence Roberts and Black mothers from showing that this category for them is *both* personal *and* political, individual *and* structural, private *and* public. He does not acknowledge that Roberts's argument reveals that a privileged motherhood rests on the abnegation of shadow mothers. He attempts to suppress arguments that actual citizen-subjects are not atomized individuals as the liberal model presumes, but rather intersectional, composite, and relational subjects in actual lived experience.

Mead's investment in the myth of the liberal citizen-subject creates a zone of affect with particular relevance for feminists, and indeed, for all women. Roberts's argument is even more deeply gendered than that of Williams, focusing on motherhood. Just as the mythology of the liberal citizen-subject is premised on the notion that having money—consumer dollars—makes one equal, it implies that having a child and a family makes one equal. Yet neither one does.

There is a connection between Williams's argument and that of Roberts. Roberts says some Black women are condemned as nonnormative because they are poor; the state takes their children away. It uses their poverty to enact a racial injury on them. Constructions of normativity and nonnormativity are constantly used to batter Black women who are poor. Williams, in contrast, is normative, respectable, wealthy—but none of that insulates her from the racial injury. So part of Williams's anger is exactly that her normativity does not matter: her demeanor as a shopper is more appropriate than the demeanor of the "saleschild" is as a clerk—but he still gets to determine where she can go and where she cannot because of racial power.

Black women and other women who find themselves not welcome in public otherwise are enticed and invited to shop by a ceaseless apparatus of advertising appeals. In such a society, being denied entry into a store because of one's race punctures the myth of undifferentiated consumption in the same way that state policies puncture the myth of undifferentiated mother-hood. The clerk at Benetton is violating the very civil rights laws whose exis-tence, Mead argues, *proves* that Roberts cannot charge racism. Ideologies of style encourage protecting the liberal citizen-subject through condemning the emotion of critical arguments such as that of Williams and Roberts. Yet, as Mead's comments demonstrate, those deploying theories of the liberal citizen-subject need not be so restrained.

Liability and Responsibility

Part of our difficulty in adequately understanding how affect may function in arguments about social justice rests on the limitations of our dominant models of responsibility. According to Iris Marion Young (2003), the domi-nant model frames responsibility as "liability," familiar from applications of criminal law: the model seeks causal connections between conscious agents and concrete harm in order to assign the agents responsibility for the dam-age they do. The model seeks (1) to "mark out and isolate responsible parties in order to absolve others"; (2) to establish that blame is attached to a viola-tion of a baseline acceptable norm; and (3) to look backward to make judg-ments about and reckon debts for actions in the past.

Williams's incident at Benetton suffers under this model, since it cannot be attached to violations by individual agents: (1) it is not clear who the "re-sponsible party" is; under the dominant model, it would appear to be only the clerk (after all, a teenager) or Benetton (after all, a company that has a "right" to do whatever it wants with its "own" property); (2) neither the buzzer sys-tem nor many other similar methods of everyday insult *count* for many audi-ences as "violation of a baseline acceptable norm"; and (3) Williams is not claiming criminal or civil damages for her mistreatment. In addition, the meaning of the injury cannot be understood in isolation. For Black women, the insults they endure are collective, cumulative, and continuing. Each new incident reopens wounds from the past. Under this model, situations that emerge from historically and socially sedimented processes—in contrast to those caused by identifiable individual or collective agents—are simply "mis-fortunes." Readers and audiences, then, can function as a "jury" under this model—some jurors finding *Williams* at fault for requiring them to hear un-necessary and inappropriate charges.

Young offers an alternative to the inadequate model of liability, drawing on important principles of feminism and antiracism to distinguish a second model that she terms "political responsibility." Five features characterize the model of political responsibility:

1. Political responsibility does not isolate some responsible parties in order to absolve others.
2. Whereas blame or liability seeks remedy for deviation from an acceptable norm, political responsibility concerns structural causes of injustice that are normal and ongoing.
3. Political responsibility is more forward looking than backward looking.
4. What it means to take up or assign political responsibility is more open and discretionary than what it means to judge an agent blameworthy or liable.
5. An agent shares political responsibility with others whose actions contribute to the structural problems that cause injustice. (2003, 11)

Young's model is different from the liability model based on the mythology of the liberal citizen-subject: that model is about individual interchangeability where someone might be excluded for *one* reason by *one* actor. Young's is an innately social view of justice, where power is wielded by groups, not just by individuals; where injuries are suffered by groups, not just individuals; and where systemic practices and processes are not misrecognized as individual, aberrant, and aleatory.

Williams's argument about the incident at Benetton is congruent with this "political responsibility" model: (1) she does not argue that either the clerk or Benetton behaved in an unusual way or should be punished; (2) she does not argue that there are acceptable norms that the incident violates; rather, she argues that this quotidian deployment of structures of power creates injustice with impunity *because* it is routine; (3) she uses the incident as a point of departure for positing the conditions of a just society. Williams's argument is an appeal for her readers and audiences to take up such a political model of responsibility.

Young's two models of responsibility turn out to be closely linked to discursive technologies of power that are used to suppress arguments about social justice. They work in tandem with ideologies of style to limit claims about group harm. Discursive technologies of power deploy tropes of civility and contempt to deflect attempts at feminist and antiracist social and political critique back on the arguer, to suppress any claim that might be made on the reader. These discursive technologies authorize certain kinds of affect, for certain kinds of rhetors, for certain kinds of arguments, yet ultimately hold liable only individuals and groups arguing for social change. Reframing Williams's argument to fit the liberal model of the citizen-subject and the liability model of responsibility leads her interlocutors to hold her responsible for her own "emotions" as well as the emotions of her audiences. She fails to fulfill properly the ideal of the autonomous, judicious, consuming citizen, and she makes us listen to her complaints about it. In this case, tropes of civility and contempt frame Williams as *personally* impolite. This reduction is a false argument: Williams has not offended anyone as an individual. Rather, her arguments are threatening to make others responsible as members of society. Here tropes of civility and contempt are deployed against feminist and antiracist arguments to protect the ideal of the liberal citizen-subject from critiques of group power.

If we think in terms of the responsibility model posed by Iris Marion Young, we can see the importance of recognizing the role that discursive policing plays inside an integrated technology of power, how appeals to normativity strengthen the very sexism they purport to reduce, and how tropes of contempt poison the well from which we all have to drink. Using contempt as a tool to deny intersectional knowledge does not establish a "level playing field" for debate about social injustice. The strictures of textual etiquette and argumentative exchange that Mead authorizes—and Williams's audiences deploy—allow people to congratulate themselves on their independence and neutrality while in effect endorsing the damage created by current social relations. These rules protect those relations from challenge and critique and in fact dismiss arguments that question their premises as unethical and therefore unworthy of a hearing.

The delivery of contempt functions as a discursive tool to deny that gender, race, and class work intersectionally to create social injury. Mead's strictures, the failure of some in Williams's audiences to see the injury revealed by her narrative, are not individual responses or rhetorical strategies, but technologies of power. The technologies operate by reducing to personal impropriety what are manifestly political arguments; this move then allows ideologically authorized moral condemnation to replace consideration of arguments about social injustice. Such technologies of power are ideologically supported methods of denying the multiple and flexible identities revealed by intersectional analysis; they serve to deny intersectional knowledge of injury and to dismiss challenges by and on behalf of those damaged through the mythology of the liberal citizen-subject.

In scholarship, punditry, and classrooms, tropes of civility and contempt serve to insulate readers from accountability—not merely accountability for the conditions in our shared social lives, but even accountability for assessing and analyzing challenges to taken-for-granted ways of thinking. Because of their skewed distribution of responsibility, because of their emphatic enforcement of the status quo, because of their frequent rhetoric of personal disparagement and ridicule, such discursive technologies provide readers with a desperate pleasure in their ability to deflect, discount, and discard arguments. They contribute to a culture of contempt. These discursive technologies of contempt encourage people to "know" a priori the moral significance of an argument. They encourage citizens to employ a *rhetorical* buzzer system that will, like Benetton, allow them to reject an argument merely by looking at its rhetorical face.

CHAPTER THREE

Anger

Grammars of Affect and Authority

A
ffect is part of the politics of style and argument of particular interest to feminist socioforensic discursive analysis. My analysis of the
trope of the angry feminist and of antifeminists' rhetorics of contempt in Chapters 1 and 2 demonstrates that it is not the *presence* or *absence*
of rhetorical affect that characterizes different political and intellectual arguments. It is not the presence of even "negative" affect laced with malice,
anger, mockery, spite, disdain, or contempt that leads to censuring feminist
authors. Negative affect is also present in antifeminist discourses, but those
authors are not routinely dismissed for being "angry," for having inappropriate affect. Angry Tropers do not deploy their cultural training program to
eject *each other* from the "economy of reason." Censuring affect is a discursive technology of power that depends expressly on whether different inflections of affect (or lack of affect) are used to *promote, negotiate,* and *challenge*
conditions of dominance. It is generally her challenge to conditions of dominance, not her affect, that leads the feminist to be condemned.

Affect is part of the authority of a text as it is constructed within a
complex matrix of institutional norms, authorial statuses, privileges, and
textual features that work together. Transforming the terms of reading to foreground inflections of politics and power allows us to consider how specific
"norms" of propriety, politeness, civility, and proper affect carry into academic
arenas conceptions that are racialized, gendered, and profoundly *classed.*
Affect is deeply entwined with creation of textual authority, but it cannot
be removed from the purposes of arguments, their claims and evidence, or

their audiences. In this chapter I touch on some ways of thinking about "civility." I also consider how some feminists in the twentieth century saw the connection between "anger" and authority. I discuss how varying the norms of discourse offers feminists opportunities to create affect that intensifies arguments that have struggled to gain a hearing. I look particularly at textual markers of vehemence in two arguments about sexual violence that demonstrate the complexity at the heart of any claims about authorial emotions and texts.

Deployment of textual vehemence appears in two texts that concern the logic and language of social responses to violence against women: attorney Cynthia K. Gillespie's *Justifiable Homicide: Battered Women, Self-Defense, and the Law* (1989) and linguist Julia Penelope's *Speaking Freely: Unlearning the Lies of the Fathers' Tongues* (1990). The two texts represent two different political positions, and consequently two different rhetorical approaches, both of which aim at similar ends: reducing gendered sexual violence and increasing social responsibility for such acts. My goal is to show that textual choices to create rhetorical force have political and ideological consequences, that rhetorical confrontation is a substantive rather than a surface issue. The issue is not whether feminists should ever use textual vehemence, but rather how, when, why, and for what purposes. Even more important is what these choices reveal about the diffuse and dispersed nature of power and the need for multiple strategies to contest it.

"Civility," Discursive Norms, and Feminist Discursive Authority

Notions of "civility" are ideals that suggest how people should relate to one another if civil society is to be ordered rather than chaotic. Edwards Shils (1991), for example, for many years Distinguished Service Professor in the Committee on Social Thought and in Sociology at the University of Chicago, considers civility to be an attitude that shows concern for the whole of society. He praises an essay of Ferdinand Mount, who argues that *civility implies including others in the same moral universe* (1973, cited in Shils 1991, 12). According to Shils, "Civility as a feature of civil society considers others as fellow-citizens of equal dignity in their rights and obligations as members of civil society; it means regarding other persons, including one's adversaries, as members of the same inclusive collectivity, i.e., as members of the same society" (1991, 12). It is significant that creating a climate of shared worth and mutual dignity is presented as a *joint responsibility of all* in civil society—although it appears in Shils's formulation that some people can be expected to demonstrate more abilities in this regard than others because of their education, place in society, and so on.

Shils also recommends a kind of "civility in manners" or "courtesy" that resembles the notions of civility that guide conventional practices of reading. This kind of civility is directed at the author, the rhetor, the one who speaks in society. Shils notes that traditional ideals of courtesy—self-restraint, gentlemanliness, and so on—involve individuals in the immediate presence of one another.[1] He argues that this kind of courtesy, adopting a "calm voice," for example, is also of importance in writing. He begins by suggesting a perhaps surprising *practical* reason for adopting a calm voice: it helps society's inevitable losers be less strained, less excitable. If they and others who may be contentious hold their anger and resentment in check, it will help calm them and perhaps others. There are also *aesthetic* reasons for speaking courteously and calmly: life and listening will be more pleasant. Finally, in his formulation, it is *morally right*:

> Civility in the sense of courtesy mollifies or ameliorates the strain which accompanies the risks, the dangers of prospective loss and the injuries of the real losses of an economically, politically and intellectually competitive society in which some persons are bound to lose. Courtesy makes life a bit more pleasant; it is easier to bear than harshness. Softly spoken, respectful speech is more pleasing to listen to than harsh, contemptuous speech. Civility in manners holds anger and resentment in check; it has a calming, pacifying effect on the sentiments. It might make for less excitability. Civil manners are aesthetically pleasing and morally right. (1991, 13)

I would argue that both of the ideals of civil society that Shils describes—treating members with equal dignity and asking all to adopt a courteous civility of tone—resonate *aesthetically*. They appear to offer a vision of the possibility of civilized debate and authorize chastising individuals who do not adhere to such standards (a common move by those using conventional reading practices).

But such ideals also ask those who argue for social justice to set aside *their* concerns to meet a standard of the common good that simply does not include them. Power has dropped out of the picture: civility is used not to have equal dialogue but to justify inequality and manage subordinate groups. The boundaries of who is to be treated with dignity turn out to be more deceptive than one might think. It is unclear what counts as "harsh, contemptuous speech," but apparently the ideals allow *some—like the Angry*

Troper—to retain the choice to speak harshly to advance their interests while condemning others as uncivil.[2]

There are strong connections among these topics: the actions of Williams's law review editors, Mead's denigration of Roberts, the ways in which our models of reason and emotion encourage us to receive textually vehement arguments, and the framing of civility as discourse etiquette. All may strike us as unexceptionable because they connect with larger ways of considering good manners as the "oil" of the wheels of civilization. Protocols of American public and academic discourses encourage such methods of arguing about oppositional positions because they link the politics of textual vehemence to broader conventions of manners. Rather than being divorced from political and social contexts, however, protocols of politeness in language and in academic discourse are related to changing middle-class norms of emotional demonstration.[3] In some ways, protocols of politeness can be seen as a kind of "politic verbal behavior," useful for maintaining interpersonal equilibrium within social groups, but they—and their violation—also have many other pragmatic and social roles that are overlooked when they are framed as conventional notions of courtesy that should be used to condemn arguments about social justice.[4] Texts are evaluated as if they were stand-ins for restrained, face-to-face conversations conducted according to the norms of white middle-class social interactions. In such a view, "raised voices," blunt terms, and confrontive claims violate standards of textual manners; textual manners are conflated with personal morals and personal character. Asking that those who present oppositional arguments rephrase them to eliminate argumentative intensity, textual emotion, rhetorical confrontation is, in such a view, merely a surface issue rather than a substantive one.

Political ends are served when readers acknowledge that authors may be addressing important problems with strong arguments, but discount the vehement text on the basis that it is "impolite" and violates social conventions. Many readers would prefer that people who are "emotional" or "out of control" withdraw from the discussion until they "calm down." My discussion here is congruent with the insights of Thomas Kochman on the essentially political nature of American social warrants of etiquette (1984). Kochman argues,

> Mainstream Americans do not see themselves as being politically shrewd, or disingenuous, when they ask members of minority groups who have felt themselves aggrieved *to stop being angry* as a *prerequisite* to negotiations aimed at discussing the nature and/or resolution of those disagreements. Rather, mainstreamers simply see themselves as

invoking what society has established as conventional procedures for handling disputations and disagreements. Such procedures require that individual negotiators on all sides remain calm and "rational" (i.e., unemotional) in presenting their views. [Mainstream Americans believe, moreover, that] to the extent that one side or other is angry or otherwise emotional, its perspective on matters is commensurably distorted. (1984, 200, emphasis added)

Rather than being "impartial," such conventions serve entrenched interests by encouraging aggrieved parties to give up part of their bargaining power—their emotional force and its consequences—*prior to* negotiation. While the *intent* of holding to such conventions may not seem so, the *effect* is political. The warrants authorize readers to treat writers perceived as angry as if they were obstreperous children, to ignore their arguments, to resist their emotional and moral force, to evade confrontation with the very real ills they may delineate—in effect, to say, "You need to calm down before I listen to you. Go to your room until you learn how to act."

Such a protocol of politeness excludes the "uncivil," without opening for our deliberation what incivility might be, what benefits accrue from our excluding it, and why it should assume such significance as to authorize ignoring arguments. Civility is not considered to constrain the audience at all, for instance, to encourage a thoughtful hearing of an argument or to consider contexts such as the climate of contempt. Focus is on the authors and their total responsibility for framing arguments in an interesting and accessible way that fits the desires of the audience; they are found at fault for superficial features of "textual politeness" but also for delivering messages that are not positive. For some readers, simply being put on notice that unpleasant social problems remain an ongoing feature of many people's lives may appear dismaying, disagreeable, divisive. Arguments about long-standing social inequalities are often delivered in terms that appear to some readers to be excessively assertive or whiny.

As a way of thinking about either texts or social relations, this deeply conventional political stance about textual etiquette does not serve any of us well: it fetishizes a specific version of discourse *etiquette* as a surrogate for discourse *ethics*, thus conflating surface issues of argument with substantive issues. It isolates textual features from their argumentative purposes. It adopts a taken-for-granted and transparent interpretation of which discursive features will count as inappropriately confrontive rather than rigorously engaging their connection to substantive argument. It neglects the differing positions of those mounting arguments and the consequent differing interpretations of their rhetorical vehemence. It overlooks the ongoing negotiation over evidence and standards that characterizes the evolution of all academic disciplines. To adopt a pose of "even-handedness" in order to chastise impoliteness "on both sides" of a civic argument ignores the role of power in establishing a context for reception of ideas. Rather than establishing a "level playing field" for civic exchange, such strictures of textual etiquette allow us to congratulate ourselves on our independence and neutrality while in effect endorsing current social relations.

In fact, perpetually derisory dismissals—and experiences such as having one's arguments greatly misrepresented or ignored—set the stage for textually vehement counterstrategies. When planning their arguments, authors who might be mislabeled, misunderstood, or misrepresented develop rhetorical strategies to subvert such dismissals. Arguers adopting such vigorous prose are not merely *expressing* anger textually, *sharing* it, or *discharging* it therapeutically. They are *employing* "anger" *rhetorically*. Rather than emotionally "losing control" of scholarly discourse, they must manipulate it—sometimes expertly—to *interrupt, disrupt,* and *invert* conventions that make their perspectives illegitimate. Not surprisingly, when appearing as part of social critique in a context inherently "political" as well as "academic," these rhetorical choices themselves become a site of contestation.

Historically, women have been positioned as subordinate to men and required to demonstrate so by proper kinds of demeanor. So the use of affect or vehement textual strategies to create authoritative arguments has been important to feminism. As Brenda Silver argues, in regard to the contested authority of Virginia Woolf's textual anger,

> To the extent that feminism, both within and without the academy, redefined anger as a site of its revisionary discourse and a legitimate critical strategy, the authority of anger itself became an increasingly contested issue. Whose voice would control the critical discourse, what tone and with it what authority would prevail, became a matter of urgency that extended beyond, but is embedded in, the criticism of feminist texts . . . the battle over anger in women's public discourse emerged again, but now the stakes were less the authority of Woolf's text [*Three Guineas*] than the authority of feminist critique and its ability to effect institutional change. (1991, 355)

Silver's comment emphasizes the discursive context in which textual anger may be employed. Since the rhetorical force of textual anger may compel attention to delegitimized viewpoints, interpreting textual anger as emotional expression rather than rhetorical performance is also a highly political act. So despite a climate saturated with conceptual and political problems about interpreting "emotional" expression, textually vehement arguments are nonetheless frequent in feminist and other oppositional academic rhetorics.

Under such circumstances, the authority of feminists to create social and legal change may become interpreted as evidence of the overwhelming power of the angry feminist. In 1992, the *Los Angeles Times* reported on action in the California legislature to increase penalties for spousal rape. California State Senator Ed Davis, representative of Santa Clarita for over a decade and formerly police chief of Los Angeles, was apparently opposed. In a moment of candor, he indicated that it was not merely the law itself he opposed, but the demeanor of the women supporting the bill:

> "We have no business passing an increase in penalties [for spousal rape] like this. We get beaten up by the women lobbyists. . . . Let's face it, we've been a little bit terrorized of late by the lobbies of women." Davis said on the Senate floor that he had opposed the bill in committee where he was confronted by "a bunch of grim-faced women glowering at me, most of them women that men would never touch." (Ingram 1992, 1)

Senator (and Chief) Davis's certainty that penalties should not be increased for spousal rape because the lobbyists favoring the law struck him as too ugly to be raped indicates the depths of resistance (and ignorance) facing women seeking justice from the legal system at the start of the 1990s. His performance resonates with the demeaning humor and bullying of Joseph Epstein and Lawrence Mead discussed in previous chapters. His witty comment reveals not a real attempt to deliberate on changes in the law, but rather a desire to show off for other men by directing ridicule and shame at women who seem not to be seeking the approval of men.

Yet practices of discursive policing like this that feminists face routinely at the scene of argument rarely succeed in silencing them. Being demeaned, demonized, and dismissed sometimes produces productive optics on power and generative rhetorical strategies for contesting it. External attacks can underscore how much is at stake in arguments over feminist issues and ideas. Efforts to insult and intimidate feminists betray a defensiveness on the part of opponents who would not have to resort to ridicule or misrepresentation if they could produce principled refutation of the ideas that challenge their privileges. Some of the best feminist scholarship emerges from creative conflict about important issues, from sites of argument that become inflamed precisely because so much is at stake. Rhetorical choices at these sites not only frame and deliver already-existing arguments but also create new insights that emanate from the exigencies of argument. Efforts to confront and contest the trope of the angry feminist often entail deployment of textual vehemence, of forceful, emotional, and colorful language as a way of mobilizing feminist affect to serve as a weapon against antifeminist affect.

I write neither to endorse nor to condemn textual vehemence, but rather to treat it as a tool that is useful for some purposes but counterproductive for others. The particular intellectual and political projects that feminists advance lead to differing rhetorical choices, choices that are *not* inherent in their personal characters or extrinsic to their ideas and arguments. Very few tools are right for all jobs, but every tool is right for some job. Finding the right tool for the right job is often the work required of feminists at the scene of argument.

Feminism attempts to advance scholarship in sociolegal and sociolinguistic studies by creating rhetorics suited for discussions in which antifeminist presumptions prevail (even when antifeminists are not personally or physically present). Gillespie and Penelope want to change the circumstances facing battered, abused, and exploited women. To do so, they craft rhetorics capable of compelling their enemies to ask and answer scholarly and social questions in different ways.

In the face of legal traditions that originally conceived of rape not so much as damage to women's dignity but rather to men's property (husbands or fathers) and that generally treated incest and domestic violence as private matters, legal activists and theorists faced daunting challenges in the late 1980s and early 1990s when they attempted to adapt the law to modern concerns and conditions. Gillespie's and Penelope's texts provide dramatically clear examples from this period of two contrasting ways to argue forcefully about gender and violence. The consistency of each author's rhetorical schema and its clear relationship to political goals disclose important aspects of the politics of textual vehemence. The authors are not chosen to be representative or comprehensive examples of women who experience anger, use anger rhetorically, or argue against sexual violence. Specifically, what interests me about Gillespie and Penelope are the different strategies they pursue and the ways in which these strategies expose and contest legal, academic, and journalistic language that sanctions, legitimates, and even rewards violence against women. Of course, all women do not experience violence in exactly the same ways. All men do not have the same kinds of relations with women and legal institutions. The strategies of two academic writers cannot stand for universal female or feminist concerns. Neither the arguments in which

Gillespie and Penelope engage nor the social practices they challenge have uniform consequences for all women or men regardless of social position. I use Gillespie's and Penelope's texts here, however, specifically to examine the ways in which writers working in a professional academic context attempt to disturb and undermine conventions of academic writing that obscure, condone, and even legitimate violence against women from all walks of life.

In *Justifiable Homicide* (1989), Gillespie argues that the legal system does not grant women the same rights to self-defense that it gives to men, resulting in numerous unjust convictions of women responding to battering by their partners with deadly violence. My illustrations come from "The Law in Action," a chapter that criticizes the gender-laden discourses of legal practices about domestic violence. These discourses effectively nullify women's judgments about the potential seriousness and ineluctability of men's violence and deny them the right to determine the nature and timing of their own (sometimes deadly) response. Gillespie implies that language is *external* to her project. She seeks mainly to replace bad discourses with better ones.

In *Speaking Freely* (1990), Penelope takes a different approach. She examines linguistic structures to reveal the ways in which, she argues, men perpetuate dominance over women. My illustrations come from "*That's* How *It Is*" and "The Agents Within." Both chapters argue that we fail systematically to identify those responsible for child sexual abuse and other acts of sexual violence in part because we permit ourselves and others to use grammatical constructions that suppress the human agency responsible for this violence. Penelope exposes injustice by calling attention to the unstated or the understated, the absences and elisions, the suppressions and denials of agency that allow people to avoid facing and taking responsibility for specific cases of sexual abuse. In contrast to Gillespie, Penelope implies that language is *internal* to her problem—in effect, that it *is* the problem, that taken-for-granted ways of constructing narratives contribute to sexual abuse. Penelope cannot rely on the commonsense model of narrative that Gillespie employs successfully because she is challenging the purported innocence and transparency of narrative through her grammatical and rhetorical analysis.

Varieties of Textual Vehemence

Differing rhetorical choices, such as the ones I examine here, can reveal fundamentally different kinds of critiques. Gillespie, I argue, works within the contradictions of existing legal discourse, helping to alter it from within. Penelope attempts to expose existing legal and social rhetoric about sexual violence as a fabricated discourse already imbued with gendered hierarchies. Gillespie uses language as if it were itself neutral, a tool for *conveying* reality. She constructs her text as a repetitive pattern of stories, as a series of dramatic narratives based on the testimonies of women brought to trial for harming the men they claim threatened and battered them. Gillespie uses irony and ridicule to reveal the less-than-generous court discourse and legal treatment of these women, to expose faulty legal requirements, institutional policies, and social logics. The stories and the outcomes that she sets forth so dramatically serve to demonstrate the unjust, even irrational, results of what many claim to be neutral social policies. In contrast, Penelope redraws the boundaries of attention, arguing not merely *with* language but *about* language, about its role in constituting the realities it purports merely to describe. Penelope draws on the form of a conventional language textbook but with a rather unconventional focus on the ways that taken-for-granted language perpetuates male dominance in society. Her formal structure, then, sets up a vivid contrast to her rather witty but inexorable expose of the ways in which people can use conventional language to rewrite apparent realities.

Neither Gillespie nor Penelope fulminates about gendered violence per se. Rather, both authors direct their vehemence at what they perceive to be unacknowledged social support and sanction for gendered violence: in the case of Gillespie, at institutional logics that undermine goals of social justice; in the case of Penelope, at conventional language that sidesteps the location of responsibility. Both must demonstrate, then, the covert power of prevailing rhetorics and uninterrogated language conventions as forces complicit in hiding power imbalances and supporting irresponsible and immoral actions. As they intervene to interrupt or redirect discussions already in progress, their rhetorical choices must respond to the ideological and political imperatives that they see at the scene of argument, not to some ideal of a full range of rhetorical options. Both Gillespie and Penelope build textual vehemence on representations of sexual violence because to do so inheres to their argumentative goals. Both "escalate" the emphasis and vehemence of their texts through elaboration, detail, and repetition, as well as frank language and ironic commentary, creating vigorous, dramatic, relentless prose. But the distinctive form of each text depends crucially on the authors' larger political goals and their consequently differing allocations of dramatic language, evidence, blame, and responsibility. Textual anger performs quite different rhetorical functions for each author, and, as I demonstrate, much is at stake for each in the rhetorical choices she makes.

Gillespie's and Penelope's rhetorical choices are important because academic and other public arguments are always matters of power. Such arguments have consequences for whether people can be battered and sexually assaulted. They influence whether others condone that battering and assault. Examining the gains and losses incurred by feminists using different strategies to challenge such social problems is vital to finding the right tools for the right job. My purpose here is not to celebrate, emulate, or denigrate specific strategies in the abstract, not to recommend one method over the other for all purposes, but to illuminate likely gains and losses incurred by different approaches to the intersection of rhetoric, affect, strategy, and social theory in both writers' texts.[5]

Gillespie: Exploit Conventions

Gillespie reproaches the legal system for not granting women the same rights to self-defense as men. Her strategies to controvert these legal policies develop an *internal critique,* one that attempts to hold the legal system to its professed intentions. To expose the failings of current legal narratives is therefore vital and central to Gillespie's argument: challenging legal policies and institutions to operate according to the ideals of equity that authorize them, she in effect establishes battered women's relations to the legal system as a *failed narrative*—a site where legal discourse effectively nullifies women's judgments about the potential seriousness and ineluctability of men's violence. Her critique particularly entails exploiting narrative conventions because it implies that problems created by faulty legal narratives can be resolved by *better* narratives.

Gillespie establishes the ur-story of legal failure by recounting a plethora of individual stories, each demonstrating what she argues to be failures of justice—numerous unwarranted convictions of women who respond to their partners' battering with deadly violence. Relying on each woman's own testimony, Gillespie constructs her narratives from the woman's point of view, thus strongly encouraging readers to adopt that narrative position. She builds textual vehemence by using a series of strong and repeated patterns of narrative and commentary, the patterns emerging as emotional waves. Introducing a sequence with explication of the point she is challenging, she then moves through a series of narratives, one to six paragraphs long, describing particular cases in which women are battered, respond (eventually) with violence, and then find themselves convicted of murder or manslaughter because of prevailing legal practices. Gillespie's narratives are both very specific—grounded in the experiences of named individuals— and very patterned—demonstrating how problems of interpretation and argument apply systematically across the cases of different individuals. The patterning is built on the very profusion of individual stories, at the same time akin and unique.

Constructing an overall narrative from the patterned specifics of individual stories contributes strongly to effects of textual vehemence. Gillespie drums away with specifics on specifics: specific cases, with names (Shirley Mae Thomas, Sharon Crigler, Lucille Valentine, Sandra King), specific violent acts done to the woman ("Each time she tried to get up he smashed her in the face with his fists and slapped and pummeled her on the face and body, harder and harder" [55]), specific injuries ("When she was arrested, she had bruises covering her entire body; her face was permanently disfigured with a scar across one eye, and her ears were almost beaten completely away" [77]), the specifics of the woman's response ("Betty closed her eyes and pulled the trigger, firing five times" [74]), and the specifics of court decisions ("Apparently, the jury did not consider either the fists or the bottle to constitute a serious threat" [59]). Gillespie's specificity develops a sense of excess in violence, of an overwhelming number of cases, of the damage that specific women suffered and found discounted by authorities. Those named by Gillespie are actors in the narrative of sexual violence: she does not provide the proper names of legal actors—judges, attorneys, jurors—despite the centrality of the legal story to her argument. Omitting the names of legal actors keeps the focus on the women's violations, both violent and legal: Gillespie suggests, by such a strategy, that she wishes not to belittle (or even identify) legal actors but, instead, to revamp systemic discourse.

Specificity combined with repetitive excess is a central strategy for Gillespie. For example, she "echoes" through quotation an inventory of unrelenting length of the household objects that violent men had used to hurt their partners:

There were, of course, many women who had been stabbed, cut, shot, and pistol-whipped. . . . [Stacey and Shupe's tally] included pistols, shotguns, knives, machetes, golf clubs, baseball bats, electric drills, high-heeled shoes, sticks, frying pans, electric sanders, toasters, razors, silverware, ashtrays, drinking glasses and beer mugs, bottles, burning cigarettes, hair brushes, lighter fluid and matches, candlestick holders, scissors, screwdrivers, ax handles, sledgehammers, chairs, bedrails, telephone cords, ropes, workboots, belts, door knobs, doors, boat oars, cars and trucks, fish hooks, metal chains, clothing (used to smother and choke), hot ashes, hot water, hot food, dishes, acid, bleach, vases, rocks, bricks, pool cues, box fans, books, and, as one woman described her husband's typical weapons, "anything handy." (57–58, quoted from Stacey and Shupe 1983)

With her own storytelling, as well as such quotations, Gillespie's "inventories" of injuries, of violent actions, of bodily hurts, increase textual vehemence through overabundance, superfluity, excess. Yet such techniques distance Gillespie from the excess itself. Readers tend to see Gillespie's emotion as *part of the story*, reflecting the story, a story of violent action and dramatic outcome. By embedding rhetorical evidence of emotion inside the story, Gillespie separates it from her own persona and thereby controls the perception of her anger as the author. As a consequence, readers tend to feel emotion that they attribute to the story, not to Gillespie, and therefore do not hold her responsible for making them uncomfortable.

Rather than analyzing and commenting on the violence itself in the narratives she relates, Gillespie builds vehemence on the surface of the violent action. She describes the violence in some detail by means of paragraphs tending to emphasize coordination rather than subordination, frequently using short, blunt clauses of the form Simple Subject–Violent Verb–Object:

> During that time [ten years] Carl's abuse of Betty had been constant and severe. He hit her, kicked her, and choked her. He had broken her nose at least five times and had knocked out several of her teeth. He had repeatedly broken her ribs, and he frequently pushed or kicked her down the stairs. She was a diabetic; and a number of times Carl hid her insulin or diluted it with water, causing her to go into a diabetic coma. He threatened to cut her head off and cut her eyeballs out. His pattern was to indulge in this sort of violence whenever he was drunk. (Gillespie 1989, 73)

Short, blunt clauses isolate the violent terms starkly, rather than relate them to larger social arguments. Gillespie does not develop vehemence by modifying the violent verbs to emphasize how violent they were or modifying the objects to emphasize how awful it was. She does not use "vivid" language— the dash of really graphic language repeats a court transcript—and thereby controls the perception of her anger as the author. In fact, the lack of affect at the level of dramatic word choices in Gillespie's text becomes itself a powerful strategy: it plays on dramatic scenes, yet appears unemotional, certainly not "angry." The strategy reinforces readers' sense of her fair-mindedness (for those readers concerned with authorial "objectivity"): she gives the impression of "simply reporting" rather than constructing a narrative.

Gillespie's vehemence also builds on patterns of lexical simplicity. Without modification, her violent nouns and verbs also repeat without great variety: *beat, hit, punch, kick, grab, kill*. Occasionally there appears a *slap* or *choke* or *pound* or *strangle* or *smash* or *stomp* or *hurl*. The effect is cumulative, accentuating the similarity of the incidents of battering, the systemic patterns underlying what might be considered private, personal behavior. Thus, Gillespie's restrained, matter-of-fact descriptions in some ways mimic the incremental, repetitive, accumulative pattern of violence that she describes. She writes, "[B]attering episodes typically encompass a number of different kinds of violence and can sometimes go on for hours. . . . Moreover, such episodes are almost never isolated incidents but are repeated over and over again, with cumulative physical and emotional damage being inflicted, and often a new beating occurring before the injuries from the last one have even healed" (52–53). Creating a similar experience in her text, Gillespie barely finishes with an episode describing a woman being beaten, grabbed, choked (usually concluding with an ironic coda on the legal outcome), when she moves to the next episode of a woman being beaten, punched, kicked, and then another being hit, kicked, strangled; the strategy becomes a cumulative assault, a dramatic appeal to empathize with the victim.

Gillespie's lexical repetition also pounds home central points with ironic effect. For example, the early part of her text is devoted to the question of adequate provocation for armed defense—permitted, in every state, when an assault is likely to cause serious bodily harm. Gillespie argues that current legal practice operates as if both antagonists were well-matched in size, strength, and skill; under that circumstance, attacking without weapons—"with hands, fists, or feet" (51)—constitutes a nonserious attack, a misdemeanor, and, therefore, does not justify an armed defense. Gillespie disagrees. Over the next several pages, she discusses both general research and specific incidents in which women were seriously harmed by their partner's "hands, fists, [and/or] feet": the phrase appears five times on two pages (51–52); subsequent pages repeat "hands [and/or] fists" three times (53–54) and "fists or feet" once (57), with reinforcement by nine additional "fists," and three additional "hands" over the whole nine pages (51–59). Gillespie's strategy is to increase the impact of the words "hands, fists, or feet" in parallel with her desire to emphasize the force and damage that the objects can cause. The single-word redundancies serve to extend the ironic and cumulative effect of the original phrase, emerging from its early repetition as a whole, and its frequent placement at the conclusion of paragraphs: one of the most powerful of rhetorical positions.

Gillespie gains a number of rhetorical advantages by exploiting traditional models of narrative to critique legal discourse. For instance, she can present a particular legal argument as failed "on its face," or "speaking for itself," in essence challenging it by declining to challenge it. For example, in a sequence over several pages she discusses the case of Dathel Shipp. The courts conceded that Shipp had believed herself to have grounds for self-defense—but not for *as much* defense as she delivered. Shipp knew her husband's background: that he had killed his first wife twenty years before and served ten years in the penitentiary for it; that he had shot Dathel in the shoulder, hip, and face when she went home to her parents rather than remain working as his prostitute and served seven years in the penitentiary for that; that when they married he had beaten her regularly, at least once requiring her to be hospitalized for broken ribs; that he harassed her constantly after the divorce and said he would kill her if he found her with another man. Thus, when he did find her with another man and started to attack her, she feared he would kill her and shot him five times in a few seconds. Charged with murder, Shipp was found guilty of voluntary manslaughter. Gillespie quotes the appellate court's own words to explain why, but rather than add her own commentary on it, she merely follows with a detailed description of the prosecution's arguments:

> "In view of the verdict, it is conceded by both the State and the defendant that the jury found that the defendant actually believed that her employment of deadly force was necessary to prevent her death or suffering great bodily harm, but that belief was unreasonable." The prosecutor had argued at trial that Dathel had "overreacted" by firing all five shots at Robert. The prosecution's position was that even if Dathel's belief was reasonable when the first two shots were fired, after he was hit . . . he had been effectively disabled; and the last three shots, including the fatal one, were unreasonable and unnecessary. (92)

Baldly reporting the arguments, without commentary, hammers the apparent absurdity home and establishes the inadequacy of the arguments that Gillespie challenges. Gillespie supplies irony and sarcasm after and between sequences describing violence, when the character of the "factual" report has already established the stage for emotional reaction. Such a location allows Gillespie to imply irony and express muted sarcasm. This is an advantage with those readers who resent authorial personas who attack power directly. Placing irony or sarcasm after the argument has been made allows the audience to distance itself from those making the judgment; it also allows Gillespie to distance herself from the act of sarcastic commentary, thus deflecting attention from her own authorial persona and stance.[6]

Gillespie draws on conventional narrative forms to tell familiar tales of innocence and injustice in which authorities misrecognize women's motivation and circumstances. She can then ridicule the results of those legal misreadings, suggesting that they produce a kind of "double bind," of "second-guessing," for battered women subjected to the mislogics of legal discourse. For example, Gillespie recounts a case in which a woman's partner, with a history of threats and battering, said he would come down in the basement to kill her and her children; so when he came down two or three steps, she shot him. She was subsequently convicted of manslaughter. Gillespie decries the legal outcome by means of a series of rhetorical questions that escalate the sense of irrationality, of absurdity:

> The Massachusetts Supreme Court, in affirming her conviction for manslaughter, said that there was sufficient evidence for a jury finding that she was not in immediate danger of death or serious injury at the hands of the deceased. Just how much closer she should have let him come before she would have been justified in pulling the trigger, the court did not say. Halfway down the stairs? The bottom of the stairs? Within grabbing distance of the two toddlers? Until his hands were around her throat? There is no justice in a criminal law that can require that sort of cold-blooded calculation of a terrified woman desperately trying to save the lives of her children and herself from a man whose avowed intention was to kill them. (72)

Gillespie's rhetorical questions here and elsewhere in her text tend to focus on the argument itself in the deeply cooperative—indeed, pseudocooperative—way of many of her ironic comments ("how much closer should she let him come . . . Halfway down the stairs?" [72]). Gillespie asks rhetorical questions that could, conceivably, be answered "legitimately"—for example, by a court that announces that women cannot shoot their attacking husbands until they advance to within three steps. By doing this, she gives a tone—albeit illusory—of fairness, even-handedness, even while confronting systematically unfair legal discourse.

Gillespie punctuates her narratives with direct sarcastic or ironic attacks on both the logic of the law and the interpretation of courts and juries. She often does so by exploiting the contrast between jury decisions and what she argues would be "reasonable," creating an oblique tone by using a "stinging" style of sentence and terms like "apparently" and "evidently," reminding readers that she draws inferences from court records.

She pushes this strategy further in the case of a woman who shot her partner as he was beating her on the head and kicking her in the stomach; she was subsequently convicted of manslaughter by a court that concluded that since her partner had beaten her before without killing her, it was not "reasonable" for her to have expected him to kill her this time. Gillespie concludes the paragraph with play on the contrast of reasonable/unreasonable, right/wrong: "It is hard to see how a woman in Verneater Chapman's shoes could overcome this presumption of once a nonlethal wife-beater, always a nonlethal wife-beater, short of letting herself be beaten to death—surely an unreasonable length to require a woman to go to prove herself right" (60–61). Note the construction of this "stinger" sentence so typical of Gillespie, concluding with an ironic slap. It begins with, and largely consists of, a low-keyed, cooperative engagement with the court's decision, pauses at a dash, then concludes with a move to a slightly different level to create ironic effect: after the dash, with "surely an unreasonable length," and "provided, of course," Gillespie becomes more earnest, more rational, lower-keyed, more cooperative, apparently seeking diligently to reconcile the court's decision with what she fears may be some "awkward" problems. Such a stance forms a powerful argumentative device, for it suggests a deep desire to align herself with the court's point of view and, therefore, an impression that she is presenting a vehement—yet at the same time moderate—critique.

In contrast to Gillespie, no overall narrative structure shapes Penelope's text. Because Gillespie relies on conventional narrative structures, because she "tells stories" about bad men, good women, and an unjust legal system, she can rely on the situations she narrates to modulate her own affect without abandoning her need to galvanize readers. Penelope calls into question exactly the conventional use of narrative structures—arguing that their common use serves to avoid identifying sexual violence by its correct name. In fact, Penelope's entire project and its rhetorical strategies require *not* sweeping readers along in narrative conventions but instead interrupting them and exposing their consequences by calling attention to the unstated, the understated, the absences and elisions, the suppression and denial of agency that enable people to avoid facing and taking responsibility for specific cases of sexual abuse.

This contrast between the two texts demonstrates some of the benefits of narrative form for Gillespie. Penelope's text, in its limited use of narrative constructions, denies its readers the more comfortable position of reading stories, instead throwing them directly into the analytic demands of linguistic argument. It also denies to Penelope one of Gillespie's greatest advantages in wielding textual vehemence: the ability to use narrative form—the reliance on narrative as an indirect method of arguing about reality—to screen her own authorial persona. Because textual vehemence creates its effects partly through appearing to violate conventions of good taste, politeness, and suppression of affect, authorial persona is always marked and often scrutinized; highly narrative arguments can deflect attention from that marked persona to compelling narrative events and the character of actors in narratives. Lacking this advantage, Penelope creates textual vehemence "in her own voice" and suffers any negative consequences. Without implying that their choices are mutually exclusive, I would argue that Gillespie benefits from some of the very discourse conventions that Penelope uses strong language to undermine and disrupt. In effect, Penelope's conceptual and political needs to challenge conventional discourse preclude her from using many of the strategies available to Gillespie, thus throwing her into a more difficult rhetorical situation.

Penelope: Disrupt Conventions

Penelope examines linguistic structures to reveal the ways in which, she argues, men perpetuate dominance over women. She traces the failure to come to grips with problems of child sexual abuse, for example, to the conventional use of grammatical structures suppressing agency. The task she sets herself is dramatically different from that of Gillespie: Gillespie encourages readers to challenge legal systems; Penelope encourages readers to challenge the way they and others allow themselves to think and speak about the world. In contrast to what I have argued to be Gillespie's internal critique—to reforge stories told through taken-for-granted language—Penelope insists on an external critique, not to reformulate narratives but to reexamine and reformulate the conventions of language that forge all stories. Challenging rather than exploiting the taken-for-granted neutrality and transparency of language, Penelope inverts, deconstructs, and expands narratives. Analyzing syntactic form, she demonstrates its implications by filling grammatical "slots" with ironic and confrontational types of questioning. She employs disruptive contrast of grammatical form and unconventional terminology as a central tool to locate as well as unpack the significance of various syntactic structures. Her strategies of textual vehemence continually deny readers the comfort of positioning themselves as outside the problems she challenges.

Penelope confronts narrative-as-usual with narrative-in-excess. She inserts overwhelming stories exactly where she is arguing that normal language practices work to obliterate such stories. She "expands" on pronouns or hidden agents, stating or restating the absent, the hidden, the unmentioned, in a compelling way that enacts her argument at the same time that it escalates the "emotional" level. In scrutinizing the documentary on incest "Kids Don't Tell," Penelope explicates the absence hidden by the film's title, "Kids Don't Tell": "*What* don't kids *tell?* They don't tell *that a member of their own family, someone who's supposed to be caring for and protecting them, is forcing them into sexual relations. They don't tell that their brother rapes them every time parents are gone,* that *granddaddy rubs against them when they sit on his lap,* that *daddy makes them pretend that his penis is a lollypop and suck on it.* That sort of information is what 'kids don't tell.' But it wasn't in the title" (142, emphasis in original). This deliberately, aggressively confrontational expansion can become both powerful and overpowering. Penelope uses shocking expansion to attack the obliqueness of "normal" reportage, to disrupt the practical, transactional demands of communication that appear to require suppression of such discourse. By forcing the narrative to reveal outrage normally elided, Penelope reveals her political position in ways that Gillespie's use of narrative allowed her to obscure. As a result, Penelope may appear to be injecting confrontation into what some might consider otherwise as a polite, sensible, straightforward discussion of a social problem.

Penelope disrupts language-as-usual by violating conventions that have tended to peel off the political and the ideological—virtually anything but the most conventional—from the discussion of grammatical form. I quote one of Penelope's sample sentences and her commentary on it at some length to show the contrast between her humorous, ironic, or sarcastic commentary and the form of academic grammatical analysis. Her example sentence: "Men regard as amusing this exaggerated fad of trying to substitute 'Ms.' for 'Mrs.'" [Dr. Crane in his nationally syndicated "Worry Clinic"] (172, 173). Her comment on the sentence: "The quotation . . . illustrates how men wield power rhetorically. . . . How does "someone" exaggerate a fad? The statement sounds even more ludicrous when we question the hidden proposition: Who is exaggerating the fad? . . . I've italicized some possible identities, and arranged them in the order of likelihood that I think Crane implied. His intended agents might be one or all of the first three or four" (173). Penelope's subsequent schematizing of alternative interpretations:

a. Men regard as amusing this fad which *women* have exaggerated . . .
b. Men regard as amusing this fad which *feminists* have exaggerated . . .
c. Men regard as amusing this fad which *someone* has exaggerated . . .
d. Men regard as amusing this fad which *everyone* has exaggerated . . .
e. Men regard as amusing this fad which *they* have exaggerated . . .
f. Men regard as amusing this fad which *Dr. Crane* has exaggerated . . . (173, punctuation and emphasis in original)

Penelope creates a challenging and ironic tone by exploiting the structural form of a grammatical discussion, explaining technical terms and syntactic relationships. Since, she argues, suppression of agency in discussions of sexual violence causes dramatic and very real damage, many of her textual examples point toward concerns with incest or rape and, in so doing, both illustrate and escalate her argument. For example, in introducing discussion of the passive voice, she provides the following schema to illustrate the structural relationship between active and passive sentences:

Agent	*Verb*	*Object*
Five men	raped	the housewife.

Object	*Verb*	*Agent*
The housewife (146)	was raped	by five men.

Penelope uses similarly confrontational terms to contrast the implications of agency that emerge through the use of passives with *be* and *get*. She provides the following contrast:

> Many women are raped every day.
> Many women get raped every day. (166)

She goes on to comment, "The *be*-passives clearly assume that whoever committed the action is also solely responsible for it. Responsibility is not imputed to the victims. But the *get*-passives force us to read them as if they had an implied reflexive pronoun: . . . *Many women get* **themselves** *raped* *every day. . . .* The *get*-passive forces us to allot responsibility to the victim(s)" (166, emphasis in original). Readers' experiences with language textbooks and grammatical schema generally do not include sarcasm or sexually direct language, so Penelope's disruptions stand as a dramatic violation of form. In addition, Penelope's deliberate decision to name "perpetrators" such as Dr. Crane and others when she pulls examples from their work pinpoints the discursive problems of specific individuals in a way that gives her criticism a bitter, attacking edge.[7]

The sudden, frequent, disruptive use of sexual and graphic language forms an important rhetorical tool for Penelope, more closely related to her central arguments than might first appear. It appears, for example, in her discussion of "false deictics": a grammatical construction in which a speaker "points" by means of words like "it," "that," and "this," but with the referent or antecedent of "it" unstated, vague, even nonexistent. Penelope explains the sexual connotations of "it" used as a false deictic, illustrating its use on a billboard for vodka displaying a "sultry, reclining woman" and the caption "Make it with Dark Eyes": "at a level we understand perfectly well, *it* refers to heterosexual coitus (fucking). . . . 'Make *it*' could mean 'be successful,' but the reclining woman clearly invites men reading the billboard to fuck her, to equate drinking vodka with fucking her" (132, emphasis in original). From this point on, Penelope uses only the term *fucking*—and in some cases, *rape*—to refer to sexual intercourse.

Although the use of terms like *fuck* violates conventions about the nature of polite and particularly academic discourse, one should not infer from their use that Penelope is not behaving properly, that she does not "know how to act." She is assuming a strategic social role in order to encourage social action. Yet conventions imply that those who argue this way may be thought of as using their shocking terms gratuitously, rather than in necessary relation to their arguments, or for shock value, as if that were a value in and of itself, like an angry person shouting just so people will look. Further, those who use the term as Penelope does—matter-of-factly slipping such a term into the text without making an explicit argument for its use—may reinforce such objections by being read as unreasonable.

Yet while certainly somewhat shocking (also possibly amusing, ironic, overbearing, and so on), the word *fucking* executes a central function in Penelope's argument. By means of it she asserts (and rather efficiently at that) a difference in *meaning* between *fuck* and *sexual intercourse* or some such apparently neutral term and asserts also that the current state of affairs makes only the former appropriate for her discussion. To declare heterosexual intercourse not a "neutral" act but, instead, "fucking" (with attendant implications of not-totally-equal-and-pleasant-things being done *to* someone *by* someone) is not merely expressive, *it is an argument.* Whether or not she has already made an explicit argument for the validity of her term, by using such a word, Penelope makes the argument at that moment. Doing so allows her to make some very powerful assertions. While it might be worthwhile for Penelope to explain to some readers why she chooses to do this and what she means by it, for her to be "reasonable" does not require such an explication. Nor does such a large generalization mean she is "unreasonable." Further, to assert (or even believe) that all heterosexual coitus constitutes "fucking" is not, in itself, "unreasonable." Such an assertion might be produced by perfectly sensible premises and a perfectly sound method of considering evidence. It is much more likely to be *wrong* than *unreasonable.* The two are not synonymous.

Penelope's use of the term *fuck* centers her argument about the nature of language and exemplifies her deliberately disruptive rhetorical strategies. To reject her argument that sexual intercourse constitutes "fucking" need not entail rejecting the rest of her argument; however, to ignore or misinterpret her use of the word is to misconstrue the purpose of her entire analysis of language. Where Gillespie can use subtle or implicit irony, Penelope must be explicit in her irony and sarcasm exactly because her argument about the nature of language and what it constructs contradicts the "common sense" of what many people "know" about language. Coming to grips with the terms Penelope uses to structure her argument about sexual intercourse echoes (but inverts) her challenge to the matter-of-fact use of conventional grammatical constructions, seeking to disrupt conventions about which words and grammatical choices "count" and which do not. She is arguing that language used matter-of-factly is *exactly* what constitutes arguments. In effect, Penelope attempts to demonstrate that conventions themselves provide no guarantees: unconventional terms can be used to further desirable goals, and conventional constructions to hinder them. Yet in using vehemence to enact her argument in this way, she runs the risk of "offending" the standards of politeness of those not yet convinced by her text to that point.

Penelope uses rhetorical questions in ways dramatically different from Gillespie, ways that contribute significantly to her distinctively vehement tone. Gillespie's rhetorical questions are closely linked to narrative frameworks: both she and the discourses she criticizes are arguing about the narrative logic of stories of legitimacy and violence, about narrative expectations, about how the events and outcomes of particular stories connect to other narratives of motivation and responsibility. In contrast, Penelope's rhetorical questions, within a structure more analytic than narrative, provide direct attacks on the logics of particular grammatical conventions. When deriding grammatical constructions creating a "pretense of objectivity," she selects the following sentences as an illustration: "The history of anger is the history of mankind. Man has *been exposed* to the effects of anger, others' as well as his own, since he was first *placed* on earth" (154, emphasis in original). She then comments on them with sarcastic rhetorical questions: "*Mankind* and *man* refer exclusively to men; if they were being used generically to include women, then we have to wonder who the 'others' are who have 'exposed' men to the effects of their anger. Angels? Fairies? Maybe sharks or rattlesnakes? . . . Men don't tolerate overt expressions of anger from women, reserving that privilege to themselves; women resort to expressing it obliquely. So, the only logical agent of *exposed* is *man*" (154, emphasis in original).

In vivid contrast to the pseudocooperative Gillespie, Penelope creates irony—or sarcasm—partly by assuming a totally *un*cooperative stance. Her rhetorical questions tend to be somewhat sarcastic requests for significant information omitted by a particular sentence construction ("How does one decide that a phrase like 'human rights' has been uttered too many times?" [172]), or the exasperated ridiculing commentary seen above ("Angels? Fairies?" [154] "How obtuse can one be?" [155]). In the example above, Penelope's choices of possible candidates ("Angels?") gives the impression of exasperation because the context demonstrates them far from real possibilities. Again, she chooses to create a sense that she has lost patience with the less-than-thoughtful, damaging constructions of language that pass muster in everyday life (running the risk that readers will judge her an impatient person, rather than a person impatient with these problems). And without narrative conventions to obscure her stance, the argumentative edge of Penelope's rhetorical questions is more salient.

The pseudocooperative Gillespie and the impatient, apparently uncooperative Penelope also locate their rhetorical questions differently and establish different relationships with regard to their overall arguments. In general, Gillespie's sarcastic or ironic attacks on prevailing legal practice frequently appear at the conclusion of one narrative, often leading to the beginning of the next, and conclude a section with a summarizing discussion of the legal problem. When these attacks take the form of rhetorical questions, they push forward her immediate argument about the vague and perhaps unreasonable demands of the court, then move to a direct bridge to the conclusion of her paragraphs ("There is no justice in a criminal law that can require that sort of cold-blooded calculation"). Placing irony or sarcasm at the end of a sequence allows Gillespie to punctuate a position she has already established and brought to her readers by means of her narrative.

While Gillespie's rhetorical questions continue to make her main argument, Penelope's rhetorical questions tend to *be* the conclusion of her paragraphs. Such a position implies that she thinks they comment on arguments that have already been made adequately, rather than one being made by means of the rhetorical question. Further, Penelope uses her rhetorical questions to comment, as Gillespie tends to do, on the immediate argument (the implications of sentences such as the one in her example, "Man has been exposed to the effects of anger") but also on arguments that swing back to connect to her overall thesis about the complicity of language in male domination. In the example above, Penelope steps aside for a moment from the specific argument at hand (the pretense of objectivity resulting from the deletion of agency) to comment on the arrogant nature of men: *equally an argument of her text*, but one focused less tightly on her current argument about anger and agency, and more on her broader arguments about syntactic structure and male violence. Again, Penelope runs the risk of offending those who believe that academic writers ought to remain "neutral," "distanced" to the very end of their arguments yet, at the same time, enacts her argument about the disciplining force of convention.

Gillespie's and Penelope's projects assign responsibility differently, with quite different consequences, particularly with regard to their demands on their readers. Gillespie's argument rides on familiar concepts of responsibility and blame. She argues that the discourse of the courts blames the wrong people in cases of violence against women: it blames specific women for their defensive behavior when their choices were controlled and limited by violent men. Since Gillespie critiques specific narratives, she can also connect blame to specific classes of individuals—judges, attorneys, jurors—thus clearly defining and segregating her "perpetrators." She almost always names individual men and women who are involved in the violent scenarios she describes, but these people are not subject to her criticism. (The batterers she believes to stand by their actions; the women, by their testimony.)[8] Her concern is to reveal the social and legal problems that result from the courts' ways of treating deadly responses to partner violence. It would be plausible, given such a line of argument, to criticize the legal actors by name. But Gillespie seldom names those she is subjecting to criticism: the specific judges, prosecutors, and others perpetrating what she argues to be injustices of the legal system. Such rhetoric leaves no one specifically "accountable" for the problems she raises, although it directs attention to the illegitimacy of certain kinds of arguments.

Most readers would agree that the relationships Gillespie describes have "gone wrong"; readers need not examine their own relationships carefully for an underlying ideological connection with the couples' violence that she describes. Gillespie establishes a very limited range of "culpability": those who engage in regular beating of their partners, perhaps those who have participated, as judge, attorney, or jury, in unjust, gendered criminal convictions. According to Gillespie's argument, justice can be achieved by replacing bad narratives with good narratives, bad faith with good faith, bad bias with equitable sensitivity. Gillespie merely demands that readers do something about a specific subgroup of people who have been treated unjustly, without demanding personal introspection and self-analysis as part of her argument (although undoubtedly some result). Because Gillespie's strong narratives reveal events that readers need not be accountable for *already,* their responses as readers need not be complicated by an assessment of their *own* complicity in the acts of sexual and legal violence she describes.

In contrast, Penelope greatly complicates such concepts of responsibility and blame. She attempts to establish that *no one* gets blamed for sexual violence against women and children, that the structure of language permits rhetorical choices that elude and evade responsibility. Penelope connects the way *everyone* talks to complicity with problems of sexual violence. She finds everywhere the grammatical constructions that trouble her and cites specific texts with named authors drawn from a wide range of public discourses: specific television documentaries, the *Boston Globe, People Magazine*, B. F. Skinner, Doris Lessing, even her own speech. These specific authorial "perpetrators" are at fault, she argues, but so are their audiences.

Penelope repeatedly and resolutely implicates audiences as well as writers: "The reporter simply gave his audience what they wanted—avoidance, obliqueness, omission, denial" (143). She further positions her audience by suggesting that authors using grammatical constructions "fool" their audiences. Words like *trick* inhabit her discussion a good deal: "writers use deictics to trick us into supplying information from our own assumptions" (130), "writers use this structure to slip their assertions past our conscious mind" (172).

Penelope's use of *we* and *they* strategically, pointedly, includes *all* of her readers (as well as herself) as willing to avoid confronting unpleasant problems caused by certain grammatical constructions: "the prevalence of [their] . . . use . . . indicates that we prefer delusion to reality—that we refuse to acknowledge our responsibility for acts committed in homes every day. . . . We don't want to hear about it, we don't want to know about it, we don't want to talk about it" (143). With regard to certain grammatical constructions that obliterate or elide agency in sexual molestation: "We aren't merely 'interpreting' in such cases, we're helping speakers maintain silence about actions they're responsible for. We become accomplices to their denial" (137–138).

Such language forces readers to turn back on themselves, reflecting on their own acceptance of such constructions. Penelope demands that her readers pay attention to taken-for-granted language, a rather uncomfortable process for those readers, since the task positions everyone as, to some degree, "perpetrators." Penelope may then appear "angrier" than her text warrants because she can make readers angry by threatening their assumptions and challenging their behavior.

Few "innocents" inhabit Penelope's argument, because she argues that everyone is implicated in allowing suppression of agency. But her net of complicity spreads still more broadly: she tries to get readers to recognize their acquiescence in a social system where the family—so often talked about as a site of love and affection—becomes a site of violence, where hatred of women is coded into the erotic. By arguing that gender problems in society interweave with its sexual relations, she demands readers' reflection on their own roles and relationships, reflection that many find disconcerting. "Men detest the women they fuck, whether they say *liberated* or *promiscuous*" (171, emphasis in original), she says, explicitly challenging the nature of *all* women's relationships to *all* men. Penelope's more complex assignment of blame includes her *readers*—not to "rescue" the persecuted or "reform" the biased but to examine themselves. And what they need to examine goes far beyond reassessing legal systems to reconsidering the foundation of their social and personal lives. Penelope's project demands strategies that are disruptive, for the project itself disrupts the ways readers conduct language "business as usual."

Penelope's choices of rhetorical strategies—and consequent reception of her arguments—are constrained by her own relationship to language and narrative, crucially different from that of Gillespie. Gillespie relies on "commonsense" representations of language as a transparent reflection of social reality; Penelope depends on technical theories of language examining how it constructs social reality. Gillespie implies that language is a tool to solve her problem; Penelope argues that language is *implicated in* her problem—in effect, that it *is* the problem. To make her argument, Penelope cannot rely on the commonsense model of language that Gillespie employs so successfully; it is the model itself that she challenges with disruptive grammatical and rhetorical analysis. As a result, Penelope faces rhetorical problems and potential objections—she must argue not merely about problems of law and sexual violence but about how language operates. Both authors must discuss the politically fraught complications of sexual violence. But Penelope must discuss complications of language analysis as well which are *also* politically fraught. Penelope has to carry, then, an additional burden recognized by many who study rhetoric: many readers' resistance to adopting a critical rhetorical eye about language they would much prefer to take for granted.

Gillespie and Penelope's goals require radical differences in their two arguments and rhetorics, differences that I would argue significantly influence how readers will come to react to positions. Gillespie focuses on bad acts; Penelope, on bad texts. Gillespie falsely cooperates with the argument she critiques; Penelope falsely analyzes it. Gillespie makes it easy for her readers to move through her argument with her; Penelope makes it hard. Gillespie sweeps her readers along; Penelope confronts them. Gillespie understates; Penelope overstates. Gillespie repeats and cumulates; Penelope interrupts and disrupts. Gillespie meets expectations; Penelope disrupts them. Gillespie makes her readers feel righteous; Penelope makes her readers feel culpable.

These dramatic differences in rhetorical strategy position Gillespie the author as low-keyed and cooperative—separated from the affect of her discussion, while Penelope appears to adopt an unnecessarily critical edge. But Gillespie's project is more reformative than radical in its requests to readers. Penelope's project radically overturns their sense of their own innocence as users of language. In a highly charged context, readers' sense of culpability becomes one of the most significant of the rhetorical choices for academic writers—most readers interpret texts that make them feel culpable with some defensiveness. For Penelope the risks appear to be higher but may well be required by her more profoundly unsettling argumentative purposes. Some might even argue that arguments asking readers to challenge deep-seated attitudes without prompting defensiveness are not doing their job.

The Politics of Textual Vehemence and Problems of Argument

I have argued that comparing the vehement strategies of Gillespie's and Penelope's texts reveals contours of academic writing with raised voices, blunt terms, confrontational claims. I have also argued that crucial differences in their strategies deeply inflect the impact of their texts: each author can be distinguished, for example, on the basis of her principles for structuring sentences and episodes, her utilizing of brutal terms and frank language, her methods for creating ironic commentary, and her assigning of responsibility and demands for action. I have also argued that recognition and reaction to such vehement rhetorics depends on who utters them and under what circumstances, particularly in the contested zone of academic and public argument that Penelope and Gillespie have entered. There one reaches—and is exposed to—a broad range of readers: in such an open arena, readers are particularly likely to hold texts accountable to conventional warrants of politeness, without considering the obstacles confronting writers who challenge dominant power relations.

In such a contested zone of argument, features such as those that distinguish Gillespie's and Penelope's texts have significant impact on both academic and more public responses to textual vehemence. I base this contention not only on my study of academic rhetoric and my observation of public discourse about the rhetoric of textually vehement women (including comments by women reviewers on the vehemence displayed by feminist arguments about gender and violence)[9] but also on several years' experience sharing Gillespie's and Penelope's texts in particular with a range of readers—colleagues, graduate students, undergraduates, and those outside the academy. My argument is informed by the differences between their readings of the two authors and mine: I find both Gillespie's and Penelope's texts to be serious, informative, forceful, interesting—even, at times, amusingly ironic. However, sharing these texts with other readers, I came to realize that only a minority react as I do. I hinge my discussion here on the fact that the great majority of these readers find both authors vehement, but Gillespie compelling and forceful, and Penelope bitter, angry, irritating. They "believe" Gillespie and discount Penelope.

Does this mean that one should favor Gillespie's strategies over Penelope's? Not at all. Simple rhetorical rules or absolutes cannot solve the problems of the politics of textual vehemence. One cannot prefer or condemn Gillespie's strategies, or Penelope's, or others that may mark themselves as textually vehement. Given the varied and flexible nature of reception contexts, the contested nature of social life and academic rhetoric, and the importance of the problems often addressed by feminist arguments, it is vital to understand the effects of textual vehemence and foolish to police them through a set of a priori rules. Every oppositional argument reflects a dialectical interplay between the undeniable risks and the undeniable possibilities of rhetorical vehemence, between situatedness and social analysis, between "affect" and "reason."

Because the costs of textual anger seem so high, readers may lose sight of why the use of textual markers of anger may sometimes be a perfectly reasonable or even desirable choice when attempting to express an argument with moral force. With antagonists waiting to pounce on putatively angry feminists, why provide them with an opportunity? Yet we also need to consider the costs of not following a path simply because we have been told not to travel on it. Textual vehemence or anger may appear in arguments of social critique asserting that current or historical conditions and policies are not desirable or equitable, but damaging, demeaning, despicable, disgraceful, divisive (see, e. g., Said 1983). As in the cases of Gillespie and Penelope, a careful analysis of their situation by aggrieved groups may demonstrate compelling reasons to use textual vehemence or anger as *a strong component of persuasion*. Textual vehemence can convey a sense of moral responsibility—and of moral revulsion—demonstrating the importance of the stakes of the debate. It can operate as a battle cry or rallying cry, drawing together into action those who already agree or who have been swayed by the argument. It can appeal to those who have not been reached by other methods. It can also operate as a site of expressive power: the power of expressing anger—not just to influence others, but also to influence oneself—not spewing forth of emotion, but constructed reflection of anger designed not so much expressively as rhetorically—to communicate rather than to combust.

In academic as well as other arguments, decisions to employ textual vehemence—and what kinds of vehemence to employ—need be assessed according to a calculus of costs and benefits relating to one's rhetorical tasks and desired effects. In the cases I discuss here, linguist Penelope asks her readers to look closely at grammatical constructions and consider their logical and ethical implications for gendered sexual violence. No small task! Attorney Gillespie asks her readers to help change the law concerning women who respond with lethal self-defense to sexual violence. High stakes indeed. Such writers may even face something of a double-bind: the problems they describe may be overlooked and ignored if not expressed with vehemence; however, if expressed with vehemence, writers may thereby alienate part of their audience.

Eschewing textual vehemence cannot ensure control over interpretation of authors' motives, intentions, arguments, or strategies. Readers interpret vehement strategies such as those used by Gillespie and Penelope within a larger context of political and cultural discourse about the relations of men and women, the legal system, and even emotional expression. Given the current contestation over social power, it would be foolish to assume that any oppositional text that calls gendered social power relations into question is safe from portrayal as "man hating" and hysterical: purported violations from conventional *opinions* (whatever their rhetoric) can always be aligned to politically constructed continua: however "positioned," the ends of any such continuum can always be deployed in counterarguments demonstrating feminist selfishness and irrationality.[10] In fact, this relentless positioning of even the most moderate of feminist positions demonstrates one of the most significant benefits—for *all* oppositional writers—of those who chose textual vehemence within academic frameworks of argument. A politics of textual vehemence does not inhere to *one* text: it is developed by understanding the details of a range of texts, a range that functions *together* as a larger cultural text. The dramatic tone of a single vehement academic text can open up the "continuum" or "scale" of texts, repositioning more moderately phrased oppositional texts as less than vehement, even sensible.

The vehemence of those challenging power relations tends to be particularly marked, particularly salient to readers. Conventional practices of reading encourage overlooking the contexts that the authors must negotiate in order to make arguments that go "against the grain" of taken-for-granted ways of thinking about social relations. Arguments about sexual violence, in particular, may be difficult for readers to encounter. In discussing serious and volatile issues, some academic authors use statistical evidence, some interviews, others theoretical arguments. Some authors may be "angry," others may not. The personal attitude or mood or feelings of an academic author is not what *matters*. It does not *matter* whether Gillespie or Penelope is "angry." What *matters* is the argument she makes to counter the injustices of violence against women.

The history of struggles for social change should make feminists and other aggrieved groups aware that there is room for humility on all sides; most strategies that work in some circumstances fail in others. Gillespie and Penelope pursue different rhetorical strategies, at least in part, because they have different tactical goals. Gillespie's strategy for action "piggybacks" on people's widespread distrust of legal systems and bureaucracies. To build allies, she taps widespread sentiments that might be mobilized for counterhegemonic purposes and mobilizes anger at bureaucracy to the service of feminism. The danger in such a strategy is that the specifically gendered nature of the problems she presents may disappear from view, and her allies may not be joining for the right reasons. When gathering allies, one may lose control of the argument. Penelope, by comparison, interrupts any coalition she might be building by pointing and repointing her audience to gender antagonisms—including casting doubt on their own behavior. While not impossible for her, it may become harder to connect those gender antagonisms to a larger social critique, beyond feminism, to galvanize allies already concerned about other issues. Neither Gillespie nor Penelope can avoid employing rhetoric that is itself connected with larger social problems; both Gillespie and Penelope insist on rhetoric that acknowledges the inevitable relationship between social power and rhetorical choices.

Partially because of the efforts of Gillespie, Penelope, and other feminist academics and activists, laws about domestic violence and the legal and popular language used to describe rape and incest have changed greatly since they wrote the texts I study here. Future feminists will not face the same scene of argument that Gillespie and Penelope confronted in the late 1980s and early 1990s. But we have much to learn from their actions, methods, and strategies. These two scholars recognized an important dimension of power when they decided to engage sociolegal and sociolinguist studies about these issues. They recognized that power did not rest solely in the courtroom, the police station, or the doctor's office. They understood that judges, prosecutors, attorneys, police officers, and doctors proceeded to treat women unfairly in part because legal theorists and lawyers did not attend adequately to the unfairly gendered dimensions of laws about domestic abuse, because linguists and rhetoricians had been insufficiently attuned to the ways in which seemingly small decisions about language had enormous consequences for women. By operating in the arenas open to them, they proved to their fellow professionals that their disciplines needed to change, that attending to feminist concerns was not a matter of placating a pressure group inside the profession but rather a matter of doing more precise, complex, and generative scholarly work. They revealed how seemingly innocent matters of sociolegal and sociolinguistic research implicated the profession as an accomplice in the mistreatment of women. Perhaps most importantly, in a scholarly world where disciplinary divisions placed important issues and questions outside the purview of researchers, they broke down barriers and expanded the social reach and scope of their fields to do worthy and socially responsible work.

CHAPTER FOUR

Tough Babies, or Anger in the Superior Position

The trope of the angry feminist sets in motion a narrative about a stock character. She is emotional, shrill, hysterical, and unreasonable, and therefore one should not pay attention to her arguments. Interestingly, as we have seen, she is often condemned in ways that are *themselves* emotional, shrill, hysterical, and unreasonable. This display of open contradiction and celebration of dominance over the feminist is a discursive technology of power. It is often mobilized by a specific antifeminist persona: the "Tough Baby." Like "Dr. Laura," the Tough Baby is a persona, but one shared by a range of antifeminist critics who echo one another in predictable rhetorical patterns. Emphasizing that the Tough Baby is a *persona* opens to comparison and scrutiny rhetorical techniques that are displayed across the particularities of specific authors and the exigencies of specific arguments. This emphasis allows us to ground analysis in textual evidence, the shared social qualities of the persona, and the ways the persona is deployed for specific argumentative purposes. Perhaps most important, it requires holding those who adopt the *ethos* of the Tough Baby accountable—not for their personal characters, not for their speaking positions, but for their rhetorical choices and the ways these choices corrupt understanding of academic arguments. The Tough-Baby persona has served as an affective core and key structure of rhetorical feeling for antifeminists from the 1990s to the present. Examining the Tough Baby's rhetorical gestures through feminist socioforensic discursive analysis can clarify broader problems about textual vehemence, social power, and warrants of politeness in academic argument.

My term *Tough Baby* is drawn from the work of political scientist Thomas L. Dumm in *united states* (1994). Dumm argues that those in dominant positions—white middle-class males like him—must take responsibility for their constructions of political and social life. He argues that their interest in establishing, solidifying, and maintaining their structures of dominance forces all others to live according to those constructions. According to Dumm,

> We men in charge proceed in opposites, countering the clean to the filthy, the hetero to the homo, the white to the black, the man to the woman; in each instance we make sex in the superior position the norm. (86)

The Tough Baby both relies on and enacts such a binary system of oppositional dominance, treating its *own* rhetorical vehemence as justified, and that of the (angry) feminist as deplorable; its own position as invaluable, and that of the (angry) feminist as ridiculous; its own (or male dominant) sexuality as imperative, that of the (angry) feminist as foolish or perverse; its own possible excesses as courageous, those of the (angry) feminist as outrageous. Rhetorically, the Tough Baby re-creates "sex in the superior position." Delivering "anger in the superior position," the Tough Baby enacts the culturally endorsed opposite to the angry feminist: the anger of the righteously indignant father. The Tough Baby constitutes itself as binary, both bully and blameless. The poses of the Tough Baby, in the textual life I describe here—their toughness and innocence—their bullying, sneering, jeering, tittering, nostalgia, bromides, bon mots, little jokes—establish "deniability" for the Tough Baby's disciplining of academic women and evasion of academic argument.

Dumm, who draws the term *tough baby* from Theodor W. Adorno's discussion of problems of masculine identity connected to German fascism (1974), is concerned with the consequences of such images of masculinity for our political life. He connects the kind of stance the Tough Baby adopts to the various kinds of physical and political violence used to perpetuate current conditions of dominance. Commenting on Adorno, he remarks:

> And yet what is at work here, for us who inhabit the superior positions, is a willingness to ignore the violence we do to remain innocent, tough *babies*. (86)

The Tough Baby tells women to "toughen up" and suffer in silence while at the same time deriding her and presenting himself as wallowing in wounded self-pity.

Tough Babies appear in many discursive arenas, but in musicology they showed up in full force in the 1990s to police the boundaries of the discipline from a perceived feminist threat. In this chapter, I examine three critics who used the persona of the Tough Baby to discipline women in musicology in the early 1990s. The three episodes demonstrate that the persona moves freely from music journalism to exchanges in academic publications to articles in refereed scholarly journals in musicology: Robert Craft in the *New York Review of Books* ("Lagoon Tunes," 1992, "Robert Craft Replies," 1992), Eric Gans in *Perspectives of New Music* (1994), and Pieter C. van den Toorn in the *Journal of Musicology* (1991). Examining antifeminist acrimony and belligerence at the scene of argument can prepare us to respond to future uses of the Tough Baby.

Arguments in the larger social arena contribute to the aggressive character of the debates about feminism and sexuality in music. The field became a particularly explosive scene of argument in the early 1990s because of the prestige of European art music in conservative circles. Classical music was positioned as a universal good to counter what was presented as the partial truths and particularisms of multiculturalism. New Right foundations supported and publicized Allan Bloom's *The Closing of the American Mind* (1988), which contended that antiracism and antisexism in the academy threatened to erase knowledge about and respect for the great traditions of European art from the age of antiquity through the Enlightenment and modernity. A foundation-funded and orchestrated public relations campaign portrayed efforts to deprovincialize, desegregate, and pluralize the curriculum at universities as savage attacks on civilization itself. Although important critical work in classics, art history, theater studies, and musicology showed that these defenders of the Western canon often showed an embarrassing lack of understanding of the nature of the art and philosophy they purported to defend, these campaigns did succeed, nonetheless, in encouraging gatekeepers in humanities fields to believe that "the barbarians are at the gates."[1]

Yet there are also specific disciplinary reasons for the scene of argument I discuss. The rancor with which musicology received arguments about feminism stems partly from its relative isolation from the "crisis of representation" that has altered the discourses of other disciplines, as well as from the relatively late introduction of feminist arguments into the field. This should not exclude feminist scholarship in musicology from normal scholarly critique. But, in fact, it did: in many cases, Tough-Baby attacks have been accepted as substitutes for scholarly critique. Rather than approaching feminist arguments on an academic plane, many responses, like the three I describe here, display a level of rhetorical outrage that leaves them unmoored from the arguments they criticize. Tough Babies, individually and together, deliver arguments to discipline and intimidate academic feminists (and by extension all women scholars) by evoking images of outraged, unreasoning women, tapping into cultural models that encourage women to suppress emotion for fear of being thought impolite, irrational, unfeminine. Such arguments are not productive challenges to even the most outrageous of academic feminist assertions; they represent, rather, the use of social etiquette warrants to supplant and suppress academic argument. They appear to deride and degrade their targets, but I would argue that, rather, they corrupt the standards of public and academic argument.

The *persona* or *ethos* of the Tough Baby is displayed when scholars choose not to present rebuttals or counterarguments, but instead decide to insult and intimidate their targets. A number of rhetorical features, taken *together*, characterize what we might consider the *tough* side of the Tough-Baby ethos: (a) it vehemently condemns the power, rhetoric, character, manners, and morals of its target; (b) it conflates the arguments of the target with those of a wide range of other people; (c) it substitutes social punditry for academic argument; (d) it appropriates to itself all that is good, true, necessary, male, and successful in nature, civilization, and religious life, assigning the rest to its target. But the Tough Baby does all this while declaring itself but a *baby*—specifically asserting its own helplessness, powerlessness, innocence; (e) it claims victim status from those it victimizes in print; (f) it both openly deploys and fervently denies its own rhetorical tools; (g) it declares its arguments to be without the personal, political, or ideological interests that, it claims, drive the arguments of its target; (h) it flaunts an openly "doubled" face, parading the transparency of its claims of innocence while hiding its allegiances and intentions.

The Tough Baby is often—although by no means always—the persona or ethos at play when scholars deploy the trope of the angry feminist, taking it upon themselves to ridicule or denounce academic feminists as "angry" rather than to criticize their arguments. Brandishing its "doubled" face, it constructs targets of straw in the face of feminists' concrete texts, celebrates male sexuality to tweak allegedly antisex feminists, presenting sexual slurs as boyish jokes. Condemning feminist vehemence vehemently, feminist anger angrily, feminist politics politically, the Tough-Baby persona is *candidly* inconsistent. All this is guilelessly academic, the Tough Baby claims; the accompanying wink, the nudge, the display of personal illogic and invective—these are central to what makes the Tough-Baby ethos. The Tough Baby seeks to wound while claiming itself to be wounded. It disciplines others according to rules it does not meet. Thus what might appear to be conjecture and contradition, were one to take the Tough Baby's argument at face value, turn out to be intrinsic to its persona—authority without responsibility.

Tough Babies substitute arguments about scholars for scholarly argument. The recurrent use of the Tough-Baby ethos in such kinds of metacommentary plays an important role in conditioning the reception of scholarly work by educated readers inside and outside the university. When aimed at nonspecialists, it exudes self-assurance and self-confidence in order to appeal to the common sense of middle-class readers who pride themselves on being educated and cultured. The rhetoric of such metacommentaries inscribes readers as wanting to preserve their private pleasures, casual habits, and uninterrogated prejudices. It advises that to succeed in doing so, they must both envy and loathe scholars who might require them to think otherwise.[2]

The Tough Baby offers for nonspecialists the illusion that he has read, considered, and become offended by feminist research. Specialists, however, are aware that it offers no insight or counter to feminist research, no understanding of the arguments of Donna Haraway, Judith Butler, or Joan Wallach Scott, or any serious feminist scholar; it is more in keeping with its interests to ridicule unnamed feminist transgressors. As I will demonstrate, features of the Tough-Baby ethos that serve such metacommentary in musicology also empower and enable similar condemnations in other academic contexts: the willingness to condemn groups of scholars wholesale, to disengage from the scholarly issues at hand, to position oneself on the side of "common sense" over careful thinking, to deploy textual vehemence not to refute arguments, but to humiliate those who argue. Given our scholarly ideals, such Tough-Baby gestures in academic prose have a compromising effect on the integrity and utility of academic argument.

Thus what may appear trivial, opportunistic, and banal in itself assumes more significance when seen, as I argue it should be, as part of a recurrent incursion of gendered policing to suppress women's academic arguments. The kinds of bromides and bon mots used by Tough Babies to delegitimate and discipline academic women appear more frequently than acknowledged both in educated public discourse and in the humanities and social sciences. Some might argue that they simply represent academic sexism or the excesses of particular critics known to be "loose cannons," or even that the targets of Tough-Baby scorn because of their own inadequacies "deserve" such attention. But there is more to account for: while, as I shall demonstrate, such metacommentary is delivered with considerable wit and vigor, it often has only a tangential relation to the academic arguments at hand, shows no knowledge of the field of feminist studies, fails to address feminist criticisms, and relies on presuppositions, evidence, and "commonsense" theorizing about the world that in other contexts the academy deems patently illegitimate. At a time when the demands of specialization are great, metacommentators signal to both critics and their readers that they do not have to engage in difficult reading of work based on new paradigms. Most scholars would reject that kind of excuse if it were presented to them directly; couching it in gender stereotypes gives it a natural and inevitable quality.

The three examples of the Tough Baby I examine are progressively more directly "academic." The first, in the *New York Review of Books*, emphasizes the feminist as sexual censor—in such a case, not only is the angry feminist outside the economy of reason, she is also outside the economy of pleasure involved in virtually any kind of male sexual discussion. This rhetorical move appears in a review by music critic Robert Craft in the *New York Review of Books*.[3] In the course of reviewing H. C. Robbins Landon and John Julius Norwich's *Five Centuries of Music in Venice* (1991), Craft comments that Landon and Norwich, while reproducing a bare-breasted portrait of Venetian musician Barbara Strozzi, fail to discuss her musical contributions as "history's only renowned female composer": "Nothing is said of her music, cantatas and arias displaying distinctive melodic and rhythmic gifts, but this oversight may be blamed on the distracting portrait of her with charms undraped" (1992, "Lagoon Tunes," 44). Craft's own desire to discuss Strozzi's musical gifts is limited to this comment, although he refers again to the sexual implications of her portrait in his final recommendation to buy the book: "Buy it for the pictures, or for the *pittoresco* period pin-up of Barbara Strozzi" (44).

Craft's discussion of the portrait's "charms" offers a little sexual titillation for some in the staid pages of the *New York Review of Books*. But it also "sets up" his next sentence, the rhetorical gesture that concerns us here. In that gesture, Craft deliberately "takes on" feminists, whom he presents as consumed with anger over men's sexual interests, as well as less-than-equal sexual arrangements. He comments,

> Feminists outraged by the foregoing phallogocentric remark should in fairness consider the sexist aspect of the female orchestras, a Venetian phenomenon famed, by the early eighteenth century, throughout Europe. (44)

In effect, Craft acts as if he anticipates an audience that he can divide into two groups: those who enjoy a little sex talk and the prudish feminists. With this gesture, Craft anticipates the reproaches of his angry feminists: if they object to him publicly tittering about the sexuality of any woman (no matter what her talents and historical contributions), they are not being "fair." While Craft's giggling prurience in a previous collection of his essays (*Prejudices in Disguise: Articles, Essays, Reviews*, published in 1974) evidences that his anxiety about the female anatomy (and willingness to reveal that anxiety in public) is of long standing, it is exactly his ability to snigger publicly that he feels called upon to defend. Yet Craft's somewhat anxious gesture also expresses a worry that feminists *will not care*—that without prodding, they might not even notice. Craft's angry feminists are powerful enough to be mentioned, yet apparently can be floored by any invocation of the magic terms of defense: "in all fairness," Craft says, "[w]e must be fair." Invoking "fairness" as an ideal for feminists confirms Craft's comment to be either fanfare or raspberry, since he is prescribing for others an ideal he himself eschews.

Craft develops this tough side of his Tough-Baby persona in replying to a single letter responding to his review, by musicologist Susan C. Cook (1992).[4] Cook, in her letter, seems more concerned with challenging Craft's facts than his freedom of speech. She makes a short, calm, limited, and perfectly reasonable argument indicating that Craft's "otherwise informative" review does a disservice to other female composers in describing Barbara Strozzi as "history's only renowned female composer"; Cook suggests other possible contenders for such a role.[5] She suggests that the manifest enthusiasm for the portrait may account for this inaccuracy, and that female musicians have often been positioned as sexually available.[6] Cook concludes her letter,

> Mr. Craft's later reference to this same portrait as a "period pin-up" not only suggests his assumption of the male gaze of his readership (why would I, a female musicologist, buy a work for a pin-up?) but perpetuates the connection between female musicality and sexual promiscuity that dogged Strozzi and her many like-minded and talented sisters and continues to make female creativity in music a suspect act of audacity where nice girls need not apply. (53)

Although Craft subsequently plays with her to imply otherwise, Cook displays not an ounce of the ethos of the angry feminist. But a Tough-Baby pose allows Craft to avoid engaging with Cook's arguments: as we shall see, he instead misrepresents them, then cleverly replies to his misrepresentations.[7]

In the light of Craft's posturing rhetoric that I quote above, the most significant claim in his reply—that Cook has misunderstood him—is particularly meretricious. Invoking Tough-Baby innocence, he denies that his review suggests *any* concerns with sexuality. *He* is "gender-blind" in all these comments, and it is *Cook* who has insisted on bringing women's sexuality into the discussion by misinterpreting his own innocent remarks. He chastises her for assuming that when he referred to the half-nude portrait of the female musician as a "pin-up portrait," he must have meant "pin-up" in the sense of a "cheesecake photo":

> [S]he can hardly be unaware that the term "pin-up" is no longer restricted to sex idols (viz. Dylan Thomas's "the pin-up poets") (53)

He continues the sentence, reproaching Cook for suggesting that only men (and, therefore, "the male gaze") would be interested in such a "pin-up portrait":

> [She can hardly be unaware that . . .] a "female musicologist" and a "nice-girl" musician could quite reasonably wish to acquire the picture of a female composer. (53)

Note that Craft plays off of, rather than engages with, Cook's criticisms. For example, he is clearly aware that it is not unreasonable for Cook to argue that when he refers to the half-nude portrait as a "pin-up," he is using the common definition of "pin-up." (The first definition in my own dictionary: "a picture that is suitable for pinning up on a wall, usually of an attractive and often voluptuous girl," followed by "a girl in such a picture." My dictionary makes no reference to an alternative use by Dylan Thomas.) But Craft does not choose simply to supply Cook and his readers with information on an alternative use. He does *not* say something like, "Cook may not be aware that I was referring to the portrait in the sense that Dylan Thomas referred to poets when he said . . ." Instead, Craft's phrasing reproaches Cook—"she can hardly be unaware" of the Dylan Thomas terminology. In other words, Cook is wrong, and not even from ignorance or for "reasonable reasons." According to Craft, Cook has dredged up an outlandishly inappropriate interpretation—the possibility that Craft meant that the half-nude portrait was interesting partly for its sexual pleasures.[8] According to Craft, Cook insists on inserting sexuality into an otherwise *innocent* discussion of a half-nude portrait of a female musician.

Craft's concluding comments offer him even greater scope to demonstrate what a Tough Baby can do with the unwitting female academic, were she so foolish as to suppose that her arguments might be considered on their merits. Craft concludes,

Vive the power of the female to "distract," in my sense, since, for better or worse, it ensures the continuation of the species and the possibility, at least, of more and greater female composers. (53)

Striking is Craft's use of *"vive"* to allude to *"vive la différence,"* evoking the image of champagne and the old roué, Maurice Chevalier toasting a lifetime of appreciation of the feminine. Note that by his use of the phrase " 'distract,' in my sense" Craft reveals that despite his declarations of innocence "to" Cook, he *has been meaning* and *does mean* "sexual distraction." In a characteristic Tough-Baby gesture, Craft replies to academic argument with social punditry, for he indicates that only with exactly these social and sexual relations can Cook get what he presents as her desire: a new generation of babies that might become female composers. Unpacking Craft's line of argument: what Cook wants is more female composers; to get more female composers, the species must continue; for the species to continue, there must be sexual congress; for there to be sexual congress, sexual relations must proceed along sexist and misogynist lines. Succinctly, Cook cannot get what she wants unless sexual relations operate exactly as men desire. The headline attached to Cook's letter furthers Craft's re-creation of Cook's point: "What's a Girl to Do?"[9] Such a line of argument, given its manifest speciousness as a response to Cook's actual text, demonstrates the persona's double tone, the tough and the innocent: to the angry feminist, so self-righteous as to be unable to understand the nuances of the text, one presents the baby face, while at the same time directing a nudge in the ribs to one's appreciative ("tough") audience.

Note that Craft's raspberries here require no "real women" at all: his coterie of angry feminists is constructed for the occasion; the mention of female orchestras—certainly not evidence of female dominance—serves only to tweak contemporary "feminists"; the bare-breasted portrait may well not even be Barbara Strozzi.[10] But the point of his jibes is not their utility against their ostensible "target," but toward the rest of his audience. In his comments on "outraged feminists" (and his reply to Cook), Craft assumes a pugilistic stance *toward* the feminists (but *for* his other audience). He darts and dances in front of what he implies to be ravening feminists, gibing at them, attempting to incite them: "Come on, punch me, see if you can get me." The Tough-Baby persona establishes itself *as* tough by such rhetorical gestures. It establishes itself as a baby by avoiding responsibility for them. The Tough Baby calls attention to his "naughty" defiance of women with a textual wink.

Craft writes for an educated public audience, relying on general cultural supports for his use of the Tough-Baby ethos and his deployment of the trope of the angry feminist. More surprising, perhaps, is my next example, the extension of both ethos and trope into the academy to infuse and authorize arguments that present themselves as academic (although not subject to peer review). Eric Gans counters criticism of his work by Rosemary N. Killam in the journal *Perspectives of New Music* (Gans 1994; Killam 1993; Killam replies to Gans in Killam 1994). Killam, in the course of developing her argument on another topic, criticizes inadequacies in Eric Gans's vision of a model of originary language and cites some feminist scholarship to offer an alternative to his originary scene. Commenting in passing on Gans's vision of a male world accompanied by objects that include passive women, his citation of only male scholarship, and his use of the "generic 'he,'" Killam primarily relies on a string of quotations from Gans to "speak for themselves," to demonstrate that when Gans posits language to be created in the matrix of men's potentially violent contestation and conflict, he fails to account for possible roles for women.

Gans chooses the occasion of his reply not to counter Killam's specific arguments; instead, he draws on her embodied gender and her use of gender as an analytic category as the basis for expressing his opinions about the discourse of *other* women and even of *others—not women*—whom he apparently feels are similar to women in their angry ethos and violations of politeness in academic discourse. He opens his reply,

> Rather than attempt to "correct" Ms. Killam's reading of my work . . . I would prefer to touch on a few issues raised by contemporary feminism and "minoritary" [*sic*] discourse in general. (1994, 86)

Creating this relationship between feminist and "minoritary" discourses and then setting his own position as outside and critical of those discourses benefit the Tough Baby in several ways: (1) such texts may challenge politically dominant discourse, and can, therefore, be accused of "complaining"; (2) such texts are authored by embodied individuals who can be said to be members of nondominant groups and can, therefore, be accused of insubordination. Thus the apparent neologism "minoritary" serves to condemn embodied men and women *not* for their ethnic backgrounds and their relative proportions in American society, but explicitly *for their speaking positions*. The only manifest connection of these texts and their authors is their *political* relation to the dominant discourse that Gans seeks to secure. To be explicit here, arguments that resemble one another not at all, that may well disagree with one another in virtually every regard, are unified by their subordinate position in relation to Gans and by their insubordination in failing to adequately respect the discourses that have moved Gans and his affiliates to positions of dominance. To use these categories in academic arguments, as Gans does, is to *enact* that dominance. To be a Tough Baby is to both openly deploy and innocently deny that dominance.

For Gans's commentary to be relevant to his critique of Killam, he must misrepresent Killam, conflate Killam's critique with the remarks of a host of unidentified feminists and women, and, more significantly, must present as indistinguishable *his own* interests and those of "civilization" and "religious tradition."[11] Argument-by-dominance infuses Gans's text: in an extended deployment of Tough-Baby gestures, he aligns his own interests with that of things dominant, the feminist's interests with things failed. Gans appears to claim for his intellectual model of originary language exactly the support of not only Western civilization and the Judeo-Christian tradition, but even of the very instantiations of them that have gained dominance in recent years: contemporary capitalism. Continuing the passage I quote immediately above, he repeats part of a passage from Riane Eisler (which Killam had quoted), commenting,

> Thus when we learn that "only in the Bible is the Goddess as a divine power entirely absent" (244), this is not offered to explain why Western civilization and its "capitalist" market system have achieved unique historical success, or why ethnography and the systematic study of other civilizations are uniquely Western achievements, but why our tradition, within which *malgre elles* Mss. Killam and Eisler operate, is *inferior* to all the others, most emphatically including those that have been driven out of business. (88, emphasis and French his)

Like his lumping together of feminists and "minoritaries," this passage reveals that Gans's argument consists primarily of a play on the concepts of dominant and nondominant—and the arrogation of the dominant for himself. By the time this passage appears (and again soon after), Gans deeply commits himself to a stance that considers his own work rigorous and intellectual but portrays the work of Killam and other feminists as foolish and political. Yet this passage, in contrast, manifests a desire to measure Killam's and Eisler's arguments only according to their usefulness for contemporary political and economic self-congratulation. Such a comment—and the degree to which it contradicts Gans's professed commitment to intellectual achievement—can be fruitfully understood by reference to the Tough-Baby persona.

Our developing understanding of the Tough Baby suggests that Gans does *not* intend us to take his argument at face value, to notice that it contradicts his major line of argument, nor does he mean the major implication of the passage: that we should measure all academic work, whatever its manifest intentions, by the degree to which it *explains* the triumph of the duo "capitalism" [*sic*] and ethnography. Nor does he wish us to think what is clearly implied by the passage—that his *own* ostensibly intellectual work on the origins of language is, under all, not intellectually rigorous and independent at all, but simply a defense and grounding for triumphalism about the powers and success of "capitalism." Rather, this apparent contradiction demonstrates that the Tough-Baby ethos magnifies its position of dominance by aligning itself with virtually *any* evidence of power and common sense, however tangentially related to the argument at hand. All the "successes"—social, historical, economic, cultural—are aligned with the Tough Baby; all "reality checks"—qualifications, objections, problems—are displaced onto the target feminist and her affiliates. The illegitimacy of this move, its deployment as a manifest self-contradiction in argument, is as *built in* as its wink. It is an enactment of dominance by demonstrating that Tough Babies do not *have* to be logical—they've "pre-won" their argument not on academic warrants, but on social warrants about tough men and angry women.

Gans's Tough-Baby credentials are based on contradiction. Expanding the scope of his critique far beyond the purportedly faulty arguments of specific individuals to those of entire classes of people, he nonetheless must acknowledge that the Tough-Baby ethos might look a little foolish deployed against even large numbers of people if they are weak, passive, minor, powerless. He positions himself, therefore, as victimized by these enormously powerful forces: he resents Killam's being allowed to refer to feminism when she criticizes him, claims that feminism is "dominant" in the academy "and elsewhere," and finds only capitulation when his publisher requires that his most recent book forgo use of the "generic 'he.'" Yet his ethos and entire argument depend exactly on his and our knowing that he outranks Killam, that men outrank women, that all the dominant positions are his and outrank all the nondominant positions that are for Killam and those others: using his terms, what Gans does is "intellectual," and what they do is "political"; what Gans offers is an originary "model," and what they offer is "mere assertion"; and so forth.[12] The alignment of Western civilization, Judeo-Christian religion, capitalism, and ethnography with his own stance might appear to undermine Gans's concurrent thesis about the success of Killam's position. The manifest contradiction of the two positions is part of the rhetoric of the wink and the nudge that characterizes the Tough-Baby ethos.

Central to the Tough-Baby ethos is also the easy assumption that the Tough Baby knows how to solve all the social problems that are judged to motivate the complaints of the (angry) feminists. Like Craft, Gans resorts to the Tough Baby's explicit social punditry: displays of nostalgia, proclamations, recommendations, condemnations—all concerning not academic arguments, but rather, conventional social roles. Gans, for example, wants to celebrate his vision of happier times, when Killam, women in general, and others producing "minoritary discourse" were proud to praise, not to criticize:

> Civilization used to be praised for providing us with the means to master our aggression, and women took pride in their civilizing influence over more violent men. But now that the level of female resentment has risen, (Western) civilization is condemned in all the ways I need not repeat, with particular emphasis on the disparagement of its Judeo-Christian religious tradition. (87–88)

Like others policing insubordinate texts, Gans seeks to explain that the social relations of previous days prevented such annoying arguments not by simple suppression, but by production: by producing ruly women unlikely to produce unruly texts. In making such an assertion, Gans conveys a capsulated history of social relations (uninterrogated on his part despite considerable investigation by many scholars) to support the crux of his argument: that in the times he celebrates, social etiquette would suppress the refractoriness of Killam's criticism—Killam being allowed to criticize him from *her own* premises rather than *his*.

Like so many Tough-Baby gestures, Gans's importing here a capsulated history of past manners and mores reveals that the persona appears willing to sacrifice any *academic* understanding of history, social theory, or textual theory for momentary argumentative gain. In this particular gesture, Gans pinpoints idealized gender relations in the past, fronts as desirable an ahistorical suggestion about the social mores of that time, then publicly censures contemporary women for (ostensibly) failing to meet those norms. This gesture assumes that *we all have agreed* on the values and benefits of the Tough Baby's idealized past world: our academic consensus is that women may be disciplined for their academic writing if it does not suit that world—but suits, rather, the world in which they live. Such a notion is patently foolish: again, this sacrifice of academic ideals for entertainment value is made with a Tough-Baby wink. Were the Tough Baby taking its academic responsibilities seriously—*not* simply taking advantage of an academic forum for personal and political display—then the Tough Baby's *own* writing should operate in a simplified world outside of history and concrete social relations. While it is possible that Gans posits such a simplified world in his own writings on the origin of language in a world of male agency, surely he would not wish to admit it. In fact, his entire Tough-Baby ethos may be adopted exactly to avoid considering that rather distressing conclusion.

Part of the "innocence" of the Tough-Baby persona is to deny the illegitimacy and invective of its own argument in order to emphasize what it suggests are those traits in the arguments of its targets. Such gestures are often couched in the form of (innocent) jokes, such as the apparently witty conclusion to Gans's response. Gans concludes that perhaps his lifetime of thinking, his elaborate research program, his many books have been wrong all along—not that language emerged in situations of conflict, but that the conflict was due to the violence of *men*. So violent and resentful are Killam and the other angry feminists he has read (despite the paucity of such rhetoric in Killam's text)[13] that he must consider classifying *them* as "the violent sex":

> But perhaps the resentful aggression that informs so many feminist texts and that peeks through in Ms. Killam's essay is a sign that it is really women after all who are the more conflictive sex, and that language emerged as a means of deferring not male but female violence. (88)

The trope of the angry feminist leads Gans to what appears to be a witty conclusion: maybe it is men who are the better, more civilized party here, and women the violent ones. Such a conclusion both presupposes feminist "resentment" and attempts to chastise Killam and other feminists for their "resentment," as if to object to social injustice is evidence of flawed character and disturbed personal psychology. The disciplining critic positions himself against the behavior of large numbers of women by promulgating cultural punditry rather than academic argument. His Tough-Baby credentials fulfilled, he summarizes his position of power by engaging in a little rhetorical dance, not unlike the self-congratulatory "superior dance" performed by Dana Carvey's character of the "Church Lady" on *Saturday Night Live*. The Tough Baby is saying, "Aren't *I* special!"

Deployment of the Tough Baby within the academic arena is by no means unusual, and, as my next example demonstrates, occurs even within the context of peer-reviewed journals, whose articles are screened to ensure their ability to contribute productively to academic discussion. Whatever the ranking of any particular journal, its willingness to condone Tough-Baby posturing suggests that it fails to understand the importance of—even the imperative to assure—accurate argument in academic discourse. Its failure to require such contributions to reflect accurately the arguments they attack demonstrates the degree to which Tough-Baby rhetorics permeate ostensibly more carefully reasoned academic discussion.

My final example, therefore, draws on a plethora of Tough-Baby rhetorical moves by musicologist Pieter van den Toorn in the process of criticizing feminist musicologist Susan McClary in the pages of the peer-reviewed *Journal of Musicology* (van den Toorn 1991, referring to McClary 1991, 1987).[14] McClary advances feminist arguments in musicology by talking about gendered semiotic codes in classical music, charging, among other things, that the codes used in some nineteenth-century symphonies may be implicated in visions of sexual violence. McClary's erudite yet lively arguments have offered occasion for considerable criticism, but much of it has been derailed by critics' enthusiastic use of social warrants authorizing attacks on the angry feminist. Much of the criticism of McClary's work operates in a climate of tainted reception rather than accurate debate. Tough-Baby attacks and the social problems that they reflect appear to have encouraged inaccuracy, impatience, and ill will in other critics of McClary who do not, themselves, adopt Tough-Baby tactics. Thus van den Toorn's attack against McClary is not isolated, although it represents a dramatically vehement and far-reaching deployment of the trope of the angry feminist and the ethos of the Tough Baby.

Like many Tough Babies, van den Toorn deploys open contradiction as a central rhetorical gesture, attempting to isolate McClary both as a bizarre anomaly and as symptomatic of the problems of women today. He charges that McClary's attempt to read cultural, political, sexual influences *in* music is to read them *into* music and to do so for ulterior, unwarranted, and ultimately "private" sexual reasons, reasons that turn out to reflect what he views as widespread political attempts to disparage and condemn men and their sexuality. His goal in mounting this argument is to infer (ostensibly from McClary's argument) her personal character and "political ideology," to reveal that it impinges on—no, *drives*—arguments that she has presented as if they were academic. Implying that McClary's arguments come from a tainted source, tormented by personal sexual problems, van den Toorn indicates,

> [T]he suggestion might be that Beethoven's music, or tonal music in general, is being placed at the service of an unrelated personal animosity. Fanned by an aversion for male sexuality, which is depicted as something brutal and contemptible, irrelevancies are being read into the music. (293)

Van den Toorn sees such personal contempt for male sexuality meshing with political stances that drag even the innocent event, artifact, or cultural activity into the political arena:

> In turn, the crusading ideology turns tyrannical. . . . Music and its appeal are judged overtly sexual-political in order that they might serve the overtly sexual-political cause. (293, 294)

With typical Tough-Baby wit and wink, van den Toorn packages these charges in a sequence that pretends to disdain the possibility of discounting McClary as "merely" an (inappropriately) angry feminist, caught up in an "ideology" that is (unwarrantedly) antimale. He then provides a "witty" "turn" to his rebuttal: readers might expect such argumentation, and, in fact, it is exactly that argument that he will deliver, after all. He cannot, *must not* refrain from its use, since it is the *only possible reply* that *can* be made to McClary's arguments:[15]

> Challenges to deep-seated convictions and beliefs are likely to be met with objections that address not the argument itself but its particular motivation. But how else could a rebuttal have been managed in the present case? Given that the issues in question do in fact involve ulterior motives in music and music appreciation, how else could the merits of the case have been assessed? (294)

Van den Toorn then turns to providing exactly the critique of personal motives that he has suggested would be illegitimate. Packaging his turn in terms of rhetorical questions—textual devices that assume that audience and critic already agree on an answer—van den Toorn demonstrates once again that the Tough-Baby persona can pick and choose which arguments are "worth" explicating—that the Tough Baby need not justify having more interest in McClary's sexual attitudes than in her evidence, her "sexual-political causes" than her arguments. In fact, by this string of arguments and rhetorical questions, van den Toorn claims, with the double "wink" of the Tough Baby, that he is justified in making personal attacks on McClary because *he* cannot understand or even find the intellectual content in her work.

Van den Toorn's argument above suggests that it is a "personal animosity" that "inflames" McClary's arguments, but also her "crusading sexual-political cause." Tough-Baby conflation of McClary and other feminists (and other women) takes place throughout van den Toorn's argument. Like other Tough Babies, van den Toorn regularly conflates specific feminist arguments—here about gendered codes in certain music—with arguments of feminists "in general"—arguments not merely about music (like Mc-Clary's), not merely about gendered sexual rhetorics (like McClary's), but even about contemporary women's roles working, rearing children, and engaging in a variety of other social roles not touched on in McClary's writings. Van den Toorn indicates that he has obtained the opinions he denounces primarily from personal interactions, as he mentions in a footnote clarifying his sources:

> These views were expressed during several informal meetings with feminist graduate students at Yale University, Spring, 1989, *but I take them to represent the socio-political undercurrent of feminism more generally*, at least as that current manifests itself in the professions. (298, f. 31, emphasis added)

In citing his informal discussion with these feminists, van den Toorn demonstrates his assumption that what one feminist thinks is what all feminists think.

This conflating of McClary's academic arguments and his impression of the "socio-political undercurrent of feminism more generally" offers much scope for Tough-Baby rhetorics. Developing a somewhat unsavory diatribe against the unruliness, perversity, and even prudishness of contemporary women, van den Toorn is quite specific about what he does not like about McClary and all these other feminists: their attempts, generally, to deplore, despise, restrict, and suppress "male sexuality":

> [Since the Civil Rights Act of 1964] feminists in search of deeper causes have taken aim at the Male Sex Drive (MSD), at male lust as malignancy, a sort of root-of-all-evil. (295)

Thus van den Toorn situates McClary's arguments not as arguments about the social imbrications of music or the gendered rhetorics involved in musical composition and reception, but as merely one more expression of the distressing modern trend in which feminists fail to appreciate men.

Rhetorical tactics to intensify and *personalize* his attack on McClary reveal that Tough-Baby van den Toorn feels no need to ground assertions about McClary's arguments in her texts. Not only does he generalize what McClary must mean from his chats with Yale graduate students, eventually to implicate all feminists and probably all women who are not nice to men—he also does the reverse. His rhetorical tactic here requires him to exaggerate the images of feminist discourse used in popular journalism to ridicule women, then personalize each argument and attribute it to McClary. This repeated strategy moves even further from McClary's arguments—to the point of attributing to McClary numerous points that she has not even raised, attitudes that she has not expressed, arguments she has not made—to create a caricature of the angry feminist:

> McClary's feminism reduces [man (*sic*)] to his sexual needs, to a groping about for release, as it were. (292)
> In reading McClary and other feminists, however, this [the history of complaints about male dominance] might never have been suspected. (295)
> What may astonish most about MSD is not, as McClary would have it, its potential for harm and abuse. (296)
> Men are not ordinarily the one-dimensional, single-minded hulks of McClary's sexual stereotypes. (295–296)
> In depicting the male-female relationship as conditioned solely by conflict (with women always losing), McClary would insist that the relationship be frictionless. (297)

The text itself does not reveal whether Tough-Baby van den Toorn assumes that his audience will be as careless as he about "the facts"—McClary's arguments—and his reconstruction of the "facts"—his fictions about McClary's arguments. Because this willingness to make assertions manifestly contradicted by McClary's texts is echoed throughout van den Toorn's critique, and because it is a tactic widespread in other critiques of McClary's work, I would have to assume that at least when deployed against feminist challenges, accuracy and fidelity give way to Tough-Baby rhetorics. But these charges clarify that the Tough-Baby ethos can go "both" ways: mount an argument against a particular feminist's arguments on the basis of the comments of other feminists, or use a particular feminist's arguments to "trigger" a response to all women it deems "feminist." Either line of argument allows wide scope for policing, since one's speaking position, not the quality of one's arguments, determines if one is to be positioned as unreasoning and (heaven forfend) man-hating.

Van den Toorn's attack on McClary establishes a base for deploying the trope of the angry feminist not merely against McClary, but against *all* feminists. Typical Tough-Baby inaccuracy and wit infuse his explicit attacks on feminism. Consider, for example, the distance between McClary's actual arguments and Van den Toorn's recapitulation of them. In her essay "Getting

Down Off the Beanstalk" for the *Minnesota Composers Forum Newsletter*, McClary argues that Janika Vandervelde's composition *Genesis II* moves metaphorically through a series of natural, cultural, historical worldviews, holding them in tension and contradiction. According to McClary, Vandervelde's "clockwork" is reminiscent of medieval music; Vandervelde's contrasting moves metaphorically capture a historical moment of the general crisis of the seventeenth century, which led to a "new secular spirit of passionate manipulation." McClary notes that this moment occasioned the emergence of certain kinds of music; for example,

> [T]he virtuosic solo violin sonata leads to the creation of specifically instrumental forms that dispense with verbal discourse altogether and that work purely on the basis of aggressive rhetorical gestures. (1987, 6–7)

One would not know this argument from van den Toorn's discussion, from which Janika Vandervelde and *Genesis II* are absent. According to his presentation, McClary is busy here presenting a "severely separatist" history of the world, "massively reductive," with "freely floating generalities." As a Tough Baby, van den Toorn can once again indicate that he is simply unable to come to grips with the unreason displayed by McClary and other feminists. Instead, he weaves quotations from McClary's language about seventeenth-century music into an attack not merely on McClary but on "contemporary feminism":

> [T]he mental gymnastics required in reconciling contemporary feminism—indeed, the "aggressive, rhetorical gestures" of that feminism, its "secular spirit of passionate manipulation"—with the socioeconomic stagnancy of the medieval era, a period in which at least half the population—McClary's half—survived socially, politically, and legally as little more than an instrument of service and barter, are beyond this particular observer. (1991, 285)

The Tough-Baby ethos here—and arguably throughout van den Toorn's critique—sacrifices much to make a joke (innocent) or mount a diatribe (tough). Except for using some of the same words, van den Toorn's comment here has nothing to do with McClary's argument. McClary and her words merely trigger a Tough-Baby diatribe about unreasoning aggressive women. Not only does van den Toorn (here and throughout his critique) misrepresent McClary's argument and manifestly fail to understand its goals, premises, assertions, and evidence, he *reiterates* what he also *demonstrates:* that he is inadequate as a commentator on McClary or on feminist arguments. Here is a set of Tough-Baby credentials: misrepresent the feminist argument, joke by using her words to create a silly scenario, attribute that scenario to her, present it as representing all feminists, use it to evoke the trope of the angry feminist, and, in case no one has noticed, *brag about doing it.*

The ethos of the Tough Baby operates as if it were above personal motivation, while its feminist targets can marshal no arguments beyond the profoundly personal. At the same time, it both openly displays and perfects the "deniability" of its own position. So there are no signals to suggest that there is anything personal in van den Toorn's arguments about how male sexuality *should* be discussed. For he takes his condemnation of McClary as an opportunity to argue that his preferred vision of male sexuality, rather than being suppressed, should be enhanced—but that even *talking* about encouraging it leads feminists to censure otherwise innocent men:

> But to recommend, therefore, that the figleaf be withdrawn, that the MSD be allowed to float like a currency, to run its course without sanction or inhibition, is to stand accused of all the awful things, of anti-social inclinations, of "sexism," "abuse," "aggression," "phallic violence," and so forth. Man is thus confined to his habitual no-man's land with fewer and fewer exits. (296)[16]

Reserving discussion of van den Toorn's argument about men's sexual expression, I merely note that he rebuts arguments about gender and sexuality in music with recommendations for the unrestrained deployment of sexuality in society—from a position that can hardly be considered "disinterested."

Beyond these references and his fanciful expansion of what he presents as (and perhaps believes to be) McClary's point of view, van den Toorn neither cites feminist cultural criticism nor shows any knowledge of it. Such knowledge might lead him to modify many an assertion—for example, the assertion that contemporary feminists are unaware that men and women in the past have *also* complained about male sex roles—toward greater accuracy:

> The complaint is in many ways an ancient one, one with which men and women have struggled for generations upon generations. In reading McClary and other feminists, however, this might never have been suspected. On the contrary, it is as if the MSD had been discovered only recently by modern-day feminists, as if the long drawn-out battle pitting male lust against the interests of women and the social

order . . . had never taken place, as if the centuries of moral, religious, legal, and literary thought . . . had never occurred. (295)

No one with even the remotest degree of knowledge of feminist studies could make such a claim. That being the case, why does van den Toorn feel free to make such a statement about a discipline or field of study of which he is ignorant? And why does the *Journal of Musicology*—a refereed journal—feel free to publish it? I am by no means suggesting that everyone should read feminist cultural criticism, or that such reading will "persuade" all scholars or make them happy. It does strike me, however, that reading the discourse of a field would be of inestimable value in mounting an attack upon it.

Van den Toorn, objecting to what he claims is McClary's strategy of lumping together all men in a (derogated) category, does not seem to object to lumping together women in general or all women feminists. At first, considering the enormously different assumptions and arguments of various kinds of feminism, one might consider this whole-scale clumping as illegitimate, and van den Toorn foolish. But I would urge reconsideration, for van den Toorn may well mean exactly what he seems to be saying—to indict (unread) all versions of feminism. According to Alison M. Jaggar, despite their various differences, their different methods of explanation and critique, feminist approaches to ethics do seem to share two common assumptions: "The first of these is that the subordination of women is morally wrong; the second is that the moral experience of women should be treated as respectfully as the moral experience of men" (1991, 97–98). Whether or not van den Toorn is open to these concerns, he uses a rhetoric that denies confronting even his own core assumptions: in choosing to ignore the research that clearly indicates that there are both sexual and economic difficulties attached to the status of women, in attempting to delegitimize and invalidate the perceptions of women about their own status, in failing to recognize that the assertions of feminists might make him uncomfortable *without* at the same time being "dubious and far-fetched," he denies manifest kinds of subordination of women and certainly fails to treat respectfully the moral experience not just of McClary but of other contemporary women.

Despite his lack of engagement with women's problems, van den Toorn resolves all these many problems with characteristic Tough-Baby confidence. After several pages of discussion of the problems that McClary, feminists, and so many other contemporary women share (and their consequent oversimplified view of the world), van den Toorn adopts a complacent tone suggesting that our current sexual relations are simply the only way for "the species" to continue, and that he has the key to solving their social-sexual problems. Once again, the Tough Baby can resolve all of the problems of McClary and other women—emotional, sexual, intellectual, academic— through social punditry. The pundit is perfectly willing, nonetheless, to chastise and correct these women, as well as advise them on the proper course not only of their lives, not only of their attitudes toward male sexuality, but even of feminism as a political movement:

> The interests of feminism are best served, it seems to me, in practical, down-to-earth terms. The arguments about sex and music are largely a form of propaganda. (297)

The Tough Baby argues that using academic discourses to argue against perceived social injustice is propaganda, while using academic discourses to argue that the status quo is no injustice is not propaganda at all.

In this whole sequence of passages, van den Toorn's Tough-Baby ethos is as "irrational" and beside the point as he is suggesting to be true of "McClary and other feminists." He talks *past* the argument. He ironically and resentfully characterizes McClary and all other feminists in one bundle and complains at the same time that women have "license to engage in a sort of negative stereotyping of another group (men), that is so hotly contested when it is directed toward women as a group" (298–299). He conflates McClary's objections to the gendered use of power with her being against "sex": sexual relations and biological males. Van den Toorn bases his critique of McClary on the assumption that she and her feminist friends are not responding to a historically developed code or cultural language for male sexuality, a code or language that changes over time. He assumes that McClary's attacks on misogyny and musical phallocentrism are attacks on some Platonic "male sexuality"—on the "essence" of it, not its historical deployment, not deployment sometimes subject to criticism from men. It is this "deep" male sexuality that he eventually chooses to defend, to essentialize, to celebrate.

Van den Toorn's rhetorical strategies—overstatement, misrepresenting and personalizing arguments, using exaggeratedly polemical labels (and initials) for agonists' arguments, and so forth—are *exactly* those that would be characterized as "inflammatory," "crazy," "hysterical," or "man-hating" if the author were a woman. Van den Toorn's own argumentative excesses, his general condemnation of (upstart) contemporary women in what purports to be a refutation of McClary's arguments, and, as we shall see, his praise for women who use textual force to subdue other women—while condemning those who use textual force to make arguments that he reads to be critical of "men"—all demonstrate well some of the specific differences between the Tough Baby and the woman condemned as the angry feminist, however rhetorically vehement her argument: McClary charges that specific pieces of dramatic and instrumental music written by men long dead, rather than being autonomous and transcendent as many have argued, are, in fact, pervaded by concerns and codes of gender that characterize (in different forms) their societies and ours. Van den Toorn replies that to suggest such a thing, McClary—the living, academic woman—is an angry feminist, unfair to men, and in doing so makes his own life and the life of other well-meaning men of today difficult. The deployment of this charge, then, is accomplished by conflating the socially ascribed roles of female musicologist and musicologist concerned with gender and reducing both to their most potent term: woman (who speaks as a woman) = angry feminist.

The very vehement argumentation that van den Toorn and other critics feel free to condemn as the work of the angry feminist is, in fact, employed with considerable dispatch in their own Tough-Baby condemnations. As should be evident from all these examples, Tough-Baby protests about feminist violations of textual etiquette or about the "angry" rhetoric of feminists not only ignore their own textual vehemence, they deploy such demands for politeness only against those whose arguments and positions they deplore. For example, van den Toorn endorses Helen Vendler's attack on several feminist texts in the *New York Review of Books* (1990). Vendler uses considerable textual vehemence in mounting her argument, uses terms such as "feeble," "gratuitous," "falsity of tone," "lamentable," "vulgarity," "deplorable," "repellent," "incoherent," and "twaddle," finds the arguments within the field "a still-unsolved tragicomic conflict" (21), and recommends that feminists not be (as, she makes clear, they so often are) "swept-up in ideological approval of third-rate work" (20). It is difficult to know what criteria—other than political position—could be used to find McClary or Killam "angry" while this attack is "womanly."

Van den Toorn draws on Vendler without expressing any reservations about rhetoric that would qualify—according to the rest of his argument—as distinctly *angry*, even "unwomanly." Rather, he uses Vendler's evaluation to condemn the "uncompromising tone" of Carolyn Heilbrun's *Hamlet's Mother and Other Women* (1990) and the "no less partisan" stance of Rita Felski's *Beyond Feminist Aesthetics: Feminist Literature and Social Change* (1989). His implication is that these feminists and McClary are to be faulted for their violations of proper textual etiquette and their hostile attitude toward others; apparently such violations do not loom so large when committed by Tough Babies. Since van den Toorn clearly does not demand "compromising

tones" of *all* academic women—only some—it is difficult to avoid the conclusion that he holds different standards according to the political position
argued, according to whose ox is being "gored." The Tough Baby apparently
uses "situational ethics" or "relativist principles" to determine who is permitted to speak vehemently about gender problems. More explanation is necessary if we are to understand why vehement rhetorics should be available to
them but not to feminists.

While van den Toorn expresses concern about charges of "phallic violence," the other Tough Babies here—Craft and Gans—develop moments of
wittiness based on the terms *phallocentric* or *phallogocentric,* suggesting that
the phallus behind such little jokes looms large as a resource for the Tough-
Baby persona. Craft, tweaking the feminists as sexually repressive, uses it in
reference to his own comments on the "distracting portrait of [Strozzi] with
charms undraped," followed by "Feminists outraged by the foregoing phallogocentric remark . . ." (1992, "Lagoon Tunes," 44). Craft's use suggests that
"phallogocentric" means "sexual," or "focusing on male sexuality." In such an
argument, *phallogocentric* has nothing to do with philosophical arguments
about the phallus, authority, and language, but only with the freedom for
men to discuss their images of male sexual desire in public. Joseph Epstein, as
part of his antifeminist diatribe that I discussed in Chapter 1, also uses the
term *phallocentric* to disparage feminists. He uses it to tweak them for assuming that anything about women might have *intellectual* interest:

> What came to be known as "gender studies" were on their way, and
> would get goofier and goofier with the passage of time, though doubt-
> less my view of the matter is, as the academic feminists would put it,
> "phallocentric." (1991, 17)

Epstein's use again ignores the philosophical origins and use of the term,
suggesting that he uses it to mean "male-centered" or "sexist." Gans also uses
the term and also creates a joke with it:

> The ease with which feminism and other minoritary [*sic*] discourses
> have reached a dominant, not to say hegemonic, position within our
> allegedly "phallocentric" culture should make us suspect what Ms.
> Killam might call the "phallaciousness" of such allegations. (87)

All three uses of "phallo(go)centric" tweak feminists by using "their own"
terminology "against them," as if arguments about phallo(go)centrism in

discourse were limited to feminists, rather than connected to Lacanian and Derridean systems of thought. The Tough Baby openly displays its ignorance of feminist discourse, but sees the *phallo-* terms as a rhetorical tool to construct feminists as preoccupied with "phalluses," which then can be reconstrued as "penises."

The reiteration of these terms built on the base *phallo-* offers insight into the construction and function of the Tough-Baby persona as it stems from our cultural constructions of masculinity. The Tough Baby separates itself from feminists and other women through its discursive denigration, and in so doing connects itself to less sophisticated forms of antiwoman commentary. Epstein's comparison of feminists to vicious dogs that I quoted in Chapter 1 alludes to a long line of ribald jokes connecting women and their sexuality to animals: for example, Mills supplies one from a "rag-mag" circulated by the students in London in 1990: "Q: What's the difference between a rottweiler and a woman with PMT? A: Lipstick" (Mills 1995, 141 [PMT is British terminology for "Premenstrual Tension," or what in the United States is often called "PMS—Premenstrual Syndrome."]). Since feminists are not the only women to have menstrual periods, all women are implicated and degraded in the joke. Such jokes also connect, full circle, to Tough-Baby allegations that feminists are indeed angry *because* they are biological women— for example, when Lee Humphries wrote a brief and apparently witty letter to a newsletter editor in response to Susan McClary's work. The letter, in its entirety: "I have read GETTING DOWN OFF THE BEANSTALK and consider that Prof. McClary's *prescriptive musicological stance* (PMS) gives rise to a phallacious analysis."[17] The Tough-Baby ethos is an innocent one, however, since this is "only a joke."

Given its intense reliance on rhetorical deployment of structures of dominance, the Tough Baby's concern with feminist *phallo-* terms represents problems of both dominance and anxiety. Part of the concern may stem from reluctance to abandon a kind of solidarity and economy of pleasure based not on sexual desire, but on establishing male sexual desire as something that is to remain mystified, always available for deployment in any of its cultural forms but never available for examination. In such a case, we might see that the Tough Baby's rhetoric focuses exactly on what women lack. The Tough Baby says, "You women dare to say 'phallus'? I'll show you a phallus!" If one interprets such a persona as more anxious than dominant, in need of protection from fear of feminists, then perhaps Sigmund Freud offers insight here. Freud argues that the display of the penis or its fetish substitutes is used to counter threats:

To display the penis (or any of its surrogates) is to say: "I am not afraid of you. I defy you. I have a penis." Here, then, is another way of intimidating the Evil Spirit. (1922/1963, 213)

Tough Babies are tough because they display—glory in—the power of the phallus. They are babies because they deny they do it.

The examples of the Tough-Baby persona at work here instantiate my argument that the trope of the angry feminist draws on taken-for-granted cultural resources to bolster feeble arguments, deflect criticism, and disguise patently "political" gendered attacks. But they also suggest that the Tough Baby draws on even more dramatically "improper" cultural resources to delegitimate feminists' (women's) academic arguments. Our social warrants, so eloquently argued by the Tough Babies, encourage some men to expect "their" women to regard them as heroes, to soothe them and provide sympathy, to fulfill their needs—or at least allow and encourage them to fulfill what they perceive as their needs. Women are supposed to be these things, and those who are not are unnatural and evil. Alas, feminists' vigorous academic arguments are the opposite of that—they *are not* soothing, they *are* critical, and they *are not* focused on *men's* concerns—all things our social warrants lead men to expect or desire. The arguments of the Tough-Baby persona imply that the problem of the feminist scholar is *not* that she is "angry," but that—by their definition of what feminism is—she is *not catering to men*. The Tough Babies' arguments suggest that our cultural assumptions further *over*determine our ready understanding of what an angry feminist is: she is the withholding mother and the withholding mistress. It is these prearranged, unarticulated role expectations that make both the trope and the Tough-Baby ethos work—that enable gendered role expectations and specifically gendered punishments for "the same" textual performances.

Rather than merely reflecting negative attitudes toward women, rather than merely revealing the waggish boyish rudeness of some academic men, use of the persona of the Tough Baby and the trope of the angry feminist are major ways for academic men to build group solidarity against the incursions of women and their arguments. Susan Jeffords describes the way that military training is set up to build an ethos of solidarity specifically at the expense of women (1989). Analogously, Tough-Baby academic rhetorics disparaging stereotypic feminists can be deployed by those aspiring to be drill instructors for academic basic training. These rhetorical strategies constitute men as a social group, with homosocial—perhaps even homoerotic—gestures that are meant to be public and vulgar. While some women, wanting to be "good girls," may also wink at these gestures ("boys will be boys"), or even conclude that the specific feminist who is targeted "deserves" such an attack ("she brought it on herself"), they delude themselves. All academic men and all academic women are implicated by such rhetorics.

Its rhetoric of disparagement and misrepresentation leaves readers with no clean way to get out of the economy of dominance established so vehemently by the Tough-Baby ethos. The rhetoric operates not just to make an exclusive community of men, not merely to isolate and humiliate individual women or feminists or all women, but to make readers dependent on and fearful of hierarchy: it replaces horizontal solidarity with hierarchical obedience. Whatever the problems of institutional practices that encourage hierarchy in the academy, academic *ideals* are themselves *not* hierarchical: they allow individuals to make claims and establish evidence that can be read, analyzed, and evaluated by others. They establish a kind of horizontal solidarity based on commitment to those ideals. The ethos of the Tough Baby, operating as the sadistic drill instructor, deliberately disrupts these arrangements to substitute a group exclusivity based on fear.

I have focused on this incursion of Tough-Baby attacks on feminists in musicology in the early 1990s in order to demonstrate its features and interconnections. The Tough-Baby persona had a long previous history and has a continuing presence in academic and civic life. Tough Babies enjoy their infancy; they never grow up. The vehemence and even vulgarity of Tough-Baby responses suggest that what animates the Tough Baby's use of the trope of the angry feminist is *not* fear from violations of politeness or problems of personal character, but concern over women academics taking their *own* standards and judgments seriously and granting *themselves* the right to assess and evaluate negatively the attitudes and actions of others—even of male colleagues, even of "senior" colleagues. While our society's discursive practices demonstrably support the use of rhetorics that humiliate, intimidate, and misrepresent rather than present counterarguments, our academic ideals, within which—*malgre lui*—the Tough Baby operates, should not.

CHAPTER FIVE

Faux Feminism and the Rhetoric
of Betrayal

At the scene of argument, the Tough Baby contributes to a climate of intimidation that makes it hard to conduct productive argument. It deploys the trope of the angry feminist in a display of animosity and contempt. Yet for some readers, the ostensible "object" of the Tough Baby's critique—the "angry" feminist—may be seen as *causing* the Tough Baby's emotional display by her "inappropriately" challenging arguments despite evidence that one need not display "angry" rhetoric to be deemed an angry feminist. The *open illegitimacy* of the Tough Baby's rhetorical moves, however, fundamentally alters the structure of argumentation by sacrificing academic standards of debate without acknowledgment. Once the trope of the angry feminist has been evoked, then all related arguments are tainted by its shadow. Entering the debate becomes deeply dangerous. Some sneer. Some remain silent. Some use the trope covertly for partisan ends.

In this chapter, I consider covert reliance on the trope of the angry feminist. Covert users eschew the dramatically hostile rhetoric of the Tough Baby but depend on its climate of intimidation to transform radical challenges into reformist and recuperative ones, to promise a "congenial," "cooperative" feminist inquiry that will maintain disciplinary structures intact. They offer to replace the angry feminist with a less annoying one. To do so, they *rely on* the trope of the angry feminist without actually asserting it. I illustrate two examples of arguments that rely on the trope of the angry feminist as deployed against feminist musicologist Susan McClary, subject of one of the Tough-Baby attacks that I discuss in Chapter 4. These two critiques rely on dramatic rhetorics of betrayal, creating paragons of acceptable feminist inquiry that can then be used to abjure McClary. A phalanx of straw allies, "stealth rules," specious disciplinary distinctions, and misrepresentations of feminist inquiry underpin these rhetorics of betrayal.

The particular rhetorics of betrayal that I describe take their form, at least in part, because of the specific disciplinary histories of musicology and feminist musicology. Within the disciplinary community of music, McClary's work on gendered and sexual semiotic codes appearing in the late 1980s and early 1990s (1987 Blasphemy, 1987; Getting Down, 1991, 1992, 1993, 1994) raises a variety of disruptive challenges. This work draws on interdisciplinary sources to question the long influential position that music is transcendent and to some degree autonomous, largely free from cultural influences. From the point of view of many musicologists, social theories cannot appropriately be applied to music, because music is not as mediated as other cultural forms. To some degree, musicology insulated itself until the late 1980s from the remarkable ferment of the "crisis of representation" that challenged the concept of "autonomous production" in so many fields in the humanities and social sciences (see, for example, Marcus and Fischer 1986).[1] An increasing number of scholars have turned to theoretical and revisionist approaches to classical music, but some critics and musicologists deplore arguments that explore the cultural situatedness of long-revered classical music or that illuminate the positive contributions and skills exhibited in long-scorned popular music. Thus the specialized (and somewhat isolated) nature of musicology itself and the attitudes of many musicologists and music critics toward discourse on music make them ill-prepared to understand McClary's arguments. Their deep disciplinary commitments lead some to rhetorics of betrayal to protect not just "music," but dominant (and rather narrowly defined) ways of arguing about music.[2]

In this frame of reference, McClary's work touches a number of nerves. McClary's writings concern the interrelationship of culture, gender, sexuality, and music in the works of such classical figures as Bach, Beethoven, Bizet, and Schubert as well as in the oeuvres of popular figures such as Madonna, Laurie Anderson, and Prince. McClary delivers her arguments with stylistic vigor and explicitly sexual references.[3] Still, it is not so much McClary's language but her assertions and conclusions that confound and disconcert some musicologists and music critics—particularly McClary's dramatic insistence that music is infused with gendered and sexualized semiotic codes, that even the music of revered classical composers such as Beethoven demonstrates such codes, and that some of these codes, like some of the ways we have of conceiving sexuality, are implicated in visions of violence.

Arguments about gender, sexuality, and the body, linked as they are with social structures and lives, always offer significant potential for interpretive anxiety and problems. The stakes in musicology may be particularly high, however: some musicologists argue that musicology has long been premised on denial of the body in relation to music and its effects (see, for example, Bohlman 1993, Cusick 1994, Maus 1993). To raise such arguments in musicology, therefore, opens up important theoretical problems in the field. Further, McClary adopts a similar stance toward *all* the music she discusses: skeptical engagement with the conditions of production and examination of the content, uses, and effects of culture. Studying both classical and popular music with similar analytic tools and attitudes represents a challenge to dominant disciplinary conceptions based on musical hierarchies that privilege certain kinds of music as singularly worthy of study and yet exempt from social critique.

Given the provocation that McClary's work represents to taken-for-granted disciplinary arrangements in musicology, it is perhaps not surprising that many of her critics appear more interested in curbing her challenges than in engaging with them. While the two critics I examine here do not use Tough-Baby rhetorics, they do rely on a set of dramatic and illegitimate strategies more easily put in play because McClary has already been positioned as the "angry" feminist. I analyze strategies of Leo Treitler's "Gender and Other Dualities in Music History" (1993) and Paula Higgins's "Women in Music, Feminist Criticism, and Guerrilla Musicology: Reflections on Recent Polemics" (1993).[4] While McClary's work should not be immune to criticism merely because she has been attacked as an angry feminist, Treitler and Higgins use some of the same unproductive strategies used by the Tough Babies. They fail to represent McClary's arguments adequately, then assume and assert what they should be proving. Like the Tough Babies, they "reconstitute" McClary's arguments rather than examine them.

These critics distinguish themselves from the contempt toward women displayed by the Tough Baby, although they rely on its presence on the scene to authorize their position. They do so not by refuting the Tough Baby, not by exposing the illegitimacy of the trope of the angry feminist, but by cordoning off the angry feminist: she is angry, they argue, but *she is not really a feminist*. They construct the possibility of a fresh ideal of feminist musicology on a new vision: the agreeable feminist.

To protect musicology from the challenges raised by McClary's work, Treitler and Higgins invoke a platonic "ideal" of feminist inquiry and feminist musicology: McClary, they can then argue, betrays this ideal. Treitler allows that a "genuine" feminist musicology might ultimately emerge some day, but argues that McClary betrays the future of such an endeavor. The function of the ideal in his argument is explicitly to serve as a foil for McClary—to establish a group whose interests McClary can be positioned as betraying. Higgins, in contrast, asserts the current and long-standing existence of a feminist musicology but argues that McClary betrays it by not devoting enough attention to its history and contemporary personnel. For both Treitler's and Higgins's arguments, I contend, feminist studies outside musicology serve merely as an idealized locus of authority that McClary can also be seen to betray—violating what they present inaccurately as its accepted scholarly standards and principles of collegiality.

I first examine how Treitler and then Higgins establish their idealized feminist musicology in order to exclude McClary's work and establish her as betraying both musicology and feminist inquiry. I then look to some of the rhetorical underpinnings they use to authorize their own positions as representatives of feminism. Since they misrepresent McClary's arguments, making of her a "straw woman," it is not surprising that they do so by means of "faux feminism," featuring "straw allies" and "straw criteria."

The Gesture: Evoking the Paragon

To Authorize a (Domesticated) Feminist Musicology

Leo Treitler evokes his "ideal" of feminist musicology most explicitly when condemning a line of McClary's research that he appears to find particularly distressing, her arguments that semiotic codes of sexual violence are central to the rhetorics of many nineteenth-century symphonies. In response, Treitler argues:

> That sort of [adversarial] exegesis cannot pass for criticism; it is, rather, an exploitation of the *idea* of gender difference in the service of political and ideological agendas for music history and criticism. When produced in the name of feminist criticism such a practice, I think, can only impede the development of the genuine article. (43, emphasis Treitler's)

Treitler endorses, then, development of a "genuine" feminist criticism that—in contrast to McClary's work—will be an endeavor without a political or an ideological agenda.[5] Further, he explicitly establishes that McClary's work threatens such an endeavor. Had McClary's work not so radically altered the terms of the debate about what might count as acceptable feminist

musicology, even to propose the recuperation of neglected women composers, as Treitler will come to authorize, would seem a political or an ideological agenda. It is important, therefore, to recognize the significance of the
authorization that Treitler provides here: Treitler's evocation of an "ideal"
feminist musicology makes a significant concession. It establishes an important precedent in a field that has generally not been hospitable to feminist
inquiry, or, for that matter, to other kinds of criticism (see Kerman 1985).

Yet the scholarly paragon Treitler evokes could hardly be described as
"feminist": no feminist scholarship is predicated on agreements not to challenge the methods of inquiry, theoretical structure, or subject matter of the
disciplines. Treitler's authorizing of even so limited an ideal of feminist musicology is in tension with other aspects of his argument which go far to defend contemporary musicology as a closed shop. For much of Treitler's critique of McClary rests on assertions of disciplinary boundary maintenance:
he argues that McClary's work should not properly be considered music
criticism, violates the disciplinary consensus to bypass some topics, and seeks
new professional license and status while actually retreading old and tired
territory. The paragon of musicology that Treitler delimits functions to control all musicologists, setting a brake on their scholarly impulses and desires.
As will become evident, the ideal of feminist musicology he authorizes can
serve only as an add-on to musicology, helping musicologists further their
distinctly ungendered main task as Treitler argues it to be currently defined,
to "understand the workings of the human imagination" (43).

What seems most threatening to that endeavor, for Treitler, is McClary's
decision to interrogate the social force of sexual codes in music. Treitler's
unfamiliarity with arguments about sexuality and social relations, evident
throughout his discussion, leads him to misrepresent McClary's arguments
as moralism rather than investigation. He appears to view feminism as requiring prudery with regard to sexuality—as emotional and evaluative
rather than as critical and conceptual. This becomes evident when he tries to
explain and counter McClary's stance toward sexual codes in music and toward the ways that sexuality has been positioned in previous articulations of
musicology. When McClary quotes misogynist and sexualized commentaries in the history of music criticism, Treitler believes that she can justifiably
express "outrage." When she instead *interrogates* the musical structures that
might have led to such criticism, Treitler assumes that to do so is to "recommend" the sexual ideas that she discusses. In other words, McClary seeks
to question what *about* the music "itself" might have led critics to impute
gender and sexuality to specific pieces of music, attempting to understand
connections among cultures, sexualities, and musical rhetorics. Treitler pre-

sumes that such inquiry can only operate on a moral plane, recommending or objecting to such imputations, recommending or objecting to the sexualities so studied. From his point of view, McClary's analytic stance betrays not only musicology, not only feminism, but womanliness itself.[6]

Treitler's misunderstanding of how feminist inquiry interrogates sexuality as a social force deeply confounds his argument, both about McClary's work and about an ideal feminist musicology. What she presents as flexible musical rhetorics expressing changing images of sexuality, Treitler reads as a claim that these rhetorics are ineluctably determined by bodily figuration. To claim that these musical rhetorics are inescapable expressions of sexual (and racial) essences is, he says, the kind of argument posited by the racial theories of the nineteenth century (he cites Stocking 1982 [1968]) and Nazi musical scholarship (he cites Eichenauer 1932). This is the tradition in which he places McClary's work, implying that following out McClary's arguments will lead to similar ends. Treitler assumes that to see music as *influenced socially* by gender means to see it as *controlled biologically* by gender. In a profound misrepresentation of McClary's work, against a plethora of evidence from her text, Treitler has taken her arguments about music, gender, sexuality, and semiotic codes in music as if they were essentialist—rather than, as she argues, historically situated, socially constructed, influenced by culture, changing over time.

Such a position would seem to offer little room for the development of a feminist musicology that might wish to consider sexual rhetorics in music. Treitler does claim, however, to support one kind of feminist musicology that would recuperate women's music. He sees such an endeavor as a form of "affirmative action," citing Edward Said as justification:

> Said has written of "the right of formerly un- or mis-represented human groups to speak for and represent themselves in domains defined, politically and intellectually, as normally excluding them, usurping their signifying and representing functions, overriding their historical reality." Here it [such affirmative action] would concern the right of women to speak themselves of the feminine in music and to judge the significance of such assessments. (38, quoting Said 1985, 91)

By interpreting Said in this way, Treitler reveals an underlying assumption at the heart of much of his objection to McClary's work: he is willing to authorize a scholarly affirmative action that permits women to talk about themselves—about women and "the feminine" in music—but *not* about the full range of their sociopolitical-conceptual concerns with regard to music, *not* about male musical concerns, *not* about epistemological problems revealed by considerations of gendered social codes in music. The role that Treitler authorizes for feminist musicologists would appear to be a tokenistic, condescending, reductionist vision of identity politics. Said's arguments authorize no such position.

Within a frame of women's identity politics, Treitler would permit consideration of sexual rhetorics in music. Despite his vehemence in condemning McClary's interrogation of male sexual rhetorics in music, when Treitler turns to authorizing feminist musicology, he does so partly on the basis of women's ability to understand their own sexuality—their ability to replace "mystical and mysterious categories of gender" with "demonstrable categories of gender difference, referred directly to immediate feelings and experiences of sexuality" (38). Such a claim puts Treitler in the awkward position of arguing *for* a kind of feminist musicology that seems to rely on assertions of *essentialized "direct experience"*—virtually what he repudiates when he represents it as part of McClary's purported scholarly program.

The most notable difference between what Treitler condemns and what he authorizes, one would have to infer, is that McClary (who looks upon such codes as socially shared rhetorics that are *not* biological) assumes that she can speak about the sexual codes appearing in music composed by men, whereas Treitler's authorization limits women to considering only women's sexuality and only in music composed by women. If this were not Treitler's underlying intention, it is difficult to understand how he might condemn McClary as if she were positing gendered, sexual musical codes that are biologically based (condemning her specifically because such a position resembles despicable and disastrous arguments of the past), then go on to authorize a feminist musicology that appears otherwise to resemble closely what he has condemned.

Treitler's arguments reveal that his assumptions about gender, music, and musicology are radically different from those of McClary: McClary argues that music and musicology have always been informed by gender, and that *this dynamic* is worthy of examination and argument—whether or not it furthers schemes of transcendent musical forms and aesthetic autonomy central to recent traditions of musicology. Treitler, rather, imagines a musicology that has never been gendered and can now "choose" or "consider" whether it can be gendered or not; he argues, in effect, that McClary does not present an attractive choice.[7] The ideal of feminist musicology that Treitler evokes cannot represent the vigorous and challenging debates of feminist studies; it can only serve as a locus of feminist inquiry that he can deploy to shun the "corruption" represented by McClary's work.

To Conserve a (Domesticated) Feminist Musicology

In the midst of widespread Tough-Baby attacks and constant repetition of the trope of the angry feminist, Paula Higgins inflects the rhetoric of betrayal similarly, disavowing McClary with an argument that contends McClary may be angry, but she is not a feminist—or not a good one. Positioning herself as a good feminist, Higgins seeks to break any perceived "chain" between the controversy over McClary's work and feminist musicology: by positioning McClary's concern with codes of sexuality as peculiar (not part of feminist inquiry), by positioning feminist musicology as long accepted (and, therefore, itself not worthy of controversy), and, as we shall see, by representing McClary as demanding a total (but nonfeminist) reconstruction of formalist musicology that will focus on the musical notes to the detriment of all other ways of studying music.[8]

Higgins frames her critique with explicit claims that the controversy about McClary cannot be a controversy about feminism because her work is not feminist "strictly speaking." Thus Higgins, early in her critique, describes the *disturbing* aspects of McClary's work as *other than* feminist:

> Indeed, despite McClary's claim of having produced "one of the first books of feminist criticism in the discipline of musicology," one wonders at times if she has not strategically co-opted feminism as an excuse for ideological guerrilla attacks upon the field—because, paradoxically, one of the book's troubling aspects is its tendency to reinscribe patriarchy everywhere. (1993, 176)

Higgins reinforces this vision of feminist musicology as separate from social and political issues as well as controversy at the conclusion of her critique, when she argues,

> Many will fail to appreciate McClary's style of criticism, and even feminists sympathetic to her in principle may find some of her methods and solutions not only reductive but counter-productive and unsettling as well. For that reason the book is perhaps best described as a work of "guerrilla musicology," with its focus on volatile social and political issues, *rather than* as a *strictly "feminist"* criticism of music. (192, emphasis mine)

Feminist musicology, as Higgins evokes it here, is an enterprise totally congruent with the tenets of dominant conceptions of musicology; that is, it is distinguished from criticism that reveals an ideological or political agenda, that challenges dominant agendas in musicology, or that advances ideas that some feminist musicologists might contest.[9]

Using the paragon of agreeable feminist inquiry, having expelled McClary's work from its walls, Higgins argues that feminism has relatively little to do with the controversy over McClary's work. She states that the "unprecedented attention" that McClary's work has received within and outside musicology is based really on McClary's purported demand that study of musical notes replace a diverse musicology. This grounding, then, permits Higgins to argue, "Much of [the 'fuss' over McClary's work] . . . has to do with setting musicological agendas as well as *strictly feminist ones per se*" (175, emphasis mine).

Evoking this paragon allows Higgins to intimate that to the degree that McClary's work challenges musicology and makes musicologists uncomfortable and angry, it is outside feminist concerns. In contrast to the work of the angry feminist, recuperative research on women—previously considered problematic because it appeared to invoke political and social issues in the pure sphere of music—can now be presented as without political agenda. This rewriting of past struggles in musicology can serve to domesticate feminist musicology: with controversial work such as McClary's excluded as outside its purview, a strictly feminist criticism of music can be construed as confined to comparatively innocuous topics like the production of women composers in history (such as Higgins's own interest in Fanny Mendelssohn Hensel [see 189, n. 67]).

Higgins uses the ideal of a "strictly" feminist musicology to distance herself and feminist musicology from McClary's controversial interrogation of how gender and sexuality may saturate musical structures and criticism. She does so by imagining a musicology that could choose to overcome its history of disrespect and disregard for women: the job of a "true" feminist musicology, then, should be to offer equal opportunity to serious women composers and women musicologists. Higgins argues that McClary does not adequately further this goal. In essence, Higgins positions McClary as betraying the "true" cause of feminist musicology as a gender lobby. Asserting the current and long-standing existence of feminist musicology, Higgins criticizes McClary for failing to meet its accepted standards and—like Treitler—for imposing political and ideological agendas on its purely neutral structures.

Yet the move to position McClary's arguments about sexuality and musical rhetorics as outside the scope of feminist musicology sacrifices much that could only be described as "feminist" without acknowledging it: without acknowledging that McClary's challenge to people's investments in sexuality and in music cuts to the core of their ideological and political assumptions about gender as well as music, without acknowledging that many critics vociferously demonstrate (sometimes in misogynist terms) the degree to which McClary offends them in that regard, without acknowledging that inquiry such as McClary's is in every way congruent with other feminist projects to reconsider gender and its hierarchies (also often greeted with outrage). This is a costly move for any feminist musicology—for it implies that "strictly feminist" things can be said without challenging any deeply held assumptions about gender and sexuality in music—or, for that matter, without in any way challenging "musicological agendas."

Faux-Feminist Ideals as a Source of Betrayal

The three parties to this debate—McClary, Treitler, and Higgins—appear to have significantly different views of feminist inquiry in musicology. McClary, in her *Feminine Endings* (1991), situates her work within an emergent community of diverse feminist musicologists who rely on pioneering work done by a previous generation of unsung feminist music scholars. Acknowledging this work, McClary seeks to open a space for discussions of how gender and sexuality constitute semiotic codes in music, how they infuse socially constituted musical rhetorics. McClary thus proposes to use gender as an analytic category to examine musical structures.

Treitler and Higgins, responding to *Feminine Endings*, argue for rather different understandings of feminist musicology and intimate that McClary's work is, accordingly, not adequately "feminist." For Treitler, feminist musicology appears to be a forum for women to talk about women's voices and women's sexuality in women's music; for Higgins, feminist musicology appears to be a gender lobby to promote the interests of women who are serious composers and musicologists. Both promise a feminist musicology that includes women, but that can be incorporated into musicology without otherwise changing the activities of music history and criticism. McClary, with her disruptive arguments, betrays this vision of a domesticated feminist musicology.[10]

What I call "rhetorics of betrayal" thus posit scholarly disagreements as the flouting of shared, incontrovertible standards or inviolate principles: breaches of faith. The force of such rhetorics—their argumentative authority—proscribes certain arguments, presenting them as violations of sacrosanct scholarly *imperatives*, not as mere differences of opinion, focus, evidence, or argumentative style. Since academic scholarship scrutinizes all arguments and evidence, with disagreement about premises and methods of inquiry commonplace, to establish such an imperative requires a specific rhetorical turn: the creation of a scholarly "paragon" of unity and consensus where deep division actually exists. Rhetorics of betrayal can then position dissonant scholars as abandoning absolute standards shared by an entire discipline; when interdisciplinary resources are in play, critics can also intimate that dissonant scholars in their own disciplines also abjure the standards of another discipline or field. Reliance on this self-constructed paragon enables critics to reformulate scholarly disunity not as contestation, but as transgression. When deployed to defend dominant orthodoxies, rhetorics of betrayal *beg* the very questions that challengers have opened for debate.

It is not the individual scholarly or argumentative failings of musicologists that make feasible the use of rhetorics of betrayal to attack feminist inquiry, but musicology's earlier reluctance to incorporate arguments from other academic fields, its consequent limited ability to receive arguments about gender as an analytic category, and the heightening of argumentative affect caused by the sophistication of McClary's arguments and the vehemence of Tough-Baby attacks.

The Underpinnings: Evoking Allies and Standards

Creation of a scholarly ideal of feminist inquiry and claims of betrayal do not stand alone in such debates. In these cases, the two critics inflect the rhetoric of betrayal differently. Treitler marshals fraudulent or counterfeit feminist allies to support his arguments delimiting the scope of feminist musicology. Higgins deploys scholarly criteria that are *not* accepted in feminist inquiry, but are, rather, idiosyncratic criteria invented ad hoc for her attack on McClary—in effect, "stealth rules," presented as if they were central to feminist studies. Further, Higgins uses contradictory "tropes of dismemberment and identity" to isolate and excise controversy from feminist studies.

Straw Allies

To quarantine the angry feminist, to authorize the agreeable "genuine" or "strictly" feminist musicology, Treitler marshals feminist scholarship from outside musicology to authorize his condemnation of McClary's "exploitation" of gender. But Treitler's phalanx of feminist straw allies buttresses his position only because he suppresses parts of their arguments, misrepresents their scholarly focus, and creates specious distinctions among disciplines.

Treitler argues that McClary's work can be distinguished from *legitimate* feminist work on sexuality and culture, such as the work of classical art historian Eva C. Keuls, citing her book *The Reign of the Phallus: Sexual Politics in Ancient Athens* (1985). Treitler argues that the physical artifacts that Keuls examines demonstrate *clear* evidence of "phallus worship" in ancient Greece, in a way that musical symbols cannot do unambiguously. But in order to marshal Keuls against McClary as he does, Treitler must suppress significant parts of Keuls's argument, leaping over and disregarding adjacent passages that contradict his use of her work.[11] Keuls argues, in those paragraphs, that the sexual power relations that Treitler finds so openly evident in her artifacts did *not* lead to scholarly acknowledgment from classicists: "[e]ven to propose the concept of a phallocracy in ancient Greece may touch a sensitive nerve" (1985, 1).[12] Treitler passes over without comment and fails to quote the paragraphs in which Keuls discusses this problem at length:

> The story of phallic rule at the root of Western civilization has been suppressed, as a result of the near-monopoly that men have held in the field of Classics, by neglect of rich pictorial evidence, by prudery and censorship, and by a misguided desire to protect an idealized image of Athens. As a Professor of Classics, I believe that an acknowledgment of the nature of this phallocracy will have the effect, not of disparaging the achievements of Athenian culture but rather of enriching our sense of them, adding yet another level to their meaning. In any case, the evidence cannot any longer be ignored. (1985, 1)

Treitler thus elides Keuls's arguments about difficulties in her disciplinary context and reception, despite their strong resemblance to his own critique.[13] He suppresses those aspects of Keuls's argument that would shed light on opposition to her work, opposition that mirrors his own objections to McClary's work.[14]

Treitler quotes Keuls to imply that she studies a legitimately, undeniably male-dominated, phallus-worshipping culture of sexuality, while what McClary finds in the musical artistic tradition is her own construction:

> This [a quotation from Keuls] raises a question about where the gender coding that is criticized in writing such as McClary's originates,

whether in the artistic tradition itself or in the writing of the critic.
(1993, 35, n. 33)

Seizing on the term *socially constructed,* Treitler appears to argue that to
evoke or reveal "socially constructed" notions is to "construct" them oneself.[15]
Keuls, he argues, does not herself construct the gender coding she discusses,
but finds it in the "artistic tradition itself"—for anyone can see that the Greeks
openly expressed male-dominant, phallus-worshipping sexuality. In contrast,
McClary must have personally invented—constructed—the gender coding
she discusses. Rather than assuming that McClary must argue for the role of
sexuality in any cultural artifact, he implies that music, by nature, precludes
any ascription of sexuality—begging the very question that McClary raises.

Treitler distinguishes McClary's work from that of feminist literary critics on grounds similar to those he applies in Keuls's case: the object of literary analysis is different from—and much less complex than—music. Treitler
argues,

[McClary] seems to work in parallel with literary critics who scrutinize the gender roles and relations in works of fiction, but in the absence of counterparts in musical works to the explicit embodiments
of such constructions in texts about men and women she must first
herself construct them out of the musical materials. (36–37)

Attempting to isolate McClary from robust feminist literary scholarship,
Treitler argues that musical texts are not analogous to written texts because
they do not show their gender explicitly. Therefore, to the degree that she
applies textual analytic methods to music, McClary improperly, illegiti-
mately creates her own text to analyze. But written texts are not the self-
evident or transparent objects of analysis that Treitler implies. Cultural objects
may be analyzed "textually," but Treitler's comment assumes that gender is
explicitly "embodied" in the words of texts in a way that few literary scholars or discourse analysts would support. A substantial body of scholarship
shows persuasively that the influence of gender on texts is not unambiguous
or unequivocal, that gender is not explicitly "expressed" in literary texts through
representations of explicitly gendered characters, as Treitler seems to think.[16]
If the role of gender in cultural artifacts were unequivocal, there would be
much less disagreement among literary scholars, and feminist literary criticism would have been long ago accepted, rather than being—like McClary's
work—hotly contested.[17]

Treitler attempts to distinguish the angry feminist from other, more agreeable feminists in other disciplines by building a fetish of music on the backs of straw disciplines—simplifying methods and objects of analysis in ways that scholars in those disciplines could not endorse. He positions art history and literary studies as places where simple, uncontested work on gender can be done, because their objects of study are explicit, accessible, malleable, more amenable to such analysis than music.[18] But in emphasizing the ineffability and inexpressibility of music, Treitler oversimplifies the complexity of art, language, and culture.

Because he is male, Treitler's credentials to represent the voice of "true" feminist scholarship in condemning McClary might seem questionable. He attempts to strengthen his credentials by mentioning three feminist scholars who, he claims, have taught him what feminist scholarship *really* is: Susan Bordo (1975 [sic, 1987]), Evelyn Fox Keller (1985), and Genevieve Lloyd (1984). Their work, he suggests, demonstrates the faults of McClary's "exploitative" approach:

> But as I owe my own sensitivity to such exploitation initially to feminist writers, especially on the history of philosophy and science, I am struck by the range of what may be known as feminist theory and criticism. (Treitler 1993, 43–44)

Only a superficial engagement with these scholars' projects could lead Treitler to cite them in opposition to McClary's general stance.[19] Rather, like McClary, they unpeel and dismember texts of various kinds (including texts sacrosanct in their own disciplines and texts that some would argue are not really "texts"); they seek to expose disabling gendered histories in the face of protests of "universality"; and they have produced responses of outrage from some in their own fields.[20] One might even infer that Treitler is engaged in a kind of disciplinary NIMBYism: feminist studies is fine as long as it's Not In My Back Yard.

Stealth Rules

Higgins agrees with Treitler that McClary's feminism is not the "real article," contending that her work is probably not feminist at all by reference to what she implies are accepted standards of scholarship in feminist studies. She reveals an elaborate and detailed set of rules of feminist scholarship that she claims McClary has violated, for example, implying that feminists everywhere would authorize Higgins to condemn the inadequate "distribution of gender" in McClary's text.

Higgins cloaks herself in the mantle of feminist scholarship to authorize her invention of a novel, and in this case fraudulent, test of fidelity to feminism—the distribution of gendered honors in McClary's acknowledgments section. To assess whether McClary meets special feminist qualifications, Higgins divides McClary's acknowledgments section into three parts, according to McClary's three categories of appreciation. Scrutinizing each type of remark, Higgins translates it into an overarching new category: for example, McClary thanks several people for "ideas, moral support, and an exhilarating sense of community"; Higgins translates this as "domestic backup." McClary thanks several people in the field for their "critical responses" which made her "work harder on [her] formulations"; Higgins translates this as seeking the "seal of approval" of the patriarchs. Guided by her reformulation of McClary's categories, Higgins argues that McClary thanks men for intellectual help and women for social support: women outnumber men in "inspiration," men greatly outnumber women as "seals of approval," and those in "domestic backup" are all women. Higgins finds this "powerfully ironic": McClary, purported to be a feminist, yet relegates "some of the best minds in the discipline" "to the stereotypical roles of nurturer, sustainer, or idea-giver" (Higgins 1993, 176).

A kind of positivist literalism animates Higgins's methods of assessment: counting, tallying, classifying, and thereby determining the meaning of a variety of features of McClary's text, particularly in relation to the appearance of feminist musicologists: number (and type) of compliments given in the acknowledgments, number (and type) of citations within the text itself, number (and type) of citations within the endnotes. Higgins implies that accepted standards of feminist inquiry authorize her to base her judgments on a specific and detailed inventory of all women mentioned in a text and an accounting for their deployment therein: how many women are discussed in the text, what kinds of women are mentioned, whether there are women who go unmentioned, whether all important women are mentioned by name, whether women are mentioned in the text itself or (merely) in the footnotes, whether all authors in anthologies are mentioned, and so forth.

Higgins justifies her use of these apparent rules of feminist criticism by explicit reference to three feminist sources (Kramarae and Treichler 1985, Pollock 1988, Spender 1989), commenting, "As feminists have been quick to note, these [acknowledgments] often set the tone of a book and are surely symbolic on many levels" (Higgins 1993, 176, f. 9). The implication of Higgins's statement is that these three sources have established gender counts as proper evaluative tools in assessing feminist work. While Higgins's statement is technically accurate—in that the three sources *do* suggest that acknowledgments are symbolic—she uses them to authorize a wide-ranging and exceedingly explicit attack in a way that they simply do not support: one source is simply an acknowledgment, the second mocks the ways that *men* have tended to relegate women to acknowledgments as helpers, and the third cites the second.[21] Rather than importing well-known criteria from feminism that feminist musicologists may in fairness be condemned for failing to meet, Higgins simply imposes private criteria that *she fails to meet in her own work.* For example, in one of her own articles contemporaneous to her attack on McClary, Higgins acknowledges (and dedicates her article) to a senior male and explicitly thanks three men and one woman (see P. Higgins 1990). While there may be important differences to account for Higgins not following in her own work the strictures she employs with McClary, surely she should explain these—explain, for example, why McClary thanking several men is seeking the "seal of approval" of the patriarchs, while her own emphatic acknowledgments of senior males avoids such problems.

No longer an intellectual and rhetorical strategy, the gender proportions in the acknowledgments section becomes, under Higgins's argument, a self-evident criterion, an *ethical* principle—one that would certainly encounter ferocious debate in any groups seriously engaged in feminist scholarship.[22] For Higgins this method of classifying and tallying is a powerful tool to demonstrate that McClary's entire text—despite attempting to interrogate gender in music—exhibits an "insidious tendency to reinscribe patriarchy everywhere" (1993, 176) by failing to cite the "proper" women in the "proper" proportions. For example, Higgins indicates that were she "permitted but a single question about McClary's book," she would ask,

> Where are the *women* in this "feminist" criticism of music? (187, emphasis hers)

Revealingly, Higgins clarifies that she does not mean "women" qua women but "*musical* women." In fact, she means *certain* musical women:

> With the exception of opera characters and a handful of late twentieth-century composer/artists, *actual musical women*—composers, musicians, musicologists, and critics—are as invisible here as in any sexist text McClary would inveigh against. (187, emphasis mine)

This rhetorical vehemence is particularly striking if one turns to McClary's text, which contains one chapter on the problems of gender and sexuality in music and musicology, two chapters on the gendered sexual codes revealed in classical music, a chapter on gender and characters in opera, and three chapters devoted to three late-twentieth-century women performer/artist/composers. Higgins does not explain why, if, as she asserts, "any sexist text" in the field talks about gender to this degree, musicology *needs* a gender lobby.

Higgins represents feminist inquiry as a series of ever-more-precise discriminations about the rhetoric of feminist scholars based on how these scholars promote feminism as a gender lobby: McClary continues to come up short. According to Higgins, feminist studies hold their scholars accountable for citing all previous women scholars by *name* in the *text*. And the reason that they must be mentioned by name in the text is not to elucidate our understanding of a line of argument, or a conceptual problem, but to give them a measure of dignity otherwise denied them. With regard to earlier women musicologists, Higgins states:

> Oddly, these staunch pioneers become *ciphers* in this feminist text, because the reference to them, tucked away in a forty-page thicket of information-packed notes at the end of the book, fails to *dignify specific authors* with mention of their studies. (177, emphasis mine)

In this argument, Higgins reveals that feminist studies allows her to criticize McClary for citing *anthologies* of work on women in music and women musicologists. Since McClary does not list each individual scholar within the anthology by name and each of their essays by title, she fails to treat them with "dignity" and makes them "ciphers." In Higgins's argument, if McClary praises women musicologists, calls them "courageous" and "pathbreaking" in her text—but does not cite each of them, by name, in the text itself—McClary virtually erases their work.[23] She can be condemned for neglecting her feminist responsibility as a gender lobbyist.

At the risk of taking Higgins's critique too seriously, since I would argue that it rests on inaccurately marshaled minutiae with little relevance to McClary's argument, I would also note that throughout her critique, Higgins conflates "feminists" with "feminist musicologists." For example, when condemning McClary for neglecting Linda Austern's work, Higgins argues that McClary seems determined to ignore any existing feminist contextual work that might bear directly on the social, cultural, or ideological history of the music she studies. (180)

Since McClary's text—both at that specific point and elsewhere—is notable in its cross-disciplinary citations of feminist work, making reference to feminist historians, literary scholars, and so forth, one would have to conclude that Higgins chastises McClary for failing to cite "feminists" or "feminist scholarship" or "women" when she *means* "feminist musicology" or "women musicologists." There is no explanation in her text for why nonmusicologists and nonmusicians do not count as "women" to Higgins.

At bottom, Higgins's distinctive method of counting the gendered distribution of honors clarifies that McClary's work is inadequately feminist because it does not foreground *in the text* the work of enough *women musicologists*:[24]

> The sole woman musicologist explicitly cited *in the 166 page text* is Linda Austern, an innovative voice in feminist criticism who has had significant training in literary studies. (177, n. 14, emphasis mine)

Animating Higgins's critique, although never articulated, is the sense that to be other than forthrightly feminist according to Higgins's criteria is to be nonfeminist and perhaps even sexist ("reinscribing patriarchy everywhere"). So, for example, Higgins censures McClary on the grounds that when McClary does cite women musicologists, it is for their work on *men*—and the *men* are cited in the *text*:

> Even the work of kindred spirit Rose Rosengard Subotnik is relegated to notes on the pages highlighting the work of Theodor W. Adorno. (177, n. 14)

Her "positivist literalist" methodology, counting names, apparently authorizes Higgins to dismiss what McClary *actually says* about the women musicologists she cites, for she neglects here the *content* of McClary's note on Subotnik, which appears to be quite supportive. McClary reports in that note,

> Rose Rosengard Subotnik has been largely responsible for bringing Adorno's work to the attention of American musicology [cites Subotnik

1976, 1978]. . . . Because Subotnik has been severely chastised for having thus brought Continental criticism into the discipline, I want to go on record expressing my gratitude to her. Hers is the richest critical work to have emerged in musicology in the last fifteen years [mentions Subotnik forthcoming, now 1991]. (175, n. 48)

By evaluating gender proportions in various tallies rather than the content of McClary's argument, Higgins engages in a line of reasoning that would be deeply contested by other scholars as criteria of "feminist inquiry" and applies criteria that, once again, *she fails to meet in her own work* (see Higgins 1990, which cites primarily male scholars).

Higgins presents her examination of the distribution of gender in McClary's text as *self-evidently* feminist. While conceding that feminism does not follow a set of rules or a single system, Higgins does not introduce her methods or criteria, explain them, or justify them, but treats them as self-evident, giving the impression that her close attention to gender proportions in text, citations, and acknowledgments is a generally accepted *feminist* method of assessment.[25] She implies its general acceptance most dramatically by the degree of detail she devotes to this type of criticism and its prominent position early in her essay. But the criteria that Higgins presents as self-evident, feminist, requiring censure when violated, are idiosyncratic criteria, "stealth rules" for academic scholarship.

Yet Higgins is not accurate. Surprisingly, since much of her vehemence and her critique rests on tallies and counts and assertions about the clear meaning of these, Higgins's critique is replete with erroneous statements about what actually appears in McClary's text and notes. I address only three of these here. In one example, contra Higgins, McClary cites Subotnik not only in regard to Adorno but earlier, two pages before Adorno is mentioned. The note "highlights"—or reinforces, or elaborates, or provides sources for—the argument of McClary's text that "music is always a political activity, and to inhibit criticism of its effects for any reason is likewise a political act" (McClary 1991, 26); the note indicates that "excellent discussions" of the political nature of the humanities are found in Edward Said (1983) and Terry Eagleton (1983), and with regard to music specifically, in Subotnik (1983). In another example, Higgins condemns McClary for not citing several scholars at specific points, without explaining that McClary cites some of those *authors* and even some of those *very essays* at *other* points in her text. So Higgins condemns McClary for not citing, at a specific point, Ellen Rosand and her essay "The Voice of Barbara Strozzi" (Rosand 1986). Higgins implies that McClary has improperly neglected Rosand's work.

Higgins entirely fails to mention that McClary cites the essay on three other occasions in her text (McClary 1991, 180, n. 24, n. 25; 205, n. 12), cites another essay by Rosand (1985) twice (McClary 1991, 180, n. 24; 182, n. 37), and mentions a forthcoming book by Rosand (now Rosand 1991) (McClary 1991, 182, n. 37). In a third example, Higgins censures McClary and corrects her purported neglect of work on the history of associating Orpheus "with effeminacy as well as homosexuality" (Higgins, 1993, 180). Higgins accompanies this charge with a note drawing attention to the work she means, such as two essays by Linda Austern (Higgins, 1993, 180, n. 24). *But McClary does cite Linda Austern on exactly that issue.* McClary mentions the extensive documentation that Austern has done and cites two Austern essays.[26] These inaccuracies leave one skeptical of the actual grounds of Higgins's condemnation.

Higgins presents her tallies and assessments as powerful enough to take up considerable space and vehemence, powerful enough to constitute a major indictment of McClary's work as a feminist, and powerful enough to override the clear meaning of what McClary actually says. Yet these are meaningless and fraudulent criteria created out-of-hand to delegitimate a patently feminist argument that does not suit Higgins's political as well as intellectual purposes for feminist musicology. Only representing these criteria as imported from outside musicology allows Higgins to palm off such specious criteria on musicology; only musicology's interest in delegitimating a major feminist challenge to business as usual allows them to appear unchallenged in a major, refereed journal in musicology.

Higgins, like Treitler, deplores McClary's position without revealing that it is part of a long-standing critical debate about the goals of feminist academic inquiry. Her silence about the existence of such a debate allows her to hide her own position, attempting to finesse a problem that ought to be directly faced: her position is that she does not want gender questioned, that she is agreeable to having divisions between the sexes to be maintained, but with more equal distributions of various goods and honors. This is a perfectly respectable position, and Higgins has every right to it. However, since it is a premise for her argument, she needs to state it clearly; she cannot assume that everyone else is or should be a liberal just because she is, or that if she does not want to interrogate gender, then no one else should. While one would not wish to condemn Higgins for promoting the role of women as a "gender lobby" in musicology, arguments resting on such unargued assumptions should not be confused with and used to condemn those engaged in the broader task of studying of gender as an analytic category.

Tropes of Dismemberment and Identity

Higgins further attempts to cordon McClary off from feminism by using tropes of dismemberment. These allow Higgins to position the most controversial aspects of McClary's work as outside feminist inquiry. Higgins finds two major features of McClary's work to be "other than" feminist. The first is research on sexuality, which Higgins does not position as part of feminist inquiry. The second is research on gender: Higgins ultimately defines feminist inquiry as involving only research on women, so that research on gender divisions or on men's gender roles does not qualify as feminist.

Perhaps most startling among Higgins's representations of feminism is her sturdy assurance, at the beginning of her critique, that McClary's investigation of sexuality and sexual rhetorics in music is not authorized by feminist inquiry.[27] Dismembering study of sexuality from feminist inquiry and feminist musicology allows Higgins to isolate McClary's most controversial move, the analysis of sexually charged rhetorics used by long-revered composers such as Beethoven. Higgins opens her essay, for example, as if she has never considered any feminist arguments that sexuality is deeply connected to, constructed by, implicated in, infused by gendered social relations; instead, she expresses bemusement and confusion about why McClary chose sexuality in music as an object of analysis ("Why sex?" [175]). Higgins does not seem to find her question answered by McClary's generous explanations for her choice: that she focuses on gendered musical codes to inform an intellectual understanding of music and of theories of meaning, to contribute to our understandings of social history, and to understand—and perhaps improve—social life and political interactions.[28] While Higgins might not understand McClary's explanations, or might feel that her own rhetorical purposes are better served by implying that these reasons are inadequate, it is difficult to see how she can mount this line of argument while claiming to analyze McClary's work from a feminist point of view.

To find the study of sexuality and cultural artifacts inexplicable requires Higgins to ignore well-known and manifestly feminist conceptions of sexuality as the "hinge" of gender relations, conceptions that have inspired a wide range of feminist research. Much feminist work is directly concerned with historical and philosophical conceptions of bodies and bodily relations.[29] Feminist topics include cultural representations of sexuality, men's sexual treatment of women, and issues of gender subordination. Much of this scholarship has focused on the ways in which literature, film, and art participate in constructing and reinforcing social attitudes and behaviors that perpetuate sexual violence, encouraging us to think of such violence as natural and inevitable, rather than as constructed by our social history and social experiences.[30] Although McClary challenges the gender purity of the musical canon, rather than literary or philosophical canons or popular genres, her work manifestly contributes to this well-known line of feminist research. Without acknowledging this long-standing tradition until much later in her critique, Higgins pokes fun at McClary for choosing sexual codes as a site of investigation. To do so is to create a feminist musicology manifestly divorced from the rest of feminist inquiry, premised on the same arrangement as Treitler is offering: to marginalize the study of sexuality and music.

A second gesture dismembering feminist inquiry allows us to pinpoint how, in Higgins's argument, McClary purportedly betrays feminist studies. McClary, like many feminist scholars, believes her task to involve interrogating *gender* as an *analytic* category—not just "writing about women." Yet the rhetorical force of Higgins's intimations of betrayal imply that, for Higgins, feminist inquiry is conducted *only* with women, and *without* men, gender, or sexuality. Thus, although she periodically disavows such a stance, much of the time Higgins argues as if feminists restrict themselves to studying *women*. The feminist inquiry that Higgins posits in her criticism, then, that she enforces through her rhetoric of betrayal, closely resembles that authorized by Treitler, which allows each gender to talk about its own work. It does not resemble feminist studies in the academy, which investigate a wide range of cultural practices, not least gendering and sexuality. Higgins's promulgation of this criterion is particularly surprising since feminists have long understood that writing about feminism and gender is not just writing about women. In fact, many believe that such a notion is ill-informed (perhaps even "antifeminist"), because it assumes that only women have gender. Assessing Higgins's seriousness about all this is difficult, since, as I have indicated, she herself writes about men—sometimes *only* about men.[31] In any case, while some feminist scholarship attempts to recuperate the history of lesser-known women or probe gendered texts, much interrogates the male-dominated history of disciplines along the lines McClary deploys in her studies of the musical canon.[32] To do so does not render scholarship inadequately "feminist."

Higgins also provides a contrasting set of gestures, however, that demand absolute *identity* between McClary's work and feminist studies (or at least feminist musicology). These gestures, perhaps inadvertently, purport to measure the present and future success of *feminist musicology* according to the success of *McClary's work*. For example, Higgins inflates specific arguments of McClary, then criticizes them as if they were the *whole* of McClary's project—even the *whole* of the project of feminist musicology. Systematically isolating different aspects of the project one by one (sometimes misrepresenting them),

Higgins considers whether *that aspect alone* can make McClary's project worthwhile. For example, one chapter of *Feminine Endings* analyzes depictions of the madwoman in opera. After discussing it, Higgins comments,

> [I]t is difficult to see how a feminist criticism of music focusing *exclusively* on negative "images of women" that saturate the mainstream male musical canon can lead to anything other than a theoretical cul-de-sac. (1993, 183, emphasis mine)

Higgins does not signal what caused her to consider this aspect of McClary's work in isolation, as if it *exclusively* represented the kind of work that McClary or feminist musicology does.[33] Perhaps it stems from Higgins's decision to move through McClary's text chapter by chapter, taking each chapter as separate and essentially unconnected to and not in dialogue with the rest of the book.

Identity and dismembered evaluation of this type is not an isolated instance for Higgins, but, in fact, part of a systematic strategy that she uses to police McClary. At one point, McClary situates her argument by explaining that it draws on already-existing understandings of music, understandings not commonly discussed, perhaps, but not, on that account, extraneous to the music; listeners, she argues, already have the cultural tools to read the semiotic codes of the music they hear. McClary provides several examples, including her own hearing of sexual longing in the *Tristan* prelude. Higgins condemns McClary's example as a "commonplace," posing the rhetorical question: "Is this the extent of interpretive insight we can hope to derive from a 'feminist' criticism of music?" (178). Setting aside the fact that McClary is arguing that the insight is "normal," *not* "new," and that Higgins knows McClary has been vigorously attacked for suggesting this "commonplace" in public, Higgins is actually making a complicated argumentative move here, worth explicating. Rather than demonstrating a concern for and commitment to feminist inquiry, it assumes that any rhetorical move or argument or statement or comment by McClary can be abstracted from its role in the argument and held up for inspection as the best and brightest thought that might emerge from a "'feminist' criticism of music."

In a related kind of dismissive gesture, Higgins holds McClary personally responsible for any distress at her apparently unpleasant research revelations. In effect, Higgins implies, neither musicology nor feminist studies is pleased with a messenger who insists on conveying bad news. For example, Higgins faults McClary for bringing to her attention the disturbing images of madwomen in opera. With no apparent irony, Higgins comments:

> Ultimately, though, one comes away dazed and confused about the larger implications of these disturbing displays of female musical insanity. What does she [McClary] suggest that we do now, burn this music? Banish it from our curricula? How are we to reconcile these metanarratives of misogyny, desire, and dread with the music we know and love? (183)

This plea displays Higgins's investment in a music exempt from critique, a response that resonates with those of other McClary critics. Higgins assumes that any negative allegations eliminate our ability to enjoy the music, to learn it, to study it ("burn it?" "banish it?"). Rather than a scholarly or critical position, such arguments demonstrate rather merely a longing that culture be pure, a desire for innocence about one's own scholarly objects of analysis, or an attachment to the role that music plays in one's own self-image.

Higgins's rhetorical gesture here fronts a criterion that, if taken seriously, would bring to a halt most feminist research as well as much other research of importance. For Higgins attempts to evaluate McClary's work by holding McClary personally responsible for solving—or telling us how to solve—any of the social problems revealed by her research. While McClary's arguments, if sound, require that we rethink many of our attitudes toward music, no scholarly precept can hold her—or any scholar—then personally responsible for reconciling resulting emotional and curricular concerns. To suggest that McClary shut up if she cannot solve the problems she sees is, whether Higgins's intention or not, a retrograde gesture to halt not only McClary's research, but any feminist scholarship that might seek or need to dislodge well-entrenched disciplinary conventions. Higgins appears willing to sacrifice the potential achievements of feminist musicology as well as many of the actual achievements of feminist and other kinds of "revisionist" or "oppositional" inquiry in other fields.

Higgins, asserting the existence of a healthy feminist musicology, uses these tropes of dismemberment and identity (as well as her stealth rules) to argue that McClary cannot be included in its community—cannot be authorized to use the label "feminist." But such a strategy conflates any "faults" of McClary with those of feminist musicology, denigrating the *line of inquiry* more than the individual scholar. Such tactics disparage and even preclude in advance not McClary's achievements, but those of feminist musicology. Higgins, fearing the disruption and unpleasantness caused by radical rethinking of fundamental categories, wishes to insulate feminist musicology from such charges. Isolating McClary is her method for doing so. Sacrificing fidelity to feminist theory and McClary's argument are the consequences.

To squelch McClary, Higgins engages in lines of argument that not only condemn McClary for opening up generative questions about gender but also ultimately, if maintained, would undermine *all* feminist inquiry in musicology.

Gender and Collegiality

The excesses of Tough-Baby attacks, the enthusiastic use of the trope of the angry feminist, the covert use of the trope for partisan purposes, and rhetorics of betrayal founded on faux feminism have been viable in musicology because of the specific exigencies of disciplinary life for feminist musicologists. Treitler, Higgins, McClary—all demonstrate in their arguments the degree to which the discipline of musicology has ignored and slighted feminist inquiry. Women composers, musicians, critics, and musicologists feel that their gender exposes them to disrespect and silencing within their discipline, whether or not they are engaged in a specifically "feminist" project (and the prominence and vehemence of the debates about McClary's work may have exacerbated these feelings).[34] Such a disciplinary history clarifies why Higgins seems to assume that feminist musicologists operate in a "zero-sum" research economy, an economy quite limited even in attention—much less in disciplinary respect and prestige. In such an economy, the term *feminist* itself becomes one of the few "rewards" that women musicologists might control. This disciplinary history, then, helps explain why these critiques lose sight of so much of McClary's actual arguments to focus on personal concerns or on whether or not McClary deserves the label "feminist" or behaves as a "good feminist" would. It also helps explain why—within the confines of this debate—nonmusicologists and nonmusicians do not count as "women" to Higgins.

This disciplinary economy of limited prestige and viciously gendered debate also makes more comprehensible Higgins's insistence on feminism as a gender lobby—but a lobby specifically for women musicologists. It also explains—although it does not justify—Higgins's desire to establish McClary as a "nonfeminist" foil to deflect controversy from and protect the endeavors of other feminist musicologists, to enforce special standards of feminist collegiality on McClary, standards not required throughout feminist inquiry or demonstrated by Higgins in her own critique of McClary.

Once McClary can be positioned as the angry feminist, she can be seen as responsible for bringing controversy to feminist musicology. Under such circumstances, in a climate of such sensitivity, critics may find themselves criticizing her impatiently and inaccurately. Higgins, for example, re-creates

McClary's arguments about feminist musicologists and then responds to her own new argument. Higgins charges that McClary is not respectful when she says that musicologists are "reticent about confessing music's effect on them." McClary, at that point, has argued that the route she has chosen is a little unusual because of the prevailing disciplinary climate of musicology: musicologists and critics, as social beings with bodies and minds, respond to that music not just cerebrally but in social and bodily ways; but they do not talk about this much because their institutional structure does not support such comments. Higgins concludes from this argument that McClary fails to grant "depth of subtlety to her own colleagues":

> That certain scholars choose not to share their subjective critiques of music in a public forum, for example, does not necessarily suggest that they do not have "feelings" about music or seek answers to many of the same questions she does. (178)

According to this comment, Higgins *agrees* with McClary: musicologists *are* reticent about these things. If scholars discuss these points in public forums or published research, her comments suggest, they might be greeted precisely as McClary has been greeted—with denigration, derision, disdain. Higgins assumes—against all the evidence of McClary's text—that McClary means that only *she* herself is subtle enough to have these feelings.

Higgins uses similar strategies of reading to conclude that McClary's picture of musicology and feminist musicologists is "unflattering" to feminist musicologists.[35] Higgins argues that McClary's criticism is "unfair" to women who are musicologists precisely because feminist musicology is so hard—because there is so much to be done and so little support for feminist musicology. According to Higgins,

> But to inject women at all into a musicological discourse overwhelmingly dominated by the notion of male genius as musicology is something of a revolutionary act. (178)

Higgins here makes a flat statement that is *exactly congruent* with McClary's own explanation of the problems in musicology's reception of feminist interests. Yet such a statement vividly contradicts Higgins's overall assessment of McClary's work: in the face of an uncongenial discipline, Higgins argues that to "inject" women *at all* is a revolutionary act; but then she criticizes McClary for "injecting," as well, some of the intellectual concerns that accompany the study of women: *gender*, and *sexuality*, and theories of *culture*.

Higgins supports work on women, but apparently *not* work examining gender as an analytic category.[36] In the face of such work, Higgins joins her male colleagues in condemning McClary.

In reading McClary's work as insufficiently gracious toward the efforts of other feminist musicologists, Higgins chooses to ignore the whole thrust of McClary's work, which is to examine discourses of music, gender, and sexuality as social and cultural formations. A stance such as McClary's would attribute the silencing of feminist musicologists to institutional and hierarchical structures rather than blaming individual women. It is hard not to be sympathetic to the underlying institutional problems that encourage Higgins and perhaps other feminist musicologists to resent the swirl of discussion about McClary's work when the efforts of women in music and musicology have been underrewarded. But women in music and musicology are not "silenced" *because of* McClary: they are not silenced because she does not praise and cite each one of them, or because they are pressured by men to prove that they are agreeable feminists, or because McClary's work absorbs the limited attention that others are willing to give to women in music and musicology. Nor are feminist musicologists freed to speak when McClary is silenced if their freedom is at the expense of studying sexuality and gender as analytic categories. Expanding the disciplinary economy for feminist inquiry should not depend on ejecting one feminist scholar in exchange for winning acceptance for a few others. It should depend on the ability of feminist inquiry to ask generative questions about gender as an analytic category.

Faux Feminism in a Promiscuous Conversation of Texts

I argued in Chapter 4 that Tough-Baby rhetorics deploying the trope of the angry feminist create a climate of intimidation through their manifestly unfair argumentation and creation of vehemence through personal and group slurs. In this chapter I have tried to demonstrate part of what I mean by such a culture of intimidation: a misshaping of argument in ways that are ultimately unproductive for an academic field. The proffering of ideals of feminist musicology that are reductive, parochial, and false to larger conceptions of feminist inquiry as a means to isolate the controversy of McClary's work is an example. Whatever the effect of such criticism outside musicology, its appearance inside musicology serves to deny the challenge that McClary's type of research represents to the powerful—and deeply gendered— conventions of musicology. It allows Treitler and Higgins to present as justified what are actually illegitimate attempts to deflect McClary's arguments. It condemns work that would be of interest to many feminists as if it failed to meet their standards. It offers a threat to other feminists who would wish to explore arguments suggested by work in other disciplines but not part of mainstream musicology.

Reference to faux-feminist inquiry as presented by Treitler and Higgins functions within a system of massive misrepresentation, disparagement, and delegitimation that authorizes those inside and outside musicology to condemn McClary's work. So, for example, Edward Rothstein in the *New York Times* (1994) bases one of his (inaccurate) attacks on McClary on Treitler's arguments. Alex Ross in *Lingua Franca* (1994) deems Higgins's evaluation of McClary "cautious, reasoned" (54), and uses her authoritatively on a number of points: for example, he cites several times Higgins's musing "Why sex?" He also quotes her rhetoric of betrayal as described above to justify censuring McClary for discussing men too much: "For one who styles herself as the first feminist musicologist, McClary spends a surprising amount of time talking about men. To return to Paula Higgins's critique: 'Were I permitted but a single question about McClary's book, I would ask: "Where are the *women* in this 'feminist' criticism of music?'" (Ross, 1994, 58–59, emphasis in Higgins). While Ross, like Rothstein, is often casual about the accuracy of his descriptions of McClary's work (McClary at no point describes herself as the "first feminist musicologist," for example), his use of Higgins's critique is symptomatic: she gives him putatively authoritative grounds to argue that real feminist scholars do not write about men.

It is socially shared language that characterizes what it means to engage in feminist inquiry in musicology. If not adequately countered, Treitler's and Higgins's representations of both McClary's work and of "genuine feminist musicology" assume the role of social "fact" (see Latour 1987). Couching their representations of idealized feminist inquiry as authorization for rhetorics of betrayal puts these representations outside direct scrutiny—as argumentative resources themselves not subjected to examination and argument. Not only do such gestures inappropriately delimit the bounds of feminist inquiry, they also call into question the element of trust—the accurate representation of other people's texts—on which we must all rely in order to think through and talk about academic questions. This is a problem of musicology in one sense. But in a broader sense it simply represents part of the corruption of academic discourse caused by cavalier use of the trope of the angry feminist.

CHAPTER SIX

Intensification and the Discourse
of Decline

As feminist scholars identify how social and cultural practices produce gender injustices, they also scrutinize scientific disciplines. Because particular understandings of biology prop up master narratives about gender, feminist scholars became interested in examining connections between scientific knowledge and social relations. Feminist biologists, philosophers, sociologists, and anthropologists began to argue that uninterrogated and sedimented layers of gender privilege inscribed in the sciences influence both disciplinary and social knowledges. The production and reception of these arguments prove a fruitful site to deploy feminist socioforensic discursive analysis. Dramatic antifeminist responses at the scene of argument revealed that there are strong *political* reasons for protecting the notion of "science" as totally pure and objective. Gender and racial differences can be argued to be natural, immutable, and innate. If "science" is positioned as sacrosanct, not to be examined by anyone but scientists (and, it turns out, not even all of them), then it can continue to serve as a "trump card" in social and political discussion, a key resource to be deployed at a crucial moment to squelch claims for social justice.

During the late 1980s and early 1990s, a public relations offensive by conservative intellectuals, activists, and publicists deployed arguments about sociobiology to explain and excuse the persistence of poverty, discrimination, sexual violence, and gender inequality. These justifications for inequality proceed from the premise that biology is not like scholarship in the humanities and social sciences; rather, biology is objective, neutral, and immune to personal or political manipulation. According to this common view, the result of scientific study is, therefore, an unimpeachable, irrefutable resource for political arguments (Herrnstein and Murray 1996, E. Wilson 2000). But the premise that science operates separately from other aspects of social life had been challenged by a significant body of work by feminists and many other scholars, including scientists, in the history, philosophy, sociology, and anthropology of science. If the image of pure and objective science was to remain available to justify conservative political work accomplished in its name (as in the case of Herrnstein and Murray's arguments about the alleged mental deficiencies of blacks), something needed to be done. Groups of conservative intellectuals, activists, and publicists—augmented by a few scientists—gave the appearance of attempting to "own" knowledge about science and medicine and any commentary on it. While illegitimate in many other ways, their gestures ignore—perhaps deliberately—neoliberal connections between biopolitics and citizenship that have become increasingly important for ordinary citizens. They ignore the importance of what Charles Briggs and Daniel Hallin term *biocommunicability*: "the productive relationship between discursive ideologies or practices and social relations . . . that focus on health and medical issues" (2007, 45).[1] Rather than acknowledging the changing roles of scientific and medical knowledge, the legitimate interest of other disciplines in production of knowledge taken as authoritative, they created an explosion of countersubversive rhetorics of demonization. They folded together an enormous body of work from widely divergent positions and misrepresented those arguments as "antiscience."

The climate of contempt toward feminist science studies was one of the conditions that Emily Martin negotiated when she wrote the text I analyze here, *The Woman in the Body: A Cultural Analysis of Reproduction* (1987). She also engages in examining the language of a social group—doctors and scientists—not always interested in cultural evidence and arguments about their practices. While many scholars in medical anthropology and sociology have chosen to study narrative, language, and representation, critical reflection on biomedical models and health care requires careful negotiation.[2] Martin joins a number of scholars who have looked closely at the way metaphor functions in thought[3] and the way that language forms a part of scientific and medical cultures. While addressing an audience of other medical anthropologists and sociologists, Martin frames her work to *change* the way medical and scientific textbooks are written. She structures her arguments to compel scientists and textbook authors to confront the importance of culture by identifying the work it performs inside their own words. She highlights questionable phrases, subjects them to withering critique through exposure, and uses a variety of rhetorical devices to demonstrate that they distort scientific evidence in order to serve sexist cultural and political ends. Martin's rhetoric of intensification anticipates and precludes many—but not all—antifeminist counterarguments (see Martin 1996).

The chapters of *The Woman in the Body* that I examine are concerned with menstruation and menopause: complex aspects of women's lives at the intersection of a variety of scientific, medical, and social discourses. Margaret Lock argues that menopause, for example, is not a "fact" but a concept "with boundaries and meanings that shift depending on the viewpoint and interest of speaker and listener" (1993, xviii). Discourses about menopause as female "castration" and decay emerged in the United States in popular books in the mid-1960s.[4] Martin's grounding in anthropology leads her to look not only at individuals' experiences of menopause but also at biological research, medical instruction, and medical practice as cultural activities influenced by discursive choices. In several chapters of *The Woman in the Body,* Martin exposes and critiques deeply sexist assumptions and presumptions situated inside biological research and medical practice. She discovers that widely used and unchallenged metaphors in biological and medical texts represent menstruation and menopause as processes of decline and decay. A number of prevalent metaphors misrepresent or suppress central and fundamental aspects of physiology, encouraging unscientific, stereotypical, teleological, and decidedly harmful interpretations of women's reproductive physiology. They impose "gendered" attitudes inappropriately on processes more effectively and accurately considered in a nongendered way. Ultimately, these metaphors have unnecessarily detrimental effects on representations of women, their physiological processes, and their medical needs.[5] Martin makes this argument to hold textbook authors accountable for their use of gendered language and metaphor—for projecting narratives of sociocultural sex roles onto physiological processes and encouraging people to see women's bodies as uniquely subject to decline. She attempts to contest or dislodge academic discourses that authorize as "medical" or "scientific" what is, in fact, the overlooked legacy of negative sociocultural attitudes toward women's bodies.

This chapter focuses on Martin's use of a set of exemplary feminist rhetorical strategies that I term *intensification.* These strategies provide textual vigor and vehemence, yet deter derision and dismissal. Using intensification, Martin contests and dislodges taken-for-granted assumptions underlying academic arguments by "hijacking" the language of the texts she scrutinizes in order to "distill" or "foreground" sexism. Intensification enables Martin to demonstrate with vigor and emphasis the problems that pervade prevalent patterns of thinking in the sciences. Her strategy reveals the contested nature of apparently "scientific" language, opens up taken-for-granted, black-boxed language—stripping the language of the allies who have treated it as fact rather than construction. In effect, textual intensification serves to reopen the black box, to reexpose its matrix and the paucity of scientific support for its claims. Rather than "eroding" and "polishing" the accepted statements in the process of "black-boxing" them, intensification "heaps" and "conglomerates," to reveal the superfluous nature of such language. What I call echoic textual intensification enables Martin and other scholars to quote, echo, aggregate, exaggerate, and in other ways appropriate the language of other people's pedagogical texts. When scholars can populate their own texts with the negative accumulation of the terms they emphasize or contest, their intensifying "retunes" the claims so they can be heard with a "new" ear. Martin's prose is textually vehement, yet the vehemence is not "hers"; it comes from her reflection of the distorted terms in the texts she analyzes.

Martin uses intensification in at least five ways. (1) She shows how a discourse of decline applied to menstruation and menopause is not a neutral description of biological processes, but rather a cultural construct dependent on metaphors of production and information-processing. (2) She foregrounds the ways in which the discourse's anachronistic voices present outmoded language and attitudes about women's reproduction. (3) She intensifies the negative terminology that permeates discussions of women's reproductive physiology. (4) She emphasizes the differences between language used for women's reproductive physiology and terms used for similar but ungendered physiological processes. (5) She accentuates the dramatically contrasting celebratory language used for men's reproductive physiology. These five methods systematically, although not exhaustively, dismantle the scientific pretensions of the discourse of decline. Martin's challenge to metaphors that have come to be taken for granted opens new questions, emphasizing the centrality of writing to the cultures of instruction in science and medicine. Her negotiation of cross-disciplinary straits depends on textual strategies for shaping ideas, creating facts, challenging claims, establishing anomalies, overturning argument. This is the constant textual struggle for allies that Bruno Latour (1987) finds central to scientific discussion.

Developing allies, for Latour, requires developing textual resources that will lead others to accept and modify claims in ways that are congruent with one's argumentative goals. According to Latour, whether or not a scientific claim is considered to be a "fact" does not rest with the claim itself, but with *later* statements at the scene of argument, with what happens when *other* authors *modify* or *shape* the claim for their own purposes. "The accepted statement is, so to speak, eroded and polished by those who accept it" (42–43).

Eventually the claim may be transformed into what Latour calls a "black box." Claims that have been placed in a black box are no longer examined. They are abstracted from their circumstances of creation. In textual matters they are removed from their origins in rhetorical choices. Martin's vehemence is created by cracking open the black box of scientific textbook language and demonstrating its grounding in the rhetoric of cultural abjection of women's bodies. Intensification does not import "politicized" rhetoric into "neutral" scientific argument, but rather, grounds its criticism by revealing the politics already present in the language being contested. I examine each of the five ways in which Martin uses that language to deconstruct her agonists' taken-for-granted, socially inscribed terms.

Underscoring Cultural Models of Production and Information-Processing

Martin argues that in describing physiological processes, physiology and medical textbooks tend to treat the body in terms of metaphorical models of (factory) production and information-processing hierarchies, models that foster conceptions of menopause as a breakdown in the authority structure of the body, and menstruation as evidence of failed production. To emphasize their latent cultural values, Martin links the negative language of these metaphors to the discussions by nineteenth-century inventor Thomas Ewbank on the world as a factory (1855) and by Langdon Winner on conceptions of technology out of control (1977). Martin piggybacks on their phrasing and echoes their arguments, to demonstrate that this history carries with it an uninterrogated ideological dimension, to demonstrate the metaphors' imbrication in culture, to set the stage for commandeering these textbook authors' language. In the case of Winner, for example, Martin argues:

> In his analysis of industrial civilization, Winner terms the stopping and breakdown of technological systems in modern society as "apraxia" and describes it as "the ultimate horror, a condition to be avoided at all costs." (Martin 1987, 45, quoting Winner 1977, 185 and 187)

Martin builds on Winner's phrasing to say,

> Menstruation not only carries with it the connotation of a productive system that has failed to produce, it also carries the idea of production gone awry, making products of no use, not to specification,

unsalable, wasted, scrap. However disgusting it may be, menstrual blood will come out. Production gone awry is also an image that fills us with dismay and horror. (46)

Several methods of intensification appear here. Martin echoes and extends a plethora of synonyms for the negative. With "horror," she echoes Winner. With "waste" and "scrap," she mirrors Ewbank's strictures. Exploiting the tumbling effect of asyndeton (omitting expected conjunctions), Martin piles her phrases of failure: "of no use, not to specification, unsalable, wasted, scrap." She does not deploy anger, but she crafts a cumulatively vehement message. The vehemence of her intensification is *not* directed toward creating a reaction with strong affect, but rather toward *magnifying* and *extending* the metaphors in the texts she challenges to reveal their relentlessly obsessive dimensions.

Intensification provides Martin with a similar strategy of excess and asyndeton to intensify the *other* terrible alternative: *no* production. To emphasize the ways in which production metaphors of science are congruent with and supportive of traditional social roles for women, Martin repeats various implications of *no* production:

Perhaps one reason the negative image of failed production is attached to menstruation is precisely that women are in some sinister sense out of control when they menstruate. They are not reproducing, not continuing the species, not preparing to stay at home with the baby, not providing a safe, warm womb to nurture a man's sperm. (47)

The use of "sinister" is a play on our culture's images of women as dangerous, as is the hyperbolic concern for women "out of control." But then Martin piles on a collection of participial phrases indicating what women are *not* doing, in order to be "sinister": "*not* reproducing, *not* continuing the species, *not* preparing to stay safe at home with the baby, *not* providing a . . ." (emphasis mine). Note that the first of the series of phrases is quite short, subsequently increasing in length, leading to a sentence structure that also echoes a sense of being "out of control," until the final, longest phrase ends the pileup and resolves it by indicating relief, a place of safety—the womb—and a lodger—the sperm.

Foreground the Remains of Anachronistic Voices

The strong emotional images created by intensification depend on the language not of the critic but of the source texts. Early in her chapter, for example, Martin refers to "remarkably vivid" medical images of menstruation from the late nineteenth century. She quotes from the work of the Cambridge zoologist Walter Heape, setting off his comment as a block quotation in the middle of the paragraph (as I do below), introducing it with the phrase "in menstruation the entire epithelium is torn away,"

> leaving behind a ragged wreck of tissue, torn glands, ruptured vessels, jagged edges of stroma, and masses of blood corpuscles, which would seem hardly possible to heal satisfactorily without the aid of surgical treatment. (35, quoting Heape from Laqueur 1986, 32)

Martin follows this block quotation with another quotation to conclude the paragraph, from the work of a famous sexologist:

> A few years later, Havelock Ellis could see women as being "periodically wounded" in their most sensitive spot and "emphasize the fact that even in the healthiest woman, a worm however harmless and unperceived, gnaws periodically at the roots of life." (35, quoting Ellis 1904, 284 and 293, from Laqueur 1986, 32)

By fronting these historical rhetorical excesses, Martin is not asserting that physicians today share the views of Heape and Ellis. But she is arguing that these historical perspectives influence our stances today; that the dramatically flamboyant rhetoric of these figures echoes today in more sober textbook prose.

Critics like Martin who connect the past to the present argue that it is difficult to see how patterns of language in *contemporary* medical knowledge today are infused with less dramatic but nonetheless similar allusions to female weakness. Because those concepts are the ones we all live with, they often appear self-evident, taken for granted, and "natural" to us. Intensification makes them visible. The verbal drama here is provided not by *Martin's* language, but by her appropriation and demonstration of past *medical* language infusing contemporary textbooks. Isolating that language through intensification demonstrates the weakness of its perspective. By quoting the dramatic terms of the past, then, she sets the stage for her further argument.

Rather than mounting dramatic accusations, Martin occasionally intensifies the evidence of the past in the present by the simple and often quite effective strategy of "allowing" *contemporary* scientists and doctors to "speak for themselves" with anachronistic voices. Martin uses this strategy as part of her critique of metaphors for menstruation when she isolates a particular "anachronistic" passage. She notes that the medical physiology textbook (Ganong 1985) is generally characterized by objective, factual descriptions until it turns to the sloughing and hemorrhaging, concluding with

> When fertilization fails to occur, the endometrium is shed, and a new cycle starts. This is why it used to be taught that "menstruation is the uterus crying for lack of a baby." (45)[6]

Martin plays here on the shock of contrast between scientific prose and folk adage/ apothegm/ saying/ idiom/ proverb. Her praise for the "objectivity" of the other descriptions in the textbook accentuates the unanswered question: why a revision otherwise purged of its outmoded concepts still contains such an adage. Apparently Martin does not believe that the qualification, "it used to be taught," makes the statement less disturbing; it continues to be taught by its presence, evoking images of sex roles that many would find inappropriate or even bizarre. (Imagine the comment differently prefaced, for example, "It amuses us now to recall that people used to say . . ." Under such circumstances, the sentence would have taken on a different rhetorical role—equally unnecessary but less odd.) A particularly powerful intensifying technique is to "let" opponents "speak for themselves": ending the paragraph with their quotation, their words. The result might be considered an "irony of silence," which recognizes that the most dramatic strategy for counterargument may be to remain silent, allowing readers to receive and consider the full force of the remarks. The technique involves pulling one's opponents' own words out of the flattening context of scientific textbook prose and situating them in a new context designed to show their significance to a new audience. One should not underestimate the affect produced at the scene of argument by this strategy of exposure.

Fronting anachronistic voices this way—or the voices of contemporary scientists and doctors who are unreflective and even foolish in their phrasing—demonstrates that sometimes even attitudes that have been contested can survive unacknowledged in current textbooks. Comments such as Ganong's demonstrate that scientific and medical textbooks sometimes *do* make "sociocultural" or "political" statements. Other reviewers of gynecology textbooks indicate that such textbooks make sociocultural statements on a regular basis.[7] Anticipating counterarguments that might claim that social language and attitudes are irrelevant to science and medicine, Martin contends that those who engage in scientific and medical research are imbued with social attitudes and their language preserves and replicates these attitudes. Scientists and physicians might wish to argue that it is exactly the methods of science that have encouraged us to "move forward" from such outmoded positions, but few if any should argue for the retention of outmoded notions that cannot be defended by current scientific research.[8]

Some who disapprove of Ganong's statement might still assert that Martin's critique is bringing politics into science, where it does not belong. The vehemence of their own language intensified in her counterargument serves to demonstrate that the *politics is already there*. As I have argued, revisionist and feminist counterarguments are often met with hostility, treated as if they seek to denounce scientific research. But the kind of argument that Martin mounts here demonstrates no failings in *scientific research*. Rather, it addresses how scientific research is reported—and distorted—by the way it becomes framed in the rhetoric of textbooks. Martin is not mounting a direct attack on or challenge to any language that scientists might wish to claim as "scientific," or "technical," but on what is, in fact, language of cultural popularization, which has practical consequences.[9] It seems unlikely that physicians and scientists would want to claim that *all* their pedagogical language and commentary are exempt from cultural influences. Few specialists in any field of inquiry would argue that textbooks reflect in any nuanced way formal inquiry or the "cutting edge" of research, but they might well dismiss criticism of scientific textbooks as not touching on the core activities of science. This does not counter Martin's critique: given that textbooks function within a cultural frame, they can be improved without challenging the nature of science.[10]

Using their own metaphors and narratives, Martin demonstrates that Ganong and other textbook authors have *themselves* obliterated any claimed separation between "culture" and "science," by deploying explicitly sociocultural constructs. By using strategies of isolation and display to emphasize this point, Martin severs her audience from Ganong's text and enlarges her circle of allies—those who would be obliged (perhaps reluctantly) to agree with her. According to Latour, "The power of rhetoric lies in making the dissenter feel lonely" (1987, 44). Intensification of its negative tone raises the stakes, for "dissenting" from Martin's argument—for defending Ganong's statement.

Intensify Negative Terminology

Martin uses various kinds of extraction and repetition to heighten rhetorical effect. Since her argument requires surveying and analyzing many source texts, she must often quote, summarize, and illustrate source passages using a variety of sentence- and paragraph-level rhetorical techniques to highlight, intensify, or comment. This argumentative technique brings to light the *patterned* use of emotionally evocative language and *metaphors* across several pages of a text or across a number of texts: a hypothalamus with estrogen "addiction," ovaries "burned out" and "senile," various kinds of "failure" and "disaster."

One way to reveal such patterns of language is to "decoct" or "purify" the text so that just its crucial terms are repeated and thereby emphasized, as Martin does in an eleven-word series, giving the effect of overwhelming excess, negatives tumbling over each other—and in so doing, much focusing and strengthening the characterization of the original passage of 130 words:

> In rapid succession the reader is confronted with "degenerate," "decline," "withdrawn," "spasms," "lack," "degenerate," "weakened," "leak," "deteriorate," "discharge," and after all that, "repair." (47)

An additional jibe: "after all that," just before the last item in the series, pushes the sense that this negativity is all unnecessary, all a choice, all too much, overkill.

Martin immediately repeats the strategy of quoting a passage, then reinforcing its negative language with her own shorter summarizing series of terms—a plethora of terms, no longer embedded in their surrounding text but highlighted, emphasized:

> The illustration that accompanies this text [of changes in the endometrium] . . . captures very well the imagery of catastrophic disintegration: "ceasing," "dying," "losing," "denuding," and "expelling." (48)

Their *embedding* in Martin's longer analysis, and their contrast to, and bundling of the negative language of the prefatory long quotations makes these sentences ironic, rather than simply their effect of excess, of being "crowded." Their strongly ironic effect resides not in the sentences *themselves*, but in their use as *accenting counter*argument in a context tightly connected to the argument they are designed to counter.[11]

Escalating and intensifying this strategy to provide a more complex, systematic, and elaborate system of repetition at the paragraph level, Martin occasionally uses multiple patterns of repetition to create a passionate and hard-hitting attack. The strategy is designed to intensify the reiterative effect of the source texts' negative images in order to develop an ironic stance toward the systematic and recurring denigration of women's reproduction in texts that purport to teach "science."

This complicated rhetorical technique can best be shown by a detailed analysis of a long passage designed to undermine or invert through intensification the negative force of the language that physiology and medical textbooks commonly use to describe menopause. Martin has previously introduced the sequence by quoting from texts that explain how the ovaries "regress," and how the hypothalamus suffers from estrogen "addiction" and "withdrawal," setting the stage for readers to consider images of collapse and deterioration. Multiple lines of repetition interconnect and reinforce the images across more than fourteen sentences, evoking the effect of Martin's multiple sources with their reoccurring figures of failure and decay. In quoting Martin's sequence here, I alter the original by numbering the sentences and changing the typeface of some words in order to clarify the interconnectedness and mounting repetitive force of the passage:

(1) In both medical texts and popular books, what is being described is a breakdown of a SYSTEM OF AUTHORITY. (2) The cause of ovarian "decline" is the "**decreasing** ability of the *aging* ovaries to respond to pituitary gonadotropins." *(3)* At every point in this system, FUNCTIONS "**fail**" and *falter*. *(4)* Follicles "**fail** to muster the strength**" to reach ovulation. *(5)* As FUNCTIONS **fail**, so do the members of the SYSTEM **decline**: "breast and genital organs gradually **atrophy**," "**wither**," and become "**senile**." *(6) Diminished*, **atrophied** relics of their former vigorous, functioning selves, the "**senile** ovaries" are an example of the vivid imagery brought to this process. *(7)* A text whose detailed illustrations make it a primary resource for medical students despite its early date describes the ovaries this way:

(8) the ***senile*** *ovary* is a *shrunken* and *puckered* organ, containing few if any follicles, and made up for the most part of *old* corpora albincantia and corpora atretica, the *bleached* and *functionless* remainders of corpora lutia and follicles embedded in a dense connective tissue stroma. (42)

(9) The illustration . . . summarizes the whole picture: ovaries *cease* to respond and **fail** to produce. *(10)* Everywhere else there is *regression*, **decline**, **atrophy**, *shrinkage*, and disturbance.

(11) The key to the problem noted by these descriptions is functionlessness. . . . (p. 43) *(12)* [B]roken-down HIERARCHY and ORGANIZATION MEMBERS who no longer play their designated roles represent nightmare images for us. . . . *(13)* We are left with breakdown, **decay**, and **atrophy**. *(14)* Bad as they are, these might be preferable to continued activity, which because it is not properly hierarchically

controlled, leads to chaos, unmanaged growth, and disaster. (42–44)[12]

This intricate pattern of repetition and variation intensifies strongly the effect of the source evidence, as the passage increasingly focuses on an overall collapse of function and control. Its main dramatic element, interwoven through the text, repeated with variations, is its vocabulary on the theme of failure. The repetition is enhanced by the patterning of five other interrelated elements:

1. A frame (beginning and ending the passage) concerned with the collapse of hierarchies or systems of authority ("AUTHORITY," "SYSTEM," "FUNCTIONS," "HIERARCHY," "ORGANIZATION MEMBERS").
2. A second frame of summaries of the (bad) state of those systems: sentences 1, 10, 12, and 13 (forms of breakdown). However, unlike the references to systems, this frame is "lop-sided," the depictions not divided equally: sentence 1 foreshadows with one "breakdown," while a crescendo of disaster concludes the passage—sentence 10 ("disturbance"), sentence 12 ("broken down," "nightmare"), sentence 13 ("breakdown"), and finally, the culmination in sentence 14 ("bad," "not properly hierarchically controlled, "unmanaged growth," "chaos," "disaster").
3. Approximately a "bell-shaped curve" of repetitions in the center of the passage of terms for failure and decay. "**Fail**," "**atrophy**," "**decline**," and "**senile**" are most frequent (appearing three or four times each); there are a total of 30 variations on this theme in 13 sentences (excepting sentence 7). The few positive terms are negated: *failing* to "muster strength," *formerly* "vigorous, functioning."
4. Approximately a "bell-shaped curve" in the length of series presenting the terms of failure and decay: beginning with sets of two (sentence 2), then three (sentence 5), peaking centrally with a list of five (sentence 10), and reducing to three (sentences 13 and 14).
5. Repetition of some terms with different grammatical functions (polyptoton), giving the passage both more variation and more coherence: notably "breakdown," "fail," "atrophy," and "function."

Note that the pattern of grammatical changes in the word *functions* operates as a micropattern of the passage as a whole: at first, there are "functions," but they are "failing" (sentence 3); then there are only ghosts of what was formerly "functioning" (sentence 6), and remainders that are "functionless" (sentence 8), finally the key result: "functionlessness" (sentence 11). The grammatical forms move, as the passage does (and as the texts quoted suggest of women's reproductive life), from shape to traces to chaos. The excess and overemphasis of the semantic and syntactic structure of this passage resembles the excess of negativity in sociocultural attitudes toward menstruation that underlies and distorts these purportedly scientific descriptions of devalued bodily processes.

The language echoed and amplified in these passages—"senile," "shrunken," "wither," "decline," "dying," "decay"—is *not* "the language of science"; it is, merely, a language of cultural life and a language of (medical and scientific) pedagogy. Intensification seeks to present the cumulative or total effect of what Martin is arguing to be the unnecessary and ultimately deleterious use of culturally based negative terms.

Emphasize Contrasting Language for Nonreproductive Physiology

Some readers might reasonably wonder, at this point, whether the textbooks' use of these negative terms should be designated "rhetorical *choices*"; perhaps they merely reflect accurate and linguistically unavoidable statements about "the way things are." However, *some* texts are able to describe menstruation and menopause *without* such terminology: Martin notes that texts in general physiology, for example, seemed to avoid such pitfalls, while Sophie Laws's 1990 survey of British medical textbooks notes that most *but not all* present "the shedding of the endometrium (the lining of the womb) as necrosis, that is death, of cells."[13] Further evidence that necessity does not drive these rhetorical choices emerges from comparing and contrasting the metaphorical language used for women's reproductive physiology to that used for analogous processes *not* associated with reproduction—such as the renewal of the lining of the stomach. This technique assumes that similar physiological processes will be described in similar ways—unless the description is influenced by some "nonscientific" criteria.

Martin develops powerfully affective counterarguments this way, for she reveals that textbooks constitute parallel but nonreproductive processes in language that is neutral or much more positive than the negative metaphors she has demonstrated to be pervasive in descriptions of female reproductive physiology. The excessive emphasis on "breakdown" and "deterioration" in descriptions of menstruation does not appear in descriptions of *other* bodily processes that also involve the "shedding of a lining." The lining of the stomach, for example, is also renewed by a continuing process of shedding and replacement; but it is described not as deteriorating but, in contrast, as producing, protecting, and renewing:[14]

> The lining of the stomach must protect itself against being digested by the hydrochloric acid produced in digestion. In the several texts quoted above, emphasis is on the *secretion* of mucus, the *barrier* that numerous cells present to stomach acid, and—in a phrase that gives the story away—the periodic *renewal* of the lining of the stomach. There is no reference to degenerating, weakening, deteriorating, or repair, or even the more neutral shedding, sloughing, or replacement. . . . In [one] account . . . the emphasis is on production of mucus and protection of the stomach wall. It is not even mentioned, although it is analogous to menstruation, that the mucous cell layers must be continually sloughed off (and digested). (50)

While the *procedure* of examining nongendered metaphors is agonistic, the language and argument structure of much of Martin's comment is not. She intensifies her findings with emphasis on a plethora of terms, matched lists of three negative and three neutral terms, grouped as a set with only one mediating conjunction (syndeton), and therefore emphasizing the myriad of rhetorical possibilities, the tumbling effect of an abundance of choices. It is only with the wry comment—"in a phrase that gives the story away"—that Martin opens and reflects on the significance of the results she has laid out for us.

Martin does not condemn these scientific writers as *deliberately* derogatory, or *intentionally* contrasting such negative and positive terms, but she does argue that the language of their contrasts is *systematic* and must, therefore, reflect either scientific or sociocultural influences. She can determine no scientific foundation for such a difference:

> Although all the general physiology texts I consulted describe menstruation as a process of disintegration needing repair, only specialized texts for medical students describe the stomach lining in the more neutral terms of "sloughing" and "renewal." One can choose to look at what happens to the lining of stomachs and uteruses negatively as breakdown and decay needing repair or positively as continual production and replenishment. Of these two sides of the same coin, stomachs, which men *and* women have, fall on the positive side; uteruses, which only women have, fall on the negative side. (50, emphasis Martin's; the "specialized medical text" cited here is Sernka and Jacobson 1983, 7)

This rhetorical strategy provides a kind of "situational irony," in which the contrast between processes calls into question the "scientific" foundations of such medical metaphors. The commentary is again even-handed, but to clarify the stakes, Martin does choose to conclude the passage with heightened textual vehemence by focusing on the distinction, which, she implies, is one of gender: "stomachs, which men *and* women have, fall on the positive side; uteruses, which only women have, fall on the negative side."

Intensification strongly hammers home the significance of the results Martin has laid out for us: someone's interests are being served here. The combination of an apparently neutral presentation of results with only the quick accent at the end puts the emphasis not on Martin's act of contestation, but on the contrast. The situation, then, raises questions about the intellectual basis of the textbook authors' rhetorical choices: Why the difference in tone? Why the systematic negative tone to denigrate women's reproductive processes? Whose interests are being served here? How? Why? Intensification thus calls into question the more dramatic implications of negative metaphors for women's reproductive processes.

Accentuate Contrasting Language for Male Reproductive Physiology

Intensification can heighten argumentative force by zeroing in on differences in language used for male and female reproductive physiology: Martin, for example, compares and contrasts the language her source texts use for those reproductive processes characterized as *male* rather than female. For instance, she examines discussions of male ejaculation, which shares some of the same qualities of shedding as menstruation, only to find that the textbooks *ignore* in describing ejaculates the very features of cell-shedding that the two substances have in common—and that are the *focus* of representations of menstruation:[15]

> Although it is well-known to those researchers who work with male ejaculates that a very large proportion of the ejaculate is composed of shedded cellular material, the texts make no mention of a shedding process let alone processes of deterioration and repair in the male reproductive tract. (50–51)

An abundance of images of female reproductive physiology, all focusing on lack of efficient productivity, on failure and deterioration, on waste and collapse, characterize these texts, as Martin has carefully delineated. But when she turns to the same textbooks' descriptions of *male* reproductive processes, she finds, instead, *celebration*. She quotes several such remarks, for example:

> "The mechanisms which guide the *remarkable* cellular transformation from spermatid to mature sperm remain uncertain. . . . Perhaps the most *amazing* characteristic of spermatogenesis is its *sheer magnitude*: the normal human male may manufacture several hundred million sperm per day." As we will see, this text has no parallel appreciation of female processes such as menstruation or ovulation, and it is surely no accident that this "remarkable" process involves precisely what menstruation does not in the medical view: production of something deemed valuable. Although this text sees such massive sperm production as unabashedly positive, in fact, only about one out of every 100 billion sperm ever makes it to fertilize an egg: from the same point of view that sees menstruation as a waste product, surely here is something really worth crying about! (48, ellipsis and emphasis Martin's)[16]

Intensification of the textbooks' heightened language of celebration allows Martin a heightened reply, achieved through an upward alteration of register with "unabashedly," then down with the everyday idiom "worth crying about," and concluding with an exclamation point (one of two in the chapter). In this case, Martin does not merely "echo" the tears of Ganong's uterus "crying for lack of a baby," but vigorously protests. Intensification uses the excesses of the textbook writers' language against them; Martin's evidence demonstrates that in these texts, just as women's reproduction is systematically denigrated, men's is systematically glorified.

Arguing about Gender

Taken together, these strategies expose and dramatize the implicit gendering of language for physiological processes. Martin's argument and rhetorical strategies are both predicated on and demonstrate the strength of a *gendered* rhetorical analysis in this particular arena. Linking sociocultural constructions of gendered social roles, examining the variations of presentation according to gender—the "neutrality" of some processes, the negativity of others, and, finally, the celebration of still others—rhetorical analysis allows

Martin to demonstrate that gender is a hinge for the (suppressed) construction of affect in medical texts.

The success of this comparison between male and female processes is both theoretical and empirical. Scholars can look critically only at what they can see from within their current social and intellectual structures. We are blind to many other things. Current awareness that there are gender roles, that they change over time, that now there is discord and confusion surrounding them—these changes in and controversies about gender make it available to us as an "edge," a "crack," a "point of awareness," an analytical tool in a way that is not the case for other "critical edges," still hidden in our intellectual blind spots, that eventually may become available to us in analyzing our methods of inquiry about the world.[17] This intellectual tool can allow us to see the social narratives behind our descriptions of reproductive physiology—to see how the creators' theories reflect their sociocultural contexts. No doubt there are more forces, more points of view, more stances, still unquestioned. That is inevitable. But clarifying those we have with the intellectual tools that become available to us will also allow us to create new scientific hypotheses and physiological descriptions that are more intellectually sound and less socially damaging.

Current sociocultural conditions allow many scholars to focus attention and criticism on *perceived* gender binaries that our society depends on to make meaning across a variety of domains—religious, educational, legal, political, and *scientific*. As a society, we have not chosen casually to depend on gender binaries, but have inherited our structuring principles with our language and our ways of posing problems. Joan Wallach Scott, discussing gender as an analytical category for historians, sees it as

> a constitutive element of social relationships based on *perceived* differences between the sexes, and . . . a primary way of signifying relationships of power. . . . For historians, the interesting questions are, Which symbolic representations are invoked, how, and in what contexts? . . . [N]ormative statements [about gender] depend on the refusal or repression of alternative possibilities, and sometimes overt contests about them take place (at what moments and under what circumstances ought to be a concern of historians). The position that emerges as dominant, however, is stated as the only possible one. . . . The point of new historical investigation is to disrupt the notion of fixity, to discover the nature of the debate or repression that leads to the appearance of timeless permanence in binary gender representation. (Scott 1988, 42–43, emphasis mine)

Scott's challenge meets with different degrees of approval from different audiences. Many scholars, like Scott, are coming to believe that gender binaries infuse all our structures of knowledge. The fact that gender is part of the structure of a variety of domains presents a challenge to some investigators. Others do not agree. Discomfort with the possibility that gender is a category shaping ostensibly scientific knowledge is not reason enough to *barricade* it from examination; interest is not a reason enough to assert its importance. To demonstrate the ways in which our thought is influenced by gender requires the force of gender as an analytic category.

The availability of gender as an analytic category does not guarantee that using it will be productive: critics cannot just colonize any argument for a gendered critique. For the gendered critique to be productive, narratives and metaphors of gender must serve an important purpose in the texts analyzed. *And that can be investigated empirically.* The feminist analysis found in *The Woman in the Body* gives us reason to believe a gendered critique does serve analytic purposes here. The implication of such arguments is that something systematic may account for the kind of framing that menstruation and menopause are given: the gendered perspective of embodied subjects who come to think about reproduction in terms of information-processing and production. Martin uses gender as an analytic tool in comparing the *negative* language for women's reproductive processes with (1) the language of analogous physiological processes that are not reproductive (and therefore characteristic of all embodied subjects), and (2) the language for reproductive processes that are characteristic of males. Martin finds the former neutral and the latter celebratory. The difference suggests that gender *is* indeed productive to investigation here: there are new factors revealed by the consideration of gender.

Arguing about Medical Metaphors

I have argued here that strategies of textual intensification *redefine* taken-for-granted uses of negative language from contested social arenas, *reemphasize* the often overlooked social imbrication of what are presented as scientifically established medical metaphors, *reopen* the textual and conceptual "black boxes" that allow authors to avoid responsibility for their rhetorical choices. The vehemence of such strategies rests not (merely) on their deployment as part of an oppositional stance and its argument, but on their *commandeering* of objectionable language presented as "neutral" or "medical," their *echoing* and *highlighting* of the language of cultural conversations that appear in the source texts, their *foregrounding* of the contemporary influences of older voices, their *emphasizing* the deeply gendered pattern of approbation for gendered physiology—and, most dramatically, their *concentrating, distilling, heaping, conglomerating* the specific language that functions to reproduce invidious gendered distinctions in language for physiological processes. Intensification demonstrating these metaphors' senescence shows how "reality" at any time is a construct dependent on the tools of that time. Reality may not be a text, but it is apprehensible to us only in textual form (see Jameson 1981). Presented to us in textual form, it can be criticized.

Rhetorical intensification firmly based on careful analysis precludes casual dismissal of such arguments on the basis that this pejorative language simply reflects "reality," not an uncommon position for readers.[18] From such a position, women's reproductive physiology *does* delimit, degrade, destroy their lives, sociocultural factors aside; the choices are a doctor's care or despair. But attempts to counter Martin's argument by marshaling "reality" as a rhetorical device would work primarily by drawing on a representation of reality that few scientists should want to support (see, for example, J. Turner 1990). All scientific knowledge is subject to being overturned by new knowledge: so even if it were possible to have an "objective reality" of menstruation and menopause (for whom, under what circumstances?), why would that reality necessarily be the view held *today*? Why not the view held in twenty-five or fifty years, when we will undoubtedly know more about people's bodies and the interactions of their physiology and their physical and sociocultural environments? Martin does not argue that science cannot produce knowledge of the world: therefore to argue that reality refutes her argument would be to say that these textbook representations she criticizes present a truth about women's bodies that exists now and forever.[19] Surely that is an untenable position.

The only scientific reality we know about experiences of menstruation and menopause has been imbricated with negative sociocultural attitudes to the degree that much research relating to it cannot stand up to methodological examination.[20] And the ways in which culture *construes* the reality of menstrual cycling need not *require* negativity, as Gloria Steinem (1978) has vividly shown.[21] Intensification is directed here not only at particular contested metaphors, but at the notion that medical conceptions are *not* language-driven, language-constituted, and thus could ever be "innocent," free from the implications that imbue all other uses of language. It also contests the notion that Euro-American biomedical languages represent the reality of menstruation and menopause, as opposed to lay languages in the United States (see Martin 1987) or lay and medical languages of other cultures (see Lock 1993).

To assume that the kind of language that Martin contests is "just a text," not harmful to women, would be to misunderstand the degree to which such textbooks and instructional materials regularly continue to present mixtures of scientific, medical, and cultural information.[22] Gynecology textbooks frequently present comments imbued with contested sociocultural attitudes.[23] In her analysis of the treatment of menstruation in contemporary British gynecology texts, Laws (1990) suggests that the kinds of rhetorical problems that Martin intensifies are common also in British gynecology textbooks and even in some professional articles about menstruation. In her analysis of the textbooks used to teach obstetrics and gynecology from the 1950s to the 1970s, Diana Scully provides numerous examples that I think most would agree to be "cultural evaluations" or "cultural recommendations" rather than "scientific knowledge."[24] Even the artwork of such textbooks may make negative statements about women and their reproduction. For example, Sue Fisher (1986) traces the "haunting" drawing of a man and a woman that was the cover illustration of *Novak's Textbook of Gynecology*, 8th Edition (Novak, Jones, and Jones, 1970). The drawing reproduces a church painting by the Florentine painter Masaccio, a depiction of the "Expulsion of Adam and Eve." Fisher argues that the woman's figure—an agonized, wailing, naked woman attempting to cover her breasts and pubic area—presents an inappropriately ideologically laden picture of women's lives and bodies.

Images, comments, and recommendations such as these represent attitudes based on taken-for-granted social attitudes, not careful evidence and analysis. Our position today allows us to recognize the problems of such past formulations; Martin encourages us to recognize similar problems in our contemporary formulations. The appearance of such in a context considered "scientific" does not insulate them from their reliance on social attitudes. It cannot protect them from charges that, rather than being neutral, they reveal as "political" that which has been proffered as "scientific." While scientists might well know the limitations of textbook language, their caveats cannot counter the cultural role that such texts play as authoritative resources. Those who make medical decisions are not "scientists" but physicians, physician's assistants, pharmacists, nurses, or people attempting to discover appropriate health care advice. For all these groups, the texts that Martin criticizes serve as authoritative sources for what most people consider to be "scientific" information about bodies and health. The very fact that these metaphors are used to teach to students or lay people the significance of purported "scientific" findings indicates that for the great majority of nonspecialists—including scientists who are specialists not in reproductive biology but in other areas of science—these textbooks and popularizations are *what counts as science.*

Further, as with all pedagogy, there are temporal problems associated with change. Sociocultural attitudes may appear to change, or start to change, or change dramatically in some populations well before textbooks reflect those changes. But some out-of-date sociocultural influences will hang on through additional revisions, and the people taught by these textbooks and popularizations continue for the rest of their lives to believe and convey the unfortunate implications of systematic, negative, inappropriate, out-of-date sociocultural influences on scientific findings. To say that what most people know as "science" is not actually science does not reduce the intellectual and social harm caused when the mantle of the Authority of Science is thrown over ideologically preconceived descriptions.

The textbooks that Martin and other scholars criticize also serve as resources for popularized discussions. Margaret Morganroth Gullette describes contemporary public discussions of menopause as a *"cultural consolidation,* a phenomenon of popular culture in which for a space of time—which can last decades—a set of beliefs and issues and verbal formulas and tropes and binaries become fixed as the only terms in which talk on a particular subject makes sense to the speakers" (1994, 93–94, emphasis Gullette's). This discourse fixes menopause as a dramatic pivotal event, a "magic marker of decline" (94). Gullette links this discourse explicitly to medical discourses as well as medicalized commercial discourses designed to sell hormone replacement therapy. The mixture of medical and popular discourse she describes permeates self-help books (even feminist self-help books, as Martin notes) and is also reinforced by the kinds of translation that take place in "medical popularizations."[25]

Physicians' working models of menstruation and menopause are by no means limited to the types of models provided in textbooks, which are only one of their textual resources. According to Lock, clinical decision-making is not based primarily on textbook knowledge or "scientific models," but, rather, flexible "folk models" based on popular cultural principles and open to both forgetting and reinterpretation (but not particularly to critical reflection) (1985, 126).[26] Lock notes that the training of medical students is designed to help them construct such practical models and does not encourage them to incorporate textbook language wholesale into their clinical work. Advanced medical students are engaged in clinical rotations and clerkships that emphasize not constant reference to texts but a case history approach involving dialectical exchange; the reference to textual material and the tempering of that knowledge into working information is, therefore, a process that relies on the personal clinical practice of the teacher. Thus use of working models does not insulate medical practitioners from social and cultural influences, or the language of inadequate textbooks. For such circumstances are exactly those where we would most expect to have interactions between general sociocultural attitudes and specific medical information.

The working models of menstruation and menopause that physicians use in clinical practice are by no means limited to the types of model provided in textbooks, which are only one of their textual resources. But the fact that physicians (like textbook authors) draw on sociocultural resources in constructing their working models is not particularly encouraging, for such sources do not present a balanced or evenhanded picture of menstruation and menopause. Laws, for example, studied British men's attitudes toward menstruation (1990). Laws argues that her interview study reveals that, at least in Britain, men's attitudes toward menstruation are linked with their oppression of women: many men denigrate menstruation because they denigrate women. Martin does not suggest that physicians *only* learn about women from medical and scientific texts, but she does imply that physicians cannot simply ignore such pejorative language as they *negotiate* their training and in practice.

Despite the scientific aspects of medical *research*, much of the *clinician's* interaction with patients is, in fact, verbal discourse and social interaction, supplemented by various medical tests and procedures. Research on the discourse and other interactions of patients and doctors,[27] and especially women and doctors,[28] suggests that interaction in medical settings is a difficult social accomplishment; that doctors' (often stereotypical) attitudes about patients' class, gender, ethnicity, and personal competence strongly influence the ways in which they interact with those patients; that the professional needs of doctors (their economic and time constraints, their need to understand patients' problems within a clinical model, and their own professional development such as need for training in surgery) all influence their interactions and treatments.[29]

Negative and culturally laden language has significant influence on the interactions of women and health care providers. The history of medical views of reproductive physiology suggests that the current profession of obstetrics/ gynecology emerges from a thoroughly misogynist past.[30] Even in the present century, doctors' confidence about their abilities to help women has led to much rather unpleasant discourse about women's useless organs and bleeding, weakness and decay, loss of femininity and downright decline. Study of the training and practices of obstetrician-gynecologists and others concerned with women's reproductive care indicates that doctors are both empowered and crippled by stereotyping and subordinating the sociocultural lives of patients.[31]

We have some evidence that doctors, taught within a biomedical model that provides inadequate counter- to negative attitudes toward women's physiology, may come to medical decisions that are influenced by their attitudes, particularly in their enthusiasm for hysterectomies.[32] The environment of medical schools remains frequently hostile to women.[33] In the 1980s, men made up 97% of the gynecologists in the United States (West 1993). Alexandra Dundas Todd (1993) argues that women come to doctors for help in understanding how they can adjust their bodies to the exigencies of their lives as social beings. But doctors do not consider information about patients' social lives as theoretically relevant to health care delivery. As a result, the doctor's technical answer assumes that the patient should adjust her social life to her body. The kind of denigration of women's reproductive physiology that Martin demonstrates through strategies of rhetorical intensification contributes to this state of affairs. Medical care does not take place in a "scientific vacuum": it is negotiated on a daily basis by embodied men and women.

Interdisciplinarity and Theologies of Argument

Several features of this scene of argument encourage the use of textual vehemence. Discursive authority in academic texts is established and maintained by a complex of factors that include the field of argument, one's agonists and allies, the centrality of one's topics of discussion, and the plausibility of one's evidence. But not all challenges to academic discussion are treated the same. Taken-for-granted notions of gender operate to signify relationships of power in a system that exists by overlooking them. Scholars' investigation of gender as an analytic category attempts to "disrupt the notion of fixity" that attends our acceptance of dominant ways of thinking about gender, "to discover the nature of the debate or repression that leads to the appearance of timeless permanence in binary gender representation" (Scott 1988, 42–43). To dislodge the appearance of "timeless permanence" is no small problem.

Arguments about gendered rhetorics, like Martin's here, are particularly revealing of rhetorical negotiation in academic argument because they directly challenge some of the ways that academic (especially "scientific") language has been represented as nonideological—in effect, as without gender. To propose that some rhetorics have a gendered history, and remain imbued with gender, opens out even more areas of contestation. Such arguments attempt to address not merely academic problems but ideological problems about whose realities will be represented, about how unacknowledged commitments to class, ethnic, gender, and other hierarchies may infuse social practices and cultural products.

Not only feminists in medical anthropology but all feminists participating in interdisciplinary discourses must engage in argumentation at contested sites where critics must address, accommodate, even reconcile *conflicting* discourse communities: readers from entirely different disciplines, with entirely different rhetorical needs and demands. Such arguments negotiate multiple disciplinary exigencies and must respond to a variety of conflicting demands. Medical anthropology is only one of many interdisciplinary discourses that open a space for dialogue and discussion *among* disciplines: to speak about language, culture, and social problems to those who accept the shaping and constitutive nature of language and those who do not; to those who assume that there is an "objective reality" and those who do not; to those who find trite or pedestrian the same arguments that others find outrageously impossible. Rhetorical force is often used when the zone of argument is broadly contested, at the intersection of feminist, nonfeminist, and antifeminist public discourse, where argument must cut across dramatically opposing audiences and groups unfamiliar with background arguments.[34]

Strategies such as rhetorical intensification challenge *both* the scientific and the *rhetorical* implications of such language: academic critics of all kinds, including medical anthropologists, use rhetoric to fight rhetoric. Rhetoric here is not a neutral technology designed for the elegant delivery of already-known ideas, but rather is a critical tool to generate new knowledge about anthropology, to expose the uninterrogated assumptions of medical practitioners and medical training. Arguments of intensification do not introduce contestation to a neutral discourse. They are not just polemics or vehicles for delivering evidence: they function as a means of interrogating the role of rhetoric as a social force, imbued with power, privileging some conclusions over others. Yet constructed as they are from the language of the texts being criticized, strategies of intensification demonstrate that "neutral" texts present taken-for-granted formulations as scientifically informed and that these formulations represent "political" positions in an already-contested contemporary discourse. Thus strategies of intensification represent a particularly adept challenge to a troubling strand of academic discourse.

Rhetorical strategies of intensification investigate the terms by which academic debates take place. Deeply entwined with the language that it criticizes, devoted to exposing that language as imbued with sociocultural prejudices, intensification emphasizes that communicating in the disciplines never "merely" conveys facts: it always also *constitutes* them. The language of a discipline, even of its textbooks, thus requires the same scrutiny as any other significant element of a discipline. Challenging gendered disciplinary metaphors is a profoundly ironic task: threatening the stability of accepted pictures of reality, emphasizing the instability of language, its inescapability as a constitutive social force. Creating arguments for multidisciplinary, conflicting audiences is also an ironic task, for it requires authors to marshal interest in a common problem from those of diverse disciplinary commitments with incompatible pictures of academic inquiry. Such sophisticated rhetorical strategies as intensification can help overcome these difficulties in cross-disciplinary debate about the implications of language and the importance of gender.

Counterargument using intensification can be a crucial part of rhetorical strategies encouraging interdisciplinary negotiations. It can heighten the disjunction between academic positions and the commonsensical ideologies that inform many textbooks. Given that the production of knowledge in the academy depends on active and constant contestation, to suppress or ignore challenges is damaging and impedes scholarly inquiry. If scientists, medical researchers, and physicians ignore challenges to the texts that in part constitute their disciplines, then these disciplines are not accomplishing their work, are not making their best contribution to academic knowledge. In the end, this matter is not simply "academic," or "rhetorical," but rather an activity that explores and contests the forces that influence our shared social life.

CHAPTER SEVEN

Ridicule

Phallic Fables and Spermatic Romance

I argued in Chapter 6 that during the 1990s, scholars who study the theories and practices of scientists came under an expressly *political* attack that sought to denigrate them and dislodge their position in the university. Proponents of this argument positioned a unitary concept of "science" as the model of all appropriate and valuable scholarship; consequently the "scientist" was positioned discursively as the "Scholar King." The essence of the argument: science is so valuable that no one should be able to examine its culture, practices, activities, or language but scientists (or, it appeared, political conservatives). Historians, philosophers, anthropologists, and sociologists of science, from all different positions including feminist, are framed as "antiscience." Further complications ensue: some science studies scholars including feminists are in fact trained and practicing scientists, but they still do "it" wrong. Once again, feminists are framed as being led astray by their anger, ideology, and irrationality. Once again feminist socioforensic discursive analysis provides tools to examine the debate.

At the scene of argument, feminist scholars deploy advanced and sophisticated rhetorical devices to analyze, interpret, critique, and counter formulations that present culturally embedded human social relations as if they were scientific representations of a natural world. The feminists I examine here look to the nexus of scientific articles, textbooks, and popular books and articles that describe human conception. They engage in various rhetorics to ridicule the ways that scientific language and narrative are infused with specific social conventions about masculinity and femininity. In some cases the material they ridicule is from research reports; in other cases, it is from textbooks and popular materials that present themselves to students and the public as accurate representation of scientific findings. All ridicule is not the same and ridiculing strategies are not interchangeable. Arguments that "science" is sacrosanct and beyond criticism offer, then, discursive resources for "dethroning." Thus this ridicule resembles what Mikhail Bakhtin (1981) calls "uncrowning power." Bakhtin argues that

> laughter . . . in general destroys any hierarchical (distancing and valorized) distance. . . . Laughter has the remarkable power of making an object come up close, . . . break open its external shell, look at it, doubt it, take it apart, dismember it, lay it bare and expose it. . . . Laughter demolishes fear and piety before an object. . . . Familiarization of the world through laughter and popular speech is an extremely important and indispensible step in making possible free, scientifically knowable and artistically realistic creativity in European civilization. (1981, 23)

Ridicule thus offers an interesting "test" to the trope of the angry feminist. Tough Babies and others use the trope of the unreasoning, fulminating angry feminist to ridicule academic authors who have argued against taken-for-granted views of gender. To do this, such critics recast all feminist argumentative strategies as textually vehement and declare that vehemence to be based on inappropriate personal anger. Such critics conflate a wide range of textual strategies and assimilate all to "anger" precisely because of the already available cultural presence of the trope of the angry feminist.

In this chapter I examine three cases where feminist cross-disciplinary critics employ textual ridicule as a tool of rhetorical analysis to isolate, identify, and invert hegemonic scientific stories, specifically this particular and peculiar narrative genre: the "phallic fable" or "spermatic romance." The vehement rhetorical strategies of these critics undermine, "deconstruct," and "deauthorize" traditional fertilization stories—"roughen" them, call them into question, display flamboyantly their source in textual practices. To develop our understanding of their strategies, I unlock the discursive moves of their incursions, exploring the nature of their critiques, how they construct their ridiculing strategies, and the possible effects of such strategies on scholarly authority, argumentation, and allies. I focus on "The Importance of Feminist Critique for Contemporary Cell Biology" (1989), written by the Biology and Gender Study Group, a group of scientists and students originating at Swarthmore (hereafter, the Study Group); "The Egg and the Sperm: How

Science Has Constructed a Romance Based on Stereotypical Male-Female Roles" (1991) by Emily Martin; and "Society Writes Biology," a chapter in *Adam's Rib*, by Ruth Herschberger (1948/1970).[1]

The "phallic fable" or "spermatic romance" is a common tale that positions the egg as passive and the sperm as active; there is often a narrative frame of romance or sexual wooing or conquest. I found one example recently by chance in *Chemistry World* (Parrington 2004). Titled "Kiss of Life? Scientists Have Found the Molecule That Triggers the Start of Human Life," the story provides a small outline,[2] then begins:

> In a well-known fairy tale a beautiful princess is woken from a deep sleep by a kiss from a handsome prince. While this may be the stuff of bedtime stories, scientists now believe that the real-life Sleeping Beauty might conceivably be the human egg. Until disturbed by the sperm, the female ovum lies effectively dormant, in a state of suspended animation in which all of its metabolic processes are switched off and the cycle of cell division is arrested. The prince among sperm that first encounters the quiescent egg acts as a wake-up call and begins embryo development. For over a century scientists have been trying to fathom how egg activation takes place. But only recently have we finally begun to identify the molecular components that mediate this fundamental event. (Parrington 2004)[3]

John Parrington's story presents the ovum as sleeping beauty, but the successful sperm is a "prince." Many of the stories emphasize the bravery of the sperm in its journey to the ovum, such as this quote from the third edition of William T. Keeton's textbook *Biological Science* (1976):

> Conditions in the vagina are very inhospitable to sperm, and vast numbers are killed before they have a chance to pass into the cervix. Millions of others die or become infertile in the uterus or oviducts, and millions more go up the wrong oviduct or never find their way to an oviduct at all. The journey to the upper portion of the oviduct is an extremely long and hazardous one for objects so tiny. Only one of the millions of sperm cells released into the vagina actually penetrates the egg cell and fertilizes it. (Keeton 1976, quoted by the Study Group 1989)

Parrington's sleeping beauty and Keeton's hazardous journey illustrate a particular and peculiar narrative genre: the "phallic fable" or "spermatic romance." According to feminist critics, scientists and science writers such as Parrington and Keeton have tended to describe cell fertilization in dramatic terms anthropomorphically congruent with socially constructed human sexual roles: males as active, and females passive. Thus "classic" accounts of fertilization represent the dramatic meeting of the "active" sperm and the "passive" egg, the "performing" sperm bringing "Sleeping Beauty" to life.[4] Traditional fertilization narratives also present a combat of sperm against environment (much like mountain-climbing), emphasizing the dramatic, dangerous, exhausting journey of the sperm as it traverses a hostile vaginal environment on the way to its destiny. Critics contend that this narrative genre provides a teleological frame that shapes views of fertilization in scientific textbooks and popularizations and may subtly influence reporting of scientific observations.[5]

The critiques I examine here exploit for ridicule their common charge that fertilization romances use language from the context of social life to report the results of biological inquiry. Their arguments and ridicule do not hinge on the social imbrications of all metaphor and narrative—which much rhetorical and textual theory would suggest is inescapable—but on *their agonists' failure to acknowledge it*. While science writers, defenders of science, and even scientists may use social representations in making what they claim to be "innocent" or merely "interesting" stylistic choices, they frequently appear unwilling to grant that these choices may have broad social significance for naturalizing social hierarchies. According to the critics, the implicit narrative demands interpretation. The science writer and scientist deny it. Ridicule then emphasizes it through excess and flamboyance.

These critics shape a discourse of ridicule by foregrounding the social imbrications and narrative construction of the stories demarcated as "scientific," and thus beyond influence by the social. They contest the phallic fable by demonstrating its narrativity, identifying (and therefore deauthorizing) its point of view. They demonstrate that the narrative is inadequate in accounting for the scientific "facts" it purports to capture but is in fact congruent with traditional representations of gender relations that have specific social and historical construction. While these strategies offer numerous possibilities for textual vehemence, ridicule in particular is created by two sources of vehemence: one is created by accenting agonists' original voices out of context or through intensification; the other involves subverting agonists' original textual strategies to demonstrate their inadequacy.

None of these critiques could properly be termed "antiscience": all seek to demonstrate that the criteria of science obviate the use of the spermatic romance; all provide much evidence, not just polemic. But all give textual mockery a role to play in stripping the cloak of neutrality from scientific texts, to demonstrate that the attitudes they present are simplistic, counter-factual, ideological—fundamentally social.

To Contest Fertilization Stories: Identify Narrativity

Martin, Herschberger, and the Study Group productively conflate "textual ridicule" with "ridicule of textuality." Their basic argument is not a ridicul-ing one: all argue that scientific narratives are grounded in and merit exami-nation as the situated, motivated rhetorical choices of scientific writers, rather than as a transparent, unmediated reflection of an underlying "real-ity." Their argument itself hardly demands ridicule. But identifying narrative *to be* narrative, metaphor *to be* metaphor, is a sound riposte to agonists' de-nial and trivialization. When textuality is systematically denied, revelation of textuality can become coterminous with ridicule of textuality.

Foregrounding textual choices in scientific argument connects these crit-ics to other projects investigating the construction of scientific texts.[6] Studies have revealed that scientific writing, like other academic writing, employs rhetorical structures to make arguments;[7] narrative appears particularly prominent in process descriptions (such as fertilization). Thus these types of scientific discourse exhibit a constitutive and inescapable "narrativity." Such socially shared narratives provide a frame so that writers can structure their descriptions of events; readers' shared knowledge of the same discourse structures allows them to comprehend those texts. Therefore, for fertilization narratives to employ narrativity does not demonstrate a "failure" of textual form. But it does provide critics with an argumentative resource against those who wish to hold scientific discourse exempt from textual indeter-minacy: the opportunity to mount attacks through narrative analysis and counternarrative.

These critics therefore object not to scientific narrativity per se, but to nar-ratives that glorify the activities of the adventurous sperm—as if that were not a rhetorical decision. In the phallic fable the sperm's movement does not result from the pressures of fluids, numbers, random movements in new environments, attraction toward specific chemical substances. Rather, the sperm exhibits an underlying sense of *purposefulness*, of *intentionality*. Such fables imply a sense of loss for the many sperm unable to fulfill their desti-nies, a sense of closure when the one (triumphant) sperm reaches what has been presented as its "goal." Martin reports that texts claim a special role for sperm: unlike the passive egg cells, sperm "have a 'mission,' which is to 'move through the female genital tract in quest of the ovum.'" The task is vital, for "once released from the supportive environment of the ovary, an egg will die within hours unless rescued by a sperm" (490).[8] Such language constructs the sperm's movement within a frame of social teleology and sexual roles. Sperm may "move" in various ways, and this movement can be observed, measured, analyzed, but they do not move with intentionality. Even if eggs were fastened and immobile, even if sperm always smashed their way into quivering and crying eggs, they would not—could not—go on "quests" and perform "rescues"—but for the rhetorical decisions made by scientists, text-book writers, and science popularizers.

To set the stage for their ridiculing criticism of these decisions, Martin uses the term *romance* in her subtitle, Herschberger talks of "patriarchal" and "matriarchal" accounts, and the Study Group uses playful labels to iden-tify narrative features. In well-developed hyperbole, the Study Group mag-nifies the nobility, dignity, and consequence of the narratives (and especially the "spermatic" protagonists) by referring to the stories primarily in glorified terms: the fertilization narratives become "sperm tales," "sperm stories," "epics," "sagas," "heroic quest myths," like "the Odyssey and the Aeneid," "a thrilling self-congratulatory story." The Study Group conveys its ironic stance by this exaggerated elevation of terms, but also by other clues: it titles one story "Sperm Goes A'Courtin,'" reminiscent of the children's folk song, "Froggy Goes A'Courtin.'" It switches terms and demotes the stories to an inferior status, the "fascinating genre of science fiction"; the falsely enthusiastic "fas-cinating genre," and, later, "thrilling . . . story"; the "self-congratulatory story," suggesting narratives disturbingly lacking in self-reflection. The Study Group also connects the reiteration of spermatic hero and quest-adventures to a mythological story script (through Campbell's [1956] mythological struc-tures). The Study Group thus plays with the theme of narrativity to poke fun: with "science fiction," they denigrate this use of scientific narrative; with "epic" and "saga," they raise it excessively; with the handy alliteration of "sperm saga," they emphasize its fatuous contrivance.

To label scientific descriptions "narrative strategies" casts doubt on the unitary "reality" of scientific portrayal by defining it as a version of storytelling—with the possibility, then, of alternative stories. Again, arguing for the presence of narrative strategies does not itself invite ridicule (such arguments are a commonplace of much academic discourse). But it forms an argumentative resource in the face of persistent assertions that scientific dis-course is above the textual problems of other academic rhetorics. The exag-gerated labels, blurring the distinctions among "high" and "low," "scientific" and "science fictional," quest saga and children's ballad, energetically insist on differences of degree, not kind. Yet even these modest methods of ridicule may repel readers who assume that using other perspectives to criticize any aspect of science constitutes an attack on Science and that Science is too important or valuable for such critique. Such an objection does not recognize the critics' underlying argument, undermining simplistic images of scientific inquiry to create more adequate ones. The objection also assumes, too facilely, that a textual perspective or social critique by its nature positions all critics (not just Herschberger) as "outsiders," despite their ongoing research work as biologists and anthropologists.

Pinpoint Point of View:
(De)Author(iz)ing Scientific Narrative

Beyond these rather modest parodic gestures, critics may "escalate" their ridicule of unacknowledged textuality by linking texts to authors. Within scientific communities, discursive conventions recognize and legitimate the ways that methodological constraints influence inquiry but ignore various social, conceptual, and rhetorical choices. Idealizations of scientific writing and rhetorical conventions of scientific discourse tend to suppress obvious signals of authorship, leading some readers to overlook the scientific author's role. Under such conditions, then, making authorship conspicuous becomes a useful method of critique.[9]

In this vein, the Study Group "exposes" authorship by demonstrating how scientific stories may vary over time or place to reflect changing social circumstances—rather than reflecting any new knowledge about biological processes. The Study Group shows the strong presence of gendered assumptions in four fertilization narratives from the same time period. In these narratives, scientists intensified their already anthropomorphic metaphors of sperm-and-egg courtship into imagined "marriages" between cytoplasm and nucleus. In four competing versions of this marriage trope, scientists in the 1930s depicted the cytoplasm as the wife and the nucleus as the husband. Perhaps not surprisingly, the versions varied according to the proposer's own style of marriage or cultural model of marriage.

For example, one British version postulated a relationship similar to its scientific proposer's own companionate marriage, the nucleus and cytoplasm as equal partners. An American version suggested that the cytoplasm (wife) dominated the nucleus (husband); in fertilization "the nucleus was subservient to the commands given it by the cytoplasm" (180), an arrangement said to be similar to the roles taken in the proposer's own conjugal relationship. An "autocratic Prussian family" served as the model for a third, Teutonic version: "The nucleus contained all the executive functions and the cytoplasm existed only to be physically acted upon by the nuclear genes" (179). A fourth version, proposed by a leading American geneticist, envisioned the cell as a more modern American family, like his own: "First, the nucleus and cytoplasm conferred; *then* the nucleus told the cytoplasm what to do" (Study Group, 179, emphasis [and consequent joke] theirs).[10] The Study Group's facetious reference to American family dynamics echoes its stance toward the "problem" of scientific authorship: a gap between professed ideals and lived actualities.

Here again, ridicule may appear justified by agonists' intransigency—boldly deploying agonists' own criteria against them. Demonstrating the *presence* of authorial point of view, even with occasional ridicule, does not vandalize the fertilization models—as with narrativity, the authorial point of view is inescapable. But, for the Study Group, *suppressing* recognition of point of view does sabotage scientific inquiry: all too many readers (not necessarily scientists) wish to claim that scientific narratives with unfortunate connotations are merely documents, "reflections of nature," tools of "science," produced through purely scientific means with no point of view. Similarly revealing counters to denial of authorly points of view have been made by contrasting narratives from various historical periods or cultures (see Misia Landau [1991, 1987], for example), or constitutive features of alternative narratives (see Bruno Latour and Shirley Strum [1986], for example). While some readers might wish to bracket such evidence as reflecting "historical" vagaries now overcome, demonstrating the role of scientific accounts as constructs—situated within and connected to social life—does undermine the aura of scientific authority surrounding narrative descriptions of biological structures, an authority implying that these representations reflect the "real" and "universal" rather than discursive practices.

Demonstrate the Narratives' "Scientific" Inadequacy

The likelihood and legitimacy of ridicule in textual criticism depends crucially on the degree to which *any* narrative description corresponds to the evidence of scientific observations. Ridicule is encouraged when a unitary teleological narrative authoritatively conceals particularly inconsistent, ambiguous, contradictory scientific observations—all present in research reports on fertilization processes. Critics argue that the phallic fable *mis*represents current knowledge about the ways that sperm and egg interact.

According to the "classic romance" of textbooks and popularizations, the spermatic brotherhood traverses a "hostile" vaginal environment, active sperm find the passive egg, and one "penetrates" or "burrows in," propelled by its forceful tail. Research indicates, rather, that sperm in many mammals must become "capacitated" by secretions from the female genital tract before it can fertilize the egg, so that the vaginal environment does not contest, but prepares, enables the sperm. The sperm has a very strong tendency to try to break away from the surface of the egg or any other cell surface it touches (important for the sperm to reach the egg in the first place); the sperm's head moves back and forth with a force ten times stronger than its relatively weak forward movement; for some species, once the sperm and egg join, the nucleus of the egg moves, "rushing" over to meet the sperm ("traversing" the "unknown inner reaches of the egg," so to speak); in mouse and sea-urchin eggs, "the sperm enters at the *egg's* volition" (Martin 1991, 497, emphasis hers); at least in mice and sea-urchins, an active egg "directs the growth of microvilli—small finger-like projections of the cell surface—to clasp the sperm and slowly draw it into the cell" (Biology and Gender Study Group 1989, 177).[11] The egg releases digestive enzymes that may help it fuse with the sperm; adhesive molecules on the surfaces of each (i.e., both) enable sperm and egg to stick together, so that the egg "traps" the sperm progressively more tightly. Martin suggests that given these features, the phrase "sperm-egg fusion," at least in the case of sea-urchins, might more properly be phrased "the egg envelopes."[12] Again, the foundation of this ridicule is the mismatch of tale and research according not to textual but to scientific criteria. The "weapon" at hand is supplied by the assertions of scientific method.

In a particularly telling argumentative move, Martin contends that the traditional narrative encourages scientists to create accounts that directly conflict with their own evidence. In such cases, language in scientists' research reports may match the narrative frame, at the cost of inadvertently distorting their own findings. For instance, Martin argues that Paul M. Wassarman reports that the sperm loses its ability to move when it fuses with the egg's surface; yet he continues to use phrasing that emphasizes the sperm's "penetration." In another example, Wassarman determines that a molecule in the egg coat binds with the sperm and designates it as a "sperm *receptor.*"[13] Martin argues that the participants' respective shapes and functions during this binding make it more appropriate to term the *sperm* the "receptor." She concludes that Wassarman's terminology may well be influenced by the emphasis on the penetrative sperm in the narrative romance, congruent with human gender roles and phallic "penetration" during sexual activity. Martin indicates,

> The imagery of the sperm as aggressor is particularly startling in this case: the main discovery being reported is isolation of a particular molecule *on the egg coat* that plays an important role in fertilization! Wassarman's choice of language sustains the picture [which his own work disproves]. (Martin 1991, 495, emphasis in original)

To demonstrate that the frame of the spermatic romance is not congruent with scientific "observation" of cell fertilization—and that its inaccuracy can influence scientific reports—establishes a powerful *internal* critique. The narrative is found lacking according to the criteria that scientists themselves use to evaluate their own and one another's work, criteria negotiated by groups of scientists as part of their procedures of inquiry. Just as scientists criticize inappropriate statistical tests or other analytic procedures, they criticize inappropriate use of terminology and other language. Demonstrating inadequacy here directly counters claims that correcting inappropriate language is peripheral to scientific purposes. It also becomes a trenchant explanation for ridicule: the metaphorical story works much better as a tool for using science to naturalize gender than it does as a way of understanding science.

Connect the Narrative to Social Representations

The critics do not ridicule because they propose replacing "faulty" tales with "pristine" stories of reproduction, conveyed in "neutral" language without reference to social life. They ridicule to contrast vividly the fable's scientific inadequacy and its social potency. They argue that the phallic fable so poorly represents current observations of fertilization that its longevity can be better explained by ideological factors, by the utility of what it suppresses about social life, rather than by what it shows about science. They do not assume that a narrative should be displaced because it elides the boundaries between "scientific" and "social"; they merely rebut scientists' own declarations that scientific work is and can be free of social influence. The rhetorical choices that unnecessarily constitute fertilization stories as existential and heroic activities thereby reconstitute them—as social rather than biological processes, or as conjointly social and biological. These critics do not attempt to "police the boundaries" between academic disciplines or between "science" and "society": they emphasize through ridicule that scientists' language violates their own professed boundaries.

But textual ridicule here does emphasize the textuality of the debate over possible assumptions about disciplinary boundaries, which encourage us to attend to "ownership" of issues. Metaphors of disciplines as "academic fields" and "academic territories," with "disciplinary boundaries," mislead us in disputes of this kind, for they encourage us to consider cross-community or cross-disciplinary arguments as "jurisdictional disputes," like arguments over which party should control land and property. A model of jurisdictional control would demand that these critiques be classified as a boundary dispute, an "irruption" of perhaps inappropriate social and language arguments into the "arena" of science, making more salient various boundary questions: Who can discuss and influence the use of scientific and quasi-scientific language? How must they construct their arguments? Who should listen? Who cares? Jurisdictional boundaries must be policed. In a jurisdictional dispute, only one party is "awarded" control.

But such a model fails here, for jurisdictional disciplinary frames sometimes do not allow us to see the number of interested parties in a dispute— particularly at a busy intersection of ideas and argument. Some of the feminist critics I analyze are biologists of one kind or another, engaged in an aspect of scientific inquiry. Others are discourse analysts directly engaged in their own disciplinary task: exploring the way that specific deployments of language constitute academic arguments and the way that such arguments serve as resources for other arguments about the "biological," the "natural," and our social life. And the language they criticize, while connected to the institutions of science, is also used to communicate about physiological processes in teaching and other situations of "lay" communication. Thus to interpret and criticize the language of fertilization narratives is to be "embedded" in many academic contexts, and to "participate in" many academic communities, not to encroach on a specially protected discourse.

For scientists and nonscientists alike, to demonstrate the "inaccuracy" of scientific metaphors or narratives delivers a strong—but not necessarily fatal—blow in arguments about their valid use. Just as narrativity and other rhetorical strategies underlie all scientific discourse, so do figures of speech and other language imbued with social purposes. And all narrative, all figurative language highlights selected features of objects at the expense of other features; things implicitly compared always fail to correspond in some ways. Therefore, to evaluate the usefulness of a scientific narrative requires sensitive questioning: What is its purpose? How "productive" of insight—especially new insight—is it? How carefully has it been examined? What does it use-fully highlight? What does it unfortunately suppress? What were its benefits, and what are its potential benefits now? What are its problems? How con-straining is it on other perspectives? How does it work in competition and collaboration with other stories?

The use of the spermatic romance burdens science writing with an entirely different linguistic and sociocultural agenda *itself* the subject of argument. Current tension and disagreement about social gender roles re-creates the metaphor: changing what, when first postulated, may have been a produc-tive, unnoticed, or commonplace view. Once some readers notice and react to the gendered metaphor's strongly marked social connotations, then its role in scientific inquiry irremediably changes and resonates with those con-notations; correspondingly, continuing to use a stereotypically negative gen-dered metaphor becomes a comment not merely on the scientific issues at hand, or the institution of "science," but also on the sociocultural context. Scientific lessons taught become also undeniably sociocultural: readers who recognize the metaphor's problems realize that the vaunted objectivity of sci-ence promotes contested sociocultural attitudes; other readers may see sup-port for "politicized" cultural attitudes in the guise of science. In either case, both men and women have to live with the consequences of a negatively gen-dered metaphorical story, a story that, as Herschberger, Martin, and the Study Group argue, influences academic inquiry, medical practice, and the activities of men and women in science.

To argue that the metaphorical story is not "social" does not adequately counter this argument. The "scientific" metaphor comes from a source do-main shared with other language communities. Of necessity and by design, it carries with it meanings inherent to its use in those communities. The metaphor's scientific meanings are parasitic on its cultural meanings; cor-respondingly, its use in the scientific context infuses that context with its sociocultural meanings. The whole point of using the metaphor is to draw on its ability to bring common meanings into science: when employed in "scientific" contexts it does not leave those meanings behind and demon-strate only "scientific" meanings.[14]

Further, the quality of "scientific" understanding is not enhanced when the narratives also present "contested" interpretations of sociocultural and gendered social relations. In effect, the romance of the sperm story creates a doubled metaphor—a biological metaphor explicated not by actual male/female relations in society, but *by another metaphor*—a metaphorical story of male/female relations. No matter what the circumstances of its original pos-tulating, no matter how "natural" and "productive" its use at that time, now the metaphorical story carries with it unnecessary conceptual and "political" connotations. The critics' ridicule capitalizes on the likelihood that some people—including some scientists—will find the story outmoded, offensive, unintelligent, perhaps unethical, even laughable.

Accent Voices and Stress Insinuations

Using ridicule to raise tactical and philosophical challenges to regimes of gendered power and knowledge runs risks of being seen as unfair to agonists. Critics counter this risk with rhetorical techniques implying that agonists' voices are fully represented; they front their own legitimacy and reliability and circumstantiate their charges by selecting and quoting specific language from the texts criticized. Martin, for example, draws from a number of texts to reveal the pervasive theme of spermatic quests that I describe earlier. By drawing together lexical and syntactic choices from different writers, critics emphasize that the problem is not isolated words used in infelicitous ways, but a systematic trope that cuts across many texts, a taken-for-granted approach. Thus mustering collected words and phrases becomes support for contentions about how pervasive the story is.

Much ground for ridicule is established when critics remove agonists' voices from their original contexts, when these voices are accented, embedded, subordinated, transformed by their new deployment in new arguments. Removing language from its original context to employ it as critical textual evidence *always* transforms it (in fact, commenting on it in any way transforms it), even when the language is not proffered in fragments. To modulate the transformation by quoting longer passages achieves a different effect, allowing agonists to amplify the story's innuendos. The Study Group, for example, lets its agonists speak more fully, but again, not quite "for themselves." Instead, it italicizes particularly egregious displays for emphasis (to make salient rhetoric that may appear "innocent" in context). The Study Group highlights crucial words in this quotation drawn from a book for expectant mothers:

> [M]yriads survive, penetrate the neck of the uterus and swarm up through the uterine cavity and into the Fallopian tube. *There they lie in wait for the ovum.* As soon as the ovum comes near the *army of spermatozoa,* the latter, as if they *were tiny bits of steel drawn by a powerful magnet, fly at the ovum.* One *penetrates,* but only one. . . . *As soon as the one enters, the door is shut on other suitors.* Now, as if *electrified,* all the particles of the ovum (now fused with the sperm) exhibit

vigorous agitation. (quoted in Biology and Gender Study Group 1989, 175–176, ellipsis and emphasis theirs)[15]

The Study Group not only highlights parts of the passage that it finds inappropriate, it forcefully and frankly summarizes the sexual or ethical implications:

> In one image we see the fertilization as a kind of martial gang-rape, the members of the masculine army lying in wait for the passive egg. In another image, the egg is a whore, attracting the soldiers like a magnet, the classical seduction image and rationale for rape. The egg obviously wanted it. Yet, once *penetrated*, the egg becomes the virtuous lady, closing its door to the other *suitors*. Only then is the egg, because it has fused with a sperm, rescued from dormancy. . . . The fertilizing sperm is a hero who survives while others perish, a soldier, a shard of steel, a successful suitor, and the cause of movement in the egg. The ovum is a passive victim, a whore and finally, a proper lady whose fulfillment is attained. (176, emphasis theirs)

Again the Study Group objects to representing biological processes as manifesting ideologically constructed, institutionally validated roles. The critics' blunt language and confrontational phrasing satirize the original passage and demonstrate their scorn for the implications of such stories: "gang-rape," "whore," "The egg obviously wanted it." Using ethical strictures and rape myths with "egg," evoking its desire for "it" (sexuality and its [fearful] pleasures), creates a ludicrous image that may in turn further challenge the same rationale when commonly used for the rape of women (as opposed to eggs). The Study Group provides other, more light amusements: categorizing the sperm as "martial" to uplift the biological scene to one of conquest, the lionizing of the sperm as steely hero, the redemption and honoring of the ovum as "virtuous lady." Further, the commentary's language structure mimics the problem/solution form of the original passage: violence and mayhem redeemed by civilized institutions such as marriage to enforce proper sexual ethics and, ultimately, happiness.

By textually ridiculing spermatic heroism and lascivious (but eventually fulfilled) eggs, the critics link earlier, more modest, apparently innocent rhetorical choices to their potentially ludicrous implications. Both highlighting terms and scornful commentary emphasize that textual moves to enhance narratives cannot be "innocent" (despite the most innocent of intentions) and that small rhetorical choices in scientific arguments can lead one, intentionally or not, to intimate that unmarried eggs are as lewd as prostitutes or wayward girls.

Switch Protagonists and Subvert Complicitous Textual Strategies

The critics argue that writers of fertilization narratives *systematically* assign to the sperm the prominent rhetorical role of protagonist. This unacknowledged rhetorical choice of spermatic protagonist therefore offers a powerful textual resource for ridicule: sabotaging falsely naturalized protagonists.

Like metaphorical and narrative structures that undergird folktales and fiction, tales of scientific discovery and description have underlying narrative architectures that relate their agents and actions.[16] Bruno Latour and Françoise Bastide argue that even quite formalized scientific arguments are similarly highly narrative and rhetorical.[17] The underlying narrative structure may encourage readers to see the "agent" of scientific texts as narrative "protagonist," with crucial rhetorical effect. In fact, Latour and Bastide argue that the decision to organize the text around the "trials" of *any* specific element, *any* agent, shapes the narrative around it and foregrounds that element—whatever its "nature"—as protagonist and even "hero." Perhaps it is not surprising, then, that Martin, Herschberger, and the Study Group focus analysis and create considerable ridicule by manipulating the role of "protagonist."

The Study Group pointedly attacks the choice of sperm as hero with the same kinds of mocking label I describe earlier as part of its attacks on narrativity. It lavishes the protagonist with labels to remind readers that choice of protagonist structures the story's events. The spermatic protagonist becomes "heroic victor," "heroic sperm," "spermatic hero," "like Aeneas," "noble survivor." The protagonist faces many difficult tasks: he "struggl[es] against the hostile uterus," "survives challenges on his journey to a new land, defeats his rivals, marries the princess and starts a new society." The dangers and his courage are so great, "We might conclude the saga by announcing, 'I alone am saved.'" The Study Group does not object to the (in any case unavoidable) narrative structures underlying scientific and semiscientific stories of fertilization, but it does object to the conceptual constraints caused by constantly reiterating sperm as hero.[18]

All three of these critical essays go beyond mocking labels and comments to employ, centrally, a simple and powerful method to ridicule and refute the phallic fable: they replace one protagonist with another. In a single ridiculing move that is (perhaps paradoxically) quite authoritative, the critics thereby substantiate and legitimate their other charges and ridiculing rhetorics. The results are dramatic and amusing.

For example, the Study Group suggests that when narratives use the language of heroics for the actions of the protagonist, then altering the protagonist—substituting egg for sperm—considerably changes the underlying argument. The Study Group argues,

> Indeed, one could make a heroic tale about the ovum which has to take a "leap" into the unknown, though its chances of survival are less than 1%. Indeed, the human ovum, too, is the survivor of a process which has winnowed out nearly all of the original 2 million oocytes, and left it the only survivor of its cohort. (185, n. 3)

Demonstrating that the usurper also has dramatic characteristics counters claims that specific, even unique spermatic qualities make it the "natural" protagonist. If the egg were chosen as protagonist, themes of *winnowing* out and *survival* pervasive in fertilization stories could be plausibly deployed "in favor of" the egg.

Such a ridiculing rebuttal demonstrates, further, that defining the protagonist is the linchpin of a series of related rhetorical decisions that work synergistically to exacerbate the impact of spermatic protagonist (or, for that matter, the plethora of spermatic protagonists). According to these critics, other structural decisions contribute. Herschberger argues that the stories do not treat gendered aspects of fertilization in the same way: males accomplish their tasks by means of *organs*, females merely by interdependent *functions*.[19] Martin argues that the stories do not treat the various entities they describe in a parallel fashion: they present the sperm as a whole entity, but the egg as a conglomeration of components; the sperm's actions are therefore part of its *purpose*, the egg's actions merely part of the *component*.[20] Martin also argues that the texts do not present potentially sensitive topics in the same way: for example, similar qualities in sperm and egg (such as their weaknesses) are not discussed in the same part of the text, allowing for invidious distinctions.[21] The sentence structure describing the two participants also varies systematically: the narratives tend to use the *passive* voice to describe what happens to the egg, the *active* voice for the activities of the sperm (Martin),[22] or they *animate* the sperm's part of the process at the expense of the egg's (Herschberger).

These disproportionate grammatical and structural decisions then become the foundation for ridiculing reversal. At one point, Herschberger simply inverts the grammatical arrangements in the fable—arrangements that implicitly valorize male agents and male processes—to valorize, instead, those of the female. Note that both accounts deny their own construction and present themselves as "straightforward": the facts are simply the facts. For example:

> *The Patriarchal Account*: The simple and elementary fact behind human reproduction is that a fertile female egg awaits impregnation in the fallopian tube, and the active male sperm must find this egg and penetrate it. (75)
>
> *The Matriarchal Account*: The simple and elementary fact behind human reproduction is that the active female egg must obtain a male sperm before it can create a new life. (81)

Mocking similarly overblown patriarchal accounts, Herschberger represents the ovum as the singular source of new life.[23] In her patriarchal account, the egg is characterized as passive, although it functions as grammatical agent. In the matriarchal account, the egg assumes responsibility for fertilization, serving as both grammatical subject and active agent. This reversing of "complicitous" rhetorical decisions punctuates with ridicule as it reveals: its impact depends on readers' understanding that such systematic decisions reinforce the original protagonist's (excessively) central role.

Redeploy Enthusiasm

Arguing that the spermatic romance tends to downplay the activities of the egg, emphasizing its *frailty*, while waxing enthusiastic about the *hardiness* and *speed* of the sperm, all three critiques create considerable ridicule by mocking the fable's disproportionate glorification of some themes over others: redeploying enthusiasm in favor of the new protagonist. Taken-for-granted themes such as *complexity, strength, resourcefulness, uniqueness, sacrifice*, and *destiny* are exposed by such redeployment.

When Herschberger swaps protagonists to form her matriarchal account, she faithfully retains the patriarchal model's valorization of the protagonist (alas, now inverted):

> Through patriarchal eyes we observed the Tom Mix bravado of the male cell and the flower-like receptivity of the female cell. In the matriarchal account, we should not be surprised to discover that the egg has become overnight the smart little administrator of fertilization, ringleader and liontamer, led on by destiny and a sense of right. The

male semen, on the other hand, is laboriously put together by one doubtful function after another. It begins to seem a miracle that it stays intact as long as it does, in time for the capable egg to extend a helping hand to the faltering sperm that comes so reluctantly to the bridal hour. (78)

In addition to denigrating the ascribed manliness of the sperm and glorifying the courageous egg, Herschberger also refocuses the attention of that interesting player "Nature" or "Destiny," from the sperm to the egg.

Herschberger reverses other themes that seem considerably more "innocent" and "straight-forward" when deployed in the familiar terms of the patriarchal account. One such theme is an enthusiasm for *quantity*—what critics claim to be the phallic fables' typical glorifying of spermatic *numbers*. In her "matriarchal" rewriting, Herschberger reverses the valorization of quantity so common in descriptions of semen, slightly changing the system of values to refocus on issues of *efficacy* as contrasted to *waste* and *error*. She also introduces the theme of *reliability* or *regularity*, which the patriarchal description often overlooks.

> *The Patriarchal Account*: It is significant that only one egg is provided each month by the female, while billions of active sperm are produced in the male for the purposes of reproduction. (77)
>
> *The Matriarchal Account*: The female system differs from that of the male in that the female egg is produced once each month with timely regularity and therefore with greater chance of being fertilized, while a margin of several million sperm is required for the fertilization of one mature egg. (85)

The patriarchal account idealizes numbers; the matriarchal account idealizes efficacy and regularity. The matriarchal account also reverses the evocation of *waste* so common to discussions of female physiology and processes, applying it to the sperm, to emphasize the "happenstansical" efforts of a particular sperm as opposed to the effective productiveness of that one egg.[24]

Herschberger also introduces the neglected theme of *size*, which the patriarchal account tends to discount in favor of the theme of *speed*, and transposes the attribution of *fragility* and *strength* from one participant to the other.[25] Quoting from her matriarchal account:

> *Matriarchal Account*: The female egg is actually visible to the naked eye, and is the largest cell in the female body and larger than any cell

in the male body. The male germ cells are unbelievably tiny, and must be magnified one hundred times in order to be visible at all. The male sperm is produced in superfluously great numbers since the survival of any one sperm or its contact with an egg is so hazardous, and indeed improbable. The egg being more resilient, and endowed with solidity, toughness, and endurance, can be produced singly and yet effect reproduction. (82)

Rather than emphasizing the long trek of the sperm with its accompanying *danger*, Herschberger emphasizes the *convenience* and *support* of the spermatic delivery system and the dangerous terrain the ovum must negotiate:

By the active pressure of the [ovum's] growth, it produces a slit in the wall of the ovary and escapes into the abdominal cavity. The sperm are provided with a continuous enclosed passageway from the testes to the penis, thus making their conveyance as simple as possible. For the female, however, there is a remarkable gap between ovary and tube, a gap which the egg must traverse alone. (83)

Note that Herschberger's inversion also draws upon the related themes of *singularity* and *companionship* or *brotherhood*. Martin notes that her sources "provide compelling information on interactions among sperm . . . [with] elements [that] include competition, hierarchy, and sacrifice" (489, n. 13).[26] Herschberger inverts the metaphorical story to emphasize the egg's staunch isolation, as it travels without help or aid or even companions in travail:

[T]he future of the new human being now depends wholly upon the courage and acumen with which the egg establishes its placenta and obtains food for the active embryo. It is clear that the sperm plays a very small and hesitant part in this larger panorama of the creation of life. We must not assume, however, that the sperm is any less essential than the egg; it is a difference in function. There is no question of superiority and inferiority. (84)

Herschberger mocks the "even-handed" patronizing responses that might be used to protest the patriarchal account. And her ovular account points to considerable narrative action beyond the climax of the phallic fable.

By implying through ridicule that boys and men need stories of heroes, these critics invert gender slurs, making themselves and women "rational," confronting silly and emotional men who require and defend valorization of the masculine in every context.

Ridicule as an Argumentative Device

The language that these critics ridicule is not isolated, trivial, or merely outmoded. It continues to appear in both scientific and popular discussions (witness my discovery in *Chemistry World*). But the force motivating these ridiculing feminist critiques is a much stronger concern about the systematic deployment of social language in arguments inappropriately sheltered from social critique: *social language recycled as scientific becomes available as support for those mounting arguments about social life.* The authority of "Science" (and its apparently rigorous designation of the "natural") thus creates an argumentative resource that can be used to justify specific social and political programs—on the basis that "Science" shows them to be universal, pervasive, natural, inevitable. This *connection*—the creation of this linguistically constituted resource—may seem to justify the textual vehemence of these critics. As a singular case, the fertilization romance might be of little importance. But as a part of a phalanx or network of social arguments, part of a system of overdetermination (Althusser 1971), it has potentially significant consequence for the daily lives of scientists and nonscientists alike. The determination of many supporters of science to be oblivious to such a connection, to trivialize linguistic matters about which they are ill-informed, may seem to warrant responses of textual ridicule, sarcasm, and other vehement rhetorical strategies.

When science is marshaled to support claims about men and women's roles in society, it is proper to study the language that makes traditional roles seem biologically inevitable. The laughter of "uncrowning power" allows us to take stock of what that language implies. Lisa Jean Moore's *Sperm Counts: Overcome by Man's Most Precious Fluid* (2007) also expresses ideas playfully through a long series of wicked puns and clever phrases, but her purpose is profoundly serious: to expose the pernicious social consequences of naïve and nostalgic representations of sperm and semen that do violence to both scientific evidence and social relations. Moore reveals how scientists' perceptions about semen as the key to reproduction led to efforts to capture and program individual sperm cells as well as to the attribution of human personalities and characteristics applied to sperm cells because of the "jobs" they perform. She then examines how sperm becomes seen as a commodity by the sperm banking industry and as an overvalued and reified piece of evidence in sexual assault cases. Moore exposes the insidious effects of a commercial culture that echoes and amplifies fears and fixations about masculinity and reproduction. Moore also examines how children's books about reproduction and health "teach" sperm to children through metaphors about heroic masculinity. She argues that these representations to children encode a childishness that then permeates adult norms, values, and taboos about the body and its functions. Like Cynthia R. Daniels's *Exposing Men: The Science and Politics of Male Reproduction* (2006), *Sperm Counts* delineates and deconstructs how scientists and popular journalists abuse scientific evidence to reduce social relations to deterministic effects of biological destiny. Like the critics I examine in this chapter, she makes her arguments through an array of witty arguments and ridicule.

Choosing ridiculing techniques opens up argumentative possibilities but also runs risks of being seen as not serious, or not scholarly. Our reading practices encourage us to question the character and motives of those who appear to violate academic (and other) conventions. We often tend to denigrate and distrust apparent transgressions of textual etiquette, inadvertently valorizing socially inscribed and politically charged politeness conventions over issues far more significant. We may dismiss ridiculing rhetoric—particularly that appearing in feminist publications[27]—as "preaching to the already converted"—merely an "in-group" device to "express solidarity." Or we may inappropriately read academic arguments as analogous to face-to-face conversations with scientists, instructors, and textbook authors wherein the critics' task is to "persuade" this [uninterested/mildly interested/oblivious/scornful] audience to agree with their criticisms and consequently alter its speaking and writing practices. The analogy assumes that an otherwise (at least grudgingly) open-minded audience will become unfriendly or hostile if it perceives itself *being ridiculed*. It also supposes that if critics are not "nice" to those they criticize, then the criticized will not want to change—and that getting them to want to change is the job of the argument. I would argue that these reading models may distort our judgment of what constitutes a good argument. Rather than interpreting textual ridicule as failure to demonstrate a serious attitude, or to adhere to academic codes of discourse, we should understand its potential for use as a legitimate and logical tool in struggles over meaning.

Reading practices that delegitimate ridicule overlook its interpretive and epistemological benefits—its potential to raise more general questions about knowledge, interests, power, and identity. Part of its contribution to clarifying meaning stems from its ability to function as another way of knowing, adding an interpretive dimension to counterargument. Sociologist Michael Mulkay, concerned with the social uses of humor, argues that in the "serious realm," we normally employ a unitary mode of discourse which takes for granted the existence of one real world, and within which ambiguity, inconsistency, contradiction and interpretive diversity are potential problems. In contrast, humor depends on the active creation and display of interpretive multiplicity. When people engage in humor, they . . . temporarily inhabit not a single, coherent world, but a world in which whatever is said and done necessarily has more than one meaning. (1988, 3–4)

Thus some of kinds of humor—and I would argue the kind of ridicule I analyze here—present an *epistemological* challenge to the unitary nature of many scientific arguments (particularly in textbooks) by emphasizing, exploiting, creating excess out of multiple interpretation. In mounting attacks both witty and excoriating, feminist critics expose—lavishly expose—overexpose—the ways in which unexamined narrative frames do social and scientific harm.

Reading practices that encourage us to bracket arguments mounted through ridicule may prevent us from acknowledging the difficulties facing academic critics—particularly in cross-disciplinary debate. Challenging gender privilege masquerading as neutral scientific discourse is no easy task. Critics must demonstrate the situatedness of scientific research to readers who generally believe in universal and transcendent objectivity. They must argue for the significance of distinctly gendered metaphors in a context that too often dismisses rhetoric as a neutral tool or emotional embellishment upon a preexisting reality that can be easily discovered through "impartial" observation and unproblematically related to others through existing language conventions. Most important, critics have to show that seemingly trivial rhetorical choices encode larger social meaning, that they stem less from scientific necessity than from uninterrogated ideological commitments to existing gender hierarchies.

Our reading practices may, further, lead us to overlook the situational logic underlying these critics' use of textual ridicule. To accomplish their discursive tasks, these feminist critics must educate and perhaps agitate. They may seek to disrupt disciplinary conventions and expand tunnel vision by adopting rhetorical and argumentative strategies appropriate to their goals. At the very least, they seek to show that scientists are situated and interested, that their knowledge is partial and perspectival. Beyond that, they try to lessen the authority of science as a support for sexist gendered metaphors and narratives that render existing power relations "natural," necessary, and inevitable. They use rhetorical contestation and ridicule to identify the existence of narratives in scientific research, to assign authorship to accounts that fuse sexism with science, to show how gendered metaphors remain in use even when they represent scientific processes poorly because they serve as ideological props for existing gender hierarchies. All of these tactics emerge from the power relations that scientific sexism helps to obscure: the cultural authority of science that gives unchallengeable legitimacy to what may be patriarchal prejudice, and the critics' consequent need to deauthorize its regimes of truth and power. In the case of these three critiques, ridicule serves to reconfigure scientific authority—as the work of individuals with interests and ideologies, and as conduits that diffuse gendered power in subtle ways that previous scholarly and disciplinary rhetorics often overlooked.

Textual mockery may further academic critics' tactical goals by its special "hailing" of the subject imagined as the ideal, maximally competent reader. If a reader is not maximally competent, he or she may not understand the ridicule.[28] It establishes a highly marked relationship between critic and text being criticized; it invites readers to observe and perhaps to share that marked relationship.[29] Whatever readers' responses, whether they join, reject, or remain agnostic, the mockery alters the relationship between the reader and scientific agonist. In addition to its tactical functions dramatically marking the relationships among critics, texts, authors, and readers, ridicule also presents a philosophical challenge to epistemologies that depend on but deny their use of social language. Both the scorn for academic ridicule encouraged by our reading practices and my call for recognition of its argumentative potential underscore the importance of understanding that rhetoric is not merely a neutral technology to be deployed interchangeably in the service of any argument but is rather a constitutive element of knowledge that is always situated in concrete historical social relations.

Textual ridicule sets the stakes for ignoring a critique rather high. It is one thing to discount the social consequences of gendered metaphors and narratives, as so many people—including academics—boldly do; it is quite another to continue to espouse notions that invite ridiculing derision. Textbook authors and scientists may well never read these critiques, or be perfectly willing to bracket such attacks as peripheral to their main interests: obtaining continuing support for science. Maintaining support for science ultimately depends on continuing social agreement that science remains "authoritative," and that is dependent on its social role. Many changes in scientific procedures have taken place not because of the vigor of opponents' arguments, but because social and intellectual pressures make holding certain notions untenable. Science, like other social enterprises, responds to a phalanx of pressures, not a single or a few critiques, however accurate and amusing.

But rather than merely "preaching to the converted," detailed ridicule based on accessible evidence creates a vivid tool for those who need to be converted, for those who need to know more, for those who need to be inspired to criticize. One ought not to be overly sanguine about overcoming the difficulties of developing intellectual allies in academic circles for shared ideological critique. To denigrate strategies that might contribute to such alliances as superficial and "merely" entertaining is short-sighted both politically and conceptually.

These ridiculing critiques assume and demonstrate that language choices are about power. Scientific language does not merely omit women or use inappropriate metaphors about them: it functions to conceal systematically the social relations that it constitutes. Scientific narratives may disguise social hierarchies as "nature" by depicting nature in socially hierarchical terms. Whether or not there could be pure unmediated language to use for science, these critics demonstrate that existing language is impure, interested, partial, and perspectival. Their satiric and parodic gestures deride it as so inappropriate that its existence can be explained only by the continuing influence of ingrained and uninterrogated ideologies of gender.

There may be no unmediated truth, but some metaphors are better than others because they reveal shared social knowledge in a clearer light. These critics show how scientists may come to use poor metaphors because their unspoken commitment to gender hierarchies warps their judgment in ways they do not yet see. Rhetorical vehemence can interrupt the truth regimes that relegate groups of people to lesser status. Dislodging these truth regimes is enormously difficult and requires extremely subtle and creative practices by feminist writers. One of these practices is their use of derisory rhetoric.

CHAPTER EIGHT

The Labor of Argument and
Feminist Futures

Structures of dominance are the condition of possibility for feminist argument. Our agency emerges as a consequence of what we must contest. The discourses we negotiate offer opportunities and foreclosures. Feminist disciplinary and interdisciplinary discourses provide multiple sites, each of them saturated with power—creating and created by institutions of power, ideologies of reading, conventions of disciplines, and the rhetoric of texts. As Judith Butler argues, these are productive sites: "The terms by which we are hailed are rarely the ones we choose (and even when we try to impose protocols on how we are to be named, they usually fail); but *these terms we never really choose are the occasion for something we might still call agency, the repetition of an imaginary subordination for another purpose, one whose future is partly open*" (Butler 1997, *Excitable,* 38, emphasis added). Butler's argument reminds us we work with the hand we are dealt. What looks like a sneer can turn into a tool.

At the scene of argument, everyone enters a dialogue already in progress. The practices and patterns that we inherit from the past are structured in dominance, working to the disadvantage of feminists and members of other aggrieved and oppositional groups. Yet if they are used in the right way, the insults, injuries, and exclusions of the past can reveal to us how power works and how social relations might be changed. Feminist socioforensic discursive analysis enables us to analyze and critique the names we are called and the words that are used to wound us. Feminist writings create new possibilities and help authorize new personalities, perspectives, and political positions.

The unglamorous, ordinary, tedious, and time-consuming labor of writing directs feminists toward new ways of knowing and enables us to see the work we want our work to do. There is never going to be an "end" to this.

It is easy to think that the "audience" of a feminist argument is a public of similar feminist readers. This is rarely the case. Feminist arguments appear in many different reception contexts. They confront deep fissures in the academic world and the broader society beyond it. They address important and volatile issues. They circulate through a broad range of intersectional publics, often through a series of echoes, misrepresentations, simplifications, and interpretations.

The terms by which we are hailed, the names we are called, the identities which we did not choose include the trope of the angry feminist. This trope and a familiar litany of similar antifeminist rhetorical moves emerged once again in the midst of the public controversy provoked by Harvard University President Lawrence Summers's remarks on women in the sciences in 2005. An economist who previously served as secretary of the Treasury during the last years of the Clinton administration, Summers delivered a lunchtime talk at a conference on "Diversifying the Science Work Force: The Movement of Women and Underrepresented Minorities into Science and Engineering Careers" sponsored by the National Bureau of Economic Research. The conference emerged in response to a long history of studies showing that widespread social, professional, and perhaps even personal practices among scientists and engineers function to impede the participation of talented women and minorities in these fields. Undesirable in themselves as manifestations of sexism and racism, these practices also violate one of the core principles of academic excellence: that researchers should be drawn from the broadest possible pool of talent. Summers used his lunchtime address to discredit the aims of the conference by presenting some personal ruminations about biology, gender socialization, and job discrimination: all areas in which he has done no research. Making no reference to the relevant work of the scientists in the room, Summers confided that he had once attempted to be nonsexist as a parent by giving his daughters trucks to play with, but he judged these efforts to have failed because the girls resorted to traditional gender roles by naming the two trucks "mommy" and "daddy." Summers presented these uncritical reflections about a nonverifiable event as possible proof that perhaps biology after all explains differences in social roles, that despite evidence to the contrary, women deprived themselves of careers in science because biological urges impelled them to be mommies because they do not want to work long hours. Summers suggested that perhaps many women just did not want to be scientists or engineers, and he opined that actual research on the issue might prove him to be correct. His comments were particularly shocking as a discredit to the purpose of the conference but were also disturbing given that during his tenure as president of Harvard, the proportion of women given tenure had dramatically lowered.

Like so many before him, Summers responded to evidence about gender discrimination with a fusion of popular punditry and quasi-intellectual bluster. Women scientists in his audience challenged Summers's views directly, referring to extensive research that disproved his speculations. They criticized his remarks as an embarrassing display of ignorance and prejudice by a university administrator whose job entailed making consequential decisions about the employment, promotion, and compensation of women and men. Yet after the meeting, journalists, pundits, bloggers, and letter writers condemned the feminists. In an orgy of vituperation, the antifeminists contended that feminist academics were angry, bitter, powerful, and dictatorial on the one hand but also fragile, emotional, and weak on the other. Once again, successful women had been invited to debate their right to exist, only to find themselves reviled and shamed for answering in the affirmative. Lauding Summers for speaking without fear, the antifeminists neglected to note that he also spoke without evidence. Summers's power as president of Harvard, as a former member of President Clinton's cabinet, and as a public figure with access to op-ed columns across the country disappeared as his defenders excused his prejudices while attacking his critics for allegedly persecuting him for simply voicing an honest opinion.

Most of the first seven related columns in the *Washington Post*, *New York Times*, and *Los Angeles Times* strongly defended Summers for one of two reasons (Wakeman and Hollar 2005). (1) His academic freedom. It was his "academic freedom" to speak, and, in a way "freedom of speech" is often represented, one's freedom is apparently absolute: if people disagree or object to your musings, they have eliminated that freedom. (2) He was correct that biological difference is a good explanation. It likely contributes to the dearth of female professors in science and math. What Summers called "the high-powered job hypothesis," "different availability of aptitude at the high end," and "different socialization and patterns of discrimination in a search" became not musings, or even hypotheses, but *truths* that the scientists in the room purportedly could not bear to hear because they were women. After about a month, more dissenting and women's voices were heard. Popular responses positioned the women as angry (Rush Limbaugh in his broadcast[1]) and hysterical (George Will in his column[2] and in his book[3]).

Women scientists and engineers appeared in Summers's speech and in the popular expressions of support for it that appeared on the pages of the

Wall Street Journal and other establishment venues as tropes, as foils for a joke, an oxymoron, and a farce. Their criticisms fueled charges that they were unfit to be scientists and engineers, that they wanted to restrict free inquiry, that they refused to acknowledge scientific evidence, that they could not bear to hear unpleasant truths, that they blamed others for their failures, and that they wanted special privileges and quotas (they were careerist).

The scientists were positioned by the trope of the angry feminist as actors in a travesty, as people whose grandiose narcissism led them to aspire to rewards greater than they deserved. In his discussion of the minstrel show, Nathan Irvin Huggins argues that travesty has often served to render social inequality as natural and inevitable. He explains,

> Travesty . . . turns on the disparity between the actor and his costume which thinly disguised pretense. The small girl with her face powdered and rouged, in the high heels, furs, and baubles of her mother; . . . To make travesty work, however, the disproportion must be obvious. No matter how she stretches and preens herself, it is impossible [end of 263] for the little girl to be her mother. Knowing that, the audience finds the pretense funny. (1971, 263–264)

Once the debate has been flagged as a travesty, subsequent arguments are intelligible only within that genre. Huggins argues that the creators of the minstrel shows knew that audiences needed no knowledge of the Roman classics to see the travesty of a black butler named Cicero or Caesar. Similarly, contemporary audiences do not need to know much about science to see the foolish imposture of the feminist scientists. The counterarguments of feminist scientists are interpreted as mere pretention, like the rotund oratory or malapropisms of the black-face actor. Feminist arguments are disabled before the argument begins; invented caricatures of "angry feminists" speak so loudly in antifeminist accounts that actual feminists cannot get a word in edgewise.

Yet the existence of a critical mass of women scientists and engineers assembled in one place capable and willing to refute sexist slurs and stereotypes reveals that feminism does not need to be approved of by its enemies in order to be effective. Antifeminist tropes gain traction in public debates so quickly in part because ridicule, contempt, and public shaming keep animus rather than analysis at the center of arguments dominated by people with vested interests in prevailing injustices and inequalities. Provoking women and fabricating controversies out of the women's responses serves as a useful distraction, a diversion from debating actual injustices and inequalities. It is also a crucible for creating a highly affective imaginary state of siege to mobilize defenders of male power on behalf of the hierarchical social order. Slavoj Žižek points to the political uses of stock characters or tropes: for example, when for a time the conservative media blamed British economic and social ills on the figure of the unemployed single mother, or when antiabortion campaigns present the typical recipient of abortion as a successful career woman selfishly neglecting her responsibility. Žižek argues that such misrepresentations are not incidental, but extremely important tactical lies in service of a larger project. "These poetic displacements and condensations," he writes, "are not just secondary illustrations of an underlying ideological struggle, but the very terrain of this struggle" (2005, 77).

Defending ourselves and other women against these attacks is necessary and useful, but it cannot consume the totality of our energies. As I argued in Chapter 1, feminist academic arguments need to focus attention on explanations, analyses, and arguments that reveal how gender functions as a social force, on exposing and critiquing the mechanisms of denial and disavowal that protect unequal power, and on generating new ways of knowing and new ways of being capable of creating a more just, decent, and honorable world. This work has to attend to the multiple, plural, intersectional, and contradictory dimensions of women's lives. Feminism cannot march under a single identity banner, tell its stories from only one point of view, or use only one methodology or theory. Every feminist argument negotiates a dialectical relationship between undeniable risks and undeniable possibilities, between affect and reason, between situated knowledge and social change. Any specific feminist academic argument inevitably participates in disciplinary debates while connecting "rhizomatically" to larger feminist debates. Its construction is, therefore, local and particular, yet also reflective of its broader goals. Toni Morrison once argued that part of the power of Toni Cade Bambara's writings was their focus on specific social objectives. To paraphrase her comment, as Avery Gordon does: "*It all depends on the work you want your work to do*" (A. Gordon 2004, 159, emphasis in original).

We can learn valuable lessons from what Juana María Rodríguez wants her work to do in her 2003 book *Queer Latinidad: Identity Practices, Discursive Spaces*. Rodríguez identifies links between lived experiences and feminist theory in generative sites that include the verbal and visual discourses of a San Francisco project for queer health, the reductive courtroom discourse of an appeal for asylum by a racialized Brazilian working-class gay man, the varied sites of "latinidad" and the complications of queer sexuality across Internet locations. Rodríguez frames her reading and writing practices across these sites as "rhizomatic," emphasizing connections among what might seem disparate trajectories, actions, and identities. She uses the metaphor of the rhizome to figure the multiplicity of identities in struggle:

> A rhizomatic reading of latinidad suggests the process through which contested constructions of identity work to constitute one another, emphasizing "and" over "is" as a way to think about differences. So latinidad is about the "dimensions" or the "directions of motion" of history and culture and geography and language and self-named entities. Even if individual narratives used to chart these discourses contradict or exclude one another, the site of rupture will itself serve as a new site. . . . The contradictions revealed in the various constructions of latinidad in fact provide the site of intervention . . . [and] can begin to be a source of new meanings. (2003, 22)

Rodríguez shows through her analyses that discourse, identity, and theory function differently according to setting. She uses the term *rhizome* to capture the notion of linkage and change in a way that may be productive for thinking about how feminist rhetorics emerge in different disciplinary and interdisciplinary contexts. Although the concept of the rhizome appears as part of the theoretical positions of Gilles Deleuze and Félix Guattari (1987) and has been deployed in feminist theory by Elizabeth Grosz (1993), Rodríguez argues that thinking "rhizomatically" also comes from the lived experience and activism of intersectional identities of women who cannot be subsumed under a singular sign—the woman, the feminist, the worker, the queer, the Latina. At Rodríguez's scene of argument, even these important identities hide that they are multiply and intersectionally constituted, that those who might or might not be members of "queer latinidad" speak different languages, have different sexual identities, come from different nations, and constantly have to renegotiate the lines that unite and divide them. Rodríguez's metaphor of the rhizome reveals the productive and generative nature of the dynamics of difference as well as the consequences of conflict. One of the things that Rodríguez shows, especially in her analysis of the group Proyecto ContraSIDA Por Vida, is that rhetorical choices can literally be matters of life and death. Rodríguez's work helps us see that part of the identity of academics comes from the social practices of which they are part: their disciplinarity, their interdisciplinarity, their subject matters, their ways of reading, writing, arguing. Rodríguez is an academic, but part of her identity comes from the imperiled community she comes from and to which she speaks. She draws on the insurrection of knowledges to make her work matter in more than one discursive arena.

Feminist argument plays out differently in different settings according to the exigencies of particular contexts and goals. Examining feminist rhetorics, claims, theories, and evidence in the light of this complex field of argument demonstrates the impossibility of defining what a "proper" feminist argument might be: To whom? In what setting? For what purpose?

Feminist arguments reproduce genetic features of previous feminism while adapting adventitiously to their own specific conditions. Thinking of feminist rhetoric in this way allows us to recognize the intertwined nature of rhetorics by interlocutors who speak both to specific controversies in their disciplines and to feminism in general. Sometimes they use feminist voices, but at other times they also deploy different voices, moving in and out of feminism in their specific claims and deployments of evidence. Feminist rhetorics are decentered, with diverse forms. Arguments, rhetorics, evidence, affects—all are shaped by their situations as well as their disciplinary or generic locations.

It is this very situated quality that gives feminist arguments their determinate features. They have multiple entry points, heterogeneous connections. They cluster around issues of emerging importance, then weaken or dissolve as they flow toward other points. Feminist rhetorics can be and must be different according to the demands at specific scenes of argument. Attempts to demand or impose one unified feminism operate at the expense of multiplicity and strength. Feminist arguments cannot return to their original "roots" because feminism works as a rhizome, not a tree. Rather than one big tree (to be pruned back or dug up), feminist arguments are everywhere, coming up through every argument. As they face different challenges, feminist arguments can be multi-, cross-, trans-, and interdisciplinary. They can be disciplinary, activist, or popular.

Feminist rhetorics require us to think carefully about the words we use, the metaphors we deploy, and the collectivities that we invoke. They can remind us that we do not generally control how our arguments are received— they exceed us, do more than we intend. Our deployment of affect is often an important part of our politics. Yet our deployment of affect is not in itself always justified, not always valuable politically and intellectually. Although valuable as a tool for political struggle, it can easily go astray. Robyn Wiegman demonstrates how affects of loss, mourning, and nostalgia have infused some feminist arguments destructively, framing intellectual ruptures across generations as discourtesies and argumentative multiplicity as bad manners (1999/2000, 2000, 2002, 2004).[4] These dynamics are understandable, but avoidable. Feminist analyses have demonstrated the danger of some of the metaphors we have used—sometimes with disclaimers—to frame debates at the scene of argument. Feminism has not been well served by its aspirations for unanimity and its neglect of the situated nature of scenes of argument. Metacommentary about the feminist movement as a totality seems especially susceptible to dangerous choices about figurative language. Metaphors of maternity and generations, for example, carry an enormous burden of cultural baggage; their ready use in the face of social pressures signals the need to rework our rhetorics rather than redeploying the very language that has hobbled women for so long. We are limited by feminist rhetorics that claim mothers must manipulate bad daughters; daughters must imitate or repudiate mothers; generations must bow under "psychic debts" to those of the past. All of these are used explicitly to limit and redirect lines of thought. Metaphors of movements and waves reify the people and moments of the past into unities, thereby hiding their sedimented histories of exclusions, sanctions, benefits, and energies. Their use in contemporary debates is often openly, explicitly, to preclude, to disparage, to shut down arguments. There is a lot of "disciplining" going on.

Respect for those who have worked in the past is sometimes misused to claim superior knowledge about the needs of the future, but also regrettably to foreclose arguments being made now. Inexperience and impatience may lead new recruits to feminism to devalue many lessons from the past. Circumstances can also structure respect as a zero-sum game: intent on verifying the value of past ideas, we can foreclose the present and future ideas of those who do not resemble us; intent on gaining respect for ourselves, we can block respect for others. Sure of the value of the feminism we have experienced, we sometimes cannot hear the voices of others, who are framing their own needs and desires for the future they live in too. The more dramatically worse social conditions become each day, the more we and they need to respond however we can, differently.

Everything that feminists have done, learned, and taught—the history of flexible and focused activism then and now—demonstrates that successes are a result of finding problems, reformulating specific goals, attending to new audiences, responding to new social conditions. The evidence of a myriad of historical, political, textual, theoretical analyses by feminist scholars demonstrates that while connection to past arguments is important, emerging futures present new problems requiring new thinking and new arguments. Each line of argument must be readied for the social and intellectual conditions of the future that will test them.

Wiegman argues that decisions about deploying affect in feminist arguments emerge from the "psychic life" of feminism, a psychic life that is not unitary or coherent, despite our desire for it to be so. Wiegman captures our need to recognize that feminist argument can and must work in multiple ways. She argues,

> There seems to me no coherent way to be in time with feminism. It is not reducible to its political function as a heuristic for making women exist in time, nor is its past fully comprehensible as the founding prehistory of our political or psychic present. This is partly because feminism's historical, theoretical, political, and epistemological dimensions do not operate together in the same sphere of articulation and hence do not cohere as a singular (or even collectivized) discourse, a knowable set of commitments, a historical origin, or an agenda of political acts and obligations—no matter how desperate we are for feminism to offer us the means to manage the incommensurable and the inexplicable, to overturn pain and indifference, to move us beyond the agony of our own unknowing. (2004, 164)

Wiegman argues that we cannot spend all our time trying to create more precise definitions of feminism. But the sites of debate she examines and similar arguments about what feminism "should be" reveal that sometimes feminists lose sight of the inescapably plural and diverse nature of feminist argument, its moves and reshapings into semiautonomous arenas. We are not well-served by a search for transhistorical and transsocial unified feminism; we cannot and should not attempt to will a universal feminism into existence merely through emphatic affirmation. But we can learn a great deal about the things that divide us and that might sporadically and strategically unite us by looking to the scene of argument and seeing how agency emerges there in the context of what we must contest. The labor of writing academic texts confines us in many ways, but it also frees us to turn our enemies into unwitting accomplices of our own emancipation by linking the labor of writing to the insurrection of subjugated knowledges.

I want to illustrate the possibilities of situated knowledge and the promise of agonistic argument by reference to what I think most readers will consider to be a most unlikely place, a scene in the 1992 motion picture *My Cousin Vinnie.* In the film, Marisa Tomei plays Mona Lisa Vito, an unemployed hair stylist from New York who unexpectedly finds herself called upon to testify in an Alabama courtroom. Nearly every aspect of Vito's character and appearance marks her as deficient by Hollywood standards. She is brash and bold, speaks with a thick Brooklyn accent, chews gum while she talks, wears dresses that are gaudy and too tight, walks with a pronounced wiggle, and appears unable to control her temper and emotions. She is white but Italian, from New York but working class, has a beautiful face and figure but has mannerisms that mark her as inadequately socialized into femininity. She has worked as a mechanic in her family's garage, a work history that in popular motion picture logic marks her as unfeminine. The film makers tap into widespread regional, class, and ethnic prejudices to portray her as an object of ridicule and derision.

Through an elaborate and largely implausible chain of cinematic plot devices, Mona Lisa Vito's boyfriend takes on the role of a defense attorney in an Alabama courtroom in order to rescue a relative on trial for murder and armed robbery. The trial hinges on the correct identification of the vehicle used by the robbers. The defense attorney calls Mona Lisa Vito to the stand as an expert witness on automotive knowledge. Although we have previously seen her glean legal information valuable to the defense from reading a highly specialized legal manual, the scene seems headed toward her humiliation on the witness stand under questioning by the prosecuting attorney.

Yet once she starts to testify, Vito shows herself to possess valuable knowledge. Her experience as a mechanic enables her to answer when the prosecuting attorney asks her what seems like a difficult technical question about what should be the correct ignition timing on a 1955 Bel Air Chevrolet with a 327-cubic-inch engine and a four-barrel carburetor. When she says she cannot answer the question, it appears as if she has been exposed as inadequate. Yet she argues that it is the question that is inadequate: it is a trick question. She cannot answer the question—and no one can answer the question—because its premises are wrong: Chevrolet did not make a 327-cubic-inch engine in 1955; the 327 did not appear until 1962; it did not appear in the Bel Air with a four-barrel carburetor until 1964. She then concludes triumphantly, "In 1964 the correct timing would be four degrees before top dead center."

Vito's rapid-fire delivery of technical terms establishes her expertise, but in a humorous way because her words still seem incongruous given her dress, demeanor, and speech. Yet she saves the day. Confronted with a photo of the skid marks made by the getaway vehicle, she explains that those marks could not have been made by the defendants' 1964 Skylark because their vehicle did not have positraction—the limited slip differential that allocates power equally to both right and left tires. She goes on to explain that the marks had to have been made by a 1963 Pontiac Tempest, which indeed turns out to be the getaway vehicle, implicating other perpetrators and absolving the defendants. At the end of her testimony, her attorney boyfriend Vinny Gambini (played by Joe Pesci) restores her to femininity by taking her hand and kissing it, saying, "You've been a lovely, lovely witness," as she smiles triumphantly, proudly, and coquettishly.

This scene in *My Cousin Vinny* succeeds as comedy, because in this case, the travesty that seems humorous leads to a reversal of the spectators' derision. Like the laughter provoked by a little girl wearing her mother's high-heeled shoes, Mona Lisa Vito's assumption of the role of an automotive expert with advanced knowledge contrasts radically with her appearance as a stereotypically unsophisticated working-class woman. But the very class position at the root of her devaluation turns out to hold the key to her emergence as a respected expert who is listened to and whose testimony wins approval and validation in court. The object of ridicule becomes the source of heroic action because she turns hegemony on its head. Foucault calls the kind of knowledge that this character in *My Cousin Vinny* displays subjugated knowledge. Subjugated knowledge is knowledge that has been dismissed and disqualified as nonconceptual, naïve, insufficiently elaborated, and "below the required level of erudition and scientificity" (2003, 7). The climactic scene in *My Cousin Vinny* taps utopian hopes that devalued people and their disqualified knowledges can solve problems and win recognition from their enemies because of it.

Off screen in real life, however, the insurrection of subjugated knowledges does not proceed so simply or easily. Linda Williams notes that courtroom scenes play a central role in melodrama because they tap into the fantasy that, in a trial, truth gets determined, wrongs get righted, and justice triumphs once and for all (2002, 264). In actual political and intellectual struggle, however, there are few once-and-for-all victories. Each moment of struggle paves the way for new possibilities, while the patterns and practices of the past never disappear. They simply become redeployed dialogically under new circumstances. The battles of the past have to be fought over and over again, albeit under new labels, terms, and conditions.

In this book, I have tried to show how feminist rhetorical analysis can help us be prepared for the future. By studying the practices, devices, figures, strategies, victories, and defeats of one distinct historical period, we learn how feminists fight on multiple fronts, how they struggle in the arenas open to them under historically specific conditions, and how a rhizomatic understanding of feminism enables us to move beyond linear narratives of progress and limited metaphors about roots, trees, and branches.

At the scene of argument, feminists confront words, categories, theories, methods, ideas, and arguments that have been structured in dominance by centuries of sexism. They enter a dialogue already in progress that places innumerable obstacles and impediments in their path. In a world where rhetoric helps to construct the realities it purports to describe, sites of argument and analysis inevitably become sites of feminist struggle. Feminists face discursive policing on many fronts. Pundits and scholars circulate seemingly endless bon mots and bromides that depict feminists as innately angry and irrational. Academic interlocutors deploy ideologies of style and charges of incivility to evade principled engagement with feminist ideas and arguments. Tough Babies wink and smirk while wallowing in wounded self-pity rather than confronting the complex claims and epistemological innovations advanced by their feminist opponents. Faux feminists resort to rhetorics of betrayal to discredit real feminists, blaming them for the absence of the ideal "agreeable feminism" that they seem certain would appear if only bad girls would stop making men nervous. Discursive policing works to protect gendered privileges inside disciplines, to warn feminists against challenging normative social roles and identities, to insulate feminism from broader movements for social justice, and to isolate feminists from their own best intellectual traditions, imaginaries, archives, epistemologies, and ontologies inside and outside the academy.

Feminist rhetoric takes place inside historical time, at discrete moments and conjunctures. Patricia Williams and Dorothy Roberts developed their arguments about Black women's rights in public and private spheres at a specific historical moment. They confronted a reactionary racist and sexist counterrevolution against the egalitarian social movements of the mid-twentieth century. Yet their ideas and arguments also spoke to longer historical frames, to discourses that have demeaned and demonized Black women for centuries but also to the tradition of critique and resistance that Black women have created in response. The anxious yet aggressive attitudes, ideas, and arguments advanced by Dr. Laura, Joseph Epstein, Jeffrey Hart, Lawrence Mead, Robert Craft, Eric Gans, Pieter van den Toorn, Leo Treitler, Paula Higgins, and Lawrence Summers also emerged from both proximate and distant historical contexts. They echoed the reactionary rhetorics dominant in journalism, politics, and academia in the post-Reagan era of hostile privatism and defensive localism in the United States, but they resonated as well with longer histories of intellectual work based on creating a normative center through expressions of countersubversive hysteria against allegedly nonnormative and transgressive "others."

Susan McClary's innovative and brilliant interventions in musicology during the 1980s and 1990s generated harsh reactions in part because challenges to dominant gender regimes played such a central role in the social, cultural, and political ferment of those years everywhere. McClary's work also drew such fervid responses because the disciplinary history of musicology kept it relatively isolated from broader intellectual currents in the humanities than was true of other disciplines. Yet McClary's bold and brave work not only advanced contemporaneous feminist ideas and arguments, it also challenged gender codes that had become deeply ingrained in Western art and music for centuries. The challenges to discourses about domestic violence and sexual abuse by Cynthia Gillespie and Julia Penelope and the critique of outdated sexist metaphorical stories in science by Emily Martin, the Biology and Gender Study Group, and Ruth Herschberger also spoke to contemporary controversies at their moment of publication as well as to longstanding practices and processes of engendering law and science.

Conflict can be unpleasant, but it can also be generative and productive. As Judith Butler argues, the abjected voice their claims through and against the discourses that attempt to repudiate them. Feminist socioforensic discursive analysis examines anger and other forms of affect as tools and tactics that can be deployed critically and strategically within argumentative contexts infused with power. Rhetorical choices by feminists and their opponents do not just reflect the gendered nature of unequal dignity, power, recognition and reward; they also constitute and contest it. Cynthia Gillespie shows how dominant discourses work to erase women's actual experiences with domestic violence and to nullify their judgments about how and when to defend themselves from it. Julia Penelope identifies how absences, elisions, and suppressions in ordinary and everyday discourses about incest and sexual abuse enable perpetrators to escape responsibility and deny dignity to their victims. Emily Martin turns the hegemony of sexist language about menstruation and menopause on its head by intensifying, echoing, and amplifying word choices that reveal misogynist anxiety, dread, and disgust. Martin, the Biology and Gender Study Group, and Ruth Herschberger deploy humor and ridicule to expose how inaccurate folk models grounded in crude sexist stereotypes permeate medical textbooks, how seemingly objective scientific stories rely on heroic and romantic metaphors that emanate from patriarchal culture rather than from the findings of scientific researchers.

Feminist rhetorics are multilayered, dynamic, flexible, and relentless. They do not seek to validate one single writing style, establish one school of thought, or continue one heroic lineage. Consistent with the uneven and intersectional nature of gendered power, however, they do attempt the difficult task that Carolyn Dever defines as building "a form of authoritative discourse whose own authoritative implications must be undone as a function of its political critique" (Dever, 2004). Feminist rhetorics proceed from the premise that rhetorical choices have political causes and consequences. They exist in history and respond to historical crises and contradictions, yet they also emerge from the intersections of many different histories all at the same time. They speak from and to social identities and embodied experiences, yet refuse to be rooted in them. They may be useful to you. *It all depends on the work you want your work to do.*

Notes

CHAPTER ONE

1. I link the trope of the angry feminist with other social resources designed to render feminism politically illegitimate. In a complex argument that draws on Judith Butler's theorizing of melancholy based on unacknowledged loss (Butler 1997 *Psychic*), Angela McRobbie argues that young women in contemporary political and popular culture experience a culturally "unintelligible rage" based on unacknowledged loss—the loss of the possibilities of feminism. They are asked to "reconcile autonomy and the possibility of achievement with compliancy with a patriarchal order which is dissolved, de-centralized, and nowhere to be seen" (2009, 122). The critique previously offered by feminism is made opaque by its reframing. "Repudiated and vilified in dominant political culture, despite having gained degrees of effectivity (in legislation and gender awareness) its only existence for a younger generation of women today is as unavowable loss. The State, media and popular culture converge in the production of female melancholia and unintelligible rage to pre-empt the re-invention of feminist politics through a wide range of individualizing strategies and techniques of the self . . ." (2009, 118–119). McRobbie argues that stereotypical framing of a mythological feminism creates repulsion in young women and leaves them without resources to analyze the sexism structured into their lives.

2. It would be useful to think of the definition of *trope* in the sense that it is used on the Web site "TV Tropes Home Page." "Tropes are devices and conventions that a writer can reasonably rely on as being present in the audience members' minds and expectations. . . . In storytelling, a trope is just that—a conceptual figure of speech, a storytelling shorthand for a concept that the audience will recognize and understand instantly. Those familiar with Stylistics might know of Roland Barthes' Codes'—it's the same idea here. . . . According to the Codes theory, a Code/Trope is an attempt to

'give meaning to what would otherwise be a series of happenings'" (http://tvtropes
.org/pmwiki/pmwiki.php/Main/HomePage).

3. My arguments here draw on Michel Foucault's theories of power, which I argue
to be particularly suitable in analyzing these discursive debates. Rather than thinking
of power as something unitary from above, used by dominant groups to impose on
others, Foucault positions power as a mobile part of *every* relation. He argues that
power is not a "thing" that one can have or not have; rather, it is always being exercised
from all points in any relation. Dominant power is one manifestation of power, but
silence, subservience, or satire can be seen as different manifestations of power, rather
than being seen as without power. "Resistance" is not external to a power relationship,
but part of it; not a stable opposition to power, but dynamic and fluid. To position
power this way allows us to see that the trope of the angry feminist is part of an apparatus of discursive power that is always fractured, mobile, being reshaped. It also
allows us to see that feminist and other discourses that "resist" or "oppose" power are
not sealed off from power, but also participate in fields of power. Nor are feminist
discourses unitary. In this view, there is rationality and logic behind power relationships, but they are not directed and controlled by specific individuals or groups. Rather,
they operate through *strategies* that both exercise power and offer opportunities for
countering it. (See Foucault 1980 History.)

4. Feminist socioforensic discursive analysis draws on theories of power, ideology,
discourse, language, and rhetoric of theorists such as Louis Althusser (1971), Nancy
Armstrong (1994, 2004), Judith Butler (1990, 1993, 1997 *Excitable*, 1997 *Psychic*,
2009), Jacques Derrida (1978), Michel Foucault (1980 *History*, 1980 Power, 2003),
Ranajit Guha (1988), George Lakoff and Mark Johnson (1980, Lakoff 1986), Seth
Moglen (2005), Michael Warner (2002), Raymond Williams (1976, 1977), as well as
recent theoretical work on affect by scholars such as Sara Ahmed (2004), Lauren Berlant (1997, 2001, 2004), Ann L. Cvetkovich (2003), Avery Gordon (2008), José Esteban Muñoz (2006), Jasbir K. Puar (2007), Eve Kosofsky Sedgwick (2003), Elizabeth
V. Spelman (1997), Imogen Tyler (2005, 2009), and Kathleen Woodward (1996, 2002,
2009). It connects these theoretical insights to the tools available for close examination of specific argumentative moves that have been developed by rhetoricians and
critical discourse theorists such as Anne Cranny-Francis, Wendy Waring, Pam Stavropoulos, and Joan Kirby (2003), Sharon Crowley (2006), Norman Fairclough (2003),
Gunther Kress (1985) and Sara Mills (1995, 2003, 2004, 2008).

5. There is abundant evidence of the systematic development of corporate conservative apparatuses to front right-wing argument and suppress social alternatives such as
feminism. Two useful sources are Linda Kintz (2002) and Ellen Messer-Davidow
(2002). Linda Kintz (2002) argues that the "think tanks" that most journalists turn to
for comments on economic and social issues are funded specifically for conservative
positions. She indicates, "Richard Mellon Scaife is a billionaire philanthropist of central importance to contemporary conservatism, beginning with Goldwater's defeat in
1964, when Scaife began helping fund the creation of the modern conservative movement in the US. He and his family have given $1.4 billion to conservative causes, estab-
lishing activist think tanks such as the Heritage Foundation, the Hoover Institution,
the Center for Strategic and International Studies, and the American Enterprise Institute, four of the most influential think tanks in the US, which provide financial sup-

port for conservative writers" (764, n. 10). "The Heritage Foundation, founded by one of the leading forces of the Christian right, Paul Weyrich, [was] allowed to conduct the initiation sessions for the 1994 newly elected members of the House of Representatives" (764, n. 8).

Messer-Davidow (2002) delineates how institutional and political structures that promoted antifeminism during the 1980s and 1990s came to fruition in recent years. Activities portrayed as conservative grassroots mobilizations were the result of conservative think tanks and legal foundations expending large sums of money to make antifeminism the official policy of society, the state, and the academy. For example, opposition to the Equal Rights Amendment led by Phyllis Schlafly's Eagle Forum and the political mobilizations on behalf of the Republican Party by Jerry Falwell, Pat Robertson, and other clergymen attempted to make the New Right seem like a grassroots movement. But Messer-Davidow's research found that funding for such New Right movements came, rather, from foundations supported by some of the wealthiest and most powerful individuals and corporations in the nation. They paid nearly $170 million between 1992 and 1994 alone to conservative academic programs, journals, organizations, think tanks, public relations campaigns, and interest-advocacy organizations. Messer-Davidow notes that private foundations gave $77 million to five conservative institutes and programs in 1995, dwarfing the $16.6 million available to progressive institutes, none of which were feminist and very few of which gave any money to academics (2002, 222). What presented itself as spontaneous and voluntary activism from the bottom up was really a synthetic product, not so much grassroots as it was Astroturf.

Messer-Davidow argues that the revanchist backlash against the egalitarian social movements of the 1960s furthered that social agenda by taking special aim at feminism and feminists as subversive, unreasonable, indecent, and perverse. Messer-Davidow argues that these attacks on feminists and feminism served strategic purposes for a broader social agenda. Just as the anticommunist red-baiting of the 1950s was not aimed exclusively at actual communists but also attempted to depict the egalitarian and democratic reforms of the New Deal era as innately subversive, antifeminism in the Reagan-Bush-Clinton years aimed to portray the achievements of the democratic and egalitarian social movements of the 1960s and 1970s as perverse and unnatural. Because gender is inscribed on the body, because sexual fears and taboos provoke primal responses, and because gendered critiques of inequality and injustice played such important roles in dethroning the normative hierarchies of the 1940s and 1950s, attacks on feminism played a primary part in the right-wing counterrevolution of the 1980s and 1990s.

Messer-Davidow also presents an important study of the different challenges faced by academic women in physics, literature, and sociology in this era. Focusing on the philosophies, truth tests, and grand theories of the disciplines, she shows how the legacies of formalism in literary studies, operationalism in physics, and scientization in sociology imposed obstacles to feminist work in those particular disciplines. Academic feminists entering the academy begin a process of change in the face of disciplinary exclusions enacted through grand pronouncements, uncritical and uninterrogated disciplinary conventions, and blind presumptions about the gender neutrality of methods, theories, and discourses imbued with male privilege.

6. The university's announcement of the new graduate program included a few pleasant remarks from the department chair and the dean, mentioning only a few details about the new program: its three emphases—race and nation, genders and sexualities, and productive and reproductive labors—and our plan to approach these areas from intersectional and transnational perspectives, with a focus on social justice and public policy.

7. Laura Schlessinger, "Save Us from Feminist Studies," *Santa Barbara News-Press*, October 9, 2008.

8. Laura Schlessinger, "More on Feminist Studies," *Santa Barbara News-Press*, October 12, 2008.

9. In a later blog, Schlessinger approves of what she claims to be a letter from a young woman who reports getting angry at her feminist professor (too much discussion of oppression), and connects the disagreement with her professor to her disappointment with her own feminist mother. According to the letter, the young woman says, "I truly believe feminists must be the most miserable people. They miss out on so much. My mother is a feminist, and she has never been happy. Thanks to you, Dr. Laura, I did not follow in her footsteps. . . . You were right when you told me the angrier the professor gets, the more 'right on' I am. She didn't care what [analysis] I provided" ("A Young Woman Does the Research on Feminist Theory," May 11, 2009, www.drlaurablog.com/).

10. Schlessinger has made this recommendation in at least two blogs within the last year. The grammatical form of the first blog indicates that feminists "go after" fetuses to kill them when they should instead "go after" the Taliban to kill them. She argues, "Feminists go after fetuses . . . let them instead go after the Taliban. I think it would make a huge statement and impact to have American women locked and loaded and protecting these young women who strive for the basic right to an education. If America's feminists would commit to such missions, I would respect and support them wholeheartedly" ("Feminists Should Go Where They Are Needed," November 25, 2008, www.drlaurablog.com/). The second blog implies that showing any respect for Iraqi cultural values with regard to women's bodies is the equivalent of "political correctness" (i.e., oversensitive). It once again positions feminists as in support of "murdering babies" and redirects them to murdering Muslims instead. She argues: "Women in Iraq wear the long black overgarments called *abayas*, and can avoid searches at checkpoints, because men are not allowed to search them, and there aren't enough female guards. This is an obvious 'PC' mistake—this is war, and such proprieties need to be put by the wayside, because people are being murdered. . . . I wish NOW (the National Organization for Women) would spend less time on rants assuring women that murdering the babies in their bodies is some kind of noble 'right,' and spend their time in the Middle East, protecting women from being used as cannon fodder" ("Where's NOW When You Really Need Them?" February 7, 2008, www.drlaurablog .com/).

11. Appeal to the emotions of the audience is one of three means of persuasion that characterize arguments created through words, according to the ancient Greek rhetorician Aristotle. An argument influences people's thinking partly through putting the audience into a certain a certain frame of mind (Aristotle calls this *pathos*). He

indicates, "Our judgments when we are pleased and friendly are not the same as when we are pained and hostile" (Aristotle 1984, 2155).

12. Appeal by the projection of the speaker's (apparent) character is another of Aristotle's means of persuasion; he terms it *ethos*. He says, "Persuasion is achieved by the speaker's personal character when the speech is so spoken as to make us think him credible [ethos]. . . . This kind of persuasion, like the others, should be achieved by what the speaker says, not by what people think of his character before he begins to speak." Aristotle argued that the chief components of a compelling ethos include good will, practical wisdom, and virtue. He says, "[There is persuasion] through character whenever the speech is spoken in such a way as to make the speaker worthy of credence; for we believe fair-minded people to greater extent and more quickly [than we do others] on all subjects in general and completely so in cases where there is not exact knowledge but room for doubt" (Aristotle 1984, 2155). See James S. Baumlin and Tita French Baumlin (1994) for discussions of ethos.

13. Recent years have not slowed the steady production of books and articles by those who wish to "inform" a larger public of the irrationality and excessive emotion of feminists (sometimes efficiently folding feminists in with other people of bad character). In recent years, for example: *Women Who Make the World Worse and How Their Radical Feminist Assault Is Ruining Our Schools, Families, Military, and Sports* (2005), by Kate O'Beirne, Washington editor of the *National Review*, former vice president of the Heritage Foundation, and former panelist on CNN's *Capital Gang*. Mike Adams, conservative Republican columnist and criminology professor at the University of North Carolina at Wilmington, includes feminist academics and students in his first book, *Welcome to the Ivory Tower of Babel: Confessions of a Conservative College Professor* (2004); in *Feminists Say the Darndest Things: A Politically Incorrect Professor Confronts "Womyn" on Campus* (2008), he indicates, "I want to find out why they hate us." Feminists are one of the targets in Jamie Glasov's *United in Hate: The Left's Romance with Tyranny and Terror* (2009). David Horowitz also includes feminist scholars on his Web site and in many books, including *Indoctrination U: The Left's War against Academic Freedom* (2009) and his book coauthored with Jacob Laksin, *One-Party Classroom: How Radical Professors at America's Top Colleges Indoctrinate Students and Undermine Our Democracy* (2009).

14. Like other strategies in the conservative "echo chamber"; see Kathleen Hall Jamieson and Joseph N. Cappella (2008).

15. This argument is based on Louis Althusser's theory of "interpellation," discussed by Sara Mills (1995). According to Althusser, discourses from a variety of social sources interpellate or "call out to us," "hailing" us as certain kinds of people. Some interpellations we consider as meant for us, others not. According to Mills, "There is an unending series of hailings, both direct and indirect, to which the reader responds or does not respond. Thus, although certain texts attempt to address themselves to the reader, she may be critical of them and may decide not to take them at face value. However . . . there are indirect effects of such interpellation. Even the hailings which are not intended for the reader, or which are intended for her and not received, nevertheless do have an effect on her" (1995, 68). Mills argues that the texts have ideological effects on readers whether they hail them in *direct* or *indirect* ways. Under the barrage

of hailings, the "dominant reading" is reinforced through its ideological intelligibility even if a reader resists it. She says, "Each text contains an ideological message which we accept (or reject) as true or obvious, and it is in this way that the reader is positioned by what I would like to class as the dominant reading. This is a seemingly coherent message which the text carries, and which the reader is supposed to find as 'obviously' what the text is about, even if s/he would like to disagree with or take issue with that message" (1995, 68–69).

16. Imogen Tyler, in her wonderful article "'Who Put the "Me" in Feminism?' The Sexual Politics of Narcissism" (2005), demonstrates that everyday public discourse repeatedly reframes contemporary feminists as narcissistic; she argues for a re-centering of narcissism as an important feminist *political* emotion.

17. We all need frameworks to account for the world, and we do not invent these independently. Instead, *our society provides us* with frameworks in terms of overarching organized structures of ideas and systematic ways for accounting for people's actions and behaviors without examining separately each thing we see. The way we are provided these frameworks is through various kinds of discourses. *Ideology* is one term we use for such frameworks. *Ideology* is a slightly pejorative term. One reason is that many people do not like to be accused of accepting a set of ideas from their society—they feel that to say so implies that they are not "independent thinkers," who examine all ideas carefully from a particular self-created point of view. This position is the result of an ideological position that characterizes American society, one that suggests that we need to be independent and free-thinking. One might say we have an ideology that values not having an ideology. In everyday discussion, the use of "ideology" tends to prefigure that the argument rests on a contrast: independent, critical, knowing people (like the author and readers) will be contrasted to political opponents whose positions are invalid (like the feminist). For historical and other reasons, "ideology" is usually used to frame the thinking of those, like feminists, who criticize hierarchical social arrangements. The term allows all such political opponents to be folded in together and treated as one; it also endorses bypassing discussion of any specific arguments in favor of disparaging persons.

18. In such discussions, *dogma* is the established belief or doctrine held by an organization, a religion, or an ideology. Its use in everyday arguments where the trope of the angry feminist appears is similar to *ideology* but emphasizes the notion that the dogma is considered all important and authoritative and cannot be disputed or doubted. *Orthodoxy* is used similarly to imply that all feminists unthinkingly obey and will not diverge from the tenets of an almost "religious" faith. The feminist's investment in considering gender as an analytic category is thus framed as a fault. The feminist can demonstrate her ability to think independently only by following the dictates of the Angry Troper and eschewing the use of gender as an analytic category. Interestingly—perhaps ironically—the feminist can demonstrate her ability to think only by not being a feminist.

19. Hart has structured claims that are more far-reaching than they might first seem. They draw on the notion that feminists are *unable* to use Aristotle's third means of persuasion through words, *logos*. While the term invokes the notion of "logic," it is not quite the same. According to Aristotle, this method operates when "persuasion is effected through the speech itself when we have proved a truth or an apparent truth

by means of the persuasive arguments suitable to the case in question" (Aristotle 1984, 2155). But reason involves using all the means of persuasion in reasoning together with others to reach decisions. By positioning feminists as "outside the economy of reason," he argues that they can only be excluded from a shared world.

20. Anne Cranny-Francis and her coauthors Wendy Waring, Pam Stavropoulos, and Joan Kirby have a useful discussion of how binaries inhibit our traditional ways of thinking about *difference*. Because binaries fold disparity into in each term, they create singularity by eliding difference. To combat the effects of overreliance on binary thinking, critics suggest a range of potentially productive strategies. Helene Cixous (1980), for example, wants to expose and emphasize the hierarchical nature of the binary. Others want to revalorize the disfavored term, shifting it to the privileged position. Audre Lorde (1984) wants to explicitly recognize the dissimilarities, distinctions, and particularities of the people and groups lumped together into the disfavored secondary term of the binary. According to Cranny-Francis et al., Lorde's politics of difference "demands relational, rather than oppositional, thinking. By placing the secondary term of the binary at the heart of the dominant term, this relational thinking deconstructs not only the power relation in which the terms are engaged, but also the meaning of each term—the dominant term (why is it defined in certain ways?), but also the absent secondary term (who does this term refer to? how is it related to their actual conditions of being?)" (2003, especially 59–60).

21. Epstein, now Lecturer Emeritus of English at Northwestern University, served almost a quarter of a century as editor of the *American Scholar*, the magazine of Phi Beta Kappa, contributing to it and other magazines his musings on a variety of topics.

22. Epstein claims, "What came to be known as 'gender studies' were on their way, and would get goofier and goofier with the passage of time, though doubtless my view of the matter is, as the academic feminists would put it, 'phallocentric.' . . . Everywhere one encountered papers, courses, conferences devoted to gender, class, and race. 'Gender, class, and race,' announced a wag (me actually), 'gender, class, and race, stop your blubbering and wash your face' " (1991, 17). Oversensitive: "Touchy, touchy, touchy. The least miscue and they book you for sexism, racism, homophobia, sexual harassment" (13). Powerful: "God pity the poor professor about whom the word goes round among graduate students that he is insufficiently (shall we say) attuned to feminism or any of the other O.K. isms" (21).

23. See, for example, the material presented in John K. Wilson (1995).

24. This paragraph is built on the productive and accessible arguments of Anne Cranny-Francis and her coauthors in their chapter "Ways of Reading" (2003, 89–138) as well as their use of Gunther Kress (1985).

25. Robinson makes this argument in the preface to *Forgeries of Memory and Meaning* in discussing racial regimes. I am not equating race with gender, but I argue that Robinson's arguments on racial regimes have generative power for understanding how contemporary power suppresses discussion of gender and justice. According to Robinson, "Racial regimes are constructed social systems in which race is proposed as a justification for the relations of power. While necessarily articulated with accruals of power, the covering conceit of a racial regime is a makeshift patchwork masquerading as memory and the immutable. Nevertheless, racial regimes do possess history, that is,

discernable origins and mechanisms of assembly. But racial regimes are unrelentingly hostile to their exhibition" (2007, xii).

26. Schlessinger, for example, provides a letter apparently from a young woman who enthusiastically identifies with "Dr. Laura" as a model, repudiating her feminist professor (obsessed with "oppression") and her feminist mother (unhappy). Hart offers, in contrast to Heilbrun, the ideal of a citizen as "a person who, if need be, can create his civilization" (2001, ix) by immersing himself in the most important books and works of Western thought and feeling.

27. Women as a group and feminists as a group have some kinds of class and racialized power, as do individuals. But they operate in a discursive arena that disables them—as it disables other groups—in arguing for social equity. Laura Mulvey argues, "It cannot be easy to move from oppression and its mythologies to resistance in history; a detour through a no-man's land or threshold area of counter-myth and symbolization is necessary" (1987, 11).

28. Robinson also reminds us, "We are not the subjects or the subject formations of the capitalist world-system. It is merely one condition of our existence" (1996, 122, quoted in Avery Gordon 2004, 202). Or, as poet Roberta Hill writes, "their fear of the dark is not my identity" (1996, "Preguntas," 91).

29. *Socioforensic* signals the centrality of systematic inquiry and evidence in crafting responsible claims about textual affect. *Socioforensic* is devised from the term *forensic,* defined as "relating to, used in, or appropriate for courts of law." This definition appears to the most prominent meaning of the term and the one I am trying to evoke and stretch. *Forensic* is also defined as "relating to, used in, or appropriate for public discussion or argumentation." I argue that the climate of contempt attempts to establish different standards for those who are aligned with social power and those who are not. What is "appropriate" for public discussion is part of what is at stake in my analysis. I append the prefix *socio* to emphasize that individual texts are occasions to consider issues of social and political power.

30. *Rhetoric* is also defined as embellishment of texts and textual flourishes. This use authorizes a notion of "mere rhetoric" used to dismiss various claims. Two uses are particularly common. The first implies that some arguments (say, scientific arguments) are packaged without any notion of persuasion. But this is a limited view of both science and argument: scientific arguments are intended to persuade their readers of a variety of issues, to marshal evidence, to establish what counts as "facts," to win allies. Richard Bauman and Charles L. Briggs (2003) examine the history of theories of language that authorize the position that science can be free of rhetoric. Many scholars demonstrate the use of rhetoric in scientific arguments, including Charles Bazerman (1988), Leah Ceccarelli (2001), Jeanne Fahnestock (2003), Alan G. Gross (1990, 2006), and Bruno Latour (1987). The second use contrasts "rhetoric" versus something like "plain speaking." This is a frame that positions rhetoric as dishonest and the language of the "plain speaker" as honest. It is, therefore, a textual device intended to persuade, i.e., rhetoric. Finally, there is also a misleading but common use of "rhetoric" for contrast to other things considered more significant, usually "reality": "rhetoric and reality," "rhetoric or reality," "rhetoric versus reality," "rhetoric meets reality," "rhetoric to reality" (from book titles and subtitles listed at amazon.com, June 2009). The frequent use of the contrast implies that rhetoric is not real and reality is

not rhetoric. The line of argument I am working in does not suggest that "reality" is not "real," but that the invocation of "reality" is always discursive, always rhetorical, and that most of what we apprehend as "real" is understood through discourse and rhetoric. In consequence, that discourse can be criticized.

31. My claims about the nature and use of "conventional reading practices" are grounded in scholarly investigation but also on experience with what may be an unusually intensive and extensive submersion in conventional practices as the director of UC San Diego's Muir College Writing Program. The program emphasized teaching rhetorical and argument analysis. In the twenty-five years of my service there, I supervised a total enrollment of nearly 36,000, observing numerous classes, reading thousands of papers and evaluations, talking to numerous instructors about what their students did and said while approaching argumentative texts. My development of the strategies of feminist socioforensic discursive analysis emerged from many years of working with the instructors of that program, and I owe them thanks for years of thinking with me about what it means to think, read, analyze, and write. My use of "conventional reading practices" includes the typical practices used by undergraduate college students but also by graduate students and the general public. As I demonstrate in several chapters of this book, these practices demonstrate themselves also in scholarly work. My experience at UC San Diego also illustrates that those trained in specialized academic discourses may revert to conventional reading practices when they deliberate as members of committees, a caution to us all.

32. I argue that the practices of judging arguments according to "conventional practices of reading" appear similar to the practices of "criticism" that Raymond Williams describes in *Keywords* 1976). Williams's discussion of "criticism" appears to focus on reception of literature and art. He argues that the early sense of "criticism" as fault-finding has become the predominant meaning. "But what is significant in the development of **criticism**, and of **critic** and **critical**, is the assumption of judgment as the predominant and even natural response. . . . **criticism** in its most general sense developed toward *censure*." (85). Social developments concerned with isolating and refining personal impressions and responses lead to their being represented as "standards of judgment." The methods for establishing these standards may have changed, Williams argues, but the assumptions have not. "What has not been questioned is the assumption of 'authoritative judgment.' . . . What is at issue is not only the association between **criticism** and fault-finding but the more basic association between **criticism** and 'authoritative' judgment as apparently general and natural processes. As a term for the social or professional generalization of the processes of reception . . . **criticism** becomes ideological not only when it assumes the position of the *consumer* but also when it masks this position by a succession of abstractions of its real terms of response (as . . . .disinterested, qualified, rigorous, and so on)" (86). Williams argues that not the term but the habit should be abandoned: "The point would then be . . . to get rid of the habit, which depends, fundamentally, on the abstraction of response from its real situation and circumstances: the elevation to 'judgment', and to an apparently general process, when what always needs to be understood is the specificity of the response, which is not an abstract 'judgment' but even where including, as often necessarily, positive or negative responses, a definite practice, in active and complex relations with its whole situation and context" (1976, 86, emphasis in original).

33. Of course, I am not equating the brutal suppression of impoverished peasants with discursive denigration of feminist academics, but the code of pacification that Guha describes provides a valuable way of thinking about language and power. It is not that peasants state their case and lose the argument in historical accounts of peasant rebellions, Guha explains, but rather that the conventions of academic argument and discourse preclude their entering the debate. I thank Jordan Camp for calling my attention to Guha's formulation.

34. Michael Warner argues, "The making of a public requires conditions that range from the very general—such as the organization of media, ideologies of reading, institutions of circulation, text genres—to the particular rhetoric of texts. . . . [T]he nature and relationship of the parties involved in the game are conditions established, metapragmatically, by the very notion of a public or by the medium through which a public comes into being. . . . Publics are essentially intertextual, frameworks for under-standing texts against an organized background of other texts, all interwoven not just by citational references but by the incorporation of a reflexive circulatory field in the mode of address and consumption" (2002, 14, 16).

35. My attention was drawn to this passage when it was quoted by Karen New-man (1991, 30).

CHAPTER TWO

1. Genevieve Lloyd, for example, argues: "Knowledge is a fiercely contested site in modern societies. Questions of who possesses it—of who is entitled to claim the genuine article—elicit strong emotions. The intensity generated by issues of evidence, of authority, and of expertise reflects a way of thinking about knowledge which has become so familiar that it is difficult to see alternatives" (2005, 195).

2. Patricia J. Williams is James L. Dohr Professor of Law at Columbia University. She earned a B.A. from Wellesley College and a J.D. from Harvard Law School. She was previously Associate Professor at the University of Wisconsin Law School and its Department of Women's Studies and a visiting professor of Women's Studies at Harvard University. She has published widely on race, gender, and the law, including the *Alchemy of Race and Rights: Diary of a Law Professor* (Cambridge, MA: Harvard U P, 1991), *The Rooster's Egg* (Cambridge, MA: Harvard U P, 1995), and *Seeing a Color-Blind Future: The Paradox of Race* (The Reith Lectures, 1997) (New York: Noonday, 1998). She was named a MacArthur Fellow in 2000.

3. Dorothy E. Roberts is Kirkland and Ellis Professor of Law at Northwestern University with a joint appointment as a faculty fellow at the Institute for Policy Re-search. She earned a B.A. magna cum laude from Yale University and a J.D. from Harvard University. She is author of numerous books, chapters, and articles in law reviews and policy journals on issues related to race, gender, and the law, including *Shattered Bonds: The Color of Child Welfare* (New York: Basic Books/Civitas, 2001) and *Killing the Black Body: Race, Reproduction, and the Meaning of Liberty* (New York: Pantheon, 1997).

4. Lawrence M. Mead III is Professor of Politics at New York University. He earned a B.A. from Amherst College and an M.A. and Ph.D. in Political Science at Harvard. He is author of numerous books, chapters, and articles on antipoverty and

welfare policy, especially in policy journals, including *Beyond Entitlement: The Social Obligations of Citizenship* (New York: Free Press, 2001) and *Government Matters: Welfare Reform in Wisconsin* (Princeton: Princeton U P, 2004). His Web site states that he became "the leading theorist of welfare reform here and abroad" (http://politics.as.nyu .edu/object/LawrenceMMead.html, accessed June 24, 2009). Mead has been singled out for special financial support from a variety of right-wing foundations, particularly the John M. Olin, Jr., Foundation.

5. I owe much of my thinking about the nature of dominant discourses in this section to the arguments of Richard Terdiman in *Discourse/Counter-Discourse: The Theory and Practice of Symbolic Resistance in Nineteenth-Century France* (1985). Terdiman points out that dominant discourses can never obliterate counterdiscourses. He argues, "In our time, dominant forms of discourse have achieved unprecedented degrees of penetration. . . . But at the same time, in intimate connection with the power of such an apparatus, discourses of resistance ceaselessly interrupt what would otherwise be the seamless serenity of the dominant, its obliviousness to any contestation. For at every level at which the discourse of power determines dominant forms of speaking and thinking, counter-dominant strains challenge and subvert the appearance of inevitability [end of 39] which is ideology's primary mechanism for sustaining its own self-reproduction" (39–40).

6. Terdiman emphasizes that dominant discourses are not a unity: "We must not be taken in by the rhetorical abbreviation in the phrase 'dominant discourse.' The moving and flowing network of practices and assumptions by which, at any series of endlessly divisible moments, social life is structured ought not be abstractly reified. . . . [D]ominant discourse is not a 'thing' but a complex and shifting formation. It is as diffuse as a way of feeling, of experiencing the body, of perceiving sensorially, of living work and leisure, of assimilating information, of communicating with others in the social world, of comprehending the organization of conflict, of experiencing the inevitable hierarchizations of social existence" (1985, 57).

7. Critics charge that such a liberal citizen-subject "is founded on faulty extrapolations by men from their misrecognition of themselves, their needs, and their histories, in a way that denies that anyone is outside the discourse of citizenship" (Miller 1993, 4).

8. According to Toby Miller, "There will always be a master command in the discourse of citizenship, that where we are constitutionally equal, we can suffer other forms of inequality with equilibrium, because in the ultimate court of personage, we are identical. The means of ensuring this equilibrium is a doctrine of equivalence that denies difference. . . . The tendency within this doctrine of equivalence is to delineate sectional from general interests very early on in such deliberations, in ways that typically function within the command metaphors of citizenship as we find it; which is to say, a white, male, heterosexual and polite capitalist norm projected out onto the world. . . . To be branded a "sectional interest" is utterly disabling under these circumstances" (1993, 221).

9. This positioning of consumption as central is part of what capitalism does to legitimate itself. While I agree with Miller's critique, my point is that consumption is one of the terms of social membership.

10. See, for example, Carole Pateman (1989), Nancy Fraser (1989).

11. Crenshaw's concept has been especially productive for women of color feminism. See, for example, Lisa Lowe's concepts of hybridity, heterogeneity, and multiplicity (1996) and Chela Sandoval's concept of differential consciousness (2000).

12. Arnold I. Davidson points out that the concept of "styles" of reasoning, while metaphorical, brings to the fore changes in thinking procedures. Drawing on Ian Hacking (1982), he indicates: "[T]he most important claims Hacking makes are that there are different styles of reasoning and that these styles determine what statements are possible candidates for truth-or-falsehood. . . . As new styles of reasoning develop, they bring with them new categories of possible true or false statement" (Davidson 1999, 125–126).

13. In the United States, emotional styles have changed historically (see Stearns and Stearns 1986, 1988). The trend has been toward increasingly "cool" styles (Stearns 1994). For changes in social control, manners, civility, and politeness, see also Norbert Elias (1978) and John F. Kasson (1990).

14. See description and criticism of these models in F. G. Bailey (1983) as well as George Lakoff and Zoltán Kövecses (1986).

15. See Arlie Russell Hochschild (1983) and Catherine A. Lutz (1990).

16. See, for example, D. A. Birnbaum, T. A. Nosanchuck, and W. L. Croll (1980), cited by Lutz (1990).

17. See Hochschild (1983) and Lutz (1990)

18. See Marilyn Frye (1983), Hochschild (1983), and Elizabeth V. Spelman (1989).

19. See, for example, Lutz (1990), Robert C. Solomon (1990), and Spelman (1989, 1997).

20. See, from feminist perspectives, Alison M. Jaggar (1989), Elisabeth J. Porter (1991), Naomi Scheman (1980), and Spelman (1989, 1997). Also, despite their differences, interesting and related arguments can be found in George Mandler (1984), Amelie Oksenberg Rorty (1980), and Solomon (1976, 1990).

21. In her argument, Spelman (1989) distinguishes attributions of "anger," considered a reasoned response to others' actions, from those of "rage," considered an "excessive" emotional response. She argues that members of dominated groups are permitted to be (or be labeled) "emotional," even "enraged," but not—because of the element of judgment involved—"angry." She contends that the vehemence of dominant groups is read as justified anger, while the vehemence of aggrieved groups is read as rage, unreasonable and out of control. In my experience, readers use the term *anger* to describe aspects of textual vehemence but consequently discount its arguments as if it were the "unreasoned," "emotional" reaction that Spelman refers to as "rage."

22. Creating arguments by means of apparent textual *un*reason might be considered to be a *reasoned* argument also. Some of the French feminists use lexicon and syntax to develop arguments that do not always appear "rational" yet are based in a reasoned argument about the influences of language forms (Nye 1989). Radical feminists may, in poetry but also in prose, use apparent *un*reason—even verbal "guerrilla theater"—to overturn notions of what they believe to be a patriarchal order inherent in language (Jaggar 1983). Nye (2004) offers an account of arguments about women and the role of reason in the history of modern philosophy.

CHAPTER THREE

1. Shils notes, "The term 'civility' has usually, both in the past and in its recent revival, been interpreted to mean courtesy, well-spokenness, moderation, respect for others, self-restraint, gentlemanliness, urbanity, refinement, good manners, politeness. All those terms have generally been reserved for the description of the conduct of individuals in the immediate presence of each other. In all of these usages, there are intimations of consideration for the sensibilities of other persons and particularly for their desire to be esteemed. Thus, it would be antithetical to civility to refuse esteem or deference to another person. Civility treats others as, at least, equal in dignity, never as inferior in dignity" (1991, 12).

2. Shils spent many years as a board member of *The American Scholar* and good friend of its editor Angry Troper Joseph Epstein, who wrote the introduction to one of Shils's books, entitling it "My Friend Edward" (Epstein 1997).

3. See especially Peter N. Stearns (1994, 1999) and Carol Z. Stearns and Peter N. Stearns (1986) but also Norbert Elias (1978), John F. Kasson (1990), and Peter N. Stearns and Jan Lewis (1998) and Carol Z. Stearns and Peter N. Stearns (1988).

4. Politeness, like emotion, is a much more complex set of discourses and practices than often acknowledged. Sociolinguistics and pragmatics are developing increasingly sophisticated ways of accounting for attributions of politeness and their consequences that will prove useful in feminist socioforensic discursive analysis. Like the analyses here, politeness studies must account for shifting definitions of power and politeness at the scene of interaction, for the difficulty of defining terms or examples specifically (given that the discourses are embedded in complex social relations), for different interpretations of what should count as polite or impolite in a given context. Useful sources are Derek Bousfield and Miriam A. Locher (2008), Robin Tolmach Lakoff and Schiko Ide (2005), Miram Locher (2004), Sara Mills (2003), and Richard Watts (2003). Toby Miller (1993) remarks that the *ethos* of "polite sociability" of some theories of citizenship depend on the exclusion of "incivility."

5. The reviews of Gillespie and Penelope, such as I have been able to find, do not discount either on the basis of textual anger, although remarks about textual affect are common in reviews and found in other reviews about gender and violence. Gillespie is now deceased; according to her obituary in the *New York Times, Justifiable Homicide* has been cited in trials across the country and was named by the Gustavus Myers Center for the Study of Human Rights as an "Outstanding Book in the Subject of Human Rights in the United States" (*New York Times,* February 3, 1993, A21). Gillespie's reviewers do not discuss specific rhetorical or stylistic structures of her text, although they describe it as "extraordinarily well-written, compelling" (Roth 1991, 381), "a chilling portrait" (Estrich 1990, 1430), with violence "stunningly portrayed" (Roth 1991, 381), "often painful reading [yet her] . . . stirring accounts of justice gone wrong, make a strong case" (Lewin 1989, 17). Some reviewers suggest that its tone is "understandably bleak . . . [but perhaps] unnecessarily dark" (Kinports 1989, 131), while others refer to the targets of Gillespie's "most scathing criticism" (Estrich 1990, 1433). Penelope is no longer working in the academy by her own choice but continues to contribute to academic dialogues. Her reviewers describe *Speaking Freely* as "witty,

serious, irreverent, and scholarly" (Kramarae 1992, 666), or "witty, lucid, and highly accessible" (Dumas 1992, 320). Cheris Kramarae indicates that Penelope's is "an impressively strong read" (667); Bethany K. Dumas indicates that the book presents "the strongest possible argument" (320) about issues that are "highly charged emotionally" (322). Dumas, in her review, writes that a male colleague said he did not want to read Penelope's book if it was "another male bashing book" (323). Because reviews are generally done by interested parties, they do not provide an adequate source for generalizations about reception of texts and arguments. For this argument about textual vehemence, I bracket consideration of both Gillespie's and Penelope's full arguments to concentrate, instead, on some of the textual features of specific chapters.

6. Each author's distinct and adept use of irony demonstrates that her use of vehement textual markers is deeply *rhetorically strategic*. While the relationship and boundaries between anger and irony are by no means clear, the textual evidence for anger closely resembles the textual evidence for irony, sarcasm, and ridicule. Interpreting and determining the role of such markers requires understanding the complex relationships possible among authors, arguments, and audiences—it may even require out-of-text knowledge. Kathy Ferguson (1993) presents an interesting analysis of feminist theory with considerable attention to the role of irony. Good introductions to the artistic and political deployment of irony and parody can be found in Linda Hutcheon (1985, 1991, 1994). See also Joseph A. Dane (1991).

7. In congruence with her recommendations to others to avoid passives and terms that hide agency, Penelope usually specifies "men" or "white males" as the promoters and benefactors of the privileges of language that she reveals. Penelope thus indicts "men" as a class (although, she concedes in her introduction, not *all* men). Despite her explicit reflection on the argumentative point that she is making by such a strategy, many of the readers assume that she does mean "all men," and that doing so demonstrates unreason and anger. Readers often react as if such strategies "condemn" large numbers of "innocent people," without regard to their individual differences—even reproach readers themselves. Readers are likely to interpret Penelope's argument as "angry" or "bitter" and "unreasonable" or "unfair" even when she has explained the grounds for this rhetorical decision. Penelope frequently creates conditions of vehemence by adopting an acerbic tone, created by making broad, bold, often graphic statements about the characters and motivations of individuals or classes of people. Readers also tend to respond negatively in certain kinds of claims referring to specific named individuals, such as Penelope's "Dr. Crane." Such cases influence readers' reception of arguments, I would argue, according to the kind of problem that the individual is said to exhibit—the kind of problem being criticized. In this case, Penelope is trying to connect the grammatical constructions used by the individual Dr. Crane with ways of talking about the world that perpetuate sexual violence by allowing us to evade its consequences. Significantly for their reception of Penelope's argument, many of her readers argue for the "innocence" of named individuals such as Dr. Crane, absolving them on the basis that they do not "know" that their constructions are so implicated, that reporters who use elisions such as "it" for "father rape" are not guilty of anything because they do not consciously "intend" to foster sexual violence by their phrasing. Under such a line of argument, persons cannot be said to contribute to social problems unless they fully and consciously embrace actions contributing directly to

the problem. For Penelope to call them by name in condemning their constructions is to be "unfair"—unreasonable.

8. Gillespie's stories assume that the woman's testimony is true, that the man had a history of battering, that the woman's description of events is accurate, and that her actions are reasonable given the provocation and situation described. With her focus on story-telling, Gillespie also encourages her readers to place themselves in the scenario, as victims of the violence. Her rhetoric consistently encourages readers to envision themselves at the scene of the violence, not at the scene of the courtroom. She inserts them into the scenario of the woman's decision-making, to encourage empathy for her problem in response, rather than inserting them into the court scenario, where the decision-making she criticizes takes place.

9. Problematic evaluation of authorial emotion is not limited to men or even non-feminists. I have frequently seen reviewers discount vehement feminist texts addressing sexual violence and the law—e.g., Teresa Carpenter's remarks on Lenore Walker's *Terrifying Love*: "Her feminist rhetoric becomes repetitive and is likely to repel the very readers who should be moved to action—police, prosecutors and—her pet peeve—'ignorant, old, white, male judges'" (1989, 17). Note that Carpenter restricts (inappropriately, I would argue) the important audience for a book on reforming legal treatment of violence against women. Erika Munk, denouncing Catharine MacKinnon's arguments about rape and pornography in the Balkan war, suggests that MacKinnon's vehemence is so powerful that readers cannot resist her (faulty) analysis: "Every woman who has watched TV has felt horror, rage and pity at the Bosnian rapes; most are understandably ill-informed about their context. The raw emotion of MacKinnon's language and the grotesque violence of the atrocities she retells can easily push women into agreeing with her analysis" (1994, 6). Note that Munk assumes that MacKinnon's vehemence renders audiences powerless to think. And much of Christina Hoff Sommers's distress with current "gender feminists," delineated in the first chapter of her book *Who Stole Feminism? How Women Have Betrayed Women* (1994), is that they are "angry" and "resentful" (which she deems not moral emotions) rather than "indignant" (deemed a "moral" emotion, but apparently not justified by any life situations facing privileged academic women).

10. As witnessed by the charges of right-wing foundation–funded Christina Hoff Sommers against academic feminists (1994); see critique by Patrice McDermott (1995).

CHAPTER FOUR

1. See discussions in Page DuBois (2001), Martha Nussbaum (1998), and Griselda Pollock (1988).

2. One of many examples is Joan Acocella's "Cather and the Academy," *The New Yorker* (November 27, 1995): 56–71. The tear sheet attached to the cover tells it all, asking in giant bold type: "What have the academics done to Willa Cather?"

3. Robert Craft, "Lagoon Tunes" (1992).

4. Susan Cook, Letter, headed "What's a Girl to Do?" *New York Review of Books* (July 16, 1992): 53.

5. In replying to Cook, Craft says he bases his comments on Landon and Norwich. Yet examination of Landon and Norwich suggests otherwise. Landon and Norwich

mention Strozzi twice. In the caption next to her picture (67, pl. 21), they describe her as "one of the leading composers of 17th century Italy . . . as talented as she was beautiful." [I]n the half-page of text devoted to her, they says she is "beautiful," and call her "a great female composer," then note that she "became the most celebrated female composer of her age (or indeed any age—there are remarkably few woman composers in the history of music)" (98). As a footnoted source of this information, the authors cite Ellen Rosand (1986). At no point in her essay does Rosand describe Strozzi in the (literally) singular terms of Landon and Norwich or Craft: she indicates that Strozzi is "one of the few known women among the many aria and cantata composers of seventeenth-century Italy" (168); "one of the most prolific contributors to secular chamber music of the seicento" (175); "an unusually gifted composer" (187); "a composer of considerable skill and highly individual eloquence" (although apparently limiting herself to arias and cantatas) (176). Rosand indicates that Francesca Caccini is "the most prominent and successful woman composer of the period" (169).

6. Our understanding of Strozzi and of Cook's concerns may be extended by consideration of a passage from Susan McClary's *Feminine Endings* (1991): "[F]or a man to enact his sexuality is not the same as for a woman: throughout Western history, women musicians have usually been assumed to be publicly available, have had to fight hard against pressures to yield, or have accepted the granting of sexual favors as one of the prices of having a career. The seventeenth-century composer Barbara Strozzi—one of the very few women to compete successfully in elite music competition—may have been forced by her agent-pimp of a father to pose for a bare-breasted publicity portrait as part of his plan for launching her career" (151). McClary's footnoted citations on this point: Ellen Rosand (1986), Anthony Newcomb (1986), and Linda Phyllis Austern (1989). McClary also cites, with regard to Renaissance courtesans and cultural production, Ann Rosalind Jones (1986).

7. Robert Craft, Letter, headed "Robert Craft replies," *New York Review of Books* (July 16, 1992): 53. Craft suggests that Cook has to "dredge up" her examples, engages in "invidious nonsense" by comparing fame over centuries, "contradicts herself" by claiming Strozzi "disappeared from history" (since her music lives on), and claims that one of Cook's sentences (which technically has a dangling modifier) is "incomprehensible" to him—apparently this renders its concerns unworthy of attention. Craft explains that the comment in his review that Strozzi was "history's *only* famous female composer" is based on Landon and Norwich's description of Strozzi as "the *most* famous" female composer in history, apparently failing to see that the two phrases are by no means synonymous and apparently believing that to declare Strozzi a one-and-only rather than one-of-several is *not* to "compare fame over centuries." Craft overlooks his own transformation of Cook's claim when he further reprimands her: "I doubt that, by itself, 'the connection between female musicality and sexual promiscuity' can have dogged 'female creativity' to the extent of having prevented the appearance of a major female composer" (53). Craft here replies to an argument *that Cook has not made*: that the connection, which she merely indicates as a problem, is *by itself* the *only* problem—the *only* reason that there has not been a "major female composer." It seems unlikely to me that Cook believes this, but whether or not she does, that is not the argument of her letter.

8. For a scholarly discussion of the issues raised by scopophilia, see Laura Mulvey (1975). For a discussion of the bared breast as a symbol other than the erotic, see Marina Warner (1985).

9. For their caption above Cook's letter, the editors chose to echo the last words of her letter, transforming them into the perplexed line of a character in a screwball comedy: "What's a Girl to Do?" Cook's original concluding words demonstrate part of what is at stake in her critique of Craft: the difficult social position and potential loss of musical contributions caused by treating the sexuality of women composers as a potentially public commodity. The editors' transformation of her words trivializes Cook's point, but it also goes further, in that it also echoes the only point in the letter where Cook refers to her *own* gender (her question: "[W]hy would I, a female musicologist, buy a work for a pin-up?"). (Bear in mind that Cook uses this question to explain to Craft why she is contending that his perspective ["gaze"] implies readers and portrait-viewers who are male.) The caption, by connecting Cook-the-female-musicologist to the personal and social problems of a nice-girl-who-might-wish-to-become-a-musical-composer-without-being-considered-sexually-available-to-all, transforms both Cook's original (rhetorical) question and her ethos. It signals what the editors re-create as the boundaries of Cook's argument: "How can 'a girl like me' make it if you guys keep bringing up sex?" By this caption, the editors pre-empt attention from Cook's argument to focus on her social and sexual position. I have not yet seen a study of such captions; I would argue it positions itself in support of Craft and his attempt to embarrass Cook. On the day Cook's letter appears, there were several other letters, with the following captions: "To Protect the Kosovars," "Democracy in Romania?" "Importing Slaves."

10. See Susan Cook, Letter, headed "What's a Girl to Do?" (1992) and Ellen Rosand (1986).

11. In the applicable part of Killam's argument, she *refers* to her own feminism, *condemns* Gans's persistent use of the "generic 'he,' " and *disparages-by-display* Gans's vision of the origins of language as a male-only proposition. (She does quote Riane Eisler [1987], who criticizes the ways in which the Bible and church hierarchies have justified male dominance.) To re-create her argument, Gans conflates Killam's limited argument with Eisler's rather different argument, and with the kinds of arguments he has seen and inferred from public nonacademic commentary such as Epstein's. He then juxtaposes this amalgam with the dominant things he claims as his own.

12. While posing as one who has been displaced by feminist power in the academy, Gans behaves as the powerful can—by denigrating and ignoring criticism. The Tough-Baby persona is tough because it holds itself above the mundane details of actually explaining carefully or responding to the arguments of agonists. So Gans indicates that he need not reply to Killam's specific arguments—and any arguments one might infer from them—because they are so trivial. However, Gans assures his readers, this does not mean he would not love to argue with a feminist some day, if only a reasonable one could be found. "I welcome any *real* argument—feminist or otherwise—about the origin of language, and would be happy to reply to any *reasoned* attempt to refute my theses" (88, emphasis added). Gans shows no knowledge in his reply to Killam of the research in feminist history, political science, and language study that offers challenges to visions of male brotherhood or male competition as the beginning of the social—or linguistic—contract, such as Carole Pateman (1988).

13. Because Killam relies on a series of quotes from Gans to carry the weight of her argument about his neglect of the possible role of women, she offers little scope for displaying much textual "anger" about Gans and his arguments.

14. In mounting her arguments, McClary does not cite van den Toorn or his work, although she does argue that previous work in musicology neglects the kinds of concerns that she fronts in her book. A version of van den Toorn's critique was subsequently published in his book *Music, Politics and the Academy* (1995).

15. With this extended set of rhetorical moves, van den Toorn apparently expresses ambivalence toward a critique of personal motives: he first affirms, then denies, then ultimately reaffirms what he presents as sad necessity—being forced to resort to discounting McClary for inadequacies of personal character (he apparently believes her not appreciative enough of classical music, not broad-minded enough about "male" sexuality, too appreciative of "female" sexuality). Describing the critique that he implies he cannot endorse, he argues, "No doubt, the foregoing is what might well have been expected by way of a reaction to McClary's arguments" (294).

16. Note similarity between van den Toorn's evocation of "to stand accused *of all the awful things*" (296, emphasis added) and Gans's comment that "(Western) civilization is condemned *in all the ways I need not repeat*" (87–88, emphasis added). Van den Toorn has confessed to (and demonstrates) difficulty articulating McClary's argument with any degree of accuracy; Gans has indicated that he is above arguing with Killam, most feminists, and most "minoritaries" (*sic*). The Tough Baby flaunts condemnation, not knowledge.

17. Lee Humphries, Letter to the editor, *Minnesota Composers Forum Newsletter*. Letter dated January 6, 1987.

CHAPTER FIVE

1. Institutionally endorsed isolation from interdisciplinary inquiry in the social sciences and humanities did not serve musicology well here because its scholars were not prepared for poststructuralist and other arguments familiar in many other disciplines by the late 1980s.

2. Because McClary's *Feminine Endings* was an early mainstream monograph of feminist musicology, critiques of it "stand for" disciplinary responses to feminist studies in a distinctive way. During the years it was written and first vociferously criticized, there was little conversation between musicology and feminist studies. Thus the representations of these critics work not only to suppress McClary's work but also, and perhaps more importantly, to signal to a broad new audience what feminist studies *is*. It is easy to forget the argumentative significance of such moves—to forget that feminist and other interdisciplinary theories and methods move slowly into some disciplines and that scholarly work valued by interdisciplinary scholarly audiences may appear shocking to those accustomed to tighter disciplinary restrictions on debate.

3. McClary's analyses are erudite, careful, and complex, drawing on various narrative and critical theories common in both the humanities and social sciences to demonstrate that gendered sexual codes are often central to the construction and interpretation of dramatic and instrumental music. Her writing adopts a tone frequently

matter-of-fact, studded with humorous, vehement, or ironic moments; she employs changes in register—from formal to informal or colloquial, from technical to sexually explicit—to illustrate her points. So, for example, she often mixes sexual metaphors and technical terminology in her descriptions to emphasize the ways in which the gendered semiotic codes play out in the music:

> As the protagonist lies in helpless exhaustion, the sluttish second theme reenters—in the key of the raised submedient rather than under the hegemony of the protagonist's tonic, as convention would demand—and toys with him, finally depleting him. (1991, 75–76)

Those of McClary's readers who protest her rhetoric often seem to assume that she means each comment to be implacably serious and abusive, where I read her to be ironic and humorous.

4. Both critics have strong credentials in musicology: Treitler has been a central figure in music criticism for many years; Higgins was appointed in 1996 to be editor-in-chief of the official organ of the American Musicological Society.

5. Treitler's accompanying gesture of presenting currently dominant conceptions of musicology as without ideology or politics is pervasive in responses to McClary's work, and fascinating in light of her explicit argument that *all* scholarship is ideological. McClary's argument relies partly on the arguments of Edward Said, who is well known for his music criticism. In the preface to his recent *Musical Elaborations* (1991), Said is critical of musicology's failure to acknowledge its ideological underpinning; earlier (1983 Opponents), he describes a religious guild system in the humanities which appears to be an apt description of the stance of many musicologists in the face of these debates.

6. This move on McClary's part is used by Treitler to justify engaging in a series of rather old-fashioned sexual jokes and comments with regard to McClary's work, as well as to develop a ridiculing radio broadcast arguing that the works she presents as demonstrating gendered rhetorics do not.

7. Treitler's arguments would be considerably strengthened were he to clarify and argue for his assumptions about sexuality, music, disciplinary strictures, arguments, evidence, and feminist inquiry. However, deploying them as presuppositions rather than analytic constructs allows them to operate within his arguments unexamined; laying them on the table would require him to defend them against the arguments raised against such assumptions by many scholars, feminist and otherwise—including McClary.

8. Rather than set an agenda for other musicologists, McClary frames her arguments to reveal her own interests; she does not demand that others follow her scholarly plans. For example, in her introduction, McClary says:

> At this moment, I cannot begin to give any kind of overview of the rich variety of approaches that appear to be emerging with the discipline [of feminist musicology]. . . . Therefore, I will only address my own work—the issues I have found most compelling. . . . The questions I have pursued in my feminist work cluster into five groups. . . . [I]t seems useful to outline them at this point. (1991, 7)

Scattered across the next few pages are the five headings for these discussions: musical constructions of gender and sexuality (7), gendered aspects of traditional music theory (9), gender and sexuality in musical narrative (12), music as a gendered discourse (17), discursive strategies of women musicians (18).

9. In the passage I quote, Higgins argues that part of what can isolate McClary and establish her work as social, political, "guerrilla"—and, therefore, *not* "strictly 'feminist'"—is that it does not meet with universal approbation among feminist musicologists. Such an apparently disingenuous statement functions primarily to mark McClary off from other feminist musicologists and to suggest that they, like Higgins, are willing to discipline McClary's controversial arguments. Higgins indicates at other points in her critique that she knows feminists often find one another's methods and solutions to be reductive, counterproductive, and unsettling. Such controversy is evident in any feminist journal as well as in the discussions about competition and conflict that appear in Marianne Hirsch and Evelyn Fox Keller (1990) and Valerie Miner and Helen E. Longino (1987). Higgins's willingness nonetheless to promulgate such a criterion is an example of the deep internal contradictions that mar both her arguments and those of Treitler.

10. While all three positions are reasonable, similar to those held by different groups of feminist scholars, none of them *encompass* feminist inquiry: failure to satisfy any one of these visions does not render work either "feminist" or "nonfeminist." While it has varied uses and is common in the academy, such "denominalism" or labeling is, in fact, antithetical to scholarly research, which hinges on what we can learn. Such an argument confuses allegiance to institutional disciplinary categories with a broader search for knowledge.

11. Treitler quotes from the first paragraph and then the fifth paragraph of Keuls's introduction. The paragraphs in between—the second, third, and fourth—present Keuls's discussion of her reception, extended into the next ten pages of her text.

12. Other feminist scholars in classics indicate that contemporary classicists do not adopt the stance of open acceptance to evidence of gender coding that Treitler implies; see, for example, Kathryn J. Gutzwiller and Ann Norris Michelini (1991) and Natalie Boymel Kampen (1995).

13. According to Keuls, "In the face of evidence for all these practices, what has been the response of Classics scholars? At best, they have habitually overlooked or interpreted away the evidence; and all too often they have openly endorsed or at least provided apologies for phallocracy (1985, 9). . . . Another school of Classicists, rather than defending the Greeks for their polarization of the sexes, denies that it occurred. . . . Apologists for the Athenians display wonderful ingenuity in defense of their idols" (10).

14. Treitler has explicitly marshaled Keuls as his ally in a concerted attempt to discredit and delegitimate McClary's work. Had he referred to, cited, included the arguments he chose to elide, he could have demonstrated how his own critique can be distinguished from the kind of scholarly resistance Keuls reports. He could use the occasion to develop further the argument that nonscholarly goals of containment and prudery do not motivate his own critique. He could use the occasion to explain more fully why he wishes McClary and, for that matter, musicology, to maintain the purity

of their object of analysis as if it were connected in only trivial ways with social relations and embodied human activities.

15. This kind of comment is based on Treitler's relative unfamiliarity with concepts of social construction. Here and elsewhere, Treitler's text moves back and forth, criticizing significantly different ways of connecting music and gender without indicating their differences: (a) explicating socially constructed ascriptions of gender, (b) criticizing them, and (c) adopting them.

16. In fact, scholars such as Nancy Armstrong (1987) and Christopher Newfield (1996) demonstrate how literary texts can be gendered without writing about women authors or images of women in texts. Paula Rabinowitz (1990) argues for a relation between gender and genre, both involving classifying and drawing boundaries, one learned from the other. Film theorist Laura Mulvey (1975) argues for the influence of gender in film, gender being connected to narrative closure and form, not just whether women happen to be on screen.

17. Discussions of gender in literary studies, like many other fields, are often acrimonious. For example, William E. Cain has collected a group of essays discussing the critical reception of feminist literary scholars Sandra M. Gilbert and Susan Gubar, whose books *The Madwoman in the Attic* (1979) and *No Man's Land* (1988, 1989) presented feminist arguments about women authors that were taken by many critics to be dramatically challenging, deeply flawed, or otherwise worthy of vehement criticism. In his introduction, Cain comments on some of the problems of the reception of that work, including the following: "[I]t is also worth noting the severity and, regrettably, the mean-spiritedness, with which their work has sometimes been criticized. . . . Gilbert and Gubar have paid a price for their accomplishments and have been roughly indicted in tones of voice that are seldom employed for male scholars of comparable importance. . . . It is one thing, however, to acknowledge that their work must be assessed and supplemented . . . it is quite another to fling polemics . . . as though they have done something disreputable and, thus, deserve no respect" (1993, xix–xx). Also useful in considering Treitler's characterization of the reception of feminist work in literary criticism are other essays in the collection, including Nancy K. Miller, "*Madwoman* Revisited" (1993) and Michele Sordi, "Caught in the Crossfire" (1993).

18. Asserting a fissure between music and other sign systems (as Treitler asserts throughout this argument) has become subject to critical debate as a move that closes music off from social and cultural criticism. McClary takes a position with regard to this debate, while Treitler behaves as though such a debate is not taking place, in order to argue that music be closed off from McClary's criticism.

19. McClary cites the same three scholars, when she argues that the "tendency to deny the body and identify with pure mind underlies virtually every aspect of patriarchal Western culture" (1991, 54). (Her reference is to Bordo 1986. Treitler cites a reprint of that essay incorrectly as Bordo 1975; the correct citation is Bordo 1987.)

20. Treitler does not mention that historians, philosophers, and scientists have sometimes greeted the arguments of these feminist scholars with as much disdain as he musters toward McClary's work. See, for example, Lloyd's preface to the second edition of *The Man of Reason* (1993) where she talks about reactions to her work. See also the diatribes about Keller and other science studies scholars in Paul R. Gross and

Norman Levitt (1997). One review of Gross and Levitt is Bennett Berger (1994); see also Andrew Ross (1996).

21. One source seems to offer no justification whatsoever for Higgins's criteria: Griselda Pollock acknowledges only her family by name, expressing the hope that colleagues and friends "will find themselves acknowledged in due place in the text" (1988, xv). Pollock's acknowledgments, then, would fail any tests of "feminist collegiality" that Higgins might use. Higgins's second source is the definition of *acknowledgment* appearing in an intriguing and amusingly polemical feminist dictionary that mocks the history of *male* literary figures appropriating *female* energy, intellectuality, and skill (see Kramarae and Treichler 1985, 28—see quotation below). Higgins's third source, Dale Spender (1989), cites Cheris Kramarae and Paula A. Treichler's definition of *acknowledgment* as "facetious—but fundamental," arguing that a "sexual double-standard" often has it that men are "intellectual beings" and women secondary, having "servicing skills." In mounting this argument, Spender is criticizing historical male literary figures who use women's authoring skills, then poorly acknowledge their support; she makes no recommendations for feminists to follow in their scholarship, recommends no proportions for a distribution of honors in women's academic texts, suggests no standard to violate in order to be considered "nonfeminist." Kramarae and Treichler's definition: "Acknowledgments: Before feminism, that portion of a book where authors acknowledged the ideas and intellectual contributions of males and the clerical and editorial assistance of females and where men thanked their wives for critically reading their manuscripts without asking for co-authorship. After feminism, the place where women authors often acknowledge the intellectual, emotional, editorial, and clerical contributions of women and sometimes of men" (1985, 28).

22. Criteria for feminist scholarship, like other scholarly criteria, cannot be created de novo by proclamation—much less by unprecedented enforcement; they are subject to argument. I am not asserting that individuals and small groups of feminists never have criteria considered appropriate for their scholarly work, merely that these must be justified and widely accepted if they are to be presented as something other than idiosyncratic or contested criteria. For example, what has come to be known as the "Montreal Massacre" has generated specific suggestions about rhetoric based on the problems presented in the case. A young man with a rifle entered a classroom in McGill University's School of Engineering, divided the women from the men, and shot and killed the women on the basis that they were "feminists." Several of the women protested that they were not feminists; but the killer explained that as students of engineering—entering a man's field—they fit his definition. He killed fourteen women, then himself. For the first twenty-four hours, there was ambiguity about the killer's selection of only women students, perhaps because the murdered students' gender was not immediately evident in the reports of the French-language press. Commentators tended to discount the killer's expressed intentions (which he wished publicized), the "philosophy" that impelled his actions, and his choice of targets, arguing that he was merely an individual psychopath. When feminists responded that a social analysis focusing on those choices was important, they were with charged "leaping on the bandwagon," taking advantage of the turmoil after the killings "for their own

agendas." Because of the killer's desire for publicity, some feminist writers have suggested or supported efforts, when discussing the incident, to *omit* the killer's name from discussion and to *include* the names of the women killed. (The latter is a regularly occurring rhetorical feature in discussions of femicide.) This is a publicly proposed, deliberately negotiated rhetorical decision related to the politics of a particular incident. I have never seen anyone criticized for violating this suggestion. See Julie Brickman (1992), Louise Maletter and Marie Chalouch (1991), Elspeth Probyn (1993), and Joanne Stato (1993). Wendy Hui Kyong Chun (1999) offers a complex discussion of the debates following the massacre.

With regard to circles of citation focusing not on "proportions" but simply on whether certain groups of scholars are simply excluded from recognition entirely, see, with regard to women in discussions of postmodernism, Meaghan Morris (1988), with regard to scholars who are ethnic minorities, Richard Delgado (1984) and Mari Matsuda (1988). In the introduction to her book of essays, Morris comes closest to choosing for *her own argument* a "proportionalist" position: arguing that theorists discussing postmodernism often use criteria that omit feminist theorizing that relates to the issue, she provides an informative reading list that includes only works signed or cosigned by women. The notes to her own articles cite the specific sources that support the points she is making, without comment or evidence of special interest in gender proportions. A substantial and growing body of research on the pragmatics, politics, and rhetoric of citations, annotations, other indicating devices, metadiscursive comments, and so on, makes clear that *like any other part of an academic text*, acknowledgments and citations are rhetorical devices, subject to rhetorical decision-making, to be debated. They are not established by fiat by a single critic.

23. McClary is actually complimenting the "courageous women [musicologists]" who fought "formidable obstacles" and "scorn" to uncover "an enormous amount of rich material: the long-forgotten music of *such extraordinary figures as* . . . [McClary follows with five early women musicians]" (1991, 5, emphasis mine). McClary's comments tend to be inclusive rather than exclusive, citing not a limited set, but as examples of a much larger set, thereby being inclusive of more work on early women musicians. McClary then, I would argue quite properly, cites the entire anthologies in which these writings have appeared.

24. Given that these kinds of counts are *not* accepted criteria for evaluation in feminist studies, it is hard to know what would count as "enough" in this regard, nor does Higgins propose specific standards.

25. This implication is furthered by several other textual decisions: The reproaches about citations follow Higgins's detailed discussion of the gendered distribution of honors in the acknowledgments, thereby authorizing themselves by the same references to "feminist" criteria. Higgins's reproaches considerably exceed the discussion of the acknowledgments, providing much more exhaustive detail; they focus, as we shall see, on allegations of neglect of women, of early women musicians, and of women musicologists; they reiterate their criticisms by means of phrasing that suggests that McClary has neglected "normal" feminist citation standards, with phrases such as "One wonders why . . ." (Higgins, 1993, 176), "One again cannot help wondering why . . ." (177), "Oddly . . ." (177), as if readers and Higgins are aware of a shared

standard that McClary has somehow missed or deliberately flouted. Higgins's attempts at precision imply that these are well-known rules of thumb and bear a deeply significant relationship to the quality of the scholarship and the degree to which it may indeed be labeled "feminist." Again, Higgins does not explain (even for the nonfeminist readers of *19th Century Music*) the importance of these criteria to understanding feminist scholarship.

26. One of the essays Higgins mentions, "Alluring the Auditorie to Effeminacie" (Austern 1988), McClary cites by title and author three times (McClary 1991, 172, n. 28; 181, n. 27; 206, n. 15) and another time refers to it by naming Austern (McClary 1991, 170, n. 7). McClary also twice cites by title and author another Austern essay, "'Sing Againe Syren'" (Austern 1989) (McClary 1991, 205, n. 12), which Higgins does not mention. Higgins, in documenting her charge that McClary ignores extant relevant work, cites a third essay by Austern, "Love, Death and Ideas of Music in the English Renaissance" (Austern 1991). McClary does not cite this third essay, one published the same year as *Feminine Endings*.

27. I use the term *startling* because feminist studies has been a central participant (at least since the early 1980s) in recent attempts to retheorize the body and sexuality. Stanton (1992), in fact, argues that women's studies has largely *shaped* the new studies of sexuality.

28. McClary's introduction provides substantial explanation for her analytic position

The connection of music and sexuality is important intellectually:

> By far the most difficult aspect of music to explain is its uncanny ability to make us experience our bodies in accordance with its gestures and rhythms. Yet this aspect is also what makes music so compelling. (McClary 1991, 23)
>
> I am interested first and foremost in accounting for how music creates such effects. (21)

The connection of music and sexuality is important to theories of meaning:

> *Any adequate account of meaning and rationality must give a central place to embodied and imaginative structures of understanding by which we grasp our world.* (24, quoted from philosopher Mark Johnson 1987, xvi, emphasis in Johnson)

Studying music from this vantage point provides insights into social history (8):

> To the large extent that music can organize our perceptions of our own bodies and emotions, it can tell us things about history that are not accessible through any other medium. (30)

The connection of music and sexuality is important socially:

> Music reflects and participates in social formation (7), serves as a public forum where models of social organization are negotiated (8), and participates "actively in the social organization of sexuality" (9). "[W]ithin the arena of these discourses . . . alternative models of organizing the social world are submitted and negotiated." (21)

The connection of music and sexuality is important politically:

> Struggles over musical propriety are themselves political struggles over whose music, whose images of pleasure or beauty, whose rules of order shall prevail. (28)

29. See, for example, Susan Bordo (1993), Judith Butler (1990, 1993), and Elizabeth A. Grosz (1994).

30. See, for example, Lynn A. Higgins and Brenda Silver (1991), Susan Jeffords (1989, 1994), Tania Modleski (1991), and Linda Williams (1989).

31. See Higgins (1990), which takes a male as its topic and comments on males and their activities, mentioning women only briefly in their roles as disruptive "concubines and women of ill-repute." This article, on a late medieval (male) composer, includes only a few women as actors. Higgins reports that young clerks were implored "to get rid of the concubines and women of ill-repute inhabiting their rooms, under pain of losing their quarterly stipends." In a note, Higgins indicates that "[t]wo clerks had been deprived of their stipends for having had concubines and for fighting with each other . . . and another was threatened with losing his unless he got rid of his concubine named Marguerite" (Higgins 1990, 9, and n. 39).

32. Examples, drawn from an enormous body of work, include in history: Leonore Davidoff and Catherine Hall (1987) and Catherine Hall (1992); in cultural studies: Susan Jeffords (1989, 1994) and Tania Modleski (1991); in philosophy and politics: Bat-Ami Bar-On (1994), Bordo (1987), Rosi Braidotti (1991), Christine Di Stefano (1991), Andrea Nye (1989, 1990), Carole Pateman (1988), Mary Lyndon Shanley and Carole Pateman (1991), and Nancy Tuana (1994); in science studies: Donna Haraway (1989) and Sharon Traweek (1988).

33. Her efforts to criticize McClary lead Higgins to disparage here a critical move that has long been of importance to feminist critique in literature, history, philosophy, and the history of science. The three feminist scholars that taught Treitler to be "sensitive" to feminist "exploitation" of gender have all done this kind of work: Susan Bordo criticizes the social and cultural view of women underpinning what she describes as the "Cartesian masculinization of thought" (1986, 1987); Genevieve Lloyd, the limited and negative role that philosophy has assigned to women (1984, 1993); Evelyn Fox Keller, the negative view of women fundamental to the deeply gendered nature of the history of science (1985). Many texts that seek to criticize the inadequacies of an existing canon or history, such as Rosi Braidotti's discussion of the history of philosophy (1991), adopt the same structure used by McClary: considering their problem first according to the (usually negative) views of such a (usually male) canon or history, then in relation to the work of contemporary feminist thinkers.

34. See, in addition to Higgins and McClary, for example, Elaine Barkin (1992) and perhaps McClary (1992), a response to Barkin, as well as reviews and reports on conferences such as Jane M. Bowers (1989), Alice H. Cash (1991), Cook (1989), and Marianne Kielian-Gilbert (1992).

35. Higgins feels free to condemn McClary not on the basis of her arguments, but on the charge that McClary's statements about feminist musicologists are not very "flattering." Higgins supports this argument by quoting a passage from McClary's foreword to Catherine Clément's *Opera, or, the Undoing of Women* (1988). In that text,

McClary indicates that American musicology has not been hospitable to feminist criticism. As Higgins quotes it, McClary says:

> [F]eminist work that is produced tends to operate within a marginalized ghetto that adds fragments of information concerning women to the already existing canon but that does not tamper with the outlines of the canon itself. It is significant that the voices calling for a feminist criticism are those of well-established men. (McClary 1988, ix, quoted in Higgins [1993, 177])

Since Higgins too agrees that musicology has a long history of being dominated by male interests, and that feminist musicology must, therefore, carve out a place in a field uncongenial to such pursuits, why should Higgins find this statement "unflattering," a condemnation of individual women in musicology or of feminist musicologists? Perhaps the full context of McClary's original statement will help us interpret Higgins's move.

McClary's statement above appears as part of her comments on a caucus of women scholars in musicology. In the sentences that appear immediately before and after the statement quoted by Higgins (represented by the ellipses here), McClary argues:

> When the possibility of feminist criticism was raised, a puzzled and some-what anxious silence was the response—in part because criticism *of any sort* is strangely absent from musicology, but in part because women scholars still feel themselves to hold a precarious position with respect to the discipline: a position that overt criticism might jeopardize. . . . Women in musicology tend to read such appeals not as open encouragement but as taunts, as invitations to professional suicide. (McClary 1988, ix, emphasis in original)

In the original passage, then, McClary is arguing that well-established men feel free to call for a feminist musicology because they are not threatened by a disciplinary structure that attacks such study. The "significance" of male voices is ironic, for McClary: it rests on the irony of male invitations being issued to a conversation that women recognize as professionally dangerous to them. Contra Higgins, McClary is supporting, not scorning, feminist musicologists, pointing out publicly their quite proper fear that such work will open them to sneers or strong condemnation. Surely the reception of McClary's work demonstrates that they are right to do so.

36. For example, the epistemological inquiries in Linda Alcoff and Elizabeth Potter (1993), Jaggar and Bordo (1990), Helen E. Longino (1990), and Joan Scott (1988).

CHAPTER SIX

1. Briggs and Hallin are concerned with biocommunicability as a form of communication within governmentality. They argue, "To analyze the role of communication in governmentality is to explore how effects of power emerge from everyday ideological constructions of how information is purportedly produced, circulated, and received, how individuals and institutions participate in this process, and how statements are infused with authority and value. We refer to this productive relationship between discursive . . . acts and practices that focus on health and medical issues . . . as *biocommunicability*" (2007, 45).

2. Note particularly the argument of Monica J. Casper (1997) on the complications of studying fetal surgery. The tradition of critical reflection on biomedical models and health care includes attention to the discourse of medical encounters: for example, Hans A. Baer (1987), Robert A. Hahn and Atwood D. Gaines (1985), Margaret Lock and Deborah Gordon (1988), Elliot G. Mischler (1984), Mischler et al. (1981), and Howard Waitzkin (1983, 1991). Scholars have probed with increasing attention the narrative and metaphorical languages that underlie ways of thinking and talking about medical knowledge: for example, Robert J. Barrett (1988), Julia Epstein (1995), Kathryn Montgomery Hunter (1991), and Cheryl Mattingly (1991), and about personal experiences of illness: for example, Howard Brody (1987) and Arthur Kleinman (1988). Some study the role of language and representation related to the epistemological and methodological stances of medical anthropology: for example, Byron Good (1994), Hahn (1995), and Kleinman (1995). Upon occasion, medical anthropologists have engaged in more closely focused textual studies such as Martin's, which, as part of its larger project, examines closely the rhetorical structures underlying medical textbooks; another example is Hahn (1987), or, as revised, chapter 8 in Hahn (1995).

3. Martin is drawing on a line of argument that frames metaphorical language as an influence on thinking: metaphors are, therefore, sites and tools of *argumentation*. While metaphorical language in academic argument may be inevitable and inescapable, the choice of which metaphors to use is subject to scrutiny and contest. See, on metaphor, Richard Harvey Brown (1977), George Lakoff (1986), George Lakoff and Mark Johnson (1980), Andrew Ortony (1979), Donald A. Schon (1963), and Mark Turner (1987).

4. Judith A. Houck discusses the history of the concern about menopause from 1963 to 1980. Gynecologist Robert A. Wilson and his wife Thelma Wilson published a paper in the *Journal of the American Geriatrics Society* indicating that both women and the medical establishment must face facts: "The unpalatable truth must be faced that all postmenopausal women are castrates" (1963, 347, quoted in Houck 2003, 104). Robert A. Wilson's subsequent book *Feminine Forever* (1966) developed this theme for a broader audience. Houck examines how the women's movement negotiated this discourse.

5. In *The Woman in the Body*, Martin seeks to construct an anthropological analysis of the reproductive life cycle as it is experienced by American women of different ages, classes, and ethnic backgrounds, with particular attention to the ways in which working-class and African American women construct views that may "resist" received medical notions. Scholars have devoted continuing attention to the complex question of understanding how women negotiate menopause. See, for example, Janette Perz and Jane M. Ussher (2008).

6. Laws (1990) provides an analogous quotation from a British gynecology textbook: "Menstruation is sometimes described as 'the weeping of a disappointed uterus'" (93). Laws indicates that British gynecology textbooks commonly used this rhetorical strategy of putting out-of-date attitudes about menstruation on the table for current conversation. Michelle Harrison reports a different use of a similar term: as a resident, she is told that she should stop scraping out uterine tissue when she feels a "gritty feeling" in the lining of the uterus. That sensation, which signals to the practitioner that the task has been adequately finished, is, she says, called "the cry of the uterus" (1983, 40).

7. See, for example, Hahn (1987), Glenda Koutroulis (1990), Laws (1990), Kathleen L. MacPherson (1981), Judith Posner (1979), Diana Scully (1980), and Diana Scully and Pauline Bart (1973).

8. Studies of medical and biology textbooks find them currently "commonsensical" and full of various kinds of social advice (see Laws 1990, for example). Hahn (1987), analyzing twentieth-century revisions of *Williams Obstetrics*, demonstrates that sociocultural notions—often ones that he finds offensive and unpleasant—are present in virtually every revision. In reply, Michael Newton argues that texts cannot incorporate all necessary "psychological and sociological information" (1987, 283). No doubt this is true, but it hardly obviates the need to criticize the arguably extraneous negative information they have incorporated or retained. Newton also asserts, quite reasonably, the attitudes toward women have changed, and it is inappropriate to judge early texts by today's standards. Newton's argument has at least two problems worth noting here: one is his assumption that the purpose of evaluating these texts is to condemn their authors, rather than to understand their position and to avoid replicating negative notions in our contemporary thinking; the other is to assume that such notions, rather than being contested in the past, were accepted by all. While historians and feminist scholars could speak to the degree to which women from 1903 to 1985 would have found acceptable the various text revisions, Hahn provides rather amusing evidence that suggests that Dr. Newton mistakes the degree to which the texts' negative images were found acceptable. According to Hahn,

> The index of the 15th edition includes the entry "Chauvinism, male, variable amounts, 1–923." In the 16th edition the entry increased to "voluminous amounts, 1–1,102." In the preface to the 15th edition, authors Pritchard and MacDonald thank Ms. Signe Pritchard for "her myriad contributions beginning with manuscript and ending [?] with index." In the 17th edition, the index entry no longer appears (1987, 280, n. 2, punctuation Hahn's; *Williams Obstetrics*: 15th Edition, Pritchard and MacDonald 1976; 16th Edition, Pritchard and MacDonald 1980; 17th Edition, Pritchard, MacDonald, and Gant 1985).

9. See Gullette (1994) for a critique of contemporary public discourse about menopause. See Antonia C. Lyons and Christine Griffin (2002) for discussion of the strategies used in four British self-help books for postmenopausal women. See Lock (1993) for a discussion of menopausal attitudes in the United States and Japan. See Jose van Dijck (1995) for a discussion of links between scientific and medical discourses and cultural dissemination (about reproductive technologies).

10. The protective "commonsense" division between "science" and "nonscience" has been interrogated in science studies and is, in any case, simply *not* applicable here. It is not merely that the subdiscipline of medical anthropology, with its study of cultures of medicine as well as medicine in cultures generally, does not rely on such distinctions, but that there are many different languages of medicine and science. See also Fisher (1995), Mischler (1984), Mischler et al. (1981), D. Silverman (1987), and Waitzkin (1983) for critiques—from different positions—of the dualism of "medicine" and "the social," and see Latour (1992) for a critique of such dualisms as "science" and "society." See John R. G. Turner (1990) for a discussion of scientists as "intensely

political animals" and Chandra Mukerji (1989) for an interesting demonstration of the role of government in maintaining a scientific workforce for possible future needs. To grant Martin's argument here, one need not join the (myriad of) debates about the subtle definitions of "interests," "politics," "society," or "cultural attitudes."

11. An interesting contrast of the effect of context results from Martin's later use of these two sentences—slightly revised—in a much shorter essay (Martin 1990, 75). There Martin builds an argument that compresses, reshapes, and refocuses material she has used elsewhere, extracting and reusing some of the most effective sentences of previous arguments. Her intrasentence revisions are slight in that essay; the significant revision is that the two "series" sentences appear one right after the other, without the long introductory quotations to which they respond in *The Woman in the Body*. Stripped of their dramatic placement in accent to the textbook passages, these sentences change in rhetorical effect. In their new setting, the sentences do not carry—for me—the same impact or irony. The difference in effect suggests that it is their *embedding* in Martin's longer analysis and their contrast to and bundling of the negative language of the prefatory long quotations that make these sentences ironic, rather than simply their effect of excess, of being "crowded." It is this experience that justifies my claim that their strongly ironic effect resides not in the sentences *themselves*, but in their use as *accenting counter*argument in a context tightly connected to the argument they are designed to counter.

12. Martin's sources cited include "regress," "addiction," "withdrawal" (Lein 1979, 84), "decline" and "gonadotropins" (Vander, Sherman, and Luciano 1985, 597), "fail to muster strength" (Norris 1984, 181), "atrophy" (Vander, Sherman, and Luciano 1985, 598), "wither" (Norris 1984, 181), "senile" (Netter 1965, 121). The longer passage quoted is "the senile ovary . . . stroma" (Netter 1965, 116). The last sentence in the passage is ironic, in the sense of representing Martin's agonists' point of view, rather than her own. I omit a few sentences of anecdote between sentences 12 and 13.

13. Laws, surveying British medical textbooks, notes that J. C. McClure Browne (1973), Derek Llewellyn-Jones (1982), and Sir C. J. Dewhurst (1981) all present "the shedding of the endometrium (the lining of the womb) as necrosis, that is death, of cells," but that Josephine Barnes (1980) does not.

14. Martin's sources include introductory physiology textbooks: William F. Ganong (1985, 776), Arthur C. Guyton (1984, 498–499), Elliot B. Mason (1983, 419 and 423), and a specialized text for medical students, Thomas Sernka and Eugene Jacobson (1983, 7).

15. Martin's sources include introductory physiology textbooks: Ganong (1985, 356), and Arthur J. Vander, James H. Sherman, and Dorothy S. Luciano (1985, 557–558).

16. Martin's source is Vander, Sherman, and Luciano (1980, 483–484). In a footnote, Martin states: "The latest edition of this text has removed the first of these sentences, but kept the second" (228, n. 79, citing Vander, Sherman, and Luciano 1985, 557). Martin does not indicate whether the sentence was removed because the authors no longer consider the mechanisms "remarkable," or because the mechanisms are no longer "uncertain."

17. I am arguing here on the analogy of art forgery and fraud, as described by Hugh Kenner at a lecture at Mt. Holyoke College, 1985. According to Kenner, when

artists make forgeries, completing works in the style of particular artists, and success-fully pass them off, they do so in the context of social attitudes and concerns about art in their own time. Later, when we look back at those forgeries, it seems incredible to us that they deceived experts at the time of their making, because to us, they are imbued with the (zeitgeist) of the era of their creation, as well as the era they are imitating. Anne Hollander (1993) makes a similar argument about how paintings of different eras represent both nude and clothed bodies according to their cultural ideals.

18. Such a position appears unlikely for many medical anthropologists: see, of many examples, Good (1994), Hahn (1995), Kleinman (1995), and Lock and Gordon (1988).

19. This is, however, the position that discourses of scientific and medical exper-tise imply. Jo Murphy-Lawless points out, "We need to develop our ability to identify the truth claims of obstetrics for what they are and for what they seek to resist or deny about women. Of course there is a problem of truth claims with all expert discourses but it is a special problem with medicine which has had the capacity to convince us of its absolute distinctiveness from other social practices, a capacity that is linked to the core argument that medicine has the power to deal with death, if not hold off death entirely. Penetrating what Foucault has described as medicine's solid scientific arma-ture is an especially critical skill for women because the truth claims of obstetrics have such enormous cultural and social power to define our lives" (1998, 23).

20. See, for example, critiques by Anne Fausto-Sterling (1985), Sioban D. Harlow (1986), and Randi Daimon Koeske (1983).

21. In a well-known column in *Ms.*, Gloria Steinem predicted different attitudes were it to be men rather than women who menstruate: "Military men, right-wing poli-ticians, and religious fundamentalists would cite menstruation ('*men*-struation') as proof that only men could serve in the army ('you have to give blood to get blood'), occupy political office ('can women be aggressive without that steadfast cycle governed by the planet Mars?'), be priests and ministers ('how could a woman give her blood for our sins?'), or rabbis ('without the monthly loss of impurities, women remain un-clean')" (1978, 110).

22. See Susan C. Lawrence and Kae Bendixen (1992), Lisa Jean Moore and Adele E. Clarke (1995, 2001), and Alan Petersen (1998).

23. See, for example, studies by Koutroulis (1990), Laws (1990), Posner (1979), Scully (1980), Scully and Bart (1973).

24. From Scully, for example: "An emotionally healthy married woman will wel-come pregnancy as a step toward maturity. The reasons for not wanting a child usually betray an underlying ambivalence toward the feminine role. They may be expressions of unconscious anxiety, conflict, or inadequacy" (Benson 1971, quoted in Scully 1980, 107). Or another: "The bride should be advised to allow her husband's sex drive to set their pace and she should attempt to gear hers satisfactorily to his . . . she is cautioned not to make her sexual relations completely passive. . . . She may be reminded that it is unsatisfactory to take a tone-deaf individual to a concert" (Novak, Jones, and Jones 1970, 726, quoted by Scully 1980, 111).

25. See van Dijck (1995) on public representations of medical information with regard to new reproductive technologies; see Patricia Kaufert (1988) on how medical research models represent menopause in explicit terms of division. Justine Coupland

and Angie Williams (2002) analyze a range of popular texts and brochures in the United Kingdom. They argue these fall into three different discourses: (1) "pharmaceutical" discourse found in brochures presents menopause as pathology to be remedied by hormone replacement therapy; (2) the "alternative therapy" discourse recommends instead changing lifestyles and using "natural" alternatives; (3) the "emancipatory feminist" discourse rejects the pharmaceutical discourse and encourages seeing menopause as a positive change.

26. See also Deborah Gordon (1988), Hahn (1985), and Pearl Katz (1985).

27. For example, Mischler (1984), Mischler et al. (1981), Waitzkin (1991), and Candace West (1984).

28. For example, Kathy Davis (1988), Fisher (1986, 1995), Merrill Singer (1987), Todd and Fisher (1993), and Todd (1989).

29. This is not to say that some doctors in some settings are not "nice" to their patients (Davis 1993); the exercise of the power of the biomedical model toward women and other patients does not require disrespectful, curt behavior, although it seems to produce it a good deal, according to Susan M. DiGiacomo (1987), Terry Mizrahi (1986), Scarlet Pollack (1984), and Singer (1987), and much of the research on the interactions between doctors and medical students and their female patients). But being a quiet patient does not imply acceptance, either (see Martin 1987 as well as Todd and Fisher 1993 on "resistance"). The vigor of the woman's health movement suggests that many Anglo-American women are seeking alternatives to limitations of biomedical discourse about their bodies (Broom 1991).

30. For example, G. J. Barker-Benfield (1976), Ludmilla Jordanova (1989), Thomas Laqueur (1990), Jo Murphy-Lawless (1988), and Sally Shuttleworth (1990).

31. For example, Gena Corea (1985/1977), Robbie E. Davis-Floyd (1987, "Obstetric," 1987, "Technological"), Brigitte Jordan (1983), Anne Oakley (1984), Barbara Katz Rothman (1985), Scully (1980), Michelle Stanworth (1987), Paula A. Treichler (1990), and West (1984).

32. See Fisher (1986) and Ruth Behar's review (1990) of *Woman in the Body* for a discussion of excessive hysterectomies. Harrison describes a compelling scene during her residency in which one doctor encourages another to remove a particular patient's ovaries because he needs some ovaries to culture (Harrison 1983, 208–210). Scully (1980), in her discussion of the training of obstetrician-gynecologists, quotes several texts suggesting that this might be the case. For example: "Menstruation is a nuisance to most women, and if this can be abolished without impairing ovarian function, it would probably be a blessing not only to the women but to their husbands" (Novak, Jones, and Jones 1975, 133, quoted by Scully 1980, 143). Or another edition: "for the woman who has completed her family, the uterus is a rather worthless organ" (Novak, Jones, and Jones 1970, 112, quoted by Scully 1980, 143).

33. See, for example, Corea (1985/1977), Adriane Fugh-Berman (1992), Agnes Miles (1991), and Jerry L. Weaver and Sharon D. Garrett (1983).

34. Martin's work appears at a rhetorical intersection, a nexus for lines of inquiry in a variety of disciplines; she must speak to scholars from many interests—feminism, science studies, literature, history, anthropology, sociology, and other disciplines on aspects of science, bodies, and medical care. Because academic conventions tend to encourage textually muted arguments, we may sometimes overlook the highly contested

nature of *all* academic argument, and the degree to which scholarship in medical anthropology has become increasingly important to scholars in a variety of other fields concerned with discourses and bodies. Part of Martin's success in reaching diverse audiences is revealed by the range of publications that reviewed *The Woman in the Body* soon after it was published. I found the following: GENERAL SCIENCE: *New Scientist* (Birke 1989). HISTORY AND SOCIOLOGY OF SCIENCE: *Birth* (Davis-Floyd 1990), *ISIS* (Hiddinga 1989), *Sociology of Health and Illness* (B. Turner 1991). SOCIOLOGY: *Australian and New Zealand Journal of Sociology* (Hanlin 1991), *British Journal of Sociology* (Hepworth 1991), *Contemporary Sociology* (Richardson 1988), *Sociological Review* (McDonald 1990). HISTORY: *Journal of American History* (Hoffert 1988). OTHER: *Hastings Center Report* (Rowland 1989), *Law and Social Inquiry* (Marcus 1990), *Michigan Quarterly Review* (Behar 1990), *Socialist Review* (A. Wilson 1989).

CHAPTER SEVEN

1. While many of the transformative and ridiculing rhetorical strategies used by Herschberger are similar to those used by the Study Group and Martin, Herschberger was writing in an earlier social and historical context. See Margaret Jackson (1987).

2. After the title and before the sleeping beauty story appears the following:

Scientists have found the molecule that triggers the start of human life.

In Short

- Initially, human eggs lie dormant, with the instruction to begin cell division switched off
- After contact with a single sperm, a huge rush of calcium inside the egg is responsible for triggering embryo development
- A lack of a family of proteins called phospholipase Cs could be a common cause of male infertility

3. A subsequent letter to *Chemistry World* from Geoff Rayner-Canham MRSC, Sir Wilfred Grenfell College, Memorial University of Newfoundland, Canada (Rayner-Canham 2004) suggested some of the difficulties of this anthropomorphic language and cited Londa Schiebinger (1999) and Emily Martin (1991) as sources.

4. The terms are selected from a passage from Gerald Schatten and Heide Schatten (1983, 29) and quoted by the Biology and Gender Study Group (1989, 177).

5. Feminist scholars have charged that the rhetoric of "science" contains narratives, metaphors, and other language expressing deeply gendered interpretations of biological processes, interpretations that may influence both scientific and medical practice. See, for example, Anne Fausto-Sterling (1985), Donna J. Haraway (1988, 1989), Sandra Harding (1986, 1991), Ruth Hubbard (1990), Evelyn Fox Keller (1985, 1992), Carolyn Merchant (1980).

6. A significant number of scholars has been concerned with anthropological, sociological, and historical reconstruction of science, including its narrative construction, for example: Françoise Bastide (1986), Gillian Beer (1983), Stephen Jay Gould (1989), Donna J. Haraway (1989), Rom Harre (1990), Debra Journet (1990, 1991), Philip Kitcher (1985), Misia Landau (1987, 1991), Bruno Latour (1987), Bruno Latour

and Françoise Bastide (1986), Bruno Latour and Shirley C. Strum (1986), Greg Myers (1990 "Making," 1990 *Writing*, 1991), Gayle L. Ormiston and Raphael Sassower (1989), Joseph Rouse (1990), Ronald Schleifer, Robert Con Davis, and Nancy Mergler (1992), John A. Schuster and Richard R. Yeo (1986), Steven Shapin (1984), and Sharon Traweek (1992).

7. The critics I analyze have considerable company in their endeavors to understand the rhetorics of science, particularly the use of metaphor. Useful works include Charles Bazerman (1988), Andrew E. Benjamin, Geoffrey N. Cantor, and John R. R. Christie (1987), James J. Bono (1990), Geoffrey Cantor (1989), Peter Dear (1991), Alan G. Gross (1990), N. Katherine Hayles (1990), Frederic L. Holmes (1991), David Locke (1992), John Lyne (1990), Marcello Pera and William R. Shea (1991), Lawrence J. Prelli (1989), and Herbert W. Simons (1980).

8. Martin has drawn her terms from various textbooks: "mission" is from Bruce Alberts et al. (1983, 796); the quest phrase is from Guyton (1984, 613); the "rescue" quotation is from Alberts et al. (1983, 796 and 804). Martin also comments in passing that scientists do not well understand the purpose of an "egg coat" protecting the outer part of the egg, and have tended to regard it simply as an "impediment" to fertilization. I would argue that categorizing something as an impediment relies on a purposive interpretation of the sperm's role.

9. Martin, Herschberger, and the Study Group are only three of many who find that idealized descriptions of scientific "objectivity" imply science is produced with no "point of view," but I read them as arguing that shared standards of inquiry can supply us with knowledge about the world. There are many aspects to these debates. Many influential feminist critics argue that a situated point of view is inescapable in doing any kind of inquiry. In this view, it is impossible to conduct any academic inquiry without a perspective, and, necessarily, a partial one. Techniques to balance one's perspective, clarify one's standards, and incorporate other perspectives make possible a kind of "objectivity" that is rigorous but not value-free. In this argument, what undermines some scientific claims and models is not that they demonstrate the kinds of perspectives delineated by the Study Group, but that they (or their defenders) claim that this is not the case. Martin, the Study Group, and Herschberger seem to agree that at least in this case, social constructions infuse our views of any biological "reality," but indicate that other research results are not congruent with the gendered metaphors they critique. I am assuming here that their critique argues that scientific knowledge is socially constructed in the general sense, since they assume that there are better views of science that may be developed through scientific inquiry. For interesting and fruitful arguments about such notions of "objectivity," see Donna J. Haraway (1988), Sandra Harding (1986, 1991), Mary E. Hawkesworth (1989), Evelyn Fox Keller (1985, 1992), and Helen E. Longino (1988, 1990, 1993).

10. The Study Group's sources here: The British companionate marriage was proposed by C. H. Waddington (1940). (G. Wersky [1978] was the source for Waddington's attitudes toward marriage.) The "wife-dominant" relationship was proposed by E. E. Just (1939). (K. R. Manning [1983] was the source for Just's attitudes toward his own conjugal partner.) The German marriage model was discussed by J. Harwood (1984). The American companionate family was proposed by T. H. Morgan (1926). (The Study Group cites G. Allen [personal communication] for indications that this

was the model of Morgan's own marriage.) The Study Group also cites, for those interested in further discussion, Scott F. Gilbert (1988); Gilbert is a member of the Study Group.

11. The Study Group's source here is Schatten and Schatten (1983). The Study Group notes that the existence of microvilli on sea urchin ova has been known since 1917, but scientists have not agreed on its interpretation, which, the Study Group indicates, is controversial. One reason for the controversy may be that gendered metaphors obscure and underplay this characteristic.

12. Martin cites work carried out by Jay M. Baltz when a graduate student in the Thomas C. Jenkins Department of Biophysics at Johns Hopkins University. She cites Jay Baltz and Richard A. Cone (1985), Jay Baltz and Richard A. Cone (1986), and Jay M. Baltz, David F. Katz, and Richard A. Cone (1988). She also cites Bennett M. Shapiro (1987) and Paul M. Wassarman (1987, 1988). And, with criticism also of their language, she cites Gerald Schatten and Heide Schatten (1984). The Study Group cites Eva M. Eicher and Linda Washburn (1986) and Gerald Schatten and Heide Schatten (1983).

13. Martin states: "[Wassarman] . . . calls the molecule that has been isolated, ZP3, a 'sperm receptor.' . . . It is as if Wassarman were determined to make the egg the receiving partner. Usually in biological research, the protein member of the pair of binding molecules is called the receptor, and physically it has a pocket in it rather like a lock. As the diagrams that illustrate Wassarman's article show, the molecules on the sperm are proteins and have 'pockets.' The small, mobile molecules that fit into these pockets are called ligands. As shown in the diagrams, ZP3 on the egg is a polymer of 'keys'; many small knobs stick out. Typically, molecules on the sperm would be called receptors and molecules on the egg would be called ligands. But Wassarman chose to name ZP3 on the egg the receptor and to create a new term, 'the egg-binding protein,' for the molecule on the sperm that would have been called the receptor" (Martin 1991, 495–496, emphasis hers, citing Paul M. Wassarman 1987, 1988).

14. Their critiques do not explicate, but rely on the understanding that the nature of metaphor and its undeniable cognitive value as a "logic of discovery" prevents metaphorical narratives from operating in isolation in a purportedly "purely scientific" argument. Since the significance of a metaphor depends on the linguistic and empirical meanings it creates and "carries" from one domain to another, the two are inextricably linked. The point of using a metaphor—whether for theoretical, illustrative, or pedagogical insight—is exactly its connection with another type of lived experience. Metaphors—in scientific texts or elsewhere—help readers to call to mind the ideas, both linguistic and empirical, that are commonly held to be associated with the referent in a given language community. Thus a shift of meaning may result from a change in the set of associated ideas as well as a change of reference or use (Hesse 1970, 160). See Richard Harvey Brown (1977).

15. The Study Group's source here is K. P. Russell (1977).

16. Landau's examination of paleoanthropological narratives of human evolution reveals that choice of "protagonist" exerted considerable influence on theoretical narratives; the crucial difference was the choice of donor-agent. Versions of what Landau calls a "narrative approach" to analyzing contemporary scientific theories suggest foci of attention for our own analysis of both the spermatic romance narrative and its

ridiculing commentary and counternarratives. In *Narratives of Human Evolution* (1991) (see also Landau 1987), Landau argues that paleoanthropology has been caught within the constraints of the stories it tells, so that it has, in effect, "told the same story over and over." Landau uses the categories proposed by Vladimir Propp (1928/1968) for the analysis of folktales to consider the structure of stories told in paleoanthropology. Propp's scheme allows identification of story elements (heroes, dragons, etc.), as well as the various relationships of these categories to each other and to the structure of the tale as a whole. Landau demonstrates how the various forms of the narrative of the "ascent of man" meet Propp's criteria and how they vary, identifying from her analysis the component crucial to differences among paleoanthropological stories: the entity considered "the donor"—the force that provides the hero ("emerging 'man'") with skills to survive.

17. Latour and Bastide (in Bastide 1986, Latour 1987, and Latour and Bastide 1986) demonstrate that the textual power that Vladimir Propp and others have used associated with the agent of a story is itself a potent rhetorical tool. The scientific article reports that the scientist has subjected its hero/substance to many trials of strength and it emerges triumphant: it is indeed the hero, radium. They argue: "The 'things behind' the scientific texts are thus similar to the heroes of a fairy tale. All of them are defined only by their performances: defeating the ugly seven-headed dragon; resisting precipitation; saving the King's daughter against all odds; finding one's way out of the tortuous kidney ducts . . . each performance presupposes a competence which, from the start, retrospectively explains why the hero withstood all the ordeals" (63–64, emphasis mine).

18. In a somewhat different gesture, Martin attacks the imbalanced presentation of roles and motives assigned the various participants in the story. Martin undermines the unacknowledged but systematic use of "manly" qualities as characteristic of the sperm by providing us with another vision of the sperm—as coward rather than daredevil. She notes: "The one depiction of the sperm as weak and timid, instead of strong and powerful—the only such representation in western civilization, so far as I know—occurs in Woody Allen's movie *Everything You Wanted to Know About Sex* *But Were Afraid to Ask*. Allen, playing the part of an apprehensive sperm inside a man's testicles, is scared of the man's approaching orgasm. He is reluctant to launch himself into the darkness, afraid of contraceptive devices, afraid of winding up on the ceiling if the man masturbates" (Martin 1991, 491).

19. From Herschberger's text: "Someday, perhaps, a democratic account of the physiology of sex will be written, an account that will stress both the functional and the organic aspects of reproduction. At present the functional is stressed only in connection with women: it is in them that ovaries, tubes, uterus, and vagina have endless interdependence. In the male, reproduction would seem to involve 'organs' only" (1948/1970, 87).

20. Martin indicates that Deborah Gordon has described such an approach as "atomism," and finds it common in Western science and medicine (D. Gordon 1988, especially 26). Martin argues that one author she analyzes "makes less of the egg's activity . . . by describing the components of the egg but referring to the sperm as a whole entity. . . . When he refers to processes going on within sperm, he consistently returns to descriptions that remind us from whence the activities came: they are part

of sperm that penetrate an egg or generate propulsive force. When he refers to processes going on within eggs, he stops there. As a result, any active role he grants them appears to be assigned to the parts of the egg, and not to the egg itself" (Martin 1991, 497–498). Martin is referring to Paul M. Wassarman (1987, 1988).

21. Martin also argues that interpretation is influenced when authors mention features of both sperm and egg as if they were distinctive to only one or the other—omitting (or omitting in that section of the text) any mention of analogous features. For example, Martin quotes a textbook's claim that the egg's lack of long-term viability is a major source of urgency in bringing sperm and egg together: "once released from the supportive environment of the ovary, *an egg will die within hours* unless rescued by a sperm" (Martin 1991, 490, quoting Alberts et al. 1983, added emphasis mine). Martin does not suggest that this information is untrue, but that its presentation—independent of similar comments with regard to spermatic longevity—serves to stress ovular weakness and, by omission, to imply spermatic strength. She further comments: "The wording stresses the frailty and dependency of the egg, even though the same text acknowledges elsewhere that sperm also live for only a few hours" (Martin 1991, 490, added emphasis mine), in response to above quotation from Alberts et al. (1983).

22. According to Martin, the egg "does not move or journey, but passively 'is transported,' 'is swept,' or even 'drifts' along the fallopian tube. In utter contrast, sperm are small, 'streamlined,' and invariably active. They 'deliver' their genes to the egg, 'activate' the developmental potential of the egg, and have a 'velocity' that is often remarked upon" (1991, 489, emphasis hers). Martin's sources cited include "is transported," "is swept" (Guyton 1984, 619; Mountcastle 1980, 609), "drifts" (Miller and Pelham 1984, 5), "streamlined," "deliver," "activate the developmental potential of the egg" (Alberts et al. 1983, 796), "velocity" (Ganong 1975, 322).

23. Herschberger seems to be concerned about responding to particularly egg-ignoring assertions in Fritz Kahn (1939/1942/1948, 29). Her paraphrase of his statement in the Patriarchal account: "No less than 225,000,000 cells are emitted from the man's body with each ejaculation—and every cell is a human being!" Her accompanying footnote: "The sperm itself is only 1/2 a human being, but such fractional qualification would ruin the esthetic veracity of [Kahn's] statement" (1948/1970, 75).

24. Martin challenges the romance's typical deployment of the theme of *waste* in relation to female processes such as oogenesis (the production of ova), suggesting that if such a theme is significant, it might more properly be applied to *male* processes. I quote Martin (who is quoting textbooks): "In a section heading for *Molecular Biology of the Cell*, a best-selling text, we are told that 'Oogenesis is wasteful.' The text goes on to emphasize that of the seven million oogonia, or egg germs cells, in the female embryo, most degenerate in the ovary. Of those that do go on to become oocytes, or eggs, many also degenerate, so that at birth only two million eggs remain in the ovaries. Degeneration continues throughout a woman's life: by puberty 300,000 eggs remain, and only a few are present by menopause. 'During the 40 or so years of a women's reproductive life, only 400 to 500 eggs will have been released,' the authors write. 'All the rest will have degenerated. It is still a mystery why so many eggs are formed only to die in the ovaries' (Martin 1991, 488, quoting from Alberts et al. 1983, 795). The real mystery is why the male's vast production of sperm is not seen as wasteful. Assuming

that a man 'produces' 100 million sperm (10^8) per day (a conservative estimate) during an average reproductive life of sixty years, he would produce well over two trillion sperm in his lifetime. Assuming that a woman 'ripens' one egg per lunar month, or thirteen per year, over the course of her forty-year reproductive life, she would total five hundred eggs in her lifetime. But the word 'waste' implies an excess, too much produced. Assuming two or three offspring, for every baby a woman produces, she wastes only around two hundred eggs. For every baby a man produces, he wastes more than one trillion (10^{12}) sperm" (Martin 1991, 488–489).

25. Martin touches on the theme of size in mocking a caption in Lennart Nilsson (1975) that purports to label a picture scientifically: "There is another way that sperm, despite their small size, can be made to loom in importance over the egg. In a collection of scientific papers, an electron micrograph of an enormous egg and tiny sperm is titled 'A Portrait of the Sperm.' This is a little like showing a photo of a dog and calling it a picture of the fleas. Granted, microscopic sperm are harder to photograph than eggs, which are just large enough to see with the naked eye. But surely the use of the term 'portrait,' a word associated with the powerful and wealthy, is significant. Eggs have only micrographs or pictures, not portraits" (Martin 1991, 491, emphasis mine). Martin is arguing that the caption used in Nilsson is inflated and inappropriate. There is no overlooking the riposte of the egg-as-dog, sperm-as-flea comparison, which emphasizes the size differential that Martin already emphasizes by the terms *enormous* and *tiny*. By delineating several implications of the word *portrait*, and wryly comparing the probable word choices held to be appropriate for the egg (given her research), Martin attempts to evoke the sense of the son of the house under a system of primogeniture—small, he may be, but he is the man of the family.

26. Martin cites also a *New York Times* report by Malcolm W. Browne (1988), and John Barth's literary rendition, "Night-Sea Journey" (1968).

27. The forums in which the essays have been published propose but by no means delimit their audiences. Martin's appearance in *Signs* (1991) suggests an audience familiar with feminist argument, social constructionism, academic discourse, and social influences on scientific and scholarly practices. The essay supplements her other work as a medical anthropologist linking culture and science: Martin's work includes *The Woman in the Body: A Cultural Analysis of Reproduction* (1987) and *Flexible Bodies: Tracking Immunity in American Culture from the Days of Polio to the Age of AIDS* (1994). An interview is Suzanne R. Kirschner and Emily Martin (1999). The Study Group, composed of scientists, feminist scholars, and students, shares a similar audience; the essay appearing first in a special issue of the journal of feminist philosophy *Hypatia* in 1988, then in Nancy Tuana's edited collection from those special issues, *Feminism and Science* (1989). Herschberger's essay presents a more complex case. Herschberger, a poet, playwright, and essayist, originally published it as a chapter in her witty challenge to stereotypical gender roles, *Adam's Rib*, in 1948 (reprinted in 1970); *Adam's Rib* was also published in England in 1954, and subsequently in Finland, Norway, and Sweden, under the pseudonym Josephine Langstaff. Parts of *Adam's Rib* have been anthologized in several textbooks. Her argument therefore has a longer history as part of public discourse—and suggests exactly the continued need for reiteration of the same arguments that may itself encourage ridicule and other textual vehemence. Sources on Herschberger: *Book Review Digest* (1948, 377–378), *The Readers' Encyclopedia*

of American Literature (1962, 462), *Contemporary Authors, Vol. 33–36, First Revision* (1973, 1978, 395–396), *American Women Writers* (1980, 286–288), *Twentieth Century Authors, First Supplement* (1959, 439), and Shira Tarrant (2006).

28. Paul R. Gross, for example, one of the leaders in calling science studies scholars "antiscience," apparently did not understand that both Martin and the Study Group were engaging in ridicule. He argues with regard to "The Egg and the Sperm," "This essay is remarkable, even among its stablemates, for angry tendentiousness. It is concerned entirely with narrative and rhetorical strategies [not scientific information]. . . . Least of all do [the data] suggest any disparagement of ova and special enthusiasm for sperm—to, that is, any ordinary and reasonable reader" (2000, 68, n. 7). Gross here deploys the trope of the angry feminist, uses "stablemates" to suggest that she and other feminist science studies scholars are animals, and concludes that anyone who might appreciate her argument is outside the economy of reason. The ridicule of the Study Group challenges Gross and his coauthor Norman Levitt also. They declare the Study Group "metaphor-mongers." They then say that the scientific language was a long time ago, that we cannot worry about what the scientists said then because they were really important scientists, that gender had nothing to do with the discussions about sperms and eggs anyway, and that it is not important because popular culture is no longer sexist anyway because on television beautiful women with lipstick and high heels wield Berettas and fight successfully (Gross and Levitt 1997, 107–148).

29. Mockery avoids the equivocation of many politeness forms often used in face-to-face interaction and other academic argument: for instance, the common prefatory comment "With all due respect" leaves listeners free to make idiosyncratic interpretations of how much respect is due, thus camouflaging the speaker's thoughts on the subject quite successfully. In contrast, mockery clarifies this relationship between critic and text criticized—"Without (a lot of/much/any) respect"—and interpellates readers from that vantage point.

CHAPTER EIGHT

1. Rush Limbaugh: "A bunch of angry feminazis took him [Summers] out simply because he spoke the truth about diversity on campus and the differences in men and women." Broadcast of the *Rush Limbaugh Show,* February 22, 2005.

2. The *Washington Post*'s George Will (January 27, 2005) wielded the epithet used to denigrate and dismiss women for centuries: "hysterical." It's derived from the Greek word for "uterus," which is presumably why Will used a form of the word no fewer than six times to patronize MIT biology professor Nancy Hopkins for telling the *Boston Globe* (January 17, 2005) that Summers's comments made her want to throw up. "Is this the fruit of feminism?" he sarcastically wondered, before broadening his hysteria smear to every person offended by Summers's musings: "Only hysterics denounce interest in those possible [gender] differences—or, in Hopkins's case, the mere mention of them—as 'bias'" (Wakeman and Hollar 2005).

3. George Will: "Is this the fruit of feminism? A woman at the peak of the academic pyramid becomes theatrically flurried by an unwelcome idea and, like a Victorian maiden exposed to male coarseness, suffers the vapors and collapses on the drawing room carpet in a heap of crinolines until revived by smelling salts and the offending

brute's contrition." (George Will, "Nature, Nurture, and Larry Summers's Sin," 2008, 250–251

4. Wiegman provides a superb analysis of the use of mourning and loss in feminist arguments and how it reflects the psychic life of feminism. Wiegman (1999) discusses Susan Gubar (1998); Wiegman (1999/2000) discusses Martha Nussbaum (1999) and Wendy Brown (1995, 1997); Wiegman (2000) discusses W. Brown (1999), Gubar (1998), and Nussbaum (1999); Wiegman (2002) discusses Gubar (1998); Wiegman (2004) discusses Gubar (1998), Wiegman (1999), and W. Brown (1997). Sianne Ngai (2001) provides a fascinating and productive analysis of the concept of envy with regard to the film *Single White Female* and the debate between Gubar (1998) and Wiegman (1999), as well as that of Nussbaum (1999) and Butler (1999).

References

Acocella, Joan. "Cather and the Academy." *The New Yorker* (November 27, 1995): 56–71.

Adams, Mike. *Feminists Say the Darndest Things: A Politically Incorrect Professor Confronts "Womyn" on Campus.* New York: Sentinel HC, 2008.

————. *Welcome to the Ivory Tower of Babel: Confessions of a Conservative College Professor.* Augusta, GA: Harbor House, 2004.

Adorno, Theodor W. *Minima Moralia: Reflections from Damaged Life.* Trans. E.F.N. Jephcott. New York: Verso, 1974.

Ahmed, Sara. *The Cultural Politics of Emotion.* New York: Routledge, 2004.

Alberts, Bruce, et al. *Molecular Biology of the Cell.* New York: Garland, 1983.

Alcoff, Linda, and Elizabeth Potter, eds. *Feminist Epistemologies.* New York: Routledge, 1993.

Althusser, Louis. "Ideology and Ideological State Apparatuses." *Lenin and Philosophy and Other Essays.* Trans. Ben Brewster. New York: Monthly Review, 1971. 127–187.

Aristotle. "Rhetoric." Trans. W. Rhys Roberts. *The Complete Works of Aristotle.* Ed. Jonathan Barnes. Princeton, NJ: Princeton U P, 1984. 2152–2269.

Armstrong, Nancy. *Desire and Domestic Fiction: A Political History of the Novel.* New York: Oxford U P, 1987.

————. *How Novels Think: The Limits of Individualism from 1719–1900.* New York: Columbia U P, 2005.

————, and Leonard Tennenhouse. *The Imaginary Puritan: Literature, Intellectual Labor, and the Origins of Personal Life.* Berkeley: U of California P, 1994.

Austern, Linda Phyllis. "'Alluring the Auditorie to Effeminacie': Music and the English Renaissance Idea of the Feminine." Paper presented at the American Musicological Society, Baltimore, November 1988.

————. "Love, Death and Ideas of Music in the English Renaissance." *Love and Death in the Renaissance*. Ed. Kenneth R. Bartlett, Konrad Eisenbichler, and Janice Liedl. Ottawa: Dovehouse Editions, 1991. 17–36.

————. "'Sing Againe Syren': The Female Musician and Sexual Enchantment in Elizabethan Life and Literature." *Renaissance Quarterly* 42.3 (1989): 420–448.

Baer, Hans A. *Encounters with Biomedicine: Case Studies in Medical Anthropology*. New York: Gordon and Breach, 1987.

Bailey, F. G. *The Tactical Uses of Passion: An Essay on Power, Reason, and Reality*. Ithaca, NY: Cornell U P, 1983.

Bakhtin, Mikhail. *The Dialogic Imagination*. Ed. Michael Holquist. Trans. Caryl Emerson and Michael Holquist. Austin: U of Texas P, 1981.

Baltz, Jay, and Richard A. Cone. "Flagellar Torque on the Head Determines the Force Needed to Tether a Sperm." Abstract for Biophysical Society, 1986.

————. "What Force Is Needed to Tether a Sperm?" Abstract for the Society for the Study of Reproduction, 1985.

Baltz, Jay M., David F. Katz, and Richard A. Cone. "The Mechanics of Sperm-Egg Interaction at the Zona Pellucida." *Biophysical Journal* 54.4 (1988): 643–654.

Barker-Benfield, G. J. *The Horrors of the Half-Known Life: Male Attitudes toward Women and Sexuality in Nineteenth-Century America*. 1st Edition. New York: Harper and Row, 1976.

Barkin, Elaine. "Either/other." *Perspectives of New Music* 30.2 (1992): 206–233.

Barnes, Josephine. *Lecture Notes on Gynaecology*. 4th Edition. Oxford: Blackwell, 1980.

Bar-On, Bat-Ami, ed. *Engendering Origins: Critical Feminist Readings in Plato and Aristotle*. Albany: State U of New York P, 1994.

Barrett, Robert J. "Clinical Writing and the Documentary Construction of Schizophrenia." *Culture, Medicine and Psychiatry* 12 (1988): 265–299.

Barth, John. "Night-Sea Journey." *Lost in the Funhouse*. Garden City, NY: Doubleday, 1968. 3–13.

Bastide, Françoise. "The Semiotic Analysis of Discourse." Unpublished manuscript. Paris: Ecole des Mines, 1986.

Bauerlein, Mark. "Critical Discussions: Bad Writing's Back." *Philosophy and Literature* 28 (2004): 180–191.

Bauman, Richard, and Charles L. Briggs. *Voices of Modernity: Language Ideologies and the Politics of Inequality*. New York: Cambridge U P, 2003.

Baumlin, James S., and Tita French Baumlin, eds. *Ethos: New Essays in Rhetorical and Critical Theory*. 1st Edition. Dallas: Southern Methodist U P, 1994.

Bazerman, Charles. *Shaping Written Knowledge: The Genre and Activity of the Experimental Article in Science*. Madison: U of Wisconsin P, 1988.

Beer, Gillian. *Darwin's Plots: Evolutionary Narrative in Darwin, George Eliot, and Nineteenth-Century Fiction*. New York: Routledge Kegan Paul, 1983.

Behar, Ruth. "The Body in the Woman, the Story in the Woman: A Book Review and Personal Essay." *Michigan Quarterly Review* 29.4 (1990): 694–738.

Benjamin, Andrew E., Geoffrey N. Cantor, and John R. R. Christie, eds. *The Figural and the Literal: Problems of Language in the History of Science and Philosophy, 1630–1800*. Manchester, UK: Manchester U P, 1987.

Benson, Ralph. *Handbook of Obstetrics and Gynecology.* Los Altos, CA: Lange, 1971.

Berger, Bennett. Review of *Higher Superstition: The Academic Left and Its Quarrels with Science* by Paul R. Gross and Norman Levitt. *Science* 264.5161 (May 13, 1994): 985+.

Berlant, Lauren, ed. *Compassion: The Culture and Politics of an Emotion.* New York: Routledge, 2004.

———. *The Queen of America Goes to Washington City: Essays on Sex and Citizenship.* Durham, NC: Duke U P, 1997.

———. "The Subject of True Feeling: Pain, Privacy and Politics." *Feminist Consequences: Theory for the New Century.* Ed. Elizabeth Bronfen and Mischa Kauka. New York: Columbia, 2001. 126–160.

Biology and Gender Study Group (Athena Beldecos, Sarah Bailey, Scott Gilbert, Karen Hicks, Lori Kenschaft, Nancy Niemczyk, Rebecca Rosenberg, Stephanie Schaertel, and Andrew Wedel). "The Importance of Feminist Critique for Contemporary Cell Biology." *Feminism and Science.* Ed. Nancy Tuana. Bloomington: Indiana U P, 1989. 172–187.

Birke, Lynda. "Mechanical Models of Women." Review of *The Woman in the Body* by Emily Martin. *New Scientist* 124.1686 (October 14, 1989): 61.

Birnbaum, D. A., T. A. Nosanchuck, and W. L. Croll. "Children's Stereotypes about Sex Differences in Emotionality." *Sex Roles* 6 (1980): 435–443.

Bloom, Allan. *The Closing of the American Mind.* New York: Simon and Schuster, 1988.

Bohlman, Philip V. "Musicology as a Political Act." *Journal of Musicology* XI.4 (1993): 411–436.

Bono, James J. "Science, Discourse, and Literature: The Role/Rule of Metaphor in Science." *Literature and Science: Theory & Practice.* Ed. Stuart Peterfreund. Boston: Northeastern U P, 1990. 59–89.

Bordo, Susan. "The Cartesian Masculinization of Thought." *Signs: Journal of Women in Culture and Society* 11.3 (1986): 439–456.

———. "The Cartesian Masculinization of Thought." *Sex and Scientific Inquiry.* Ed. Sandra Harding and Jean F. O'Barr. Chicago: U of Chicago P, 1987. 247–264.

———. *Unbearable Weight: Feminism, Western Culture, and the Body.* Berkeley: U of California P, 1993.

Bourdieu, Pierre. *Outline of a Theory of Practice.* Trans. Richard Nice. New York: Cambridge U P, 1977.

Bousfield, Derek, and Miriam A. Locher, eds. *Impoliteness in Language: Studies on its Interplay with Power in Theory and Practice.* New York: Mouton de Gruyter, 2008.

Bowers, Jane M. "Feminist Scholarship and the Field of Musicology: I." *College Music Symposium* 29 (1989): 81–92.

Braidotti, Rosi. *Patterns of Dissonance: A Study of Women in Contemporary Philosophy.* Trans. Elizabeth Guild. New York: Routledge, 1991.

Brickman, Julie. "Female Lives, Feminist Deaths: The Relationship of the Montreal Massacre to Dissociation, Incest, and Violence against Women." *Canadian Psychology* 33.2 (1992): 128–143.

Briggs, Charles L., and Daniel C. Hallin. "Biocommunicability: The Neoliberal Subject and Its Contradictions in News Coverage of Health Issues." *Social Text* 93 25.4 (2007): 43–66.

Brodkey, Linda. *Academic Writing as Social Practice*. Philadelphia: Temple U P, 1987.

Brody, Howard. *Stories of Sickness*. New Haven, CT: Yale U P, 1987.

Broom, Dorothy H. *Damned If We Do: Contradictions in Women's Health Care*. North Sydney, NSW: Allen and Unwin, 1991.

Brown, Richard Harvey. *A Poetic for Sociology: Toward a Logic of Discovery for the Human Sciences*. Chicago: U of Chicago P, 1977.

Brown, Wendy. "The Impossibility of Women's Studies." *Women's Studies on the Edge*. Ed. Joan Wallach Scott. Special issue of *differences: A Journal of Feminist Cultural Studies* 9.3 (1997): 79–101.

———. "Neoliberalism and the End of Liberal Democracy." *Edgework: Critical Essays in Knowledge and Politics*. Princeton, NJ: Princeton U P, 2005. 37–59.

———. *Politics Out of History*. Princeton, NJ: Princeton U P, 2001.

———. "Resisting Left Melancholy." *boundary* 2.26 (1999): 19–27.

———. *States of Injury: Power and Freedom in Late Modernity*. Princeton, NJ: Princeton U P, 1995.

Browne, Malcolm W. "Some Thoughts on Self-Sacrifice." *New York Times* (July 5, 1988): C-6.

Butler, Judith. "A 'Bad Writer' Bites Back." *New York Times* (Op. Ed., March 20, 1999).

———. *Bodies That Matter: On the Discursive Limits of "Sex."* New York: Routledge, 1993.

———. "Discussion." *The Identity in Question*. Ed. John Rajchman. New York: Routledge, 1995. 129–144.

———. *Excitable Speech: A Politics of the Performative*. New York: Routledge, 1997.

———. *Frames of War: When is Life Grievable?* New York: Verso, 2009.

———. *Gender Trouble: Feminism and the Subversion of Identity*. New York: Routledge, 1990.

———. *The Psychic Life of Power: Theories in Subjection*. Stanford, CA: Stanford U P, 1997.

Cain, William E., ed. *Making Feminist History: The Literary Scholarship of Sandra M. Gilbert and Susan Gubar*. New York: Garland, 1993.

Campbell, Joseph. *The Hero with a Thousand Faces*. Cleveland, OH: Meridian, 1956.

Cantor, Geoffrey. "The Rhetoric of Experiment." *The Uses of Experiment: Studies in the Natural Sciences*. Ed. David Gooding, Trevor Pinch, and Simon Schaffer. New York: Cambridge U P, 1989. 159–180.

Carpenter, Teresa. "The Final Self-Defense." Review of *Terrifying Love: Why Battered Women Kill and How Society Responds* by Lenore Walker. *New York Times Book Review* (December 31, 1989): 17.

Cash, Alice H. "Feminist Theory and Music: Toward a Common Language. School of Music U of Minnesota Minneapolis 26–30 June 1991." *Journal of Musicology* 9.4 (1991): 521–532.

Casper, Monica J. "Feminist Politics and Fetal Surgery: Adventures of a Research Cowgirl on the Reproductive Frontier." *Feminist Studies* 23.2 (1997): 232–262.

Ceccarelli, Leah. *Shaping Science with Rhetoric: The Cases of Dobzhansky, Schrodinger, and Wilson*. Chicago: U of Chicago P, 2001.

Chun, Wendy Hui Kyong. "Unbearable Witness: Toward a Politics of Listening." *differences: A Journal of Feminist Cultural Studies* 11.1 (1999): 112–149.

Cixous, Hélène. "Sorties." *New French Feminisms*. Ed. Elaine Marks and Isabelle de Courtivron. Amherst: U of Massachusetts P, 1980. 90–98.

Clark, Candace. *Misery and Company: Sympathy in Everyday Life*. Chicago: U of Chicago P, 1997.

Cook, Susan. Letter, headed "What's a Girl to Do?" *New York Review of Books* (July 16, 1992): 53.

———. "Women, Women's Studies, Music and Musicology: Issues of Pedagogy and Scholarship." *College Music Symposium* 29 (1989): 93–100.

Corea, Gena. *The Hidden Malpractice: How American Medicine Mistreats Women*. Updated Edition. New York: Harper and Row, 1977/1985.

Coupland, Justine, and Angie Williams. "Conflicting Discourses, Shifting Ideologies: Pharmaceutical, 'Alternative' and Feminist Emancipatory Texts on the Menopause." *Discourse and Society* 13.4 (2002): 419–445.

Craft, Robert. "Lagoon Tunes." Review of *Five Centuries of Music in Venice* by H. C. Robbins Landon and John Julius Norwich. *New York Review of Books* (April 9, 1992): 43–44.

———. Letter, headed "Robert Craft replies." *New York Review of Books* (July 16, 1992): 53.

———. *Prejudices in Disguise: Articles, Essays, Reviews*. New York: Knopf, 1974.

Cranny-Francis, Anne, Wendy Waring, Pam Stavropoulos, and Joan Kirby. *Gender Studies: Terms and Debates*. Houndmills, Basingstoke, Hampshire: Palgrave Macmillan, 2003.

Crenshaw, Kimberlé. "Demarginalizing the Intersection of Race and Sex: A Black Feminist Critique of Antidiscrimination Doctrine, Feminist Theory and Antiracist Politics." Special Issue: Feminism in the Law: Theory, Practice and Criticism. *U of Chicago Legal Forum* (1989): 139–167.

Crowley, Sharon. *Toward a Civil Discourse: Rhetoric and Fundamentalism*. Pittsburgh, PA: U of Pittsburgh P, 2006.

Cusick, Suzanne G. "Feminist Theory, Music Theory, and the Mind/ Body Problem." *Perspectives of New Music* 32.1 (1994): 8–27.

Cvetkovich, Ann L. *An Archive of Feelings: Trauma, Sexuality, and Lesbian Public Cultures*. Durham, NC: Duke U P, 2003.

"Cynthia K. Gillespie; Advocate for Rights of Battered Women Was 51." Obituary. *New York Times* 142 (February 3, 1993): A21.

Dane, Joseph A. *The Critical Mythology of Irony*. Athens: U of Georgia P, 1991.

Daniels, Cynthia R. *Exposing Men: The Science and Politics of Male Reproduction*. New York: Oxford U P, 2006.

Davidoff, Leonore, and Catherine Hall. *Family Fortunes: Men and Women of the English Middle Class, 1780–1850*. Chicago: U of Chicago P, 1987.

Davidson, Arnold I. "Styles of Reasoning, Conceptual History, and the Emergence of Psychiatry." *The Science Studies Reader*. Ed. Mario Biagioli. New York: Routledge, 1999. 124–136.

Davis, Kathy. "Nice Doctors and Invisible Patients: The Problem of Power in Feminist Common Sense." *The Social Organization of Doctor-Patient Communication*. 2nd Edition. Ed. Alexandra Dundas Todd and Sue Fisher. Norwood, NJ: Ablex, 1993. 243–265.

————. "Paternalism under the Microscope." *Gender and Discourse: The Power of Talk.* Ed. Alexandra Dundas Todd and Sue Fisher. Norwood, NJ: Ablex, 1988. 19–54.

Davis-Floyd, Robbie E. "Obstetric Training as a Rite of Passage." *Medical Anthropology Quarterly* New Ser. 1.3 (September 1987): 288–318.

————. Review of *The Woman in the Body: A Cultural Analysis of Reproduction* by Emily Martin. *Birth—Issues in Perinatal Care* 17.3 (1990): 169–171.

————. "The Technological Model of Birth." *Journal of American Folklore* 100.398 (1987): 479–495.

De Lauretis, Teresa. "Eccentric Subjects: Feminist Theory and Historical Consciousness." *Feminist Studies* 16.1 (1990): 115–150.

Dear, Peter, ed. *The Literary Structure of Scientific Argument: Historical Studies.* Philadelphia: U of Pennsylvania P, 1991.

Deleuze, Gilles, and Félix Guattari. "Introduction: Rhizome." *A Thousand Plateaus: Capitalism and Schizophrenia.* Trans. Brian Massumi. Minneapolis: U of Minneapolis P, 1987. Reprinted as Chapter Four: "Rhizome." *Postmodern Literary Theory.* Ed. Niall Lucy. Malden, MA: Blackwell, 2000. 92–120.

Delgado, Richard. "The Imperial Scholar: Reflections on a Review of Civil Rights Literature." *U of Pennsylvania Law Review* 132 (1984): 561–578.

Derrida, Jacques. "Signature Event Context." *A Derrida Reader: Between the Blinds.* Ed. Peggy Kamuf. New York: Columbia U P, 1991. 80-111.

————. *Writing and Difference.* Trans. Alan Bass. Chicago: U of Chicago P, 1978.

Dever, Carolyn. *Skeptical Feminism: Activist Theory, Activist Practice.* Minneapolis: U of Minnesota P, 2004.

Dewhurst, Sir C. J., ed. *Integrated Obstetrics and Gynaecology for Postgraduates.* 3rd Edition. Oxford: Blackwell, 1981.

Di Stefano, Christine. *Configurations of Masculinity: A Feminist Perspective on Modern Political Theory.* Ithaca, NY: Cornell U P, 1991.

DiGiacomo, Susan M. "Biomedicine as a Cultural System: An Anthropologist in the Kingdom of the Sick." *Encounters with Biomedicine: Case Studies in Medical Anthropology.* Ed. Hans A. Baer. New York: Gordon and Breach, 1987. 315–346.

Dijck, Jose van. *Manufacturing Babies and Public Consent: Debating the New Reproductive Technologies.* New York: New York U P; Houndmills, Basingstoke, Hampshire: Macmillan, 1995.

Dillon, George L. *Contending Rhetorics: Writing in Academic Disciplines.* Bloomington: Indiana U P, 1991.

DuBois, Page. *Trojan Horses: Saving the Classics from Conservatives.* New York: New York U P, 2001.

Duggan, Lisa. *Twilight of Equality: Neoliberalism, Cultural Politics, and the Attack on Democracy.* Boston: Beacon, 2003.

Dumas, Bethany K. "Deconstructing the Patriarchal Universe of Discourse." Review of *Speaking Freely: Unlearning the Lies of the Fathers' Tongues* by Julia Penelope. *American Speech* 67.3 (1992): 320–324.

Dumm, Thomas L. *united states.* Ithaca, NY: Cornell U P, 1994.

Eagleton, Terry. *Literary Theory.* Minneapolis: U of Minnesota P, 1983.

Eichenauer, Richard. *Musik und Rasse.* Munich: J.F. Lehmanns Verlag, 1932.

Eicher, Eva M., and Linda Washburn. "Genetic Control of Primary Sex Determination in Nature." *Annual Review of Genetics* 20 (1986): 327–360.

Eisler, Riane. *The Chalice and the Blade.* San Francisco: Harper, 1987.

Elias, Norbert. *The History of Manners. The Civilizing Process: Vol. I.* Trans. Edmund Jephcott. New York: Pantheon, 1978.

Ellis, Havelock. *Man and Woman: A Study of Human Secondary Sexual Characteristics.* London: Walter Scott, 1904.

Epstein, Joseph. "The Academic Zoo: Theory—in Practice." *Hudson Review* 44.1 (1991): 9–30.

———. "My Friend Edward." Edward Shils. *Portraits: A Gallery of Intellectuals.* Chicago: U of Chicago P, 1997. 1–29.

Epstein, Julia. *Altered Conditions: Disease, Medicine, and Storytelling.* New York: Routledge, 1995.

Estrich, Susan. "Defending Women." Review of *Justifiable Homicide: Battered Women, Self-Defense, and the Law* by Cynthia K. Gillespie. *Michigan Law Review* 88.6 (1990): 1430–1439.

Ewbank, Thomas. *The World a Workshop: or the Physical Relationship of Man to the Earth.* New York: Appleton, 1855.

Fahnestock, Jeanne. *Rhetorical Figures in Science.* New York: Oxford U P, 2003.

Fairclough, Norman. *Analysing Discourse: Textual Analysis for Social Research.* New York: Routledge, 2003.

Fausto-Sterling, Anne. *Myths of Gender: Biological Theories about Men and Women.* New York: Basic Books, 1985.

Feagin, Joe R., and Melvin P. Sikes. *Living with Racism: The Black Middle-Class Experience.* Boston: Beacon, 1994.

Felski, Rita. *Beyond Feminist Aesthetics: Feminist Literature and Social Change.* Cambridge, MA: Harvard U P, 1989.

Ferguson, Kathy. *The Man Question: Visions of Subjectivity in Feminist Theory.* Berkeley and Los Angeles: U of California P, 1993.

Fisher, Sue. *In the Patient's Best Interest: Women and the Politics of Medical Decisions.* New Brunswick, NJ: Rutgers U P, 1986.

———. *Nursing Wounds: Nurse Practitioners, Doctors, Women Patients and the Negotiation of Meaning.* New Brunswick, NJ: Rutgers U P, 1995.

Forgas, Joseph P., ed. *Social Cognition.* New York: Academic P, 1981.

Formanek, Ruth, ed. *The Meanings of Menopause: Historical, Medical, and Clinical Perspectives.* Hillsdale, NJ: Analytic Press. Distributed by Lawrence Erlbaum Associates, 1990.

Foucault, Michel. *The History of Sexuality.* Vol. 1. New York: Vintage, 1980.

———. *"Society Must Be Defended": Lectures at the College De France, 1975–1976.* New York: Picador, 2003.

———. "Truth and Power." *Power/Knowledge: Selected Interviews and Other Writings.* Ed. Colin Gordon. New York: Pantheon, 1980. 109–133.

Frankenberg, Ruth. *White Women, Race Matters: The Social Construction of Whiteness.* Minneapolis: U of Minnesota P, 1993.

Fraser, Nancy. *Unruly Practice: Power, Discourse, and Gender in Contemporary Social Theory.* Minneapolis: U of Minnesota P, 1989.

Freud, Sigmund. *Jokes and Their Relation to the Unconscious.* Ed. and trans. James Strachey. New York: Norton, 1963.

———. "Medusa's Head." *Sexuality and the Psychology of Love.* Ed. Philip Rieff. Trans. Joan Riviere. New York: Collier, 1922/1963. 212–213.

Frug, Mary Joe. *Postmodern Legal Feminism.* New York: Routledge, 1992.

Frye, Marilyn. "A Note on Anger." *The Politics of Reality: Essays in Feminist Theory.* Trumansburg, NY: Crossing, 1983. 84–94.

Fugh-Berman, Adriane. "Tales out of Medical School." *Sexual Harassment: Women Speak Out.* Ed. Amber Coverdahl Sumrall and Dena Taylor. Freedom, CA: Crossing, 1992. 80–84.

Gaines, Kevin K. *Uplifting the Race: Black Leadership, Politics and Culture in the Twentieth Century.* Chapel Hill: U of North Carolina P, 1996.

Gallop, Jane. *The Daughter's Seduction: Feminism and Psychoanalysis.* Ithaca, NY: Cornell U P, 1982.

Ganong, William F. *Review of Medical Physiology.* 7th Edition. Los Altos, CA: Lange, 1975.

———. *Review of Medical Physiology.* 12th Edition. Los Altos, CA: Lange, 1985.

Gans, Eric. "Remarks on Originary Feminism." *Perspectives of New Music* 32.1 (1994): 86–88.

Geertz, Clifford. "A Lab of One's Own." *New York Review of Books* (November 8, 1990).

Gilbert, Sandra M., and Susan Gubar. *The Madwoman in the Attic: The Woman Writer and the Nineteenth-Century Literary Imagination.* New Haven, CT: Yale U P, 1979.

———. *No Man's Land: The Place of the Woman Writer in the Twentieth Century.* Vol. 1. *War of the Words.* New Haven, CT: Yale U P, 1988.

———. *No Man's Land: The Place of the Woman Writer in the Twentieth Century.* Vol. 2. *Sexchanges.* New Haven, CT: Yale U P, 1989.

Gilbert, Scott F. "Cellular Politics: Ernest Everett Just, Richard B. Goldschmidt, and the Attempt to Reconcile Embryology and Genetics." *The American Development of Biology.* Ed. Ronald Rainger, Keith R. Benson, and Jane Maienschein. Philadelphia: U of Pennsylvania P, 1988. 311–346.

Gillespie, Cynthia K. *Justifiable Homicide: Battered Women, Self-Defense, and the Law.* Columbus: Ohio State U P, 1989.

Gioia, Dana. "Can Poetry Matter?" *Atlantic Monthly,* 267.5 (1991): 94–106.

Glasov, Jamie. *United in Hate: The Left's Romance with Tyranny and Terror.* Nashville, TN: WND, 2009.

Good, Byron. *Medicine, Rationality, and Experience: An Anthropological Perspective.* Cambridge, UK: Cambridge U P, 1994.

Gordon, Avery. *Ghostly Matters: Haunting and the Sociological Imagination.* 2nd. Edition. Minneapolis: U of Minnesota P, 2008.

———. *Keeping Good Time.* Boulder, CO: Paradigm, 2004.

———. "Something More Powerful Than Skepticism." *Keeping Good Time: Reflections on Knowledge, Power, and People.* Boulder, CO: Paradigm, 2004. 187–205.

Gordon, Deborah. "Clinical Science and Clinical Expertise: Changing Boundaries between Art and Science in Medicine." *Biomedicine Examined.* Ed. Margaret Lock and Deborah Gordon. Dordrecht: Kluwer, 1988. 257–295.

————. "Tenacious Assumptions in Western Medicine." *Biomedicine Examined*. Ed. Margaret Locke and Deborah Gordon. Dordrecht: Kluwer, 1988. 19–56.

Gould, Stephen Jay. *Wonderful Life: The Burgess Shale and the Nature of History*. New York: Norton, 1989.

Gramsci, Antonio. *Selections from the Prison Notebooks*. New York: International, 1971.

Griffin, Farah Jasmine. *If You Can't Be Free, Be a Mystery*. New York: Simon and Schuster, 2001.

Gross, Alan G. *The Rhetoric of Science*. Cambridge, MA: Harvard U P, 1990.

————. *Starring the Text: The Place of Rhetoric in Science Studies*. Carbondale: Southern Illinois U P, 2006.

Gross, Paul R. "Bashful Eggs, Macho Sperm, and Tonypandy." *A House Built on Sand: Exposing Postmodernist Myths about Science*. Ed. Noretta Koertge. New York: Oxford U P, 2000. 59–70.

————, and Norman Levitt. *Higher Superstition: The Academic Left and Its Quarrels with Science*. Baltimore, MD: Johns Hopkins U P, 1997.

Grosz, Elizabeth. "A Thousand Tiny Sexes: Feminism and Rhizomatics." *Topoi* 12 (1993): 167–179.

————. 1994. *Volatile Bodies: Toward a Corporeal Feminism*. Bloomington: Indiana U P, 1994.

Gubar, Susan. "What Ails Feminist Criticism?" *Critical Inquiry* 24.4 (1998): 878–902.

Guha, Ranajit. "The Prose of Counter-Insurgency." *Selected Subaltern Studies*. Ed. Ranajit Guha and Gayatri Chakravorty Spivak. New York: Oxford U P, 1988. 45–84.

Gullette, Margaret Morganroth. "Menopause as Magic Marker: Discursive Consolidation/ Strategies for Cultural Combat." *Discourse* 17.1 (1994): 93–122.

Gutzwiller, Kathryn J., and Ann Norris Michelini. "Women and Other Strangers: Feminist Perspectives in Classical Literature." *EnGendering Knowledge: Feminists in Academe*. Ed. Joan E. Hartman and Ellen Messer-Davidow. Knoxville: U of Tennessee P, 1991. 66–84.

Guyton, Arthur C. *Physiology of the Human Body*. 6th Edition. Philadelphia: W. B. Saunders, 1984.

Hacking, Ian. "Language, Truth, and Reason." *Rationality and Relativism*. Ed. Martin Hollis and Steven Lukes. Cambridge, MA: MIT P, 1982. 48–66.

Hahn, Robert A. "Divisions of Labor: Obstetrician, Woman, and Society in *Williams Obstetrics*, 1903–1985." *Medical Anthropology Quarterly* New Ser. 1.3 (September 1987): 256–282.

————. *Sickness and Healing: An Anthropological Perspective*. New Haven, CT: Yale U P, 1995.

————. "A World of Internal Medicine: Portrait of an Internist." *Physicians of Western Medicine: Anthropological Approaches to Theory and Practice*. Ed. Robert A. Hahn and Atwood D. Gaines. Dordrecht: Reidel, 1985. 51–111.

————, and Atwood D. Gaines, eds. *Physicians of Western Medicine: Anthropological Approaches to Theory and Practice*. Dordrecht: Reidel, 1985.

Hall, Catherine. *White, Male, and Middle-Class: Explorations in Feminism and History*. New York: Routledge, 1992.

Hall, Stuart. "Gramsci and Us." *Marxism Today* (June 1987): 16–21.

Hanlin, D. Review of *The Woman in the Body* by Emily Martin. *Australian and New Zealand Journal of Sociology* 27.1 (March 1991): 125–127.

Haraway, Donna. *Primate Visions: Gender, Race, and Nature in the World of Modern Science*. New York: Routledge, 1989.

———. "Situated Knowledges: The Science Question in Feminism and the Privilege of Partial Perspective." *Feminist Studies* 14.3 (1988): 575–599.

Harding, Sandra. *The Science Question in Feminism*. Ithaca, NY: Cornell U P, 1986.

———. *Whose Science? Whose Knowledge? Thinking from Women's Lives*. Ithaca, NY: Cornell U P, 1991.

Harlow, Sioban D. "Function and Dysfunction: A Historical Critique of the Literature on Menstruation and Work." *Culture, Society, and Menstruation*. Ed. Virginia L. Olesen and Nancy Fugate Woods. Washington: Hemisphere, 1986. 39–50.

Harre, Rom. "Some Narrative Conventions of Scientific Discourse." *Narrative in Culture: The Uses of Storytelling in the Sciences, Philosophy, and Literature*. Ed. Christopher Nash. New York: Routledge, 1990. 81–101.

———, ed. *The Social Construction of Emotions*. New York: Blackwell, 1986.

Harrison, Michelle. *A Woman in Residence*. New York: Random House, 1983.

Hart, Jeffrey. "A Lost Lady." Review of *When Men Were the Only Models We Had: My Teachers Barzun, Fadiman, Trilling* by Carolyn Heilbrun. *New Criterion* 20 (2002): 65.

———. *The Making of the American Conservative Mind: National Review and Its Times*. Wilmington, DE: Intercollegiate Studies Institute, 2006.

———. *Smiling through Cultural Catastrophe: Toward the Revival of Higher Education*. New Haven, CT: Yale U P, 2001.

Harwood, J. "The Reception of Morgan's Chromosome Theory in Germany: Inter-war Debate over Cytoplasmic Inheritance." *Medical History Journal* 19 (1984): 3–32.

Hawkesworth, Mary E. "Knowers, Knowing, Known: Feminist Theory and Claims of Truth." *Signs: Journal of Women in Culture and Society* 14.3 (1989): 533–557.

Hayles, N. Katherine. "Self-Reflexive Metaphors in Maxwell's Demon and Shannon's Choice: Finding the Passages." *Literature and Science: Theory and Practice*. Ed. Stuart Peterfreund. Boston: Northeastern U P, 1990. 209–237.

Heilbrun, Carolyn. *Hamlet's Mother and Other Women*. New York: Columbia U P, 1990.

———. *When Men Were the Only Models We Had: My Teachers Barzun, Fadiman, Trilling*. Philadelphia: U of Pennsylvania P, 2002.

Hepworth, Mike. Review of *The Woman in the Body* by Emily Martin. *British Journal of Sociology* 42.1 (1991): 160.

Herrnstein, Richard J., and Charles Murray. *The Bell-Curve: Intelligence and Class Structure in American Life*. New York: Free Press, 1996.

Herschberger, Ruth. "Society Writes Biology." *Adam's Rib*. New York: Harper and Row, 1948/1970. 71–87.

"Herschberger, Ruth." *American Women Writers*, Ed. Lina Maniero. New York: Ungar, 1980. 286–288.

———. *Book Review Digest*, Bronx, NY: H.W. Wilson, 1948. 377–378.

————. *Contemporary Authors, Vol. 33–36, First Revision.* Detroit, MI: Gale Research, 1973, 1978. 395–396.

————. *The Readers' Encyclopedia of American Literature.* New York: Crowell, 1962. 462.

————. *Twentieth Century Authors, First Supplement,* Ed. Stanley Kunitz. New York: H. W. Wilson, 1959, p. 439.

Hesse, Mary. *Models and Analogies in Science.* Notre Dame, IN: U of Notre Dame P, 1970.

Hiddinga, Anja. Review of *The Woman in the Body* by Emily Martin. *ISIS* 80.3.303 (1989): 571–572.

Higgins, Lynn A., and Brenda R. Silver, eds. *Rape and Representation.* New York: Columbia U P, 1991.

Higgins, Paula. "Tracing the Careers of Late Medieval Composers: The Case of Philippe Basiron of Bourges." *Acta Musicologica* 62.1 (1990): 1–28.

————. "Women in Music, Feminist Criticism, and Guerrilla Musicology: Reflections on Recent Polemics." *19th-Century Music* 17.2 (1993): 174–192.

Hill, Roberta. "Preguntas." *Philadelphia Flowers: Poems.* Duluth, MN: Holy Cow, 1996. 89–91.

Hirsch, Marianne, and Evelyn Fox Keller, eds. *Conflicts in Feminism.* New York: Routledge, 1990.

Hochschild, Arlie Russell. *The Managed Heart: Commercialization of Human Feeling.* Berkeley: U of California P, 1983.

Hoffert, Sylvia D. Review of *The Woman in the Body* by Emily Martin. *Journal of American History* 75.1 (1988): 228–229.

Hollander, Anne. *Seeing through Clothes.* Berkeley: U of California P, 1993.

Holmes, Frederic L. "Argument and Narrative in Scientific Writing." *The Literary Structure of Scientific Argument: Historical Studies.* Ed. Peter Dear. Philadelphia: U of Pennsylvania P, 1991. 164–181.

Horowitz, David. *Indoctrination U: The Left's War against Academic Freedom.* New York: Encounter, 2009.

————, and Jacob Laksin. *One-Party Classroom: How Radical Professors at America's Top Colleges Indoctrinate Students and Undermine Our Democracy.* New York: Crown Forum, 2009.

Houck, Judith A. "'What Do These Women Want?' Feminist Responses to Feminine Forever, 1963–1980." *Bulletin of the History of Medicine* 77 (2003): 103–132.

Hubbard, Ruth. *The Politics of Women's Biology.* New Brunswick, NJ: Rutgers U P, 1990.

Huggins, Nathan Irvin. *Harlem Renaissance.* New York: Oxford U P, 1971.

Humphries, Lee. Letter to the editor. *Minnesota Composers Forum Newsletter.* Letter dated January 6, 1987.

Hunter, Kathryn Montgomery. *Doctors' Stories: The Narrative Structure of Medical Knowledge.* Princeton, NJ: Princeton U P, 1991.

Hutcheon, Linda. *Irony's Edge: The Theory and Politics of Irony.* New York: Routledge, 1994.

————. *Splitting Images: Contemporary Canadian Ironies.* Toronto: Oxford U P, 1991.

――――. *A Theory of Parody: The Teaching of Twentieth-Century Art Forms.* New York: Methuen, 1985.

Ingram, Carl. "Senate Votes to Toughen Law on Spousal Rape." *Los Angeles Times* (August 15, 1992): 1.

Jackson, Margaret. "'Facts of Life' or the Erotization of Women's Oppression? Sexology and the Social Construction of Heterosexuality." *The Cultural Construction of Sexuality.* Ed. Pat Caplan. New York: Tavistock, 1987. 52–81.

Jaggar, Alison M. "Feminist Ethics: Projects, Problems, Prospects." *Feminist Ethics.* Ed. Claudia Card. Lawrence: U P of Kansas, 1991. 78–104.

――――. *Feminist Politics and Human Nature.* Totowa, NJ: Rowman and Allanheld, 1983.

――――. "Love and Knowledge: Emotion in Feminist Epistemology." *Women, Knowledge, and Reality: Explorations in Feminist Philosophy.* Ed. Ann Garry and Marilyn Pearsall. Boston: Unwin Hyman, 1989. 129–155.

――――, and Susan R. Bordo, eds. *Gender/ Body/ Knowledge: Feminist Reconstructions of Being and Knowing.* New Brunswick, NJ: Rutgers U P, 1990.

Jameson, Frederic. *The Political Unconscious: Narrative as a Socially Symbolic Act.* Ithaca, NY: Cornell U P, 1981.

Jamieson, Kathleen Hall, and Joseph N. Cappella. *Echo Chamber: Rush Limbaugh and the Conservative Media Establishment.* New York: Oxford U P, 2008.

Jeffcoate, Sir Norman. *Principles of Gynaecology.* 4th Edition. London: Butterworths, 1975.

Jeffords, Susan. *Hard Bodies: Hollywood Masculinity in the Reagan Era.* New Brunswick, NJ: Rutgers U P, 1994.

――――. *The Remasculinization of America: Gender and the Vietnam War.* Bloomington: Indiana U P, 1989.

Johnson, Barbara. "The Alchemy of Race and Style." *The Rhetoric of Law.* Ed. Austin Sarat and Thomas R. Kearns. Ann Arbor: U of Michigan P, 1994. 261–274.

Johnson, Mark. *The Body in the Mind: The Bodily Basis of Meaning, Imagination, and Reason.* Chicago: U of Chicago P, 1987.

Jones, Ann Rosalind. "City Women and Their Audiences: Louise Labe and Veronica Franco." *Rewriting the Renaissance: The Discourses of Sexual Difference in Early Modern Europe.* Ed. Margaret G. Ferguson, Maureen Quilligan, and Nancy J. Vickers. Chicago: U of Chicago P, 1986. 299–316.

Jordan, Brigitte. *Birth in Four Cultures: A Crosscultural Investigation of Childbirth in Yucatan, Holland, Sweden and the United States.* Montreal: Eden, 1983.

Jordanova, Ludmilla. *Sexual Visions: Images of Gender in Science and Medicine between the Eighteenth and Twentieth Centuries.* Madison: U of Wisconsin P, 1989.

Journet, Debra. "Ecological Theories as Cultural Narratives: F. E. Clements's and H. A. Gleason's 'Stories' of Community Succession." *Written Communication* 8.4 (1991): 446–472.

――――. "Forms of Discourse and the Sciences of the Mind: Luria, Sacks, and the Role of Narrative in Neurological Case Histories." *Written Communication* 7.2 (1990): 171–199.

Just, E. E. *The Biology of the Cell Surface.* Philadelphia: Blakiston, 1939.

Kahn, Fritz, M.D. *Our Sex Life: A Guide and Counsellor for Everyone.* Trans. George Rosen, M.D. New York: Knopf, 1939. 2nd Revised Edition, New York: Knopf, 1942, 1948.

Kampen, Natalie Boymel. 1995. "Looking at Gender: The Column of Trajan and Roman Historical Relief." *Feminisms in the Academy.* Ed. Domna C. Stanton and Abigail J. Stewart. Ann Arbor: U of Michigan P, 1995. 46–73.

Kasson, John F. *Rudeness and Civility: Manners in Nineteenth-Century Urban America.* New York: Hill and Wang, 1990.

Katz, Pearl. "How Surgeons Make Decisions." *Physicians of Western Medicine: Anthropological Approaches to Theory and Practice.* Ed. Robert A. Hahn and Atwood D. Gaines. Dordrecht: Reidel, 1985. 155–175.

Kaufert, Patricia. "Menopause as Process or Event: The Creation of Definitions in Biomedicine." *Biomedicine Examined.* Ed. Margaret Lock and Deborah Gordon. Dordrecht: Kluwer, 1988. 331–349.

Keeton, William T. *Biological Science,* 3rd Edition. New York: Norton, 1976.

Keller, Evelyn Fox. *Reflections on Gender and Science.* New Haven, CT: Yale U P, 1985.

———. *Secrets of Life/ Secrets of Death: Essays on Language, Gender and Science.* New York: Routledge, 1992.

Kerman, Joseph. *Contemplating Music: Challenges to Musicology.* Cambridge, MA: Harvard U P, 1985.

Keuls, Eva C. *The Reign of the Phallus: Sexual Politics in Ancient Athens.* Berkeley: U of California P, 1985.

Kielian-Gilbert, Marianne. "Feminist Theory and Music Conference, Minneapolis, June 1991: Questions on Ecstasy, Morality, Creativity." *Perspectives of New Music* 30.2 (1992): 240–242.

Killam, Rosemary N. "Women Working: An Alternative to Gans." *Perspectives of New Music* 31.2 (1993): 230–251.

———. "Writing Music Culture for Calamity Jane, Water, and Other Dangerous Women (with Minimal Apologies to Clifford and Lakoff)." *Perspectives of New Music* 32.2 (1994): 194–198.

Kim, S. "Hegemony and Cultural Resistance." *International Encyclopedia of the Social and Behavioral Sciences.* Ed. Neil J. Smelser and Paul Baltes. New York: Elsevier, 2001. 6645–6650.

Kinports, Kit. "Women on the Verge." Review of *Justifiable Homicide: Battered Women, Self-Defense, and the Law* by Cynthia K. Gillespie and *Terrifying Love: Why Battered Women Kill and How Society Responds* by Lenore Walker. *American Bar Association Journal* 75 (1989): 129–131.

Kintz, Linda. "Performing Virtual Whiteness: George Gilder's Techno-Theocracy." *Cultural Studies* 16.5 (2002): 735–773.

Kirschner, Suzanne R., and Emily Martin. "From Flexible Bodies to Fluid Minds: An Interview with Emily Martin." *Ethos* 27.3 (1999): 247–282.

Kitcher, Philip. *Vaulting Ambition: Sociobiology and the Quest for Human Nature.* Cambridge, MA: MIT P, 1985.

Klamer, Arjo, Donald M. McCloskey, and Robert M. Solow, eds. *The Consequences of Economic Rhetoric.* Cambridge, UK: Cambridge U P, 1988.

Kleinman, Arthur. *The Illness Narratives: Suffering, Healing, and the Human Condition.* New York: Basic, 1988.

———. *Writing in the Margins: Discourse between Anthropology and Medicine.* Berkeley: U of California P, 1995.

Knize, Megan S. "The Pen Is Mightier: Rethinking the 'Gladiator' Ethos of Student-Edited Law Reviews." 2008. Unpublished paper. Available at http://works/bepress.com/megan_knize/.

Kochman, Thomas. "The Politics of Politeness: Social Warrants in Mainstream American Public Etiquette." *Meaning, Form, and Use in Context: Linguistic Applications.* Ed. Deborah Schiffrin. Washington, DC: Georgetown U P, 1984. 200–209.

Koeske, Randi Daimon. "Lifting the Curse of Menstruation: Toward a Feminist Perspective on the Menstrual Cycle." *Lifting the Curse of Menstruation: A Feminist Appraisal of the Influence of Menstruation on Women's Lives.* Ed. Sharon Golub. New York: Haworth, 1983. 1–16.

Kouri, Jim. "Duke Rape Case All Too Common." *LibertyPost.org.* December 17, 2006. Available at www.libertypost.org/cgi-bin/readart.cgi?ArtNum+169955&Disp=4. Accessed July 28, 2007.

Koutroulis, Glenda. "The Orifice Revisited: Portrayal of Women in Gynecology Texts." *Community Health Studies* 14 (1990): 73–84.

Kramarae, Cheris. Review of *Speaking Freely: Unlearning the Lies of the Fathers' Tongues* by Julia Penelope. *Signs: Journal of Women in Culture and Society* 17.3 (1992): 666–671.

———, and Paula A. Treichler. *A Feminist Dictionary.* London: Pandora, 1985.

Kress, Gunther. *Linguistic Processes in Sociocultural Practice.* Geelong, Victoria: Deakin U P, 1985.

Lakoff, George. *Women, Fire, and Dangerous Things: What Categories Tell Us about the Nature of Thought.* Chicago: U of Chicago P, 1986.

———, and Mark Johnson. *Metaphors We Live By.* Chicago: U of Chicago P, 1980.

———, and Zoltán Kövecses. "The Concept of Anger." *Metaphors of Anger, Pride and Love: A Lexical Approach to the Structure of Concepts.* Zoltán Kövecses. Philadelphia: John Benjamins, 1986.

Lakoff, Robin Tolmach, and Sachiko Ide, eds. *Broadening the Horizon of Linguistic Politeness.* Philadelphia: John Benjamins, 2005.

Landau, Misia. *Narratives of Human Evolution.* New Haven, CT: Yale U P, 1991.

———. "Paradise Lost: The Theme of Terrestriality in Human Evolution." *The Rhetoric of the Human Sciences: Language and Argument in Scholarship and Public Affair.* Ed. John S. Nelson, Allan Megill, and Donald N. McCloskey. Madison: U of Wisconsin P, 1987. 111–124.

Landon, H. C. Robbins, and John Julius Norwich. *Five Centuries of Music in Venice.* New York: Schirmer, 1991.

Laqueur, Thomas. "Female Orgasm, Generation, and the Politics of Reproductive Biology." *Representations* 14 (Spring 1986): 1–82.

———. *Making Sex: Body and Gender from the Greeks to Freud.* Cambridge, MA: Harvard U P, 1990.

Lashgari, Deirdre, ed. *Violence, Silence, and Anger: Women's Writing as Transgression.* Charlottesville: U P of Virginia, 1995.

Latour, Bruno. "One More Turn after the Social Turn." *The Social Dimensions of Science.* Ed. Ernan McMullin. Notre Dame, IN: U of Notre Dame P, 1992. 272–294.

———. *Science in Action: How to Follow Scientists and Engineers through Society.* Cambridge, MA: Harvard U P, 1987.

———, and Françoise Bastide. "Writing Science—Fact and Fiction." *Mapping the Dynamics of Science and Technology: Sociology of Science in the Real World.* Ed. Michel Callon, John Law, and Arie Rip. London: Macmillan, 1986. 51–66.

———, and Shirley C. Strum. "Human Social Origins: Oh Please, Tell Us Another Story," *Journal of Social and Biological Structures* 9.2 (1986): 169–187.

Lawrence, Susan C., and Kae Bendixen. "His and Hers: Male and Female Anatomy in Anatomy Texts for U.S. Medical Students, 1890–1989." *Social Science and Medicine* 35.7 (1992): 925–934.

Laws, Sophie. *Issues of Blood: The Politics of Menstruation.* Foreword by Margaret Stacey. Houndmills, Basingstoke, Hampshire: Macmillan, 1990.

Lein, Allen. *The Cycling Female: Her Menstrual Rhythm.* San Francisco: Freeman, 1979.

Lewin, Tamar. "When Justice Goes Wrong." Review of *Justifiable Homicide: Battered Women, Self-Defense, and the Law* by Cynthia K. Gillespie. *New York Times Book Review* (December 31, 1989): 17.

Llewellyn-Jones, Derek. *Fundamentals of Obstetrics and Gynaecology. Vol. 2. Gynaecology.* 3rd Edition. London: Faber and Faber, 1982.

Lloyd, Genevieve. "Knowledge." *New Keywords: A Revised Vocabulary of Culture and Society.* Ed. Tony Bennett, Lawrence Grossberg, and Meaghan Morris. Revised Edition. Malden, MA: Wiley-Blackwell, 2005. 195–197.

———. *The Man of Reason: "Male" and "Female" in Western Philosophy.* Minneapolis: U of Minnesota P, 1984.

———. *The Man of Reason: "Male" and "Female" in Western Philosophy.* 2nd Edition. Minneapolis: U of Minnesota P, 1993.

———. "Rationality." *A Companion to Feminist Philosophy.* Ed. Alison M. Jaggar and Iris Marion Young. Malden, MA: Wiley-Blackwell, 2000. 165–172.

Locher, Miriam A. *Power and Politeness in Action: Disagreements in Oral Communication.* New York: Mouton de Gruyter, 2004.

Lock, Margaret. "Anomalous Aging: Managing the Postmenopausal Body." *Body and Society* 4.1 (1998): 35–61.

———. *Encounters with Aging: Mythologies of Menopause in Japan and North America.* Berkeley: U of California P, 1993.

———. "Models and Practice in Medicine: Menopause as Syndrome or Life Transition?" *Physicians of Western Medicine: Anthropological Approaches to Theory and Practice.* Ed. Robert A. Hahn and Atwood D. Gaines. Dordrecht: Reidel, 1985. 115–139.

———. "The Politics of Mid-Life and Menopause: Ideologies for the Second Sex in North America and Japan." *Knowledge, Power, and Practice: The Anthropology of Medicine and Everyday Life.* Ed. Shirley Lindenbaum and Margaret Lock. Berkeley: U of California P, 1993. 330–363.

———, and Deborah Gordon. *Biomedicine Examined.* Dordrecht: Kluwer, 1988.

Locke, David. *Science as Writing*. New Haven, CT: Yale U P, 1992.

Longino, Helen E. "Essential Tensions—Phase Two: Feminist, Philosophical, and Social Studies of Science." *A Mind of One's Own: Feminist Essays on Reason and Objectivity*. Ed. Louise M. Anthony and Charlotte Witt. Boulder, CO: Westview, 1993. 257–272.

———. *Science as Social Knowledge: Values and Objectivity in Scientific Inquiry*. Princeton, NJ: Princeton U P, 1990.

———. "Science, Objectivity, and Feminist Values." *Signs: Journal of Women in Culture and Society* 14.3 (1988): 561–574.

Lorde, Audre. *Sister Outsider: Essays and Speeches*. Freedom, CA: Crossing, 1984.

———. "The Uses of Anger." *Women's Studies Quarterly* 9.3 (1981): 7–10.

Lowe, Lisa. *Immigrant Acts: On Asian American Cultural Politics*. Durham, NC: Duke U P, 1996.

Lubiano, Wahneema. "Like Being Mugged by a Metaphor: Multiculturalism and State Narratives." *Mapping Multiculturalism*. Ed. Avery F. Gordon and Christopher Newfield. Minneapolis: U of Minnesota P, 1996. 64–75.

Lutz, Catherine A. "Engendered Emotion: Gender, Power, and the Rhetoric of Emotional Control in American Discourse." *Language and the Politics of Emotion*. Ed. Catherine A. Lutz and Lila Abu-Lughod. Cambridge, UK: Cambridge U P, 1990. 69–91.

Lyman, Peter. "The Domestication of Anger: The Use and Abuse of Anger in Politics." *European Journal of Social Theory* 7.2 (2004): 133–147.

———. "The Politics of Anger: On Silence, Ressentiment, and Political Speech." *Socialist Review* 11.3 (1981): 55–74.

Lyne, John. "Bio-Rhetorics: Moralizing the Life Sciences." *The Rhetorical Turn: Invention and Persuasion in the Conduct of Inquiry*. Ed. Herbert W. Simons. Chicago: U of Chicago P, 1990. 35–57.

Lyons, Antonia C., and Christine Griffin. "Managing Menopause: A Qualitative Analysis of Self-help Literature for Women at Midlife." *Social Science and Medicine* 56 (2002): 1629–1642.

MacPherson, Kathleen L. "Menopause as Disease: The Social Construction of a Metaphor." *Advances in Nursing Science* 3.2 (1981): 95–113.

Maletter, Louise, and Marie Chalouch, eds. *The Montreal Massacre*. Trans. Marlene Wildeman. Charlottetown, PEI: Gynergy, 1991.

Mandler, George. *Mind and Body: A Psychology of Emotion and Stress*. New York: Norton, 1984.

Manning, K. R. *The Black Apollo of Science: The Life of Ernest Everett Just*. New York: Oxford U P, 1983.

Marcus, George E., and Michael M. J. Fischer. *Anthropology as Cultural Critique*. Chicago: U of Chicago P, 1986.

Marcus, Isabel. "A Sexy New Twist: Reproductive Technologies and Feminism." *Law and Social Inquiry* 15.2 (Spring 1990): 247–269. [Review includes *The Woman in the Body*.]

Martin, Emily. "The Egg and the Sperm: How Science Has Constructed a Romance Based on Stereotypical Male-Female Roles." *Signs: Journal of Women in Culture and Society* 16.3 (1991): 485–501.

————. *Flexible Bodies: Tracking Immunity in American Culture from the Days of Polio to the Age of AIDS*. Boston: Beacon, 1994.

————. "Meeting Polemics with Irenics in the Science Wars." *Science Wars*. Ed. Andrew Ross. Durham, NC: Duke U P, 1996. 61–79.

————. "Science and Women's Bodies: Forms of Anthropological Knowledge." *Body/Politics: Women and the Discourses of Science*. Ed. Mary Jacobus, Evelyn Fox Keller, and Sally Shuttleworth. New York: Routledge, 1990. 69–82.

————. *The Woman in the Body: A Cultural Analysis of Reproduction*. Boston: Beacon, 1987.

Marx, Karl. "Human Emancipation." *Citizenship*. Ed. Paul Barry Clarke. London: Pluto, 1994. 137–140.

Mason, Elliott B. *Human Physiology*. Menlo Park, CA: Benjamin Cummings, 1983.

Matsuda, Mari. "Affirmative Action and Legal Knowledge: Planting Seeds in Plowed-Up Ground." *Harvard Women's Law Journal* 11 (1988): 1–17.

Mattingly, Cheryl. "The Narrative Nature of Clinical Reasoning." *Journal of American Occupational Therapy* 45 (1991): 998–1005.

Maus, Fred Everett. "Masculine Discourse in Music Theory." *Perspectives of New Music* 31.2 (1993): 264–293.

McClary, Susan. "The Blasphemy of Talking Politics during Bach Year." In *Music and Society: The Politics of Composition, Performance and Reception*. Ed. Richard Leppert and Susan McClary. Cambridge, UK: Cambridge U P, 1987. 13–62.

————. "Constructions of Subjectivity in Schubert's Music." *Queering the Pitch: The New Gay and Lesbian Musicology*. Ed. Philip Brett, Elizabeth Wood, and Gary C. Thomas. New York: Routledge, 1994. 205–230.

————. *Feminine Endings: Music, Gender, and Sexuality*. Minneapolis: U of Minnesota P, 1991.

————. "Foreword. The Undoing of Opera: Toward a Feminist Criticism of Music." Catherine Clement, *Opera, or the Undoing of Women*. Trans. Betsy Wing. Minneapolis: U of Minnesota P, 1988. ix–xviii.

————. "Getting Down Off the Beanstalk: The Presence of a Woman's Voice in Janika Vandervelde's *Genesis II*." *Minnesota Composer's Forum Newsletter* (1987).

————. "Narrative Agendas in 'Absolute' Music: Identity and Difference in Brahms's Third Symphony." *Musicology and Difference: Gender and Sexuality in Music Scholarship*. Ed. Ruth A. Solie. Berkeley: U of California P, 1993. 326–344.

————. "A Response to Elaine Barkin." *Perspectives of New Music* 30.2 (1992): 234–238.

McCloskey, Donald N. *The Rhetoric of Economics*. Madison: U of Wisconsin P, 1985.

McClure Browne, J. C. *Postgraduate Obstetrics and Gynaecology*. 4th Edition. London: Butterworths, 1973.

McDermott, Patrice. "On Cultural Authority: Women's Studies, Feminist Politics, and the Popular Press." *Signs: Journal of Women in Culture and Society* 20.3 (1995): 668–684.

McDonald, Maryon. Review of *The Woman in the Body* by Emily Martin. *Sociological Review* 38.3 (1990): 588–591.

McRobbie, Angela. *The Aftermath of Feminism: Gender, Culture and Social Change*. Los Angeles: Sage, 2009.

Mead, Lawrence M. *Beyond Entitlement: The Social Obligations of Citizenship.* New York: Free Press, 2001.

———. *Government Matters: Welfare Reform in Wisconsin.* Princeton, NJ: Princeton U P, 2004.

———. "Is Complaint a Moral Argument?" *Child, Family, and State.* Ed. Stephen Macedo and Iris Marion Young. New York: New York U P, 2003. 134–147.

Memmi, Albert. *The Colonizer and the Colonized.* Trans. Howard Greenfield. New York: Orion, 1965.

Merchant, Carolyn. *The Death of Nature: Women, Ecology, and the Scientific Revolution.* New York: Harper and Row, 1980.

Messer-Davidow, Ellen. *Disciplining Feminism: From Social Activism to Academic Discourse.* Durham, NC: Duke U P, 2002.

Miles, Agnes. *Women, Health and Medicine.* Philadelphia: Open U P, 1991.

Miller, Jonathan, and David Pelham. *The Facts of Life.* New York: Viking Penguin, 1984.

Miller, Nancy K. "*Madwoman* Revisited." *Making Feminist History: The Literary Scholarship of Sandra M. Gilbert and Susan Gubar.* Ed. William E. Cain. New York: Garland, 1993. 87-104.

Miller, Toby. *Cultural Citizenship: Cosmopolitanism, Consumerism and Television in a Neoliberal Age.* Philadelphia: Temple U P, 2006.

———. *The Well-Tempered Self: Citizenship, Culture, and the Postmodern Subject.* Baltimore, MD: Johns Hopkins U P, 1993.

Mills, Sara. *Discourse.* Second Ed. New York: Routledge, 2004.

———. *Feminist Stylistics.* New York: Routledge, 1995.

———. *Gender and Politeness.* New York: Cambridge U P, 2003.

———. *Language and Sexism.* New York: Cambridge U P, 2008.

Miner, Valerie, and Helen E. Longino, eds. *Competition: A Feminist Taboo?* New York: Feminist, 1987.

Mischler, Elliot G. *The Discourse of Medicine: Dialectics of Medical Interviews.* Norwood, NJ: Ablex, 1984.

———, Lorna R. Amarsingham, Stuart T. Hauser, Samuel D. Osherson, Nancy E. Waxler, and Ramsay Liem. *Social Contexts of Health, Illness, and Patient Care.* Cambridge, UK: Cambridge U P, 1981.

Mitchell, Michele. *Righteous Propagation: African Americans and the Politics of Racial Destiny after Reconstruction.* Chapel Hill: U of North Carolina P, 2004.

Mizrahi, Terry. *Getting Rid of Patients: Contradictions in the Socialization of Physicians.* New Brunswick, NJ: Rutgers U P, 1986.

Modleski, Tania. *Feminism without Women: Culture and Criticism in a "Postfeminist" Age.* New York: Routledge, 1991.

Moglen, Seth. "On Mourning Social Injury." *Psychoanalysis, Culture and Society* 10 (2005): 151–167.

Moi, Toril. *Sexual/Textual Politics: Feminist Literary Theory.* New York: Methuen, 1985.

Moore, Lisa Jean. "Extracting Men from Semen: Masculinity in Scientific Representations of Sperm." *Social Text* 20.4 (2002): 91–119.

———. *Sperm Counts: Overcome by Man's Most Precious Fluid.* New York: New York U P, 2007.

————, and Adele E. Clarke. "Clitoral Conventions and Transgressions: Graphic Representations in Anatomy Texts, c1900–1991." *Feminist Studies* 21.2 (1995): 255–301.

————. "Traffic in Cyberanatomies: Sex/Gender/Sexualities in Local and Global Formations." *Body and Society* 7.1 (2001): 57–96.

Moraga, Cherrie, and Gloria Anzaldua, eds. *This Bridge Called My Back: Writings by Radical Women of Color.* New York: Kitchen Table, Women of Color, 1981.

Morgan, T. H. *The Theory of the Gene.* New Haven, CT: Yale U P, 1926.

Morris, Meaghan. *The Pirate's Fiancée: Feminism, Reading, Postmodernism.* New York: Verso, 1988.

Mount, Ferdinand. "The Recovery of Civility." *Encounter* XLI (1973): 31–43.

Mountcastle, Vernon. *Medical Physiology,* 14th Edition. London: Mosby, 1980.

Mukerji, Chandra. *A Fragile Power: Scientists and the State.* Princeton, NJ: Princeton U P, 1989.

Mulkay, Michael. *On Humour: Its Nature and Its Place in Modern Society.* Cambridge, UK: Polity in association with Basil Blackwell, 1988.

Mulvey, Laura. "Changes: Thoughts on Myth, Narrative, and Historical Experience." *History Workshop* 23 (1987): 3–19.

————. "Visual Pleasure and Narrative Cinema." *Screen* 16.3 (1975): 6–18.

Munk, Erika. "What's Wrong with This Picture?" *Women's Review of Books* 11.6 (1994): 5–6.

Muñoz, José Esteban. "Feeling Brown, Feeling Down: Latina Affect, the Performativity of Race, and the Depressive Position." *Signs: Journal of Women in Culture and Society* 31.3 (2006): 675-688.

Murphy-Lawless, Jo. "The Obstetric View of Feminine Identity: A Nineteenth Century Case History of the Use of Forceps on Unmarried Women in Ireland." *Gender and Discourse: The Power of Talk.* Ed. Alexandra Dundas Todd and Sue Fisher. Norwood, NJ: Ablex, 1988. 177–198.

————. *Reading Birth and Death: A History of Obstetric Thinking.* Bloomington: Indiana U P, 1998.

Myers, Greg. "Making a Discovery: Narratives of Split Genes." *Narrative in Culture: The Uses of Storytelling in the Sciences, Philosophy, and Literature.* Ed. Christopher Nash. London: Routledge, 1990. 102–126.

————. "Stories and Styles in Two Molecular Biology Review Articles." *Textual Dynamics of the Professions: Historical and Contemporary Studies of Writing in Professional Communities.* Ed. Charles Bazerman and James Paradis. Madison: U of Wisconsin P, 1991. 45–75.

————. *Writing Biology: Texts in the Social Construction of Scientific Knowledge.* Madison: U of Wisconsin P, 1990.

Nelson, John S., Allan Megill, and Donald N. McCloskey, eds. *Rhetoric of the Human Sciences: Language and Argument in Scholarship and Public Affairs.* Madison: U of Wisconsin P, 1989.

Netter, Frank H. *A Compilation of Paintings on the Normal and Pathologic Anatomy of the Reproductive System.* The CIBA Collection of Medical Illustrations, Volume 2. Summit, NJ: CIBA, 1965.

Newcomb, Anthony. "Courtesans, Muses, or Musicians? Professional Women Musicians in Sixteenth-Century Italy." *Women Making Music: The Western Art Tradition.* Ed. Jane Bowers and Judith Tick. Urbana: U of Illinois P, 1986. 90–115.

Newfield, Christopher. *The Emerson Effect: Individualism and Submission in America.* Chicago: U of Chicago P, 1996.

Newman, Karen. *Fashioning Femininity and English Renaissance Drama.* Chicago: U of Chicago P, 1991.

Newton, Michael. "Commentary on Hahn's *Divisions of Labor.*" *Medical Anthropology Quarterly* New Ser. 1.3 (September 1987): 283–287.

Ngai, Sianne. "Jealous Schoolgirls, Single White Females, and Other Bad Examples: Rethinking Gender and Envy." *Camera Obscura* 47 16.2 (2001): 177–229.

Nilsson, Lennart. "A Portrait of the Sperm." *The Functional Anatomy of the Spermatozoan.* Ed. Bjorn A. Afzelius. New York: Pergamon, 1975. 79–82.

Nisbett, Richard E., and Lee Ross. *Human Inference: Strategies and Shortcomings of Social Judgment.* Englewood Cliffs, NJ: Prentice-Hall, 1980.

Norris, Ronald V. *PMS: Premenstrual Syndrome.* New York: Berkeley, 1984.

Novak, Edmund R., Georgeanna Seegar Jones, and Howard Jones, Jr. *Novak's Textbook of Gynecology.* 8th Edition. Baltimore, MD: Williams and Wilkins, 1970.

———. *Novak's Textbook of Gynecology.* 9th Edition. Baltimore, MD: Williams and Wilkins, 1975.

Nussbaum, Martha. *Cultivating Humanity: A Classical Defense of Reform in Liberal Education.* Cambridge, MA: Harvard U P, 1998.

———. "The Professor of Parody." *New Republic* (February 22, 1999): 37–45.

Nye, Andrea. *Feminism and Modern Philosophy.* New York: Routledge, 2004.

———. *Feminist Theory and the Philosophies of Man.* New York: Routledge, 1989.

———. *Words of Power: A Feminist Reading of the History of Logic.* New York: Routledge, 1990.

Oakley, Ann. *The Captured Womb: A History of the Medical Care of Pregnant Women.* New York: Blackwell, 1984.

O'Beirne, Kate. *Women Who Make the World Worse and How Their Radical Feminist Assault Is Ruining Our Schools, Families, Military, and Sports.* New York: Sentinel HC, 2005.

Ormiston, Gayle L., and Raphael Sassower. *Narrative Experiments: The Discursive Authority of Science and Technology.* Minneapolis: U of Minnesota P, 1989.

Ortony, Andrew, ed. *Metaphor and Thought.* Cambridge, UK: Cambridge U P, 1979.

Parrington, John. "Kiss of Life? Scientists Have Found the Molecule That Triggers the Start of Human Life." *Chemistry World* 1.2 (2004). 38–40.

Pateman, Carole. *The Disorder of Women: Democracy, Feminism, and Liberal Theory.* Cambridge, UK: Polity, 1989.

———. *The Sexual Contract.* Stanford, CA: Stanford U P, 1988.

Penelope, Julia. *Speaking Freely: Unlearning the Lies of the Fathers' Tongues.* New York: Pergamon, 1990.

Pera, Marcello. *The Discourses of Science.* Trans. Clarissa Botsford. Chicago: U of Chicago P, 1994.

———, and William R. Shea, eds. *Persuading Science: The Art of Scientific Rhetoric.* Canton, MA: Science History Publications, 1991.

Perz, Janette, and Jane M. Ussher. "'The Horror of This Living Decay': Women's Negotiation and Resistance of Medical Discourses around Menopause and Midlife." *Women's Studies International Forum* 31 (2008): 293–299.

Petersen, Alan. "Sexing the Body: Representations of Sex Differences in Gray's *Anatomy*, 1858 to the Present." *Body and Society* 4.1 (1998): 1–15.

Pfeil, Fred. *White Guys: Studies in Postmodern Domination and Difference*. London: Verso, 1995.

Pollack, Scarlet. "Refusing to Take Women Seriously." *Test-Tube Women: What Future for Motherhood?* Ed. Rita Arditti, Renate Duelli Klein, and Shelley Minden. London: Pandora, 1984. 138–152.

Pollock, Griselda. *Vision and Difference: Femininity, Feminism, and Histories of Art*. London: Routledge, 1988.

Porter, Elisabeth J. "Reason, Passion and Objectivity." *Women and Moral Identity*. North Sydney, NSW: Allen and Unwin, 1991. 88–119.

Posner, Judith. "It's All in Your Head: Feminist and Medical Models of Menopause (Strange Bedfellows)." *Sex Roles* 5 (1979): 179–190.

Pratt, Mary Louise. *Toward a Speech Act Theory of Literary Discourse*. Bloomington: Indiana U P, 1977.

Prelli, Lawrence J. *A Rhetoric of Science*. Columbia: U of South Carolina P, 1989.

Pritchard, Jack A., and Paul C. MacDonald. *Williams Obstetrics*. 15th Edition. New York: Appleton-Century-Crofts, 1976.

———. *Williams Obstetrics*. 16th Edition. New York: Appleton-Century-Crofts, 1980.

———, and Norman F. Gant. *Williams Obstetrics*. 17th Edition. New York: Appleton-Century-Crofts, 1985.

Probyn, Elspeth. *Sexing the Self: Gendered Positions in Cultural Studies*. New York: Routledge, 1993.

Propp, Vladimir. *Morphology of the Folktale*. Austin: U of Texas P, 1928/1968.

Puar, Jasbir K. *Terrorist Assemblages: Homonationalism in Queer Times*. Durham, NC: Duke U P, 2007.

Rabinowitz, Paula. *Women's Revolutionary Fiction in Depression America*. Chapel Hill: U of North Carolina P, 1990.

Rayner-Canham, Geoff. "No More Sleeping Beauty." Letter in *Chemistry World* 1.5 (2004): 24–25.

Richardson, Laurel. Review of *The Woman in the Body* by Emily Martin. *Contemporary Sociology* 17.2 (March 1988): 239–240.

Roberts, Dorothy E. "The Child Welfare System's Racial Harm." *Child, Family, and State*. Ed. Stephen Macedo and Iris Marion Young. New York: New York U P, 2003. 98–133.

———. *Killing the Black Body: Race, Reproduction, and the Meaning of Liberty*. New York: Pantheon, 1997.

———. *Shattered Bonds: The Color of Child Welfare*. New York: Basic Books/Civitas, 2001.

Robinson, Cedric. "Manicheanism and Multiculturalism." *Mapping Multiculturalism*. Ed. Avery Gordon and Christopher Newfield. Minneapolis: U of Minnesota P, 1996. 116–125.

———. "Preface." *Forgeries of Memory and Meaning: Blacks and the Regimes of Race in American Theater and Film before World War II.* Chapel Hill: U of North Carolina P, 2007. vi–xvii.

Rodríguez, Juana Mariá. *Queer Latinidad: Identity Practices, Discursive Spaces.* New York: New York U P, 2003.

Rorty, Amelie Oksenberg, ed. *Explaining Emotions.* Berkeley: U of California P, 1980.

Rosand, Ellen. *Opera in Seventeenth-Century Venice: The Creation of a Genre.* Berkeley: U of California P, 1991.

———. "Seneca and the Interpretation of *L' incoronazione di Poppea.*" *Journal of the American Musicological Society* 38 (1985): 34–71.

———. "The Voice of Barbara Strozzi." *Women Making Music: The Western Art Tradition, 1150–1950.* Ed. Jane Bowers and Judith Tick. Urbana: U of Illinois P, 1986. 168–190.

Rose, Tricia. *Longing to Tell: Black Women Talk about Sexuality and Intimacy.* New York: Farrar, Straus and Giroux, 2003.

Ross, Alex. "A Female Deer? Looking for Sex in the Sound of Music." *Lingua Franca,* (July/August 1994): 53–60.

Ross, Andrew, ed. *Science Wars.* Durham, NC: Duke U P, 1996.

Roth, Susan. Review of *Justifiable Homicide: Battered Women, Self-Defense, and the Law* by Cynthia K. Gillespie. *Signs: Journal of Women in Culture and Society* 16.2 (1991): 379–381.

Rothman, Barbara Katz. "Childbirth Management and Medical Monopoly." *Women, Biology, and Public Policy.* Ed. Virginia Sapiro. Beverley Hills, CA: Sage, 1985. 117–135.

Rothstein, Edward. "Did a Man or a Woman Write That?" Column, "Classical View." *New York Times* (Sunday, July 17, 1994): H25.

Rouse, Joseph. "The Narrative Reconstruction of Science." *Inquiry* 33.2 (1990): 179–196.

Rowland, Robyn. Review of *The Woman in the Body* by Emily Martin. *Hastings Center Report* 19.3 (May–June 1989): 40–42.

Rubin, David. *Everything You Wanted to Know about Sex but Were Afraid to Ask.* New York: McKay, 1969.

Russell, K. P. *Eastman's Expectant Motherhood,* 6th Edition. New York: Little, 1977.

Said, Edward. *Musical Elaborations.* New York: Columbia U P, 1991.

———. "Opponents, Audiences, Constituencies and Community." *The Anti-Aesthetic: Essays in Postmodern Culture.* Ed. Hal Foster. Seattle, WA: Bay, 1983. 135–159.

———. "Orientalism Reconsidered." *Cultural Critique* 1 (1985): 89–107.

———. *The World, the Text, and the Critic.* Cambridge, MA: Harvard U P, 1983.

Sandoval, Chela. *Methodology of the Oppressed.* Minneapolis: U of Minnesota P, 2000.

Schatten, Gerald, and Heide Schatten. "The Energetic Egg." *The Sciences* 23, 5 (1983): 28–34.

———. "The Energetic Egg." *Medical World News* 23 (January 23, 1984): 51–53.

Scheman, Naomi. "Anger and the Politics of Naming." *Women and Language in Literature and Society.* Ed. Sally McConnell-Ginet, Ruth Barker, and Nelly Furman. New York: Praeger, 1980. 174–187.

Schiebinger, Londa. *Has Feminism Changed Science?* Cambridge, MA: Harvard U P, 1999.

———. *The Mind Has No Sex? Women in the Origins of Modern Science.* Cambridge, MA: Harvard U P, 1989.

Schleifer, Ronald, Robert Con Davis, and Nancy Mergler. *Culture and Cognition: The Boundaries of Literary and Scientific Inquiry.* Ithaca, NY: Cornell U P, 1992.

Schlessinger, Laura. "Feminists Should Go Where They Are Needed." (November 25, 2008). Available at www.drlaurablog.com/.

———. "More on Feminist Studies," *Santa Barbara News-Press* (October 12, 2008).

———. "Save Us from Feminist Studies," *Santa Barbara News-Press* (October 9, 2008).

———. "Where's NOW When You Really Need Them?" (February 7, 2008). Available at www.drlaurablog.com/.

———. "A Young Woman Does the Research on Feminist Theory." (May, 11, 2009). Available at www.drlaurablog.com/.

Schoeman, Ferdinand. "Statistical Norms and Moral Attributions." *Responsibility, Character, and the Emotions: New Essays in Moral Psychology.* Ed. Ferdinand Schoeman. Cambridge, UK: Cambridge U P, 1987. 287–315.

Schon, Donald A. *Displacement of Concepts.* London: Tavistock, 1963.

Schuster, John A., and Richard R. Yeo, eds. *The Politics and Rhetoric of Scientific Method: Historical Studies.* Dordrecht: Reidel, 1986.

Scott, Joan Wallach. "Gender: A Useful Category of Historical Analysis." *Gender and the Politics of History.* New York: Columbia U P, 1988. 28–50.

Scully, Diana. *Men Who Control Women's Health: The Miseducation of Obstetrician-Gynecologists.* Boston: Houghton, 1980.

———, and Pauline Bart. "A Funny Thing Happened on the Way to the Orifice: Women in Gynecology Texts." *American Journal of Sociology* 78 (1973): 1045–1051. Reprinted in *Changing Women in a Changing Society.* Ed. Joan Huber. Chicago: U of Chicago P, 1973. 283–288.

Sedgwick, Eve Kosofsky. *Touching Feeling: Affect, Pedagogy, Performativity.* Durham, NC: Duke U P, 2003.

Selzer, Jack, ed. *Understanding Scientific Prose.* Madison: U of Wisconsin P, 1993.

Sernka, Thomas, and Eugene Jacobson. *Gastrointestinal Physiology: The Essentials.* Baltimore, MD: Williams and Wilkins, 1983.

Shanley, Mary Lyndon, and Carole Pateman, eds. *Feminist Interpretations and Political Theory.* University Park: Pennsylvania State U P, 1991.

Shapin, Steven. "Pump and Circumstance: Robert Boyle's Literary Technology." *Social Studies of Science* 14 (1984): 481–520.

Shapiro, Bennett M. "The Existential Decision of a Sperm." *Cell* 49.3 (1987): 293–294.

Shils, Edward. "The Virtue of Civil Society." *Government and Opposition* 26.1 (1991): 3–20.

Shuttleworth, Sally. "Female Circulation: Medical Discourse and Popular Advertising in the Mid-Victorian Era." *Body/ Politics: Women and the Discourses of Science.* Ed. Mary Jacobus, Evelyn Fox Keller, and Sally Shuttleworth. New York: Routledge, 1990. 47–68.

Silver, Brenda. "The Authority of Anger: *Three Guineas* as Case Study." *Signs: Journal of Women in Culture and Society* 16.2 (1991): 340–370.

Silverman, D. *Communication and Medical Practice: Social Relations in the Clinic.* London: Sage, 1987.

Simons, Herbert W. "Are Scientists Rhetors in Disguise? An Analysis of Discursive Practices within Scientific Communities." *Rhetoric in Transition: Studies in the Nature and Uses of Rhetoric.* Ed. Eugene E. White. University Park: Pennsylvania State U P, 1980. 115–130.

———, ed. *The Rhetorical Turn: Invention and Persuasion in the Conduct of Inquiry.* Chicago: U of Chicago P, 1990.

Singer, Merrill. "Cure, Care, and Control: An Ectopic Encounter with Biomedical Obstetrics." *Encounters with Biomedicine: Case Studies in Medical Anthropology.* Ed. Hans A. Baer. New York: Gordon and Breach, 1987. 249–265.

Solomon, Robert C. *A Passion for Justice: Emotions and the Origins of the Social Contract.* Reading, MA: Addison-Wesley, 1990.

———. *The Passions.* New York: Doubleday, 1976.

Sommers, Christina Hoff. *Who Stole Feminism? How Women Have Betrayed Women.* New York: Simon and Schuster, 1994.

Sordi, Michele. "Caught in the Crossfire: Critical Situations of Gilbert and Gubar's Madwoman and No Man's Land." *Making Feminist History: The Literary Scholarship of Sandra M. Gilbert and Susan Gubar.* Ed. William E. Cain. New York: Garland, 1993. 271–300.

Spelman, Elizabeth V. "Anger and Insubordination." *Women, Knowledge, and Reality: Explorations in Feminist Philosophy.* Ed. Ann Garry and Marilyn Pearsall. Boston: Unwin Hyman, 1989. 263–273.

———. *Fruits of Sorrow: Framing Our Attention to Suffering.* Boston: Beacon, 1997.

Spender, Dale. *The Writing or the Sex? Why You Don't Have to Read Women's Writing to Know It's No Good.* Oxford: Pergamon, 1989.

Stacey, William A., and Anson Shupe. *The Family Secret: Domestic Violence in America.* Boston: Beacon, 1983.

Stanton, Domna C. "Introduction: The Subject of Sexuality." *Discourses of Sexuality: From Aristotle to AIDS.* Ed. Domna C. Stanton. Ann Arbor: U of Michigan P, 1992. 1–46.

Stanworth, Michelle, ed. *Reproductive Technologies: Gender, Motherhood and Medicine.* Minneapolis: U of Minnesota P, 1987.

Stato, Joanne. "Montreal Gynocide." *Violence against Women: The Bloody Footprints.* Ed. Pauline B. Bart and Eileen Geil Moran. Newbury Park, CA: Sage, 1993. 132–133.

Stearns, Carol Z., and Peter N. Stearns. *Anger: The Struggle for Emotional Control in America's History.* Chicago: U of Chicago P, 1986.

———, eds. *Emotion and Social Change: Toward a New Psychohistory.* New York: Holmes and Meier, 1988.

Stearns, Peter N. *American Cool: Constructing a Twentieth-Century Emotional Style.* New York: New York U P, 1994.

———. *Battleground of Desire: The Struggle for Self-Control in Modern America.* New York: New York U P, 1999.

————, and Jan Lewis, eds. *An Emotional History of the United States*. New York: New York U P, 1998.

Steinem, Gloria. "If Men Could Menstruate: A Political Fantasy." *Ms.* (October 1978): 110.

Stocking, George W. *Race, Culture, and Evolution: Essays in the History of Anthropology*. Chicago: U of Chicago P, 1982 [1968].

Stotsky, Sandra. "Conceptualizing Writing as Moral and Civic Thinking." *College English* 54.7 (1992): 794–808.

Subotnik, Rose Rosengard. "Adorno's Diagnosis of Beethoven's Late Style." *Journal of the American Musicological Society* 29 (1976): 242–275.

————. *Developing Variations: Style and Ideology in Western Music*. Minneapolis: U of Minnesota P, 1991.

————. "The Historical Structure: Adorno's 'French' Model for the Criticism of Nineteenth-Century Music." *19th-Century Music* 2 (1978): 36–60.

————. "The Role of Ideology in the Study of Western Music." *Journal of Musicology* 2 (1983): 1–12.

Tarrant, Shira. *When Sex Became Gender*. New York: Routledge, 2006.

Terdiman, Richard. *Discourse/Counter-Discourse: The Theory and Practice of Symbolic Resistance in Nineteenth-Century France*. Ithaca, NY: Cornell U P, 1985.

Todd, Alexandra Dundas. "Exploring Women's Experiences: Power and Resistance in Medical Discourse." *The Social Organization of Doctor-Patient Communication*. 2nd Edition. Ed. Alexandra Dundas Todd and Sue Fisher. Norwood, NJ: Ablex, 1993. 267–285.

————. *Intimate Adversaries: Cultural Conflict between Doctors and Women Patients*. Philadelphia: U of Pennsylvania P, 1989.

————, and Sue Fisher, eds. *The Social Organization of Doctor-Patient Communication*. 2nd Edition. Norwood, NJ: Ablex, 1993.

Tomlinson, Barbara. *Authors on Writing: Metaphors and Intellectual Labor*. Houndmills, Basingstoke: Palgrave Macmillan, 2005.

Traweek, Sharon. *Beamtimes and Lifetimes*. Cambridge, MA: Harvard U P, 1988.

————. "Border Crossings: Narrative Strategies in Science Studies and among Atomic Physicists at Tsukuba Science City, Japan." *Science as Practice and Culture*. Ed. Andrew Pickering. Chicago: U of Chicago P, 1992. 429–465.

Treichler, Paula A. "Feminism, Medicine, and the Meaning of Childbirth." *Body/Politics: Women and the Discourses of Science*. Ed. Mary Jacobus, Evelyn Fox Keller, and Sally Shuttleworth. New York: Routledge, 1990. 113–138.

Treitler, Leo. "Gender and Other Dualities of Music History." *Musicology and Difference: Gender and Sexuality in Music Scholarship*. Ed. Ruth A. Solie. Berkeley: U of California P, 1993. 23–45.

Tuana, Nancy, ed. *Feminism and Science*. Bloomington: Indiana U P, 1989.

————. *Feminist Interpretations of Plato*. University Park: Pennsylvania State U P, 1994.

Turner, Bryan S. "Review Article: Missing Bodies—Towards a Sociology of Embodiment." *Sociology of Health and Illness* 13.2 (1991): 265–272. [Review includes *The Woman in the Body*.]

Turner, John R. G. "The History of Science and the Working Scientist." *Companion to the History of Modern Science.* Ed. R. C. Olby, G. N. Cantor, J.R.R. Christie, and M.S.J. Hodge. New York: Routledge, 1990. 23–31.

Turner, Mark. *Death Is the Mother of Beauty: Mind, Metaphor, Criticism.* Chicago: U of Chicago P, 1987.

Tyler, Imogen. "Against Abjection." *Feminist Theory* 10.1(2009): 77–98.

———. " 'Who Put the "Me" in Feminism?' The Sexual Politics of Narcissism." *Feminist Theory* 6.1 (2005): 25–44.

van den Toorn, Pieter C. *Music, Politics and the Academy.* Berkeley: U of California P, 1995.

———. "Politics, Feminism, and Contemporary Music Theory." *Journal of Musicology* 9.3 (1991): 275–299.

Vander, Arthur J., James H. Sherman, and Dorothy S. Luciano. *Human Physiology: The Mechanisms of Body Function.* 3rd Edition. New York: McGraw-Hill, 1980.

———. *Human Physiology: The Mechanisms of Body Function.* 4th Edition. New York: McGraw-Hill, 1985.

Vendler, Helen. "Feminism and Literature." *New York Review of Books* xxxvii.9 (May 31, 1990): 19–25.

Waddington, C. H. *Organisers and Genes.* Cambridge, UK: Cambridge U P, 1940.

Waitzkin, Howard. *The Politics of Medical Encounters: How Patients and Doctors Deal with Social Problems.* New Haven, CT: Yale U P, 1991.

———. *The Second Sickness: Contradictions in Capitalist Health Care.* New York: Free Press, 1983.

Wakeman, Jessica, and Julie Hollar. "Stand by Your Man: Mostly Male Pundits Defend Male-dominated Science." *Extra!* (May/June 2005): 23–24.

Ware, Vron. *Beyond the Pale: White Women, Racism and History.* London: Verso, 1992.

Warner, Marina. "The Slipped Chiton." *Monuments and Maidens: The Allegory of Female Form.* London: Weidenfeld and Nicholson, 1985. 267–293.

Warner, Michael. *Publics and Counterpublics.* New York: Zone, 2002.

Wassarman, Paul M. "The Biology and Chemistry of Fertilization." *Science* 235.4788 (January 30, 1987): 553–560.

———. "Fertilization in Mammals." *Scientific American* 259.6 (1988): 78–84.

Watts, Richard J. *Politeness.* New York: Cambridge U P, 2003.

Weaver, Jerry L., and Sharon D. Garrett. "Sexism and Racism in the American Health Care Industry: A Comparative Analysis." *Women and Health: The Politics of Sex in Medicine.* Ed. Elizabeth Fee. Farmingdale, NY: Baywood, 1983. 79–104.

Wersky, G. *The Visible College.* New York: Holt, Rinehart, and Winston, 1978.

West, Candace. " 'Ask Me No Questions . . .': An Analysis of Queries and Replies in Physician-Patient Dialogues." *The Social Organization of Doctor-Patient Communication.* 2nd Edition. Ed. Alexandra Dundas Todd and Sue Fisher. Norwood, NJ: Ablex, 1993. 127–157.

———. *Routine Complications: Troubles with Talk between Doctors and Patients.* Bloomington: U of Indiana P, 1984.

Wiegman, Robyn. "Difference and Disciplinarity." *Aesthetics in a Multicultural Age.* Ed. Emory Elliott. New York: Oxford U P, 2002. 135–156.

———. "Feminism, Institutionalism, and the Idiom of Failure." *differences: A Journal of Feminist Cultural Studies* 11.3 (1999/2000): 107–136.

———. "Feminism's Apocalyptic Futures." *New Literary History* 31 (2000): 805–825.

———. "On Being in Time with Feminism." *Modern Language Quarterly* 65.1 (2004): 161–176.

———. "What Ails Feminist Criticism? A Second Opinion." *Critical Inquiry* 25.2 (1999): 362–379.

Will, George. "Nature, Nurture, and Larry Summers's Sin." *One Man's America: The Pleasures and Provocations of Our Singular Nation.* New York: Crown Forum, 2008. 250–252.

Williams, Linda. *Hard Core: Power, Pleasure, and the "Frenzy of the Visible."* Berkeley: U of California P, 1989.

———. *Playing the Race Card: Melodramas of Black and White from Uncle Tom to O.J. Simpson.* Princeton, NJ: Princeton U P, 2002.

Williams, Patricia J. *The Alchemy of Race and Rights: Diary of a Law Professor.* Cambridge, MA: Harvard U P, 1991.

———. *Open House: Of Family, Friends, Food, Piano Lessons and the Search for a Room of My Own.* New York: Farrar, Straus and Giroux, 2004.

———. *The Rooster's Egg.* Cambridge, MA: Harvard U P, 1995.

———. *Seeing a Color-Blind Future: The Paradox of Race.* The Reith Lectures, 1997. New York: Noonday, 1998.

Williams, Raymond. "Criticism." *Keywords: A Vocabulary of Culture and Society.* New York: Oxford U P, 1976. 84–86.

———. "Structures of Feeling." *Marxism and Literature.* New York: Oxford U P, 1977. 128–135.

Wilson, Ara. "Take Back the Body." Review of *The Woman in the Body* by Emily Martin. *Socialist Review* 19.3 (1989): 131–136.

Wilson, Edward O. *Sociobiology: The New Synthesis.* Twenty-Fifth Anniversary Ed. Cambridge, MA: Belknap P of Harvard U P, 2000.

Wilson, John K. *The Myth of Political Correctness: The Conservative Attack on Higher Education.* Durham, NC: Duke U P, 1995.

Wilson, Robert A. *Feminine Forever.* New York: Evans, 1966.

———, and Thelma A. Wilson. "The Fate of Nontreated Postmenopausal Women: A Plea for the Maintenance of Adequate Estrogen from Puberty to the Grave." *Journal of the American Geriatrics Society* 11 (1963): 347–362.

Winner, Langdon. *Autonomous Technology: Technics-out-of-Control as a Theme in Political Thought.* Cambridge, MA: MIT P, 1977.

Woodward, Kathleen. "Against Wisdom: The Social Politics of Anger and Aging." *Cultural Critique* 51 (2002): 186–218.

———. "From Anger . . . to Anger: Freud and Feminism." *Freud and the Passions.* Ed. John O'Neill. University Park, PA: Pennsylvania State U P, 1996. 73–96.

———. *Statistical Panic: Cultural Politics and Poetics of the Emotions.* Durham, NC: Duke U P, 2009.

Young, Iris Marion. *Political Responsibility and Procedural Injustice*. Lawrence: U of Kansas, Dept. of Philosophy, The Lindley Lecture, 2003.

Žižek, Slavoj. "Afterword: The Lesson of Ranciére." Jacques Ranciére, *The Politics of Aesthetics: The Distribution of the Sensible*. New York: Continuum, 2005. 69–79.

Index

Barbara Tomlinson is Associate Professor of Feminist Studies at the University of California, Santa Barbara. She is the author of *Authors on Writing: Metaphors and Intellectual Labor*. In 2009, she received the Academic Senate Distinguished Teaching Award, University of California, Santa Barbara.